Missionary Memories
How God Leads

Missionary Memories
How God Leads

by
Dr. Robert Chick

To my wife and kids, you mean the world to me. To all those who supported our ministry all these years with prayer, encouragement, and support - thank you!

Table of Contents

Acknowledgements

Above all, I want to acknowledge God who made me, saved me, called me, and kept me all these years. I look forward to an eternity with Him. Then, there are the most important people in my life, my family. My wife put up with me throughout this project and, you will see as you read, throughout these many adventures and misadventures. She is and always has been an encouragement and example of great patience when dealing with my rather fragile personality. I love her more than words can express and I'm sure I should have used many more words to express that in our life together. Our children have been the source of many an adventure and now we're thrilled to add grandchildren to the adventure. There are many fellow missionaries, pastors, writers, friends who have played a part in my life, for which I'm grateful. A special thanks to Anne White who helped in the editing of this personal project as a favor. She has been one of our "adopted" daughters for many years.

Preface

This project started in an effort to combat burn out. It was many years into our ministry and I was about to quit to go live under a bridge as a hermit. Then I started to think of how God worked in and through my life. I remembered the good times. I remembered the bad times. I remembered God was always there in every up and down I faced. I started remembering and chronicling my journey with God into ministry. I intended for these little stories to encourage me by seeing how God was always at work. It worked. God worked. It's been a long time since I started this project and my wonderful wife, Beth, convinced me it might encourage other believers. So, I started sharing these in blogs and social media posts. I received quite a few encouraging responses and was honored when others requested my permission to use different stories in their own devotions and teaching situations.

Appointed

We know that all things work together for good for those who love God, to those who are called according to his purpose. (Romans 8:28 WEB)

It all began with an airport. At least for me it began in an airport. I was sitting, minding my own business, glancing up from my book to watch the strange passengers wander to and fro, when I felt the Lord trying to tell me something. No audible voice, no graffiti on the airport walls to make things clear. Just some time reading and my heart starting to talk about mission work. Granted, the previous couple of years at Bible college probably laid some groundwork in my thinking. I shared my feelings with Beth, my wife, and she received the same inclination while I was away. Things seemed to fit together. But, where, when, and how were the questions yet to be answered.

An application here, an application there, and then we waited. We heard from a couple missions who talked about raising support. That didn't appeal to us so we said our polite, "Thank you. But, no thank you." Then there was silence. A year of silence until our son was born to break up the quiet of our home. Like a birthday present, we received a call from the mission asking us to come and be interviewed.

After months of waiting, our application for missionary service finally bubbled its way to the top of the prospective missionary stack. The initial information was sufficient to garner their interest in our family. We were asked to come to their home office, in New Jersey of all places, for a personnel interview.

As a young couple just finishing school, we couldn't afford such a trip. We could barely afford to pay rent and then eat. We often observed there was too much month at the end of the paycheck. We knew God called us to consider missions and He was opening a crack in the door. But, God also knew we were poor as church mice. A newborn baby, Joel, and a two-year-old, Ellice, stretched our finances to the limit. How could we make the trip?

The Lord provided someone, although I cannot remember who, to pay for our plane tickets to New York City and back. With Joel in a basket and Ellice holding my hand we climbed aboard our first air flight as a family. Beth's brother and his family offered us a room in their home while her aunt provided a car. Cold, (it was December) unsure what was ahead, and ready to see what God had in mind, we looked forward to our first face to face meeting with a mission board.

The next morning we arose, looked at a map, and began our journey. Our first stop was a local church. Although Joel would accompany us to the meetings, Ellice was scheduled to enjoy the day at the church daycare center. That was another provision from the Lord. We couldn't afford to pay for

1

daycare. The Lord placed the need on the pastor's heart and the costs were covered. Locating the mission offices was next on our list.

I discovered quickly I didn't like the roads in New Jersey. I'm sure there is someone, somewhere, who understands the flow and pattern of the highways and side streets but it escaped me as we wandered from place to place. Did you know you can't turn left in New Jersey? At least that was my impression. I'd get a bead on our destination and be thwarted by the ubiquitous no left turn signs. This gave new meaning to the phrase turned around.

Eventually, we located the office on Main Street and entered the hallowed halls we read about in the history of the mission. We were greeted by a friendly Mr. L and met other potential candidates awaiting the barrage of questions and meetings scheduled during the evaluation. Armed with the meager information gleaned in reading the history of the mission, we thought we were ready for the challenge.

Most meetings were straightforward and direct. Even the psychiatrist was quick and felt we just might fit in with the missionary mindset. (It goes to prove you really can fool some of the people some of the time!) The most grueling and nerve-wracking interview was with the board.

We were ushered into a long conference room and instructed to sit at one end of the long conference table while five board members occupied the other end with the president of the mission in the center. I asked to move closer and was promptly told to remain where I was seated. The questions followed.

We were not sure how to answer or what they wanted to hear. It's a strange human habit to turn over in our minds and try to discover hidden meaning behind a question instead of just answering the clear question. We knew God brought us to this point. We were taken off guard as questions centered around many cultural issues and none surfaced in relation to my work as a broadcast engineer. Beth and I provided answers which were honest and direct. Our response to some questions was, "We don't know." We finished, exited the room, and waited. We were not sure how things would turn out. We sat in the front room as deliberations were held behind closed doors.

Chatting with other candidates helped to pass the time but didn't assuage our concerns. One candidate couple departed after meeting the psychiatrist. Another couple departed promptly after their board interview and another was instructed to undertake some biblical studies and then return at a later date. Whew, I'd been to Bible college. In the end, we were the only couple left in the room.

Members of the mission passed through the room, making a particular fuss over baby Joel. It was quiet and tense as we waited.

Finally, we were asked back into the board room. We were accepted as missionaries. Praise the Lord! We weren't sure what God had in mind when we left Lexington the day before. Now we were sure. This was a definite answer to His plans for our life.

With relief, we left the conference room and relaxed on the couch in the foyer. We were IN! Into what was still a question. Neither of us were familiar with all the details of becoming faith missionaries. This we would learn in the years to come. Right then we were in the door. God called, we listened and we were accepted. Whew!

Little did we know, at that happy juncture in our lives, what God was going to do in and through us in the years ahead. With excitement in our hearts and on our lips, we returned to share the good news with family, friends and our home church.

It's like that between us and God. He leads, He guides, but He doesn't reveal the answers until we persevere to the end. Maybe you're in the midst of a change. It becomes clear at the end. At least we can count on that.

Raising Support

For the Scripture says, "You shall not muzzle the ox when it treads out the grain." And, "The laborer is worthy of his wages." (1Timothy 5:18 WEB)

Growing up I heard missionaries share their ministries in church. My most vivid memory was being bored out of my skull. The endless slides, monotone speeches and sad appearances distracted me from the work God was performing around the world. How could God condone boring people to death? Maybe I missed the point when I was young. Then again, maybe the point wasn't clear.

My desire was to be different. But, I wasn't a dynamic public speaker. As a matter of fact, I was afraid to speak in front of more than one person, and one person made me nervous. Here the Lord carefully molded me and taught me, through the help of other believers, to present the ministry from very humble, stumbling beginnings to eventually preaching and teaching. God can mold a mushy lump of clay into something useful!

Unbeknown to me, God started a couple of years before we were appointed. We regularly attended the Young Adult Sunday School Class at our church. A friend of mine, Chip, was teaching class. Chip completed his seminary education and was about to move to Pennsylvania. This left our class in need of a teacher. Chip approached me to take over the class.

I was resistant to the idea. I didn't think I was prepared. I didn't know enough to teach a class of young adults, many of whom were more educated and churched than me. I was too young. God used Chip to get me moving. He had confidence in my knowledge of Scripture and ability to take over the class. God used this experience to teach me to speak in public and share the ministry.

As appointees with TWR we shared our new-found direction and calling in life at every opportunity. We were dismayed to find not everyone felt as excited as we did. Church, family, and friends provided a gamut of responses from contagious joy to curiosity to downright concern for our mental welfare. Some thought it a great step of faith while others thought we were crazy to enter into a faith ministry. Then there were those who just couldn't quite figure out what was happening so they just smiled and said, "Very interesting."

It's like a magic potion. Start talking about raising financial support and people suddenly develop attention deficit disorder. If you're in front of a church board their eyes start to glaze over and shoulders slump. Everybody knows everyone else needs support. The pastor knows, the board knows, the missionary knows but no one wants to talk about it. Why? Because if they discuss it they will be challenged to make a final decision, yes or no.

Our support need wasn't quickly or spectacularly met as we had hoped and prayed. For three years we worked on raising our support. We met with pastors, shared with churches, individuals, friends, and family. All our efforts resulted in only modest commitments of support. It is exciting, now, after many years of ministry, to see these first partners still underwriting our ministry. With few contacts, we were on our own to find churches, discover the denominations which were for or against the ministry, and seek opportunities to share the ministry and our financial need.

We made a choice concerning our support. It was God's support to raise and maintain. We chose not to share, from the pulpit, our financial need or plea for funds. Our goal was to present what God was doing in our lives, the ministry and the world, then pray. Pray for the Lord to work in people's hearts. When asked about our needs we were more than glad to share the financial need. We felt this was the Lord's guidance.

During our initial deputation, we weren't as sure of our calling because of the meager results and became discouraged. We questioned whether God really called us to serve or if we had only followed our personal desires. Now, with 20/20 hindsight, we look back and see how the Lord blessed us again and again by meeting our needs in regular support and personal needs over the years.

One day after three years of deputation we talked about the situation. Our leads had run dry. Our energy was run down. I could only afford so many days off from my job and still provide for the family. We discussed the plus and minus factors of our deputation and determined to wait another thirty days to see what would happen. If the Lord provided a significant increase we'd continue forward. If there wasn't a change we would resign. It was a tough decision to place a fleece before the Lord. We asked for a direct yes or no response. We committed ourselves to act accordingly, regardless of personal desires and dreams.

A couple of weeks later things didn't look good. Then we received a visit from the mission area representative. We expected a proper lecture on our lack of forward momentum. The representative had other ideas in mind.

TWR needed someone on Guam right away. Would we be interested? We didn't know where Guam was located. We didn't have our support. No problem, he told us, our support would be covered for a one-year term of service. After that we'd return to the USA to raise the remaining support. We gave the offer careful thought. About ten minutes was all it took to see God was sending us forward in an unexpected way. We agreed. They wanted us there in less than three weeks!

It's amazing how much packing you can do, how fast you can quit a job, how many friends you can tell, and how much rejoicing you can enjoy in a few short weeks. Our furniture and belongings were sold, discarded, or stored in friends' basements and attics until we were left with just a few suitcases.

We climbed aboard a plane, stopped in California for a couple days to visit my brother and Disneyland, then on to Hawaii and finally Guam. What a whirlwind of emotions and changes moved through our family. We headed across the Pacific to a little dot on the map we didn't know existed only a few weeks earlier. God brought us this far . . . now what?

God, at times, wants us to understand more fully that He is in control. During these times He cleanses us from our own accomplishments and reveals His hand of grace and provision.

Going to GUAM

In nothing be anxious, but in everything, by prayer and petition with thanksgiving, let your requests be made known to God. (Philippians 4:6 WEB)

When Beth and I moved to Kentucky to continue my education, we were not interested in mission work. The word missionary was not in our vocabulary nor was it one of our desires. I attended Bible college since we were sure the Lord called us into the ministry. However, I jumped to the wrong conclusion and studied for a pastoral ministry.

I learned about preaching, preparing sermons and the wonders of becoming a pastor. With the pending arrival of our first child I went back to work as a radio engineer. I held the appropriate license, had the experience and it paid the bills.

I worked in radio, studied for the ministry and waited for our first child. Daily life kept Beth and me busy. Along the way a number of missionaries from around the world crossed our path and we discovered they were people, just like other people, only living and working somewhere else. As I studied, the Lord made it clear we were not to be in a pulpit ministry. One of my homiletics professors, after hearing me preach, asked, "Are you sure you want to do this for a living?"

With an engineering background, an uncertainty from my homiletics class and a need to determine where God was leading, we decided to at least take a glimpse at mission work. I figured the mission field didn't need engineers so it was a safe step. Wrong! God showed us several ministries very interested in my training and abilities. Finally, we were ready to give in and consider missions. I put my last request before the Lord, "Father, if we are going into missions, I'd really like to stay in the United States."

I'm convinced that God has a great sense of humor. Guam, as you may know, is a territory of the United States! We got what I prayed for. God moved us into missions and kept us in the "USA" . . . sort of! What a hoot! Here we were headed to Guam, a small dot in the Pacific we could barely find on a map.

I never really liked to travel. My first airplane flight was at the age of twenty-one. I flew from Florida to Cincinnati to attend the wedding of a close friend from high school. It was quite an experience which I'll never forget. It was during this flight, sitting in an airport terminal, waiting for the next flight that God spoke to me and called me into the ministry. I should have figured there was going to be some relation between airplanes and the ministry.

Compared to that short jump across the US the flight to Guam seemed endless. With two children in arms we traveled seven hours to Hawaii and then another seven hours to find Guam. I think it's amazing a pilot can locate such a small chunk of rock in the middle of nowhere. I'm reminded of the verse from Revelation, "The sky was removed like a scroll when it is rolled up. Every mountain and island were moved out of their places." (Revelation 6:14 WEB) Think of the startled face on a pilot flying toward Guam after that happens!

It was still dark when we arrived. Our first glimpse of the island as the plane made its approach revealed a massive number of lights twinkling in the darkness. We couldn't remember a place with so much wattage devoted to nighttime. We gathered our baggage, departed from the customs area and wondered how anyone would find us. We didn't know anyone on the island. We didn't know anyone on the staff. None of the Guam staff knew us. We approached the exit and saw smiling faces holding up a copy of our prayer card.

We walked outside into the tropical night for the first time. Describing the humidity, heat and weight of the tropical climate doesn't do justice to the impact we felt after hours in the dehydrated atmosphere of the airplane. The relief to find friendly faces, helpful hands and to walk again on shaky legs, was an encouragement as we struggled against the needed sleep and jet lag. We never knew what jet lag was until we crossed fourteen time zones!

We rode down the strange paved streets. They really did have paved roads on the island. The cars appeared normal and there was even a McDonald's restaurant! The children were thrilled. It was soon clear our meager information concerning Guam was outdated. We envisioned dirt roads, grass huts and half-dressed natives with bones in their noses. Instead we found asphalt, island shirts, concrete houses and modern conveniences.

A field of visions whisked by the car windows. We were pleased to find an apartment with a view across the graveyard to the Pacific Ocean. It was beyond our wildest dreams. The mission even provided a temporary car for our use. The new adventure began with a good night's rest.

Whoever views the Christian life as calm and quiet hasn't lived long as a believer. Change abounds everywhere. We discovered this on the mission field. What we expected was different from what God provided. It was worth the risk, if we considered following God a risk, to step forward and follow God's lead to see where He put us.

Guam was not what we envisioned; it was better, far better. God knows what He's doing. We just need to walk forward, wait and see!

Preparing the Way

But having food and clothing, we will be content with that. (1 Timothy 6:8 WEB)

Prior to the mission field God worked to prepare our hearts for His plan. During college God guided and prepared us for the ministry and a different lifestyle.

We moved to the sleepy little village of Wilmore, Kentucky. This was a community where you didn't need to lock your doors. Bicycles sat outside without fear of theft.

One day at Fitch's IGA, the local grocery store, I discovered I forgot my checkbook. No problem. Mr. Fitch nodded to the cashier, a note was placed in the register. I went home with my groceries and could pay him later. Mr. Fitch is gone now but I remember his love and kindness to struggling college students.

We were so encouraged, we contemplated having a family. Sure enough, it wasn't long before we discovered our first child was on the way. I looked for a job. Beth wanted to work part time until Ellice was born and then be home full time. I was hired as Chief Engineer for a couple of radio stations in Lexington. I was on salary, the hours were flexible, and it was a perfect fit for a student with classes to attend.

The pay was not spectacular. After I received my pay and paid the bills we were left with about $20.00 to survive for another month. Things were tight but we enjoyed God's provision. We didn't starve; we lived a simple life.

Simplicity was one of the keys to Wilmore. Walking from home to the college was one of my favorite events. Our neighbors knew our names, children played in the school playground and the town was quiet.

We enjoyed sitting on our small front porch. We planted trees in our yard. It was a new housing area, and we watched the street develop. The city water tower was visible through our bedroom window. Every night a cross shone bright from the top of the tower. When the curtains were open there was comfort in the glow cast on the walls. God provided our home and He gave direction.

In my junior year God guided me to change jobs. I became Assistant Chief Engineer to another pair of radio stations. I was not the boss, but they paid better. Six months after I was hired we were appointed as missionaries. I let my boss know we would eventually depart and I needed time for deputation. Lou was great. He had no objections and encouraged us in our ministry.

The work was good, hard, honest work. Our bills were paid. As our last days in the USA approached, we realized we had nothing. Well, almost nothing. I sold my piano, the only piece of furniture with any value. Most of our furniture was tossed out, used furniture. Our income barely kept us in our home. Our children, two by this time, enjoyed a happy life at home. They didn't know anything different.

Our parents lived in other states. Ellice was almost ready to start kindergarten and Joel was learning about sleeping in a "big" bed. Memories were all that tied us to the USA. No home, no stash of stuff, even our car was from the recycled car lot. This was God's preparation.

We arrived on Guam with no ties to things back home which would draw us away from the mission field. No home to maintain at a distance. Even the pay was an increase in salary!

These are the things which can pull a missionary's heart to draw him back to the comfort and safety of his homeland. God kept these out of our life or removed them from our hearts before sending us to another land with a new culture, a new experience in His grace and care.

Within a few days of our arrival on Guam, we knew how to get around the most basic areas of the island. We established a bank account, visited the offices and transmitter site and learned more of how things work on the mission field. We were amazed at the wonder and glory of God's provision which brought us to this new home.

We served fourteen years on the island of Guam. During those years God provided us with numerous opportunities to minister and serve within the confines of the mission, the local church and providing a helping hand with other mission organizations in the region.

Some of the staff were worried that the apartment was too small and the car was only available for a few days. I had to start work as quickly as possible. Time to settle into a new culture was not in the plan. But it didn't take as long as we thought to feel a part of the ebb and flow of island life.

In all this God calmed our hearts, our fears and provided us with grace to understand His provisions. We were expecting grass huts and primitive conditions. We arrived to a modern apartment building. It was small, but so was our family. It definitely worked. We were excited, thrilled, and blessed to be where God called us.

For some the thrill of expectation prior to arrival on the mission field is often dashed when things are not as advertised. We've seen people arrive and then quickly look for a way to return to the home they know, the comfort of family and a lifetime of memories. Beth and I were prepared by God for this change even though we didn't know it. He does provide!

Pray for the Dead!

If Christ is in you, the body is dead because of sin, but the spirit is alive because of righteousness. (Romans 8:10 WEB)

On weekends I like to sleep in and enjoy a rested start to the day. I consider sleeping late to be anything past seven in the morning. My wife, Beth, felt this was way too early for anyone to stir. When we were first married I'd arise early and wander about our small apartment. After an hour or so of reading, looking out the window and boredom, I'd wander back to the bedroom.

Snuggling up to my lovely sleeping wife I'd whisper, "Are you ever going to get up?" It sometimes took a few renditions, with increased volume, before she would open one eye and see me smiling down at her. It was then I would look innocent and say, "Oh, were you still asleep? I didn't mean to wake you." She never believed me.

One Saturday morning on Guam, we were awakened to the mournful sounds of what must have been a dying moose or other large animal outside our apartment. Our daughter, Ellice, and son, Joel, came bounding into our room and climbed across the bed so we could see the unusual looks on their faces. It was a mixture between concern and curiosity.

"What's up, guys?" I asked them as they scampered across the covers, elbows and knees thumping us to wakefulness. Beth opened one eye and sniffed to see if there was breathable air.

"There are people across the street," said Ellice, "doing weird things."

"In the graveyard?" I asked. I piled up my pillows and slid to a sit against the headboard.

"What sort of things?" asked Beth, finally opening the other eye peeking from the safety of her blanket.

"Making weird noises and burning stuff," responded Ellice, curling her nose as if she were smelling a rotten apple.

"Let's take a look," I said. I tossed off the covers; Beth pulled them close and burrowed deeper. The children and I headed to the front door.

Our flat was situated on the second floor of a four unit apartment across the street from the local cemetery. The graveyard was sandwiched between the road and the shoreline. We surveyed the fence-bound graves. A lot of people stood next to gravestones or wandered around looking for a lost relative's last resting place. Once the graves were identified each person or family stood by a particular stone with flowers in hand.

Near one end, under the shade of a concrete cabana, stood the local priest. Dressed in flowing regalia and donning a spectacular liturgical hat, he chanted some liturgy in Latin or the local language. The people responded at the appropriate time with somber melodies in agreement. Back and forth the invocation was proclaimed and the musical affirmation responded.

11

The people, with priestly guidance, were praying for their relatives to depart purgatory and enter heaven. Candles, invocations, penance all struggled together to assure them the dead would rise again to Heaven. Uncertainty brought them back year after year.

It was an eerie sight which chilled our hearts. Their religion held no concrete answers. Their faith reminded us again of God's grace and love. Heaven awaits us, we are sure. It is not our candles, music, or attendance which opens the pearly gates. It is the saving grace God has provided through His Son on the cross.

We are staunch believers in the security of the believer. God has brought us into His kingdom and we are His. "My Father, who has given them to me, is greater than all. No one is able to snatch them out of my Father's hand." (John 10:29 WEB)

With our children we watched people, unsure of their eternal destination, giving all they could to possibly enter the Kingdom of Heaven.

The need is great . . . the workers are few . . . PRAY.

First Sight of the Antennas

But what does it say? "The word is near you, in your mouth, and in your heart;" that is, the word of faith, which we preach: (Romans 10:8 WEB)

On the day of our arrival on Guam, we were driven to the southern end of the island to the village of Malesso (Merizo). As we approached from the west we could see the impressive towers and antennas God used to reach into the Far East to over a third of the world's population. Our hearts leapt with joy and tears welled up in our eyes to see these steel and aluminum behemoths rising from the ridge of Mount Schroeder.

We rounded the southern tip of the island, drove up the mountain, down a dirt road and arrived at the transmitter building. Here I would be working with other engineers and technicians to bring the saving message of the Gospel to millions of people at the press of a button. This was a new world. I worked in commercial radio for many years prior to God's calling to TWR but not on the scale of these large antennas and not in the shortwave world.

George took us on a tour of the building and the antenna farm. It would not be until later, when I was working, that we'd hear the actual programs being aired. People from all over the USA and the world were gathered - no, brought together by God to use the wonder of modern electronics to make us fishers of men with a very long fishing pole.

As an engineer, I have a special fascination and love for electronics and radio in particular. When we're driving through cities I spot radio towers and antennas and then try to determine the type and purpose for each installation. This isn't something on Beth's list of things to do when traveling. However, in this case the scientific purpose of the antennas was of no interest as my heart jumped for joy realizing their eternal purpose was more than the flow of electrons and wave forms. In these wires flowed the message of everlasting life and eternity to the hearts of the listeners.

The difference between my previous experience in radio and what lay ahead took shape. This wasn't a job, this wasn't an occupation to keep the family fed and clothes on our backs. This was a calling from God to do whatever the Lord had for us to do in order for others to hear, understand, and respond to the marvelous message of salvation and love from God through his son Jesus the Christ.

Extreme Weather

He makes the storm a calm, So that its waves are still. Then they are glad because it is calm, So he brings them to their desired haven. (Psalm 107:29 30 WEB)

We arrived on Guam in June 1983. That was a good time of year. There were seldom, if any, storms in that season. It was hot and humid, normal tropical weather, but the typhoons were months away. It didn't take long to discover the intensity of the tropical sun.

Only a few minutes without a shirt or sun screen and a sun burn was evident by the lobster red color of our skin. Those who spent hours in the sun at a lake in New York found twenty minutes in Guam's sun sufficient to make their evening miserable. Sunshine was to be carefully metered until the clouds filled the sky and even then it was dangerous.

In the fall, the wind and rainy season began and so did the higher possibility for a typhoon. It was our first fall when we experienced this marvelous outpouring of nature. We weren't sure what to expect. A handbook was provided by the local government. Basically, everything needed to be tied down, picked up and otherwise removed from the open. The unseen force of the wind is very powerful. Once you've lived through a typhoon or a hurricane or a tornado you quickly identify with Jesus teaching on the Holy Spirit as a wind which comes unseen but with great power.

Watching our island neighbors provided certain clues concerning storms. Over the years we became accustomed to their reactions and gauged our response to a pending storm based on their inherited senses. While the weather service proclaimed disaster early and warned everyone to board up their windows, we watched the island residents. When the Chamorros started to bolt plywood to their windows we started to enclose our home, as well. It was quite a process.

Each home had a collection of storm boards fitted to the numerous windows around the house. The newer homes had aluminum fittings which were easier and, theoretically, secure. The older plywood boards, which our home sported, were rather bulky to carry around and wedge in the brackets for each window. If the wind started to billow around the neighborhood this became something like hang gliding with a plank on your back. Numerous dance steps could easily be developed by paying careful attention to newbies attempting to put storm boards up when the wind was too high.

With hammer in pocket and boards pulling at my hands in an attempt to fly free, I began the ritual. It was a rite of passage for new arrivals on the island. Many thumbs, fingers and hands were scarred and inflamed during the initial experience.

14

Each window sported a set of metal brackets for the storm boards. Unfortunately, the brackets were larger than the boards. This taxed the imagination with ways to fill the gap between the wood and the bracket. Digging through the clutter of the shed, pieces of scrap wood were gathered as shims to prayerfully keep the boards in place. The trick was to hold the board in place while nailing small pieces of shim to a thin piece of plywood before the next gust of wind ripped the plywood from your hands and flung it across the yard.

With the numerous storms we quickly learned the ins and outs of protecting our home from the pending storm. As many typhoons came close but not quite to the island it was often a practice exercise only. However, there is that first heavy strike of wind which starts the memories flowing for the rest of your life. During the height of one storm we watched a chicken fly down the road . . . backwards!

The might of the wind forcing the massive palm trees to bow in obedience was impressive. Watching cars and trucks bounce up and down, sometimes turned over or moved to a different parking place, was clear evidence this invisible force was something to be reckoned with, carefully, and in respect. This strength was evident driving home after a particular storm.

A colleague and I were operating the transmitters through as much of one storm as possible. We arrived early, while it was still a moderate wind with rain, and parked in front of the transmitter building. As the storm built to its peak we busied ourselves resetting the transmitters from overloads caused by swaying antennas. The battle turned in favor of the wind about two hours before the end of the shift as winds blew rain through the air chambers into the transmitters.

The transmitters were shut down, air chambers sealed against the horizontal rain and we waited out the storm. It was still raging when the shift ended and we decided to make a daring drive homeward. We were both new to the island and discovered this was a poor decision. Praise the Lord we arrived home safely through the dangers along the twenty-minute drive.

Driving back to the site later that day I was amazed at the immense damage to the island. Small wood homes and shacks were destroyed and downed telephone poles provided a high-tech canopy above the roads. The wire antennas were broken in sections and the transmitters needed some drying and repairs.

Beside the numerous typhoons, Guam is also center to the most earthquakes worldwide. There are shimmers and shakes every day. Most go unnoticed but some have a major impact. Within a few months of our arrival there was an earthquake in the night just prior to the arrival of a typhoon. Joel, three years old at the time, came into our room and said with all honesty, "Mommy, it's earthquaking and typhooning here. Let's get out of here!" A few years later he was an old pro for both natural occurrences, and provided a calming effect on other newcomers to the island.

There is one aspect of typhoons which is difficult for some people to deal with. There is a confined aspect as the storm passes over the island. One fall my mother was visiting for a few days and was the lucky participant in a passing typhoon. Being a bit on the claustrophobic side she was not pleased with the closed house during the 12 hours we waited for the storm to pass. We would often find her peeking through the cracks between the boards to catch a glimpse of the open sky.

Yet, there is beauty in the winds whirling and the swaying of the palm trees. A quick investigation of the fibrous material in the palm tree explains its ability to bend with the wind and why they are always still standing after the storm passes. A particularly large storm passed directly over the island one year. As the winds threatened to implode our home for several hours it became suddenly calm and quiet. Stepping outside and into the street we looked up to witness clear sunny skies. We were in the "eye" of the storm. This lasted about a half hour before the winds began to increase, from the opposite direction, and we were forced back into the house to ride out the backside of the storm.

The after effects of storms were usually more difficult to deal with than the passing winds and rain. For days, sometimes weeks, the approaching storm would dump water onto the island until it could soak up nothing more and the streets and low lands began to flood. Pushing the clouds ahead of the storm and pulling others within its swirls, the weather was less than amicable. When the storm passed it took the clouds and rain away.

Within hours of the storm passing the skies were cloudless and the sun shone with a vengeance. Heating the super saturated island, the humidity levels rose above the normal 85 percent to almost 100 percent. Since the storm knocked out the power, thus stopping the water pumps, we were left in a sweltering condition with no place for relief. The few offices which had generators and air conditioning become favorite havens to escape from the heat and humidity. Working long hours became a blessing.

The antennas, used to reach the far east, consisted of wire structures suspended between towers. With counter weights, up to eight tons, the force of God's wind became clear as these massive weights bobbed up and down like a fishing float on the river. The first few days after a storm were times for all hands to help with the reconstruction or repair of these life-giving antennas. It was dirty, tiring, and hard work.

When weeks later a letter arrived from a new believer who entered into our heavenly family because they heard the first program when the antenna was repaired, it all became more than worth the effort. We need to remind ourselves of the bigger picture and not get bogged down in the immediate hard work.

Roach Invasion

He said, "Throw it on the ground." He threw it on the ground, and it became a snake; and Moses ran away from it. (Exodus 4:3 WEB)

Nobody that I know likes roaches. They are disgusting little creatures you work a lifetime to eliminate from your home. As I was growing up the thought of finding a roach in our home was scandalous. Like everyone else, when they appeared we would quickly eradicate them by a heavy implementation of chemical weapons from the Raid company.

Guam was the perfect breeding ground for these critters. But Guam spawned no ordinary roaches. They ranged in size from miniscule to several inches. They could fly and would bite if handled. They loved cardboard boxes, especially stored in the outdoor cupboard, dark places and moisture. With the high humidity of the island there were always places for the enemy to expand their family tree. Their appearance was timed for when guests arrived or some other special event.

I remember scratching at something in my sleep one night. Suddenly I realized that the "something" was moving across my leg! God's design of the human mind is amazing. Within microseconds my mind went from la-la land to perfect alertness. I sprang from the bed with a shout, tossed off the covers and watched the immense night stalker dive for cover under the edge of the waterbed.

Beth, needless to say, was a bit startled at my sudden night time desire to remake the bedding. Six words, "there's a roach in the bed," and she too sprang to life, leapt from the comfort of the bed, grabbed a can of Raid and joined the hunt. Ten minutes later, the bed a mess, and our nerves on edge, we crushed the invader into another life, prayerfully down below. All hopes of a good night's rest were banished as we cautiously returned to bed. For hours, we thought any movement might indicate another invader. The next day we were very tired indeed!

Another night I was at a church board meeting until late in the evening. When I arrived home, I was greeted with a trophy board of roaches. It seems Beth and Ellice disturbed a piece of furniture, long sitting dormant, and unleashed an invasion. They achieved the upper hand and created the trophy to demonstrate their hunting prowess.

Like roaches, the schemes of Satan can be found anywhere and everywhere in this world. It only takes the projection of Jesus' perfect light to find the enemy running for cover. As believers, we must be vigilant to notice that touch, however light and unexpected, which signals something isn't right. It's then we need to jump, bring our thoughts to focus on God and call for the holy exterminator.

Island Church

Let us consider how to provoke one another to love and good works, not forsaking our own assembling together, as the custom of some is, but exhorting one another; and so much the more, as you see the Day approaching. (Hebrews 10:24 25 WEB)

One source of encouragement no matter where you travel in the world is to gather with other believers to worship God and learn from His word. The first few Sundays on the mission field were experimental. We visited each church, checking their beliefs, children's programs, and the quality and integrity of their preacher. It was interesting when we arrived at a church without a pastor and found it to be God's choice for our family. In no way was this a slight against the other churches, their members or organization. It was the Lord leading and providing for our family's needs after three years of deputation.

During the next fourteen years we would all be involved in many different ways in the growth and changes which would affect the local church. Serving in positions such as Sunday School Superintendent, Junior Church Superintendent, Deacon, Elder, Choir Director, Vacation Bible School teacher, music leader and audio consultant and installer, we watched the church change, grow, and work through difficult and good times. It was God's leading and we were thrilled to be part of His plan for the church and the many people who passed through the doors.

Things are not always as orderly as an engineer and theologian would appreciate. For years the large church parking lot was total chaos during every service and event. People parked anywhere. Some tried to make rows but regularly cars were blocked by those who needed to depart, making the end of services a bit nerve wracking for those who needed to be somewhere else. I suggested marking the lot for years. "Let's organize the parking lot," I proclaimed, "and we will fit in more cars than usual without the hassles when people come and go." My suggestion was ignored for years. Even while serving on the elder board I was unable to garner support for such a simple change for the church. In other areas of ministry, the church was very organized and functioned well. The Sunday services, mid-week prayer services, and special events were carefully planned and executed. Parking was another category all together. Finally, when I moved to the deacon board, I had my chance.

One sunny Saturday morning I brought my family to the church property. With string in one hand, spray paint in the other and a collection of measuring instruments and plans in my mind we went to work. Carefully measuring the space for the cars, putting them in an order which facilitated traffic flow into the back of the lot and out the front, we painted parking lot lines on the pavement. It took all day, lots of white paint, and some very energetic children to get it accomplished. Praise the Lord there was not a cloud in the sky so things dried quickly.

Come Sunday morning, with a little help from carefully placed deacons and youth to provide driving directions, the cars came, parked and departed without the usual confusion and frazzled nerves. When we departed from the island, the church board presented me with a beautiful photo in a nice frame showing all the parking lines to remind me of the church and all the work there.

There are times we need to poke one another to get things done. Sometimes that doesn't work. It may be God telling us to stop poking others and start poking ourselves. How often do we poke others with our suggestions and don't look in the mirror to see if God is telling us to get the job done?

The Music of Children

*He is ever lending generously, and his children become a blessing.
(Psalms 37:26 ESV)*

One of our greatest pleasures at church involved the entire family. On several occasions, we participated in or directed and worked in children's musicals. Ellice and Joel were the first participants, followed by the rest of the family. Beth directed several productions while I had the joy of participating as Psalty the Sailor and Patch the Pirate.

These were great times of working together and presenting the Gospel message in a format understood by all the island residents. Each performance would fill our church and provide opportunities to share and demonstrate the message of God's salvation. Many of the children found this a time for discovering God's message as they participated.

As Patch, I presented a unique character to the children and a source of humor for observant adults. Between acts I would move the patch from one eye to the other before I returned to the platform. Some noticed and tried hard not to snicker during the program. To children, pirates are ominous folks shrouded in mystery and intrigue. Patch was a little less dangerous but children's imaginations would still go wild.

One day, a few weeks after one of the Patch the Pirate programs, Beth and I were walking through the new island mall. A young girl who apparently attended the church program was also at the mall that day. Later, her mother told us, "My daughter saw you walking in the mall. She pointed your direction and said, 'There's that pirate.' Then she made us walk on the other side of the mall." Eventually I met the young lady and she discovered I was not quite the evil pirate she envisioned.

Children in the neighborhood would hear tales of the pirate who lived in the house in the middle of the street. They would peek through the fence when they thought no one was looking. If I was out in the yard they would cross over and walk on the other side of the street to keep from being shanghaied and hauled off as slave labor. They got over it.

These programs, the music, the participants, the island people's love for music and children provided numerous opportunities for talking and sharing the word of salvation with others. Our children were instrumental in our involvement.

Children are a wonderful lot. They can entertain, amaze and aggravate all in a matter of minutes. Their imaginations run wild and their enthusiasm is inexhaustible. Young hearts are looking for truth and the Gospel speaks directly to their need. We need to be careful and use every opportunity to share God's love with these little ones. Sometimes it may take the attention of a pirate. At other times it only takes a quiet conversation.

Directing the Choir

Now these, the singers, the heads of fathers' houses of the Levites, were in the chambers of the temple free from other service, for they were on duty day and night. (1 Chronicles 9:33 ESV)

Another aspect of church life we enjoyed was the choir. Several directors helped guide our small numbers through the first few years. Then there was a vacuum and I was asked to pick up the baton and direct the choir. This continued for most of the next twelve years and built many bonds of fellowship, ministry and service in the church body. This was a new ministry for me. I had been in many choirs, and involved with music for years. I felt I might be successful. Little did I know the Lord was going to keep me in that position for so long and teach me many things about directing. .

Take fifteen to thirty people, depending on the time of year, from five or six nationalities, most of whom do not speak English as their mother tongue, add some church choir music and the fun begins. One of the biggest challenges was picking music which was suitable for the church and the abilities of the choir members. My accompanist, Cindy, was excellent and would play anything I put on the piano. This helped tremendously.

Many of the choir members could not read music and some had questionable singing abilities. Each piece needed sufficient time for the choir to work through each part before bringing everything together to worship the Lord on Sunday morning. The Christmas and Easter Cantatas always brought in the most participants.

One time I had Beth sing soprano. At the time, she was singing alto and didn't want to move. I told her plainly, "Dear, I need at least one person in the soprano section who can read music and pronounce the English language so it is understood." She agreed and the resulting piece was beautiful and blessed our hearts as well as the congregation.

Working in music and the church allowed us to fellowship with others around the island from different denominations. One result was the formation of a choir for the Billy Graham Crusade.

In the 1990s Dr. Graham's message was to be simultaneously aired, via satellite, to a multitude of locations around the globe. On Guam it would be tape delayed to compensate for the time differences. As part of the local presentation a choir was formed from the evangelical churches on the island. Many of our choir members joined and it was a blessing for all who participated. Beth and I were also privileged to participate with solos.

Several thousand people came to the field house at the University of Guam to hear the choir and Dr. Graham. For four nights, the Lord brought the message of salvation through this servant to the people of Guam in an unusual and dramatic way. Hundreds came to the Lord through the messages. Beth and I participated in the counseling section of the crusade as well and were able to witness to residents who came forward in response to the invitation. What a blessing to be part of this personal, one on one ministry of God's saving grace.

I look forward to hearing the Heavenly Angels singing before God's throne. Then it will be a wonder to join in the ultimate chorus to worship and praise our creator. If you have trouble holding a melody, don't worry, the day will come, and last for eternity, when you will be able to sing with perfect pitch before the perfect God of the universe.

On the Right Page

My heart is steadfast, God, my heart is steadfast. I will sing, yes, I will sing praises. (Psalms 57:7 WEB)

For many years I worked in the church as a worship leader. At times others would help out and alternate but mostly I led the services for over ten years. The advantage of such a long period of service was forming close relationships with accompanists, special musicians and the church staff. After a few years I was very comfortable with both Cindy (the choir accompanist) and Jane who played for the worship services. This was a time when most church music came from the hymnal and praise choruses were accompanied by the piano.

Each Sunday morning, I would stand beside the quarter-grand piano as Jane, and sometimes Cindy or another pianist, checked out the hymns for the morning. Our goal was to ensure we used the same tempo and appropriate dynamics for each piece of praise to God. With this out of the way I could lead the service without the necessity of looking over to the piano to provide cues or directions. God worked with us to make things run smoothly, most of the time.

One morning Jane and I discussed the hymns. The timing was this for this hymn and yes there was an unwritten fermata I would insert into that hymn. We knew where we were going and how to get from one to the next. Jane played the end of the last hymn for the service and I sat down and we waited for the service to begin.

I stepped up to the podium, asked the congregation to rise and turn to hymn such and such, then waved my hand to set the time and listened as Jane played the last line of the hymn for the introduction. I followed along to confirm the right melody. My hands were lifted to start everyone simultaneously. We sang the first few words and I realized something was terribly amiss. I listened to the next phrase. I was singing the same words and melody as the congregation. Jane, on the other hand, was playing a totally different melody.

I signaled for the congregation to stop singing as Jane stopped playing and turned to see what was the matter. After I sauntered over to the piano, Jane and I discovered the problem. I started to laugh and took a moment to regain my composure. Then I stepped back to the podium. It was one of those one in a million events. The last line of the last hymn for the morning was almost identical to the last line of the first hymn. When Jane and I completed our routine walk through the hymns she forgot to turn back to the first hymn. So, I heard the right introduction, the congregation heard the right introduction, Jane played the right introduction, but it was the wrong page on the hymnal.

We both laughed as Jane flipped back to the correct page in the hymnal. With renewed vigor the entire congregation sang the correct hymn with the correct melody and the remainder of the service went smoothly. Jane and I found it to be humorous for years to come.

Sometimes we find our Christian life starting on one note and suddenly lost in another melody. We have to laugh, seek God's face and start again with renewed vim and vigor for His calling. When the master director gets our attention, the music is glorious harmony between our walk and God's direction.

A Missing Page - Winds of Change

Yahweh will save me. Therefore, we will sing my songs with stringed instruments all the days of our life in the house of Yahweh. (Isaiah 38:20 WEB)

One thing I always enjoy is leading singing. Waving my hands to and fro to keep people in time and hearing their voices joined together in song is a delight. Whether it is a choir or a congregation, I get chills as voices blend in praise to God. But, sometimes things don't go the way you plan them.

One Sunday morning C was playing the piano for hymn accompaniment. As usual before the service began I went through each hymn with C to ensure we were in sync with the same musical terms and tempo. A fermata here, repeat there, modulate here all worked together to help bring the congregation into God's presence. We were ready and the start of the service approached.

I lifted my hands and heard the correct introduction. The congregation sang with beautiful voices and we could sense the presence of the Lord as we sang a hymn of praise and adoration to God. The song rose and fell as we tried to express the dynamics of the composition. Voices blended in unison during the verse and then filled out the score of parts in the chorus. I closed my eyes, waved my hands and listened.

Halfway through the second stanza C suddenly stopped playing. The congregation and I kept singing. I opened my eyes and glanced toward C. There she sat with her hands in her lap smiling at me. Some members of the congregation glanced her way as we finished singing the hymn. A capella is almost always beautiful but usually part of a plan.

I indicated the next hymn title and then the number. I dislike for worship leaders to just spout out numbers like they make perfect sense to everyone. I don't know anyone who has the numbers memorized. I always like to hear the name since it helps prepare the heart. Everyone turned their pages and when they found their place they looked up in anticipation. I raised my hands hoping the piano would join us once more.

C played in her usual perfect style. Since we sat in different sections of the church, I couldn't talk to her until after the service. When everything was over, I worked my way through the fellowship and conversation to find C chatting happily with her husband and friends.

"C?' I said to get her attention.

"Yes?' she replied, turning to smile at me.

"Did I offend you or do something wrong this morning?' I asked quietly.

She looked at me quizzically and said, "No, why?"

"Well," I paused to consider how to make a simple question complicated, "you stopped playing halfway through the first hymn. Didn't you like that hymn?"

She laughed, put her hand on my shoulder and replied, "I love that hymn. But I took the pages out of the hymnal so I could spread them all out on the piano. As I played the breeze from the ceiling fan picked up that piece of music and it slipped between the music holder, the keyboard and right down inside the piano under the strings. I didn't have any music to play. You know I can't play without music." We both laughed and then tried unsuccessfully to extract the music from the piano.

The winds of change, in this case a ceiling fan, altered our direction for the morning and provided another humorous episode. As far as I know that piece of music is still inside the piano waiting to be let out from behind the bars of string. The breeze caught our attention and called for a change of plans. After that Sunday, we started leaving the music in the folder or turning off the ceiling fan over the piano.

Sometimes God takes pages from our lives unexpectedly and hides them out of sight. Like C we might find ourselves at a sudden loss, unable to continue. Then we must wait until God calls for the next page. It's then we start looking around to see if God is calling for a change. We stop taking things for granted. They just might blow away in a heavenly breeze.

Has God brought a sudden wind into your life? Are things out of place, hidden or beyond reach? Maybe it's time to see if God wants your attention on something else. Wait. Wait and watch for God to direct the next song of your life. Then you will be back in sync with the heavenly director singing in your heart the wonders of His grace.

Being Robbed!

But know this, that if the master of the house had known in what watch of the night the thief was coming, he would have watched, and would not have allowed his house to be broken into. (Matthew 24:43 WEB)

One year just before our furlough we were busy with church services, special music and making preparations to visit family, church and friends in the USA. We were excited about our ministry. We gathered listener letters to share, culled through our photographs and slides and organized our travel plans.

I remember spending weeks picking slides, borrowing slides, and writing a script. We wanted to express the work of God through the ministry. We wanted to show our personal involvement in God's work. We asked colleagues to read letters, with appropriate accents of course, and operate the recording studio. The operation cost us a few cookies and cans of soda! Missionaries will do just about anything for a good bag of cookies and cold drink. This was the age of the missionary slide show. Today it is Power Point and videos or DVDs.

DVDs were not available to the general public during those years. However, videos were becoming affordable and rental shops were opening even on Guam. Three days before our departure we borrowed a colleague's video player then a couple videos from another friend and scheduled an evening to rest, relax and enjoy the high-tech entertainment with Ellice and Joel. We worked on cleaning and preparing the house during the day and watching a video at night. This may have been the start of our famous Friday video and pizza nights.

Sunday came around and we jumped into the church services with enthusiasm. This Sunday we shared a little of our ministry, went to lunch with friends, visited others during the afternoon and then returned for the evening service to sing in a quartet. When we finally reached our home we were tired, very tired.

Ellice and Joel struggled to stay awake long enough to change into pajamas and crawl into their beds. They were asleep before we finished kissing them goodnight and leaving their rooms. Beth and I went through our routine lock up procedure and headed to the bedroom.

I deposited my pants on the chair beside the bed, we brushed, cleaned and climbed into bed. It was about twenty seconds before we were both deep in sleep. Our sleep was so deep I don't remember dreaming, just waking up the next morning ready to finish our packing. We were scheduled to depart that evening.

In the morning I reached for my pants and noticed my wallet sitting on top. I thought, "how curious" and then dressed. Wandering down the hall to the

27

living room I thought it odd the front door was open. I glanced in the children's rooms and they were still asleep. Beth was comfortable in our bed. Suddenly I realized things weren't right.

Cautiously I walked back into the living room and looked around. Something was wrong but I couldn't put my finger on the problem. Slowly I began an inventory of the room until my eyes rested on the cabinet between the living and dining room.

My radio receiver was where I left it. But the new stereo was gone! Our TV was still there but the borrowed video player was gone! I began to shake with the realization we were robbed while asleep in our own home.

I surveyed the front rooms and found the kitchen window screen was slit where the burglars entered the house. Apparently, we missed this window in our late night, tired, lockup procedure. I woke Beth up and explained what happened. We were both shaken by the experience. We called the police.

With more precision and detail than I expected, the Guam Police Department came, took finger prints and our detailed report including serial numbers and descriptions. They were relieved to discover only a few items taken.

One officer turned to us and said, "I'm glad you didn't wake up while they were in the house."

I gave him a quizzical look and asked, "Why?"

"Because," he replied directly, "if they were confident enough to break in while you were home they were probably armed. Most thefts on the island are by teenagers who only break into empty homes. When someone breaks into a house where people are sleeping they are very dangerous."

The Lord worked overtime to protect us by providing a busy schedule. Suddenly I remembered my wallet on top of my pants. I extracted it from my pocket and looked inside.

The credit cards, bank cards, photos and miscellaneous items were still inside but, sure enough, the cash was gone. About $100 in cash was taken directly from my wallet less than two feet from where I was sound asleep and I didn't hear a thing. Praise the Lord for keeping our eyes and ears shut throughout that night.

We never recovered the money, stereo or video player. It was several years before we could afford to replace them. It was also years before we felt completely safe in our own home at night. Our lockup procedure was carefully followed each evening and then the house checked each morning.

The thieves never returned. Slowly we learned to leave the feelings of invasion behind us. The event had shaken our confidence and feeling of security. Through the break-in God taught us His love and care and protection were beyond anything we could imagine.

Flying Chick Boy

But those who wait for Yahweh will renew their strength. They will mount up with wings like eagles. They will run, and not be weary. They will walk, and not faint. (Isaiah 40:31 WEB)

When we moved into our first Guam home I saw the opportunity to improve my amateur radio station by attaching a tower to the back of our concrete home. This also provided ready access to the roof. This is important on a tropical island. Annually you need to clean the roof and paint it white. That'll reduce the inside temperature several degrees on a clear day. A few stakes in the ground, a couple clamps on the roof, and everything was safe and secure. Joel was very observant while I was installing the radio tower.

A day or two later, Joel and his friend were playing in the yard. Beth and I had a simple rule for discipline when the children were young. If we told them not to do something after the first occurrence then there was no more excuse for disobedience. The problem with this mode of instruction was ensuring all bases were covered, before something terrible happened. It's amazing how many little things in life you don't remember when trying to set out the ground rules.

One day, Beth was sitting and reading in the living room. She heard a thud, thud, thud resound through the concrete walls then silence. A few minutes later she heard the same series of thuds. At first she thought it was the washer shaking the house until she realized concrete houses usually don't shake. During earthquakes they shake but this wasn't an earthquake.

Glancing out the dining room window she heard the same thud, thud, thud and then witnessed two very young boys (about three years of age) flying off the roof to land in the yard. They looked at each other then smiled with obvious glee and rushed toward the back of the house and the very convenient radio tower.

Across the roof they ran with capes made from blankets flying from their backs. In their enthusiasm, they leaped again only to find Beth waiting like a policeman at the end of their flight. I wonder if Superman ever met his mother after jumping from a tall building. Beth wasn't happy.

A new rule was quickly laid down before someone was hurt in his imaginative use of available materials and access. They were disappointed with the new rule but glad they weren't sitting on hot, sore bottoms at dinner time.

A few years later we visited with folks we met from the Naval Air Station. They were the proud and harried parents of a couple energetic and imaginative boys as well. While we enjoyed conversation and fellowship they pulled an old parachute from the closet.

Their children would use the material in a number of ways including building forts, tossing things in the air, etc., to entertain themselves. As they handed the parachute to James his eyes lit up with glee and expectation. Along with Ellice and Joel he went out the door, clutching the parachute to his chest.

As a quick last-minute reminder Beth shouted to them, "No jumping off the roof with the parachute!" James turned to look at us and was crestfallen as he slumped out the door to play.

Our friends turned to us and said, "We never thought of that. Why would you think of that?"

Beth calmly replied, "We know our son. Given the chance he would jump off the tallest building with a napkin if he thought he could float to the ground."

Just like our boys, we tend to know God's rules but ignore them until we hear a thundering voice of correction. Common sense to do some things and not others is a gift from God. As Calvin, a cartoon character, once said, "I have lots of common sense. I just choose to ignore it." Let's listen as God prompts us, from our hearts, to live in obedience before the hand of correction falls.

A Doorkeeper in the House of God,

For a day in your courts is better than a thousand. I would rather be a doorkeeper in the house of my God, Than to dwell in the tents of wickedness. (Psalms 84:10 WEB)

(An excerpt from our March 1985 prayer letter written by Beth.)

As I was considering our work with the mission and reading this passage, I felt that "we" as missionaries are "door keepers" at the house of our God. I considered the great privilege involved. Yet, in the world's eyes, we do not perform work that is either prestigious or comfortable.

Jesus is the "door" to heaven. He is the only way. And as believers we are standing at the door to show the world where He is, the doorway to heaven.

Not all of our work is thrilling. But as a doorkeeper in God's house, work is part of our duty. In the end we discover that truly it is "better" in His courts as a simple doorkeeper than to dwell with the wicked.

In the Mail Department here where I work, essential and exciting work is accomplished. But it is not always the answering of spiritual questions and letters, the sending out of tracts, or helping to provide biblical counseling. Sometimes envelopes and stamps must also be licked, and stamps placed on the envelopes in order for the information to reach our listeners.

There is also the necessity of stamping tracts and lessons with the mission address. Otherwise non-believers couldn't correspond with us, we wouldn't receive information for prayer from listeners, and then we wouldn't be able to encourage believers as they grow in faith. Every day is not spent just searching Scripture for an appropriate, prayerful verse to help a listener. There is also the filing of listeners' cards and the typing of envelopes.

Much of this may sound like mundane, routine work and not perfect for someone good in math and science. Still, the listeners will not receive answers to their searching unless this work is done.

Bob could also tell you the same. At the broadcast station in Merizo it's not all climbing towers and making major transmitter upgrades. Most of the time is spent performing routine maintenance to reduce OFF AIR time. This is what Bob calls dusting and cleaning. On the 6 PM to 2 AM shift, transmitter upgrade/maintenance is only done when there is a failure. Yet, while working PM shifts, Bob hears the word of life going out over those four super power transmitters in four different languages at a time. He hears God's word going forth to a needy world.

What a joy it is to be a "doorkeeper." How privileged to lick stamps, scrub floors, and maintain transmitters so that MILLIONS can hear the Gospel of our Lord and Savior Jesus Christ.

Glowing Light Bulbs

The night is far gone, and the day is near. Let's therefore throw off the works of darkness, and let's put on the armor of light. (Romans 13:12 WEB)

Occasionally we'd have visitors on Guam. Sometimes they were relatives but occasionally a group of visitors arrived from one of our target areas to experience the ministry first hand. Such was the case with our Japanese listeners. Through our partner in Japan a number of listeners, along with workers in the Japan office, came to meet us face to face. Many of our guests came to salvation through the programs they heard from KTWR. To celebrate we held a picnic at the transmitter site in Merizo. Our staff cooked local food on large open grills made from old fifty-five gallon barrels. We added fixings and drinks and celebrated God's work through the ministry. I worked with a colleague to cook burgers, short ribs and goodies for ninety- seven people!

Throughout the day's festivities we demonstrated the transmitting equipment and attempted to explain shortwave radio propagation. We were thrilled when a couple of folks in the group listened intently to the technical explanations and then the discussion of the Gospel message. They were not believers! In the course of the celebration they too heard and understood God's message of salvation. They gave their lives to Christ that day and returned to their homeland members of our eternal family.

Amazingly not everyone in life is familiar with the fascinating world of radio frequencies and their effects on the environment. In truth, most people are afraid of electricity and anything electronic. They don't understand how it works and frankly, don't want to know. As long as the light comes on with the switch they're happy. During this visit we demonstrated the magical effects of RF radiation from an antenna.

I took a burned out fluorescent light bulb then walked up hill from the transmitter building until I was underneath the transmission lines. A transmission line is a bunch of wires which connect the transmitter to the antenna. (That's the technical explanation.) It's through these lines the radio waves reach the antenna and then radiate thousands of miles to the target areas.

I held the four foot long bulb vertical with a hand on each end. Then I slid the upper hand down the tube. The lamp then started to glow through the interaction of the high power shortwave signal and the gas inside the tube. It's fascinating and fun to watch and experience.

Our Japanese guests were amazed, a bit skeptical, and frightened. I asked for a volunteer to hold the bulb. There was a unanimous refusal from the crowd. Finally, Hitoshi, our Japanese colleague living on Guam, carefully walked to where I was standing and took hold of the lamp. He tilted it sideways to make sure it wouldn't shock him or produce some dangerous result. His friends cheered him on as he waved the lamp like a light saber from Star Wars.

There are a lot of things God calls me to do in life. Many of them frighten me. I've found faith and strength stepping into these callings. It's there I discover the power of God working in my life. I just need to get past the glowing light and put my hand to the lamp.

Whitewashed Roofs

"Woe to you, scribes and Pharisees, hypocrites! For you are like whitewashed tombs, which outwardly appear beautiful, but within are full of dead people's bones and all uncleanness. (Matthew 23:27 ESV)

Housing on Guam was different from the ubiquitous wooden frame houses in the USA. Individual homes were built more like apartment complexes with concrete walls, ceilings and floors. Local earthquakes and typhoons made this a good solution to the island housing needs. There were advantages and disadvantages to the design.

One of the advantages was obvious as I setup my amateur radio gear. I purchased a small radio tower from a departing missionary and an antenna from a departing enlisted man at the Naval Air Station. I eliminated the need for guy wires and special mounting base by standing the tower next to the house and anchoring it to the concrete ledge protruding all around the roof. It was a great solution, easy to implement and provided great access to the roof.

Roof access was vital to survival in the tropical climate. With concrete construction, most of the houses sported flat roofs. Take a slab of concrete the size of a house, add in regular earthquakes and cracks develop. In addition to the cracks, the moisture in the air ("low" humidity was 85%) was an incentive for mold to grow in leaps and bounds on the roof, turning it black.

If you studied solar heating you would recognize that black is a great color to collect heat. Unfortunately, we wanted to reduce the heat in our home, not increase the Easy Bake Oven effect. In order to reduce the cost of electricity from air conditioning there was a semi-annual schedule to paint the roof a beautiful and blinding white.

The local hardware and paint stores made a fortune on roof paint. Some paints were reputed to have anti mold formulas. This special formula demanded a higher price. We tried it once but the mold returned just as quickly as with cheaper paint. Applying the paint to the roof was a laborious task preceded by a thorough cleaning of the surface.

Cleaning the surface required using a power washer. These gas-powered, high-pressure washers worked great. They performed several functions at the same time. First, they removed the unwanted mold and loose paint from the roof. For the family member inside the house the washer revealed the areas where cracks had developed by flooding the house with water. Finally, the high-pressure water stream quickly removed flesh and muscle down to the bone if you weren't careful which way the nozzle pointed. I know from experience!

Discovering the cracks in the ceiling was good. This was the first part of the second step to recondition the roof. After the water dried, tar was applied to the long and sometimes deep cracks on the ceiling. The patchwork quilt was then covered by a thick layer of shining white paint. A cloudy day was best for painting so the reflection didn't hurt the eyes. The finished product was beautiful to behold, plus it provided a functional result. Painting the roof white could reduce the interior temperature of the house about 10 F degrees on a sunny day.

Painting complete, radio tower attached to the house, things were in order to live in the tropics another year or two. The entire job was simplified by the ready access to the roof via the radio. We lived in a white washed bunker ready for the next storm.

Jesus called the religious leaders white washed tombs because they looked good on the outside and were filled with death on the inside. Our home was first cleansed by the blood of Christ on the inside and then white washed to remove the exterior mold and decay. Often we concentrate on the outside appearance while the inside is in shambles. A clean exterior may make the inside feel cooler but it doesn't clean it up. It may be a good time to stop looking at the roof and start cleaning the inside.

Children and Neighbors

For to you is the promise, and to your children, and to all who are far off, even as many as the Lord our God will call to himself." (Act 2:39 WEB)

Children are fascinating to watch around the globe. Arriving as the foreigners on our little island, our children had to deal with being the outsiders. Just as adults must find their fit into society children also must learn how to relate to and play with the other children in a new culture.

Ellice and Joel were only five and three when we arrived on Guam. They didn't notice the differences in skin color or even the accents prevalent on the island. To them their neighbors were just other children. As children they wanted to play!

In our first apartment there were only four flats and no children. The shack next door was home to a couple young children but there was no chance for us to allow our children out to play. Within a month we moved from this small flat to a house in a nice neighborhood. It didn't have the nice view of the ocean but it was a large house with a bedroom for each of our children.

Ellice and Joel played out in the yard hoping to become friends with the neighborhood children. There were many. Most of the children were Chamorro (island natives) or Filipino. As the children played about the neighborhood they eventually noticed our two blond and bleached children playing in our yard.

Our children sat on the curb and watched the other children play and waited. Unfortunately, the local children were not very friendly to strangers. Occasionally one would cross the street and actually kick Ellice or Joel and then dance back home laughing at the foreigners.

I wanted to give these children a piece of my mind, something I can seldom afford to give away. Ellice and Joel didn't appear too upset and were very stalwart as they waited. Each day they played and sat, played and sat, and occasionally received some abuse from the other children.

Their faithfulness in waiting patiently had a slow but definite impact. The reaction from the local children became less violent and eventually stopped. In a couple of weeks, they started to talk with the new neighbors. It was then that our children had a chance to share some of their life in the USA as they answered questions about where they came from and why we were there.

As the years went by the opportunities to witness to our closed neighbors were enhanced and opened through the faithfulness of our children. The next summer we held Bible Clubs in our home and most of the neighborhood children attended. A couple of them received Christ as their Savior.

When school started Ellice and then later Joel were involved in school activities, clubs, and events so the doors opened more and more to witness to the neighbors. Opportunities were opened to witness not only to neighbors but also to teachers as our children stood proudly for their Savior in a class where they were one of maybe two other foreigners.

Jesus said we need to be like children in our faith. Sometimes we need to be like children with our neighbors. It may take a while for them to notice but God's presence in our lives will become evident.

Out of the Lips of Children

At that time Jesus declared, "I thank you, Father, Lord of heaven and earth, that you have hidden these things from the wise and understanding and revealed them to little children; (Matthew 11:25 ESV)

If you travel west from Guam toward the USA you'll find China. Usually you travel east to the USA. But things aren't always as you'd think. It was cheaper to fly to Hong Kong first, purchase a ticket to the USA and then fly to the USA. Go figure. There's something strange about airline ticket pricing. So, on our first furlough we decided to visit Hong Kong and take a one-day trek into mainland China. We settled into a small apartment in Hong Kong and prepared for the big day.

We boarded a bus in Hong Kong and headed toward the China border. When we arrived at the border we were inspected, checked, and passed on from station to station. With our money changed and bags in hand we entered China ready for a firsthand peak at our biggest target area. While everyone else on the bus was going to visit relatives, we were the only family on "tour." After crossing the border, we met our private translator and our driver and climbed into a small van.

We rode around and enjoyed the sites and learned more about the people. During our tour we had a chance to chat with the translator. The driver wasn't interested in conversation and the translator indicated we should be quiet about certain subjects so he would not report her to the authorities.

Our translator made a comment after Ellice began singing, "Jesus loves me this I know." Ellice wanted to share the Gospel of Jesus with the people of China. She knew this was why we were living on Guam and so she wanted to help in our ministry. Thus, the conversation turned to the Gospel.

Turning to face us and not be heard by the driver, our translator meekly let us know she was Christian. She had heard the Gospel over the radio! What a marvelous confirmation of God's work in our lives. The work to minister to this vast nation was having an impact. We were encouraged as God provided us with a face to face confirmation. "So shall my word be that goes forth out of my mouth: it shall not return to me void, but it shall accomplish that which I please, and it shall prosper in the thing I sent it to do." (Isaiah 55:11 WEB) We have no information about the young lady's name or what she's done since this meeting but pray for her walk with the Lord in a nation which opposes her belief.

We were also interested in visiting a Chinese home if possible. Finally, after many inquiries, our translator gained access to a three- story home. We were informed this was a single family home but if that was true it was a very large family. As we wandered through the rooms to the balcony on the top floor, we discovered why they allowed us to tour their home.

Little girls with long, blond, curly hair were unknown in their culture. They were fascinated with a little girl sporting a head of long, blond, curly hair. Almost everyone in the house reached out to touch Ellice's hair. Personal space is a different story in China.

In America people don't like to be caught staring at another person. If we're watching someone and they turn our direction we quickly look away and pretend we're doing something else.

During the trip, we were taken to visit a large department store. As we walked through the building we noticed a couple of things. First, we were the only people in the store besides the employees. This was not an average Chinese shop but designed for visitors. Second, we realized everyone was staring at us. When we turned and saw them watching they kept right on watching and didn't attempt to turn away. The store had lots of goods for sale inside and a small bumper car ride outside.

We decided to allow Ellice to ride the bumper cars. It's not fun if you're the only participant. So we paid to have our translator drive one of the cars. It took a bit of convincing and coercion to get her to agree to drive the little car. It wasn't a matter of her driving but the combination of her driving and our paying the bill. This show of generosity was not in her frame of reference. When she started the ride her smile and joy was more than we needed in repayment for the kindness.

Since it was an all-day tour we stopped for lunch. The tables were full, conversation was loud and energetic. There was a pause in the restaurant's din of conversation as we entered and took our place around the round table. The table was large so we could all sit, including the translator but not the driver (who went off on some unknown function while we ate) to enjoy a preset meal. A white tablecloth hung over the edges and rice bowls were placed at each seat. The only utensils provided were chop sticks.

One item missing was a napkin. I looked about to see if other tables had these, in my opinion, essential items. They did not. I soon discovered the purpose for such a large tablecloth. Glancing down at the overhanging cloth on my table I saw the remains where others wiped their mouth, hands, whatever on the cloth in lieu of napkins. On the next visit to China, I vowed to bring my own tissues, for lunch if nothing else!

The food was tasty and plentiful. I don't remember all the dishes we received but one caught Joel's attention. A large fish of some sort was brought out on a platter and placed in the middle of the table. It was split open and broiled, but the head and tail were still attached. Like the other dishes we all reached to the platter and removed a portion with our fingers to eat over the rice bowl in front of us. The bowl provided a nice catch for anything which missed the lips and fell.

Joel leaned forward and stared at the fish. He didn't attempt to reach for any of the meat. After a couple of minutes, he looked at Beth and me and said,

39

"That fish is looking at me!" The fish was situated with the head and eyes towards Joel's seat. He wasn't about to eat something which was staring him in the face. We turned the fish the other way and Joel then enjoyed the tasty meal.

When we finally departed the country, it was back through the border. In the time it took us to enter the country, visit a museum, see a reservoir, shop in the stores, eat lunch, drive about and return to the border, the exchange rate changed. It changed in our favor and we received more money when we turned in our script than we paid to receive it. It was a free day after all!

Children say the most unexpected things at the most embarrassing times. Ellice was open about her faith and love for our translator. If not for her honesty we never would have known to pray for our young translator and her faith.

As adults, we miss things we once saw as children. It seems our observations are hampered with age. Jesus made it clear wisdom was hidden to the wise and open to the child. Maybe it's time we started acting like children in our faith and see what God wants us to see.

Timing is Everything

Blessed is the man who fills his quiver with them! He shall not be put to shame when he speaks with his enemies in the gate. (Psalms 127:5 ESV)

A missionary furlough is not an extended vacation. On the contrary, furloughs are full of adventure, new sights, new sounds, and lots of work and travel. Schedules, transportation and lodging are a big part of setting up a furlough. For our first furlough one church provided us a nice home. No rent, furnished, and the only bill we had to pay was the telephone. Go figure.

For the first few weeks of furlough we didn't occupy the house; we traveled. We retrieved the old car we left with friends. Next we drove around the eastern USA visiting friends and churches. As we drove from place to place Beth didn't feel well.

We thought she was having problems with jet lag. We visited a pastor friend and his family in Georgia and they also noticed Beth was having difficulty. The wife, Susan, worked in a pregnancy counseling center and made a suggestion. Maybe Beth wasn't sick. Nope, couldn't be. At least it wasn't what we were planning.

With a simple test, we discovered our third child was on the way to join us during furlough. As we say, designed in Hong Kong and assembled in the USA! With this mystery resolved it was easier to deal with the travel schedule.

Eventually we rented a truck in Kentucky and piled it full of our belongings, then drove to our furlough home in Missouri. During our stay in the missionary home I learned how to use a riding lawn mower and even how to re-roof the house alongside the church members. Our children attended the Sunday School and Awana clubs when we were in town, and friendships developed.

Since furlough is a time for raising funds and partnering with new churches I disappeared for days at a time to visit other cities. There I tracked down churches and shared the ministry with pastors and anyone willing to listen. Slowly our support was pledged and our son's arrival approached.

In March of 1986 we were scheduled to participate in a special missionary service in the church that provided our housing. Beth wasn't feeling well enough to attend the service so I took Ellice and Joel. Sunday School went well as I taught a lesson. In the worship service I sang special music and led the congregational singing. As soon as the special music was over someone came down the aisle and informed me it was time to take Beth to the hospital.

I left the children with friends and headed home. We were quickly off to the hospital and found it was a booming day for babies. There was no room at the inn so to speak! For the first half hour Beth occupied a gurney in the hallway. Finally, we received a private room because all the semi-private rooms were full.

41

The labor hall was bursting at the seams so when it was time for the big event we stayed in the room where James Alexander was born at just before 1 p.m. I watched a Star Trek episode on the room's television and held Beth's hand at the same time. I really did pay attention to the birth but it was nice to have a distraction when things were boring! HA!

By late afternoon Beth and James were comfortable in their beds in the hospital and everything was in order. I hurried back to pick up my stuff at the house and then was off to church for the evening service.

To start the service, I read the passage: "Then he said to his disciples, 'The harvest indeed is plentiful, but the laborers are few. Pray therefore that the Lord of the harvest will send out laborers into his harvest.'" (Matthew 9:37 38 WEB)

I preached in the evening service and started with a poor joke about bringing more workers into the harvest field! Timing is everything they say and this was a day of good timing.

Awards and Arms

For everything there is a season, and a time for every purpose under heaven: (Ecclesiastes 3:1 WEB)

On our first furlough Beth, Joel and Ellice spent most of their time in our furlough mission home and with the small Bible church in O'Fallon, Missouri while I was out visiting churches, pastors and supporters. Since Beth was pregnant this worked well. She could establish a permanent obstetrician and get things in order about the house. Ellice was in school. She attended J.L. Mudd Elementary School.

J.L. Mudd Elementary School was a short bus trip from our home. Each morning we watched Ellice walk down the street to the corner and wait for the familiar yellow colored Blue Bird school bus. Why they called them Blue Bird buses when they were yellow is a mystery. There were other young children in the neighborhood so Ellice had the chance to make friends at home and at school. Unlike Guam she was just one of the crowd, not a pale faced foreigner.

Along with school Ellice and Joel were busy with the Awana programs at the church. The church, although small, was filled with gracious, loving hearts ready and willing to share the Gospel and ministry with as many as possible. Each week Ellice and Joel would sing, play games, learn verses and get to know the other children in the church and neighborhood. Beth was also part of the teaching and fun each week.

Ellice and Joel had a blast and earned a number of awards during the year. One highlight was attending the awards night. In the spring, there was a big night planned and Ellice was to receive a special award. She was excited all day and could hardly wait.

Just after dinner she went outside to play on the swing set. There was still an hour before the ceremony. I glanced out the window and watched as she started walking slowly back toward the house. The look on her face made it obvious something was wrong. Her joyous smile was gone and she looked serious.

Ellice came in and told us she fell from the swing. At first, she didn't want to say anything because she wanted to go to the ceremony. Her arm hurt. We looked at the arm, considered waiting until after the ceremony but it was obvious a visit to the emergency room was necessary.

I drove her to the hospital in St. Joseph's and explained the incident to the staff. Beth took Joel and attended the Awana awards to receive Ellice's award. This may sound routine but I'm not a lover of hospitals, needles, doctors or anything associated with hospitals, needles or doctors. After I worked in a hospital for four years I avoided walking through the doors like there was a plague inside. It was a miracle I was able to attend the birth of all my children!

That evening Ellice and I were killing time waiting for an available doctor in the emergency room. A doctor finally came to us and smiled as we repeated the details of the accident. A few minutes of examination, one X-ray and it was a definite break. Not only was it a break but it would require a "closed reduction" to complete the break and set the arm correctly. It was too late in the evening for the surgery so a temporary cast was applied, the operation scheduled for the next morning and we returned home with the news.

Ellice was a sad little puppy that evening. Not only had she missed receiving her special award, "Sparky of the Year," but now she had to go back to the hospital for surgery. Surgery was uncertain territory for Ellice. This was not the first broken bone but the first requiring surgery. I don't believe she slept well that night.

The next morning Beth and I took Joel to stay with friends and headed to the hospital. Ellice was a trouper. It was apparent she was concerned but she did well as they dressed her, gave her medication to sleep and started an IV.

The procedure was quick and short. Basically, they completed the break then set and cast the arm. Fortunately, this does not require opening the arm. It sounds rather brutal but was necessary to ensure a clean and straight healing process. A few hours later Ellice awoke and was groggy for a while, then had some pain but recovered rather quickly.

As a second grader Ellice was not going to slow down just for some broken arm. She pressed on, had a great time as school let out for the summer and ignored that stiff arm as she played, jumped, ran and did all the things a little girl does to have fun.

I wonder why things happen when they do. They don't always make sense and sometimes seem brutal. Ellice missed her award but gained strength in her ability to deal with accidents, and even hospitals. I'm not sure why God allowed this to happen but I do know it was for a reason. Sometimes we need to just wait and listen to discover the good from a bad situation.

Flat Roofs

"When you build a new house, you shall make a parapet for your roof, that you may not bring the guilt of blood upon your house, if anyone should fall from it." (Deuteronomy 22:8 ESV)

Our daughter Ellice started first grade on Guam and continued in the second grade during our first furlough. We enrolled her in J.L. Mudd Elementary School. I suppose Mr. Mudd was a famous person but the name always struck me as funny.

The process was simple and she joined other young girls and boys to learn about reading, writing, and arithmetic. (How do you get the Three Rs with one "R," a "W" and an "A?") The school was not far from our furlough home but she rode a bus each day.

One day we received a note from her teacher. The teacher requested a conference to discuss our darling daughter. Ellice was strong willed but loved school and having fun. Her grades were just fine and she appeared to get along well with the other children in the neighborhood. We were curious why we needed a conference. I unfortunately had a schedule to keep so Beth met with the teacher.

The teacher was careful to choose her words. To soften the obvious bad news, she first commended Ellice on her good spirit and good grades. She was doing well with the other students. The problem was her perceptions of reality. The results of our daughter's drawing class revealed Ellice might need psychological help.

The teacher continued to explain the situation. There was a drawing assignment. Ellice was to draw a simple house with trees representing her real home. Searching through her desk drawer the teacher withdrew Ellice's work and placed it on the desk.

"It's obvious," stated the teacher using tones of concern and an air of authority, "Ellice doesn't have a complete grasp on reality."

Pointing out details of the drawing, she continued, "Here we have a house with a flat roof and the trees are inside out. We both know," she continued, indicating it was a well-established fact, "houses have pointed roofs and trees are pine or leafy trees. It seems Ellice has conceptual problems."

Beth looked at the drawing, looked at the teacher and almost laughed out loud. Ellice drew a perfectly good representation of our home on Guam. We have flat roofs on Guam. We have palm trees in our yard which look like inside out trees. Beth explained this difference and that Ellice was well aware of how our house looked. The teacher was both surprised and amazed.

The teacher's understanding of the world was limited by her experience and she had not considered Ellice's background during the evaluation. This was not the first time such misunderstandings would occur in the life of our children. The remainder of her time at J.L. Mudd was great.

Just like our daughter we're not always understood. Sometimes as Christians we assume people understand our point of view, our background. Misunderstandings quickly develop and people can get offended. It's important to sometimes explain the parapet on our roof or the palm tree in our yard. It's sometimes necessary to open our own eyes to see the palm tree in the yard of someone else.

Car Trouble - Doubled

But the salvation of the righteous is from Yahweh. He is their stronghold in the time of trouble. Yahweh helps them, and rescues them. He rescues them from the wicked, and saves them, Because they have taken refuge in him. (Psalms 37:39 40 WEB)

During a one-year furlough we drove many miles in our 12-year-old Ford. It was a great car. It was big, comfortable, had cruise control, and included what I called "frost bite" air conditioning. This was really great in the summer months. But even with a good car, things go wrong. This furlough was no exception to the rule.

In the fall I traveled without Beth and the children so Ellice could attend school. One of my trips was to the Mississippi delta town of Memphis. We had a few contacts through a former TWR missionary. One couple graciously offered me a bed in their home for a few days while I worked through the church yellow pages in attempts to meet pastors and increase our support.

One day in the middle of Memphis the car motor stopped. A couple little coughs, a little spurting and then dead. Great, I'm in a city I don't know, staying with people I just met, and my car dies. With no other option I found a pay phone and called my host.

He had a heart with a desire to serve the Lord whenever possible. He listened to my plight and said he would be down as soon as possible. I called a tow truck and the car was hauled to a shop somewhere in the city for repairs. My friend took me back to the house and offered to bring me down for the car the next day when it would be ready.

The middle of the afternoon the following day we rode in his restored Chevy (very nice) to pick up my car. I was never sure where the shop was located. When I entered the shop it was ready and I proceeded to pay the bill.

With our home on Guam using a bank established in Hawaii and now living temporarily in Missouri, things got a little tedious. The owner of the shop processed my credit card with a phone call for authorization. After a couple minutes, he informed me there was a problem with the card. I asked him to try again. He did. The authorization center still insisted I needed to talk with my bank. This wasn't likely since my bank was on a small island thousands of miles away.

My friend saw I was a bit upset. He offered to pay the bill to get the car back on the road and I could send him the money later. Praise the Lord! Here was a man I only met a couple days before willing to pay my bill and trusting me to drive back to Missouri and send him a check. The Lord surely provides in unexpected ways. I returned home and mailed a check to my friend to clear up the debt I owed.

Things went well for the next couple of months. But, sometimes small unexpected items can cause large problems. The second failure occurred on a busy day driving along the interstate through the hectic and confusing traffic of Saint Louis.

The whole family was returning from a Sunday morning meeting in a small town across the border in Illinois. The service went well and we were looking forward to a relaxing afternoon. Fortunately, the traffic wasn't too heavy as we pointed our Ford toward home.

In the middle of the intertwining of interchanges and roads I was out in the left lane to pass a slow driver. Suddenly, instantly, the motor stopped. No sputter, no hesitation, no signs, just completely dead. Praise the Lord we had just crested a small rise in the highway.

Using gravity and our initial inertia I navigated the car across the four lanes between faster cars to the shoulder and rolled to a stop. Two small children, a pregnant wife and a dead car. What would we do now?

This was before the ubiquitous cellular phone and there were no emergency phones within sight. I exited the car, opened the hood, and gazed at what was obviously an automobile engine. At least that's what the mechanics call it. Lots of tubes, wires, and mechanical looking gadgets which had names I didn't know.

With a look of understanding I climbed back into the car and authoritatively informed Beth, "It's dead." Beth is a perceptive person and knew I didn't have a clue what was happening. Her graciousness abounded as she nodded, accepted my evaluation and then asked what was next.

I didn't know. As I contemplated walking to the next exit a car pulled up behind us and stopped. An unknown lady with a car phone offered assistance. We knew none of the shops or mechanics so I called a friend at the church who was a machinist and car mechanic. If he didn't know how to fix the car he would know the best man for the job.

The lady who provided the phone call also provided a ride home for Beth and the children as I waited for Mr. Mechanic (our friend) to send a tow truck. When the truck arrived, the driver introduced himself as Mr. Mechanic's friend and we headed toward home. I was dropped off at the house and the car continued to be towed to Mr. Mechanic's home in the country.

The next day we were taken to Mr. Mechanic's home for a nice evening meal and to take a look at the car. At first he didn't show signs of interest in helping fix the car. When I explained we were more than willing to pay for repairs his attitude changed.

We later discovered other missionaries came to the church and expected all their needs, repairs, and work to be provided free of charge. After we explained this was not the case for us, because we knew he needed to earn a living and we had a fund to help with such repairs, he was glad to do the work.

All he asked was to be reimbursed for the parts he might need. We shook hands in agreement and then walked to the garage to inspect the car.

It took only a few minutes for him to determine the fuel pump was not pumping fuel. The problem wasn't the pump but the cam (whatever that is) that activated the pump. Removing the front of the engine, he was surprised to discover the bolts were very loose. As he went deeper he found the cam swinging freely inside the cover.

Things started to make sense. When the car was repaired in Memphis, which included opening this portion of the engine, they didn't properly torque the bolts, causing the cam to come loose, the fuel pump to stop pumping and me to be stranded on the side of the highway.

Praise the Lord for faithful and willing servants such as Mr. Mechanic to discover the problem quickly, tighten the bolts and watch us drive home after a great country dinner.

While I learned something about cars and mechanics, I am sure Mr. Mechanic learned something that evening as well. Not all servants of the Lord expect everything for free. The laborer, both missionary and mechanic, is worthy of his wages. It's a two-way street!

Snow

For he says to the snow, "Fall on the earth;" Likewise to the shower of rain, And to the showers of his mighty rain. (Job 37:6 WEB)

Living close to a metropolitan center of Saint Louis in O'Fallon, Missouri, our year in the USA provided a number of new experiences for Ellice and Joel. I remember the first time it snowed at our furlough home.

Joel was too excited to sit still or wait to don all the necessary cold weather coat, hats, gloves, boots, etc. He squirmed and tried to escape outside while Beth struggled to keep him warm. Ellice was home from school that day. Unfortunately, she was very sick and only vaguely remembered some snow.

Joel went out in the yard and did all the things children do in snow. James, not his future brother but a friend's seventeen-year-old son, graciously played with the little island boy who had never seen snow.

One of the first things Joel learned was how to make snow angels. Within minutes we had an army of angels guarding our house on every side. Ellice watched from the window, upset that she had to stay inside.

The snow angels were followed by snowmen, snowball fights, more snow angels and lots of laughter. Snow was tracked in the house, wet clothes covered the surfaces of the spare room, but then it became only a fading and memory.

When I think of snow I remember fourteen years later when we were living in Austria. Joel and the whole family lived for years on Guam with the tropical weather and cook outs on the beach at Christmas time. A cold winter Christmas was something new. Turn it into a white Christmas and a whole new world of adventure opens up.

Joel was watching a television show with Evan and James one day. It was a story which took place in winter time. The children in the story rolled up snow and made a snow man. Joel, with that older brother superior air of experience, confidently explained to his younger brothers, "That doesn't really happen. It only works like that because of special effects. It's only a television show. Real snow doesn't do that."

Beth and I heard this and just laughed. Joel looked at us funny and we said, "Just wait Joel. Just wait 'til it snows."

During our first autumn in Austria it snowed as expected. The boys put on the cold weather coats, hats, gloves, boots, etc. and ten minutes later headed out to discover what could be done with snow. Yes, Joel, you really can roll up snow and make a snow man! It wasn't just television, it was real life. He was astonished as he put the head on his first Austrian snowman.

They made a snowman to guard the steps from the street. They made a snowman on the front of our car that looked like he'd been run over. They made snowmen all over the apartment complex. We discovered not everyone in the apartment complex liked snowmen, but we did.

Sometimes we read God's word and say, "That's only then, not now. It's just a special effect for Scripture." We just can't believe in our hearts that God will really do some of the miracles from the Bible. Then we let go of our hearts and open the door and venture into His world. There we discover snowmen are real, miracles do happen, and it isn't just a book.

Trains

When King Ahaz went to Damascus to meet Tiglath-pileser king of Assyria, he saw the altar that was at Damascus. And King Ahaz sent to Uriah the priest a model of the altar, and its pattern, exact in all its details. (2 Kings 16:10 ESV)

I was always fascinated by trains as I grew up. One of my neighbors was a model train aficionado. A corner of his basement was filled with his extensive HO gauge train diorama. It included switch cars, steam locomotives, diesels, freight and passenger trains. There were villages, tunnels, bridges and little people and cars to complete the model. The detail of those miniatures was amazing.

My brothers and I would spend hours watching our neighbor operate the complex controls to maneuver the trains through tunnels, over mountains, loading and uploading cargo, all in miniature. When something went wrong, he'd crawl under the table and then pop the upper part of his body through a hidden hatch to reach the interior of the diorama and effect repairs or adjustments.

Years later, married with children, the urge to play with HO trains returned. So when our children were young I purchased a small HO set for Christmas. We put together a board and a layout which would fit under our son's bed. We were on Guam at the time. Guam has a highly corrosive atmosphere. The tracks rusted, the train lurched and it was not the most successful experiment. It was fun while it lasted but it didn't last too long.

Later I purchased books, which have long been lost, about trains of all sorts. Once, after we were married, Beth and I took the Amtrak train across Florida.

Other than that, my closest experience with trains was watching them fly by my aunt's house as I hid in a nearby thicket. My brothers and I would carefully place pennies and nickels on the iron tracks. When we heard the train coming we would hightail it to the nearest bush and wait for the massive train to roll by and squash our farthings into thin wafers. Our parents weren't happy we played near the tracks so we didn't tell them. Unfortunately, our collection of wafer thin coins was a dead giveaway.

We were told tales of trains derailed by young boys putting pennies on the tracks. This was the parental ploy to keep us away from the dangerous train traffic. The thrill of the adventure made our squashed nickels valuable to us if to no one else.

I never rode on a train, except miniatures at amusement parks, while growing up. It would be years later, as an adult, when I'd enjoy close encounters with trains. First, I needed to have children. Many of the best things in life are excused by the presence of children.

On the south side of Saint Louis stands a railroad museum. During one of our furloughs we lived near Saint Louis. About an hour north is the town of Quincy where my parents lived at the time. Being so close, my father came down to visit. The next day Dad, Joel and I drove over to see the massive engines and learn some of the history of the US rail service. There were no trains on Guam and Joel had never ridden a train.

Not only was Joel impressed by the massive size and detail of these machines but Dad and I were also thrilled with the visit. We climbed aboard different engines from different periods of US history. Getting that close without becoming an engineer was enthralling.

There was a great difference between the models created, filling many basements, and the real thing. It wasn't until we touched a real locomotive engine that we comprehended the enormity of these behemoths. All my life I looked at pictures and watched movies with trains. I imagined what it would be like to stand in the cab with all the knobs and levers. Never did I fully understand the massive weight and power involved until I came face to face with a real steam train.

The word of God also fascinated me from childhood. I could see there was great detail in the revelation of God. My imagination would run wild trying to realize some of the images about heaven and eternity. Trying to understand the true nature of God is difficult in the theoretical realm of the imagination. It was not until I was a believer and started to know God face to face that the finer details were revealed.

When I touched God, I started to understand my theological model was just not large enough. When I stood at a distance and considered God through the writings and exposition of others, then God was manageable and easily contained. As I stood in His presence the immensity of God was overwhelming. God is not the artistic creator my mind imagined but much more.

As there are minute details in the construction and operation of a steam engine, well beyond my vision while visiting a museum, there are aspects of my God which I can't even imagine are missing in the overwhelming wonder of what I've already discovered.

Non-believers spend a lot of time analyzing and categorizing God within the confines of human logic. At a distance, in theoretical consideration, God is easily managed and contained. Unfortunately, there are also believers who keep looking at models of God and not the real thing. They develop systematic theology, carefully constructed confessions and church polity to pander to human nature which likes to manage and confine God. It's safe and comfortable.

It's like a steam engine. We can imagine the inner workings and think we have it all figured out. It's easy to manage and confine at the theoretical level. But those who work on the locomotives, who touch and handle the inner workings, understand the true function which produces such power. Good theory may produce a good steam engine. But good theory is only theory and won't get us from point A to point B.

Good theology is not God. Until we invest in a hands-on approach with God we maintain a safe distance which is easily managed and confined. When we allow God to have hands on in our lives we discover we can't manage things, much less cautiously confine God's work. Maybe it's time we started looking at the real thing, up close and personal, and not just our human reconstruction. It might be time to step away from the theory books and put our hand to work with God. Then we will discover the true nature of God's presence in our lives.

The Last Week

We know that all things work together for good for those who love God, to those who are called according to his purpose. (Romans 8:28 WEB)

A few weeks before we returned to Guam from our first furlough we packed all our belongings into a twenty-foot container. I moved one chair to load it on the truck and found a lost tape recorder. At least I found all the pieces from the recorder. The recorder had been carefully dismantled as much as possible by a young man.

Joel always enjoyed trying to discover how things worked. Taking them apart was fun. Putting them back together was a bit of a problem, as he was only six. It was then that Beth and I decided it would be better to give him old items to dismantle and keep the good ones working until he learned how to put them back together.

We tossed out the recorder parts, finished packing the container and sealed the doors before a truck hauled it away. We prayed it would arrive in Guam in one piece. Finally, we were ready for our last week of furlough.

It all began on a Monday morning as we prepared to drive to my parents' home. The car was experiencing cooling problems. Unfortunately, I was not well versed with cars and in the course of checking things sprayed my right arm with scalding water from the radiator, creating third degree burns up my arm.

Dancing and shouting about the gas station, I hurried to wash my arm with clean cold water and then climbed back in the car. With my arm propped on the back of the seat and my teeth gritted together we began the two hour journey to Quincy.

I was able to maintain control over the pain. We even stopped along the way and picked up some ice cream at Dairy Queen. We arrived with my pain controlling grin and settled down in the home of my parents.

Mother was concerned, as a mom should be, but I refused to visit a doctor for two days. When I finally went to see the physician, they were amazed I could still stand and talk coherently. The nurse took my blood pressure and looked at me strangely. I asked what the problem was and she responded, "I don't understand how you can still be conscious!" Burn ointment and clean bandages were prescribed and I returned to my parents' home to live through the ordeal.

During the week we were prone to spill things. It was so dramatic my parents started feeding us on the porch to keep from destroying the dining room carpet. By Friday things were settled down. I could sleep better and the pain in my arm was lessened.

My father and I took Ellice and Joel to the park for some fun. Sitting at a picnic table we watched both children climb on the equipment. They were having a grand time. Then it happened. Ellice was almost to the top of a fifteen-foot jungle gym when she fell off backwards flat onto the ground.

I had visions of the broken arm from the spring. The cast had been removed the week before. I was also concerned about her back. I jumped from the picnic bench where Dad and I were having a quiet talk and ran across the park to Ellice. Dad commented later, "I didn't know you could run that fast!"

When Dad and I reached Ellice, she was definitely in pain. A few minutes later an ambulance arrived so Ellice and I headed to the hospital while Dad took Joel back to the house to let the others know what had happened.

Fortunately, there was nothing wrong with Ellice's neck or back. She did, however, break the same arm which had just healed from her earlier accident. So she acquired another cast, our nerves were shot, and we went back to the house to try and recover. Praise the Lord the injury was not more severe.

Driving back to the Saint Louis area, we stayed the night with friends. In the morning baby James rolled off the bed and smacked into the dresser. Adding this to Ellice's cast, my bandaged arm, and a twenty-hour trip back to Guam, things were a bit tense. We finally boarded the safety of the airplane and sighed in relief, waiting to arrive in Hawaii, the first stop of our journey home.

God was gracious and worked through his faithful servants to provide us with a few days of rest and relaxation on Oahu. Our hotel was paid and some extra funds provided to see the island.

With Ellice's broken arm and my burned arm, the beach, one of Hawaii's famous places, was off our list of places to visit. We drove around the island of Oahu, enjoyed the sights and sounds and the experience of a new culture.

Finally, we boarded the plane back to Guam, our home, and the ministry God placed in our hands. Each step of our furlough was in his hands and covered by his love, grace, and care.

I'm not sure what God was telling us in these adventures. It sure didn't seem fun at the time. But I know there was good from this. My burned arm, Ellice's broken arm and James' banged head were to produce fruit. Maybe it was just patience and reliance on God. If not for His presence I think we would have gone nuts.

All Things Small and Smaller

The small and the great are there. . . . (Job 3:19 WEB)

Guam was a home for many interesting animals. One of my favorites was the gecko. This small lizard-like creature could be found in almost any room of any building. They climbed walls, decorated your windows, and even scurried across your hand to escape your underwear drawer while encouraging a startled scream at their unexpected appearance.

One of the first nights on Guam I remember lying half asleep in the bed listening to the new noises of the island. Somewhere between coherence and dreamland I suddenly heard someone laughing in the darkness of the room. I sat up and looked around as my eyes penetrated the miniscule light of the room. No one was there. I settled down again and listened intently. There it was again! Definitely someone laughing, and near our bed!

Sitting up quickly enough to arouse Beth we both sat and listened for the movement of the intruder. After a few minutes there was another laugh. Switching on the light, we found the room empty. Well, it was almost empty. On the wall above the door was a gecko. Occasionally he, or she, would emit a sound ominously similar to the laugher of a human.

Many years later we were accustomed to the noise and didn't notice except when visitors would awaken in the night suspecting someone was sneaking in their room. Geckos also served a useful purpose other than scaring you to death by jumping off a door onto your head as it was being opened. They ate smaller bugs.

Mosquitoes in particular were their normal feast. In the spring, when the termites would swarm, it was a regular feeding frenzy as the windows would be darkened by an army of geckos slurping up the flying insects.

The first spring we were on Guam, we were enjoying a warm evening out in the yard. Just before dusk there was a strange movement in the grass. From seemingly nowhere, dozens of toads began hopping into the yard like the plagues upon Egypt. They spread across the lawn and stopped and waited.

Slowly a cloud began to rise about the house and from the boonies (jungle) behind the house. It was a termite swarm! The number of flying critters was incredible. The frogs whipped out their tongues with lightning speed, enjoying their smorgasbord on the wing.

Having no experience with such an event we went inside and closed the doors. But termites are small creatures. With a determination powered by nature they entered every crack, crevice and hole in the windows and doors to cover the walls and furniture throughout the house. We didn't know they were attracted to the light as they continued their invasion of our home.

Beth went ballistic. The bugs were more than she could handle. I wasn't much help squashing bugs on the walls and dresser, leaving telltale bloody marks. Joel was quick to recognize his mother's distress, grabbed some tissue and began helping with the destruction process. There were dead bugs all over the place. It wasn't a restful evening when they finally stopped their attack.

Although all the moving dots were extinguished we failed to see all the new residents in our beds until we attempted to curl up for the night. This was quite an experience we didn't want to repeat. Fortunately, better late than never, someone taught us about the critters.

In the following years we learned to turn off the lights inside the house. A porch lamp was left burning with a bucket of water underneath. The bugs would fly toward the light then fall into the water and drown. While it may sound cruel it kept them out of the house.

I am reminded of the land of Egypt when God sent the plagues. Gnats went everywhere. They were in the houses, the bowls, the morning coffee. Yucky! I can appreciate the Egyptians' willingness to set God's people free. I was ready to set everyone free just to clear my house that night.

A Special Christmas

For there is born to you, this day, in the city of David, a Savior, who is Christ the Lord. (Luke 2:11 WEB)

While growing up, Christmas was for me always a special time in our home. After I was married and became a father we also worked to make "special days" fun and exciting for our children. Special events surround Christmas in our home and at church.

In the fall of 1986 the mission decided to hold a special Christmas broadcast. That was the first year we would broadcast not only the normal schedule from 6:00 p.m. to 1:30 a.m. but throughout the night.

In those special programs were testimonies from our staff. They shared their Christmas traditions and the story of Christmas. The programs were produced by the staff on Guam on a voluntary basis. Even manning the transmitters during this extra shift in the night was voluntary. The staff in our Hong Kong office heard of the event and joined in, eager to make extra special programs in various Chinese languages.

Beth, the children, and I worked all day for these special broadcasts, operating the transmitters and audio equipment. Presents, food, and games were brought along to the transmitter site for this special time.

There was an exciting moment as transmitter number three developed a problem. With three other transmitters beaming out the Gospel, working on the output stage was a bit touchy. RF (radio frequency) burns are very nasty. Everything inside the transmitter is alive even when the power is turned off to the box. The antenna which usually broadcasts the message becomes a receiving antenna, funneling the power from the other four transmitters back into the system.

With Beth's assistance I was able to locate the failure in one of the large variable vacuum capacitors in the output tuning network. The unit was changed, the transmitter re-tuned and programs continued for the remainder of the day. I took the old capacitor and made a desk lamp out of the unit. It wasn't necessarily pretty but it was very functional and unique to be sure!

It was several months before we received letter responses to the programs. People were thrilled with the special celebrations broadcast that Christmas Day. As far as I know, this tradition has continued every Christmas since. Special donations were given to add these unique and extra set of programs to the schedule as we celebrated Christ's incarnation with our listeners.

Throughout God's Word traditions are celebrated. Some are biblically mandated and others encouraged from historical events. I believe it is also important for us to start and maintain traditions which are marker stones of God's work in our lives and ministries.

Turkey Day in the Tropics

Continue steadfastly in prayer, watching therein with thanksgiving;
(Colossians 4:2 WEB)

Christmas wasn't the only holiday we celebrated overseas. Since Guam was a U.S. territory, most of the mainland holidays made their way to Guam to be added to the local historical holidays. Thanksgiving Day was celebrated regularly with the abundance of food, fellowship and games.

Most of the staff on Guam came from the mainland and were familiar with Thanksgiving. Teaching our Asian colleagues about the holiday was fun and they quickly learned to enjoy the food if nothing else.

One year we took the opportunity to gather together as a staff to celebrate. The celebration included dressing up in costumes. Thanksgiving provided many different remembrances.

During the 80s the Space Shuttle missions were also beginning and developing man's reach into space. One Thanksgiving a gentleman from one of our home churches came to Guam. The island serves as an alternate landing site for the shuttle so he was there "just in case."

The day before Thanksgiving a typhoon came through the area, creating a mess and interrupting the power and water systems. But a good American holiday is not to be passed by idly. Some things are worth the extra effort.

We lit the gas on our stove, dressed the turkey, and cooked until the house was a bit warm. The lack of electricity for fans or air conditioning didn't help. Fortunately, the electricity returned just before we ate to provide a bit of light and a cool breeze from the fan.

Our guest, along with other friends on the island totaling twenty-five, came and we celebrated big time. Lots of food and fun. As we neared the ending of the meal there was a small problem. There was still no water.

Actually, the lack of water was quite a problem, especially with the mess created by having a dinner for twenty-five people! Add in the problem of toilets and other amenities and this made the later afternoon interesting.

Praise the Lord for fifty-five gallon barrels! Over the years missionaries have used these barrels to ship their goods from country to country. We used a container, the modern larger square version of the "missionary barrel." However, some of these drums were still shuffling around the island when we first arrived.

Knowing there were occasional water problems we acquired a couple drums, placed them under the down spouts of our roof and they were filled by the seasonal rains on the island. With this ready supply of water at hand the solution presented itself.

Out to the barrels we all went to clean our faces, hands, and a number of the dishes as well. Not conventional but functional to be sure. Everyone standing around the barrel waiting their turn added more opportunities for great conversation and fun.

Each year we celebrated this homeland tradition with friends and family and the requisite turkey. For us this was one of the special memories we wanted for our children. We hope they remember them and enjoy them as much as we do.

God calls us to remember His provision. That year He provided, even in the midst of the storm.

Streams

. . . then shall the lame man leap like a deer, and the tongue of the mute sing for joy. For waters break forth in the wilderness, and streams in the desert; (Isaiah 35:6 ESV)

Growing up in Ohio I spent many days playing in the local streams. Our home was in the middle of a greenbelt community. No matter which way you turned you had to exit the community through some portion of the local forest. Throughout the forest surrounding our town ran a small stream which emptied into the local lake.

Occasionally my friends and I would spend time floating on the lake in a row boat and pretend to fish. But, since I didn't like to clean or eat fish, we would toss back into the lake whatever we caught. The adventure was the fishing, not the catching.

Fishing required sitting on the shore or renting a row boat and money was in short supply. The next best thing to the lake for fun was the local stream. Many adventures took place around the stream. With my friends I explored every inch and every crook and every cranny of the stream.

Country streams are miracles to behold. As a young man I could spend days exploring the banks, rocks, and wildlife found in and around a stream. Skipping from rock to rock was a great pastime for a young man. My friends and I would take bets on how far we could go along a stream before slipping on a rock and getting wet. I still enjoy walking along and wading through small streams.

When Beth and I had children, I looked forward to introducing our children to the wonder of a forest stream. On Guam these are few and far between. In fact, the only streams were deep in the jungle and hard to get at without a machete and plenty of bug spray. With the ocean all about the island we didn't spend time learning about streams on the island. So the wonders of a cool stream had to wait a few years.

When we visited friends in Georgia there was a chance for Ellice and Joel to experience a cool freshwater stream. While we waited for a break in the events at the camp meeting there was an opportunity to walk about the complex, through the woods and visit a small stream nearby. Here was my chance to teach Ellice and Joel the fun of a cold mountain stream.

It didn't take much coaxing to get them in the water. They stood beside the stream, watched the fast-flowing waters and wondered what it would be like. One or two toes were dipped in to see how cold it was. It was cold. They had a choice, jump in or walk away. They decided to jump in.

Within minutes they were both splashing through the cold water still in their clothes. We didn't bring swimsuits; it wasn't on our list of meeting requirements. Soon they were sliding down rocks with the mild current. I'm not sure if they remember that day but I do.

I think God introduces us to refreshing streams at the right time. Like the Psalmist says, "He leads me beside quiet waters. He restores my soul." Sometimes we have to dip our toes in first to see if we have the stamina to jump in. Once we make that commitment we discover the refreshing wonder of God's streams.

Letters of Encouragement

When this letter has been read among you, cause it to be read also in the assembly of the Laodiceans; and that you also read the letter from Laodicea. (Colossians 4:16 WEB)

Since I've been blessed with a missionary career involving radio broadcasting I can attest to the great need for communication. This is a two-way street. Missionaries often feel cut off from their extended family, homeland, and supporters.

All missionaries should communicate with their supporters, family, and friends on a regular basis. This may be accomplished via prayer letters, email updates, and occasional telephone calls. It's vital for a missionary to keep those interested in the ministry up to date on the encouraging and discouraging work of God in their lives and ministry.

Letters and communication are not only vital to the missionary relationship with their supporters, family, and friends but also with their listeners. The goal of radio mission work is the spiritual life of the listener. Each detail of the electronics, each file in the computer database, each program created is for reaching the listener with a message of God's grace, love and salvation.

Beth worked in the Listener Mail Department on Guam for many years. The numerous letters she read to me were constant sources of encouragement. Through these letters we heard about lives changed, souls saved for eternity and the results of God's Word broadcast to the world.

Today, we hear from our listeners via the postal system, internet email, telephone calls, texting and faxes. For those who visit the target countries there are also first-hand reports of God's work in the world. Through these responses I'm continually encouraged in my calling from God.

I remember one specific letter on Guam. A listener heard a weak signal from a location outside our target area. The programs were beamed to the west and this listener was writing from the east. He was listening to the small signal which leaks off the backside of the antenna.

Even a small signal with the word of God is sufficient to change a life. This man heard the word of salvation, gave his heart to the Lord and sought to serve God. I was curious. I took the letter and searched it for details of the date and time he listened.

Taking this information, I went home and consulted my past work schedules. There it was. The same date and time this man indicated he heard the life-giving words. I was the one on duty to press the transmitter buttons so this message could be heard so far away. Praise the Lord for such small things as pressing buttons. This was a letter of encouragement from a listener that reached directly to my heart.

Many times I've seen and heard missionaries discuss their sadness about being forgotten soldiers on the field of battle. They're encouraged by friends in church, pastors and even family to pursue God's work in their lives. They're encouraged, sent to the field and left to survive on God alone. Now this is possible, but God called us to work together throughout the ministry, not just in the preparation.

God does place His servants in situations where they rely on Him and Him alone. Our faith and trust in God grows in these situations. He also places His servants where He uses fellow believers to encourage and lift up the servant in their duties and life away from "home." Training a missionary, raising his support and sending him to the field is not the end of the matter.

For a missionary to be a true partner in ministry, communication must flow to the missionary as well as from the missionary. In the years my family lived overseas we were encouraged by a few churches and individuals who took time to send email, drop a letter in the post, and even cards for birthdays.

As an encouragement we strived to answer each letter, card, email, or other contact we had with our co-laborers. Simple little notes describing what was happening in the family, the new things the children learned, how the church was growing or shrinking, praises for God's hand of mercy and prayers for situations of struggle all built a bond between the missionary and the supporter.

Through these simple messages we began to know one another better and better. When we saw each other on furlough there wasn't a need to struggle for names and relevant conversational information because we were already in touch.

Fire up that typewriter, sharpen your pencil, put ink in your pen, click out words on the computer, send a text or dial the telephone. Build a bond of fellowship, ministry and encouragement between you and the missionary. Don't be worried the missionary is too busy.

If he claims he hasn't time to communicate with you then honestly, he is too busy and headed for burn out and should consider whether this is God's plan or his own. On the other hand, his response may be delayed but he (or she) will still be encouraged by your prayer and care to contact him.

Create a conversation with a fellow sinner turned saint. Forge a bond between with a normal guy or gal responding to a special call. You both struggle with living a faithful life for God and serving Him with your lives. There is a common bond found only in the savior you cherish, praise and place your hopes upon.

Yap and Ulithi

*Let them give glory to Yahweh, and declare his praise in the islands.
(Isaiah 42:12 WEB)*

Working with electronics on the mission field is a different type of ministry than most people consider when thinking about mission work. With the modernization of mission work there is an increasing need for electronic technicians, computer programmers and others to support and bring the messages prepared by teachers and preachers to the world. These skills provided me with an opportunity to help other missions and ministries in the Pacific region.

Beth prayed for chances to see other islands and countries in the region. The only problem was she didn't specify who would do the traveling so I was the lucky recipient to her answered prayers.

One of my first trips was to the small island of Yap. This is one of the many islands in the Federated States of Micronesia. The island boasted one paved road from the airport into the capital city. It was a beautiful road to handle the dozen or so vehicles existing on the island. During WWII the island was occupied by the Germans who built a canal right through the middle, effectively making two islands out of one.

Pacific Missionary Aviation maintained a passenger and cargo service for the residents to the smaller outlying islands and atolls. These small planes provided a vital link for the residents as well as the missionaries serving in these remote areas. Their radios needed occasional service and no one on the island was available for such work. Not being an avionics technician but being familiar with radio I was asked to come and install their repaired radio and adjust the antenna system.

Landing on the small runway was a thrill. Going through the grass hut they called the International Airport Terminal was also interesting. Due to drought conditions there was water only thirty minutes a day. The pilot had duties to attend so I had some free time.

I was taken on a small tour of the island by the pilot's assistant, a local Yapese youth, in one of the few trucks on the island. I experienced the wonder of the villages spotted about the island and some of the culture as he explained things in his halting English.

The next day I completed the work on the radio and a test run was necessary. Packing the plane, we scheduled a trip to the atoll of Ulithi. Each bag, and passenger, were carefully weighed on an industrial scale. (Some of the rather large island ladies didn't like this idea.) With this information the weight was distributed about the passenger seats and cargo hold for a smooth flight. I was permitted to ride in the copilot seat as there was no copilot. We flew northward over endless empty ocean until a small dot appeared on the ocean. That was our destination.

The runway went from one shore of the narrow island to the other. Just enough room to stop the plane, if all went well. We circled as I thought about the short runway and the big airplane. As the pilot lowered the plane and our wheels touched ground we heard a series of smacking sounds. Rolling past the small terminal we stopped, turned, and taxied back to the terminal. The pilot opened his window and shouted a number of commands to the boys on the runway.

When I asked what was the problem he turned to me and said, "They forgot to cut the grass like I told them last time I was here. That was what we heard, the grass hitting the propellers and the wings as we landed." The boys dispersed, grabbed machetes and began to chop down the high grass before we returned to the relative safety of Yap.

God used this small plane to bring supplies and missionaries to the outlying islands. The silver plane was a symbol of hope and witness of God's provision to these people. It takes an airplane to reach some people and radio to reach others. God works in wondrous ways and I'm glad He allowed me to see some of His handiwork.

Pohnpei Dance

But sanctify the Lord God in your hearts; and always be ready to give an answer to everyone who asks you a reason concerning the hope that is in you, with humility and fear: (1 Peter 3:15 WEB)

A missionary friend on Guam worked with Moody Bible Institute to provide training for local pastors on the islands. Each summer, four to six weeks would be scheduled for classes sponsored by Moody Bible Institute and staffed with some of their professors as well as teachers and pastors from the missionary community on Guam. One year I was asked to come and teach two weeks of classes.

The attendants of the Summer Institute for Pastors came from the small islands and atolls throughout the Federated States of Micronesia. Some pastors would travel for days on the ocean in open canoes to reach the small island of Pohnpei and learn more of God's word. Their desire was to improve their skills and abilities to pastor on their home islands.

I was housed at the Hotel Pohnpei with a beautiful view overlooking one small bay and a neighboring peninsula. The room was actually a small hut made from the ubiquitous palm branches arranged, woven and placed on the walls and roof of the wooden frame. Looking throughout the hotel compound, you could determine the age of the latest home improvement by the color of the thatching on the roof. The more brown there was, the older the hut. Regularly the roofs and walls were replaced from the always available supply of palm branches on the island.

One of the beauties of this construction was the ready availability of materials. Incredible as it may seem the woven roof actually deflected the rain which came several times a day. With the high inner walls and a gap just below the ceiling there was even some room for a little breeze. Security - well that was not the real issue. Don't leave anything of value in a room with palm branches for walls.

The second advantage of the construction was the ability of little creatures to climb in and out of the weaving to build their tiny homes, raise families, and look for food. To eliminate the chance of ingesting the discarded materials from these creatures, each room included a protective sheet carefully suspended above the bed to catch what fell during all hours of the day. I looked up there once. That was a mistake!

The housing was not the highlight of my visit. Teaching these pastors in their native dress ranging from suits to grass skirts was a challenge. Fortunately, they all understood English, making my job easier. Their interest in the word of God and expanding their understanding of scriptural interpretation, application, and memorization should be emulated by many believers.

They studied hard. They studied each day when there was no class and looked with nervousness toward the test which would be given the final day. They didn't receive their certificate without demonstrating a working understanding of the material presented.

One day the discussion turned to the subject of dancing. This was a chance to work with the cultural differences.

One pastor raised his hand and inquired, "Sir, what do you believe about dancing and the Bible?"

I immediately realized this was a precarious situation. The previous teacher was sitting in the class watching the progress of the lessons. He was not scheduled to depart for another day. I knew his opinion on many things including dancing, drinking, smoking and the like. In most areas we agreed but not in all.

I stepped forward and placed my hands palm down on the edge of the long table and stared into the pastor's eyes. I paused to consider my answer and I could tell they were all interested in my response. I was also well aware of the nature of dance in their various cultures. It's through dance they share their history and stories. Still, I had to respond as I felt the Lord lead.

"Gentlemen," I began, "I must tell you. I have strong convictions concerning dancing. I don't dance."

There was silence in the room. Their faces showed signs of disappointment. The departing professor showed signs of agreement, glad to hear me make this statement.

"But," I continued, "my conviction is, not to do anything that makes me look absolutely stupid. I can't dance! So, I don't dance. However, David danced as he brought God's ark into Jerusalem. The Israelites danced in joy before the Lord when they escaped from Pharaoh's soldiers. Dance has a place and purpose in many cultures and I find no biblical admonition against dancing as a whole."

There was a sign of relief throughout the room. These men were willing to change their entire culture if the Scriptures called them to such change. This is the same conviction we must show as we walk with the Lord in this world. Sometimes God calls us to change, and sometimes, just to follow.

Pohnpei Preaching

Preach the word; be urgent in season and out of season; reprove, rebuke, and exhort, with all patience and teaching. (2 Timothy 4:2 WEB)

I once spent two weeks on the island of Pohnpei teaching at the Summer Institute for Pastors. On the second Sunday I was asked to attend the local church and present the sermon from God's Word. This was an honor and I was thrilled with the opportunity.

After a little discussion with my teaching colleague I discovered there were certain rules concerning preachers in the local Baptist church. First I needed to wear a tie. This was the first problem.

After living on Guam for many years, I no longer owned a tie much less an appropriate shirt for a tie. Traveling about the islands, my wardrobe consisted of colorful, flowered, island shirts and the occasional formal Filipino Barang. Discussing this island wardrobe with my colleague from Chicago, the land of suits, ties and fancy dress, he looked in his room and brought out a nice tie I could borrow. When he saw the shirt it was intended to adorn, he just shook his head and wandered away mumbling something about the island lifestyle versus good Christian tradition. I held the two up in a mirror and thought, cool! But somehow I doubted my wife would agree. Her sense of fashion was much better than mine. She had great sense. I didn't, and still don't.

So on Sunday morning I put on my best flowered shirt and donned the requisite tie for the service. It would have made a fashion statement anywhere in the world; maybe not a good fashion statement but a statement nonetheless. An hour before the service my ride arrived in the form of a pickup truck, loaded with the driver's wife and mother-in-law.

On Pohnpei a pickup truck is considered a family vehicle, something to be treasured. Men are also to be treasured and, unfortunately, considered of more value than women. Thus the wife and grandmother were required to sit in the back of the truck while I was motioned to sit up front with the driver. I try not to make cultural waves when I travel. Watching grandma, not a young lady, creak out of the cab and start to climb into the back of the truck, I just couldn't keep quiet. After a few minutes of discussion, and insisting on my love for a good open breeze, the wife, not the aged grandmother, was installed inside the cab while I rode in the back of the truck. Grandma and I had a great view and cool breeze as we bumped and jostled our way along toward the inner part of the island. Considering the heat and lack of air-conditioning, it was probably the coolest place in the vehicle.

Down dirt roads and up the side of a mountain, we arrived at the concrete church and were greeted by the elders of the church. They were excited about the morning service and people could be seen arriving in the occasional pickup truck but mostly on foot. I joined the church leaders in a prayer meeting in preparation for the service. We asked God to bless the meeting, guide me to say the right words, and to touch the heart of someone new that morning. The prayer ended so we had time to chat. While talking and waiting for the prescribed time the head elder turned and asked, "Where is your jacket?"

"Jacket?" I asked. "What jacket?"

"The preacher must wear a jacket," replied the pastor with a knowing nod of his head.

"It is tradition in the church from the time the first missionaries came to our island," responded the sincere elder. He was concerned their guest speaker, me, was underdressed.

I told them I didn't own a suit coat or sports jacket. I liked the island lifestyle and clothing. After a few moments of consternation and a few wagging heads, one elder jumped up, smiled at the rest and went to a cabinet in the open air room. Proudly, he pulled a wool suit coat from the closet which, unfortunately, fit over my shoulders. I was obliged to adhere to their traditions. I donned the hot and itchy coat and we headed into the church.

The singing was impressive, the enthusiasm evident and the room hot. I was starting to understand the feelings of a log on an open fire. No fans, no air-conditioning, no breeze worked to accentuate the warmth of my wool coat. This was not going to be easy.

I opened my Bible and began to preach. For the next forty minutes I shared the word of God. I had to stand arm's length from the pulpit to keep from dripping on my notes. The pages of my Bible began to curl from all the dripping perspiration.

Just before I reached the flashpoint of the human body, I apologized, turned to the elders, and asked if I could remove my jacket. I was about to faint. They looked at each other, mumbled a few words, shook a few heads, and then agreed it was permissible. I continued the service cooled by the evaporating moisture in my drenched clothes. I was a human swamp cooler.

Tired, dried out and ready to sit down I concluded my message. I asked if anyone was interested in coming forward for salvation, dedication, or prayer. Praise the Lord the message was well received. A couple people came forward for prayer.

I returned the wool coat to its treasured closet and thought about the first messengers of the Gospel coming to the island. I wonder about the wisdom of some early missionaries. Insisting a tropical island don their attire was silly then and is silly now. Clothes don't make the believer, it is their relationship with God. Granted there are times we must all get uncomfortable to be God's servants. This wasn't one of them. Sometimes we must get uncomfortable because those before us set an unusual example. What examples are we leaving in our wake? Will future servants of God be glad we passed through or wonder about our sanity? Maybe it's time to take a little survey and see where our traditions just might be altered for the present and future generation of Christians.

Pohnpei Church Meal

On the first day of the week, when the disciples were gathered together to break bread, Paul talked with them, intending to depart on the next day, and continued his speech until midnight. (Acts 20:7 WEB)

When I was invited to teach at the Summer Bible Institute for Pastors on the small tropical island of Pohnpei, I felt very honored. It was a privilege to open the word of God with these men and women. During two weeks of teaching, God used me to expand his church in the islands. I have never seen these islands and probably never will. Some of the participants spent two weeks in outrigger canoes, going from island to island in the Pacific Ocean just to attend these training sessions sponsored by Moody Bible Institute.

Like many churches food is important. I can't count the number of potluck meals I've been to in churches around the world. My wife, Beth knows what I think of most church dinners. Being a bit cynical I see them as an opportunity for the wife to fix some dish her family wouldn't eat at a regular meal, and then pawn if off on the unsuspecting church family. Remember, it's a church family. As good Christians, we wouldn't dare say the meal tasted like last week's sweepings off the floor. "Oh yes, Sue, that was delightful," we say, while looking over her shoulder for the nearest waste bin. When you add in all the little rugrats scooping up the good stuff at the front of the line, I'm not a big fan of church potluck dinners. But I still attend. I think it is a sense of duty, even in the face of death by experimental casserole.

On Pohnpei, when the service was over, there was a long spread of food in the covered area. There was no fellowship hall or kitchen. The covered area was a large cabana covering a bunch of picnic tables. There was enough food for a small army. "Oh great," I thought, "another potluck." But let me make one thing clear: These folks could cook! This was great food! I just might start enjoying potluck meals once more.

The pastor, elders and I were ushered through the line to fill up our plates, take a seat and enjoy the local delicacies. I realized no one else was eating and there was still a lot of food still on the table.

The pastor filled me in on what was happening. He said this was a weekly event. The remaining food would be put on plates and delivered to people who were sick, or otherwise unable to attend the service. Once the church members were ministered to, the remaining plates were given to needy families in the area until all the food was gone. An impressive show of Christian care to the neighborhood.

As we sat, ate, and conversed, the people of the church sang beautiful songs of Christ and His deliverance. Their voices blended perfectly and it added a soothing background to our discussion on the history of the church and the response of the people from the island. As we completed our dining

73

and continued to converse, the ladies began to sway and wander about between the tables.

Not knowing precisely what was happening, I watched out of the corner of my eye until they were behind me and I was left to guess at the coming events. I did notice each lady carefully picked up her purse and carried it with her. With one hand they were searching the contents for some special item. The music grew louder as the ladies approached from behind us. The elders and pastor showed no concern and kept expanding their explanation of the history of the church. I didn't think the church was so large to have such a long, detailed history. I looked their direction and nodded my head in feigned interest. I really wanted to know what these singing ladies were doing behind my back.

Suddenly I heard a *psst, psst* and felt a cool liquid sprayed under each of my arms. It was all I could do to resist the urge to jump up and shout, "Whoa! What was that?" The fragrance of perfume soon reached my nose, and I realized they were baptizing our smelly bodies with the sweet scent of ladies' perfume. Each lady passed behind me, the pastor and elders and anointed us with a double sound and squirt.

After a dozen women added their personal perfume to our shirts, we were smelling pretty good. Although the mixture of fragrances was a bit unusual, it was a welcome relief from an hour of preaching in a wool suit coat! Not a bad tradition on an island with an average temperature of 88 degrees Fahrenheit!

I remembered Scripture talked about a number of women who ministered to Jesus. One used perfume to anoint Him for death. Judas complained about the waste. These ladies used their perfume to deal with a unique situation. They weren't wasteful but helpful. Waste and help, these two are often confused in our rush to be zealous. Let's just pause, enjoy the smell of the perfume and the work of God.

Pohnpei Honor

Let the elders who rule well be counted worthy of double honor, especially those who labor in the word and in teaching. (1 Timothy 5:17 WEB)

As a teacher at the Summer Institute for Pastors held on the island of Pohnpei, I was considered an honored guest by the islanders and the students at the seminars. Sometimes it can be a lot of fun to discover new traditions in new cultures. Discovering I was in a position of honor was unique. I didn't know how unique until the last day of the seminary. The day a teacher departed was a day of celebration with gifts given and honor shown..

There were many "Thank you" and "Please come back" comments. During my two weeks of teaching we developed a bond between cultures, founded on the word of God and our faith. A number of island crafts were given to remind me of my time in their midst. One gentle servant of God presented me with a hand carved wooden fish. The surface was carefully smoothed by brush strokes from a palm branch. Still others presented necklaces of sea shells and other items they valued in their homes.

One woman soaked a fragile handmade headdress of flowers in perfume all night to place on my head and show honor to her teacher. The wave of perfume rolling down my face was almost suffocating but I dare not remove such a show of distinction. Another loving student created a similarly fragranced lei from the luscious island flowers.

After all the goodbyes, thanks and a time of food and fellowship I was placed in the back of a pickup truck. I leaned into the wind as they drove around the city and surrounding village. I was on display so all could see the teacher who came to help them learn more about God and how to serve Him. Needless to say, I was a touch embarrassed by all the attention. I only came to the island to serve God with the gifts He gave me. I wasn't expecting this demonstration.

The pickup trip ended at the airport where all the students, friends and other curious islanders watched until I climbed the stairs of the airplane and it took off toward my home on Guam. I watched them gathered at the runway fence, smiling and waving until we were out of sight. As I sat back, I was thankful for the overpowering fragrance of the flowers. A number of passengers, all from a tropical island, added to the airplane's internal smell and it wasn't good. Here was a small blessing in the form of fragrant flowers.

As I climbed off the plane, Beth had the most unusual look on her face. During the flight I had forgotten about the leis and crown of flowers on my head. I think seeing her husband with a flower wreath on his head and wearing shell necklaces was more than she expected. It was something new to remember.

I went to fulfill God's call to teach and train others in the word of God. I received a training course in cultural integration and cooperation. It wasn't what I expected but exactly what God knew I needed. It's nice when we can look back on obedience and see God's hand in the results, complete with flowers and fish.

Diamonds, A Girl's Best Friend

Let your beauty be not just the outward adorning of braiding the hair, and of wearing jewels of gold, or of putting on fine clothing; (1 Peter 3:3 WEB)

The concept of mission work was something new for our family as God called us into the ministry. Our daughter, Ellice, was young but interested in God and teaching other people about Jesus in her own childlike manner.

For three years we visited churches, shared with friends, and put hours each day into raising our support for the mission field. When asked we would tell Ellice, and later our son Joel, we were preparing to tell others about Jesus. Two years later we discovered we were headed to the Pacific to proclaim the Gospel into China and the Far East.

While we were still in the US we were thankful I had a boss who was understanding. Often I took afternoons off from work and disappeared over the weekend to share at churches in the area. Occasionally we would take a weekend to visit my parents in Illinois.

My father was always tinkering something together in the basement. It might be as simple as a pot holder or as complex as a nuclear power station. Well, maybe just a ham radio transceiver. While growing up I was always fascinated with the projects and tests he made in the basement. Everyone needs a basement to keep exciting things such as volt meters, old record players, radio gear and assorted other odds and ends.

Bringing my children to visit Grandpa was always exciting. It didn't take them long to discover the miraculous neat stuff in the basement. Grandpa was a genius! He could build or fix anything! No two ways about it, Ellice and Joel thought Grandpa was the world's answer to anything electronic or mechanical, not to mention a bastion of wisdom.

On each visit my dad would take one of the two children aside for a one-on-one experiment and construction project. There were flashing lights to be wired together, radios to listen to and even the occasional conversation with some ham radio operator across the globe while sitting in Grandpa's lap. During one of these visits Grandpa decided his first and only granddaughter needed some jewelry.

My dad took a heavy piece of copper wire and a ten cent coin then called to Ellice and headed to the marvelous, mystical, basement workshop. The two were gone for over an hour before they emerged. Dad was smiling and chuckling while Ellice was beaming and holding out her hand.

"See Daddy," she said as she approached, "Grandpa made me a dime on ring!"

The ten cent piece, a dime, soldered to a ring of copper perfectly fitted to my daughter's finger could well have been a multi-faceted diamond stone in her heart and eyes. It was handmade with love to a precise fit for her only. What more could a granddaughter want from her Grandpa?

From that day on, the ring was worn on all occasions. Everywhere Ellice went, she was wearing her dime on ring. On Sunday she wore it to church. In the lower classrooms of our church, a separate church service was held led by the Asian residents of our area. They were great people and dedicated to the proclaiming of God's word.

However, children are children. One of the young children took a shine to Ellice's special ring and it disappeared. It was never recovered but not forgotten. The memory would come to light as soon as we arrived on Guam.

On our first evening on the island we were guests of another missionary family. This was standard in the mission. Dealing with jet lag is difficult enough without trying to prepare an evening meal and not burn down the house. The first few evenings any missionary arrived or returned to the island they were guests of other staff families.

This evening we met and were hosted by the Chen family. Eddie and Ruby are wonderful people and delighted to help us with our first evening meal on the island. We found their home on our map, drove over, and knocked on the door.

Eddie opened the door, welcomed us, and entreated us to enter. As we passed through the door Ellice looked carefully at Eddie, then Ruby.

"I don't like Chinese people!" she proclaimed as a simple statement.

Beth and I were aghast. Eddie and Ruby didn't miss a lick and just kept right on being gracious and wonderful to this new missionary family. With apologies and a desire to strangle our daughter we sat down and began to converse and learn about each other.

In the course of our conversation we had a chance for an aside chat with Ellice. We soon discovered she was still mad about her ring missing from the service at our home church. We praise the Lord for the careful and gracious treatment by our hosts. They welcomed us and made us feel at home.

In the years following, fourteen on Guam, we became close friends with the Chens and often recalled and laughed about this first evening. Ellice and Joel were friends with their children as well.

Children are honest about their feelings; not always timely, but honest. Ellice's honesty allowed her to draw closer to the Chens as they discovered something of her missing treasure and she discovered something of the treasure in the new family she met.

As adults we might learn a lesson. We can learn a little better timing but be honest with one another. It sure keeps the air clear and the relationships honest and on solid ground. Our Lord was honest with those He met. Still, He loved them and gave Himself up for them. Maybe we can learn to do the same.

Years later when I discussed the matter with my daughter, she reminded me of something I forgot. After the dime on ring was lost my dad compensated by creating a penny bracelet. Same general idea: a piece of wire, a coin and some solder. While I was writing this, I received a note from Ellice telling me she still has the bracelet. She discovered the best jewelry in the world in one of her boxes. As she remembered her Grandpa she cried with good memories of fun times. It doesn't fit anymore but it is among her collected treasures. The simple things of life are often the things we cherish the most.

Jesus Loves Me

For God so loved the world, that he gave his one and only Son, that whoever believes in him should not perish, but have eternal life. (John 3:16 WEB)

After flying for two days, and what seems like a thousand hours, a traveler will arrive at the airport on the island of Guam. It was our family's first international trip. It was our family's first air flight. When we departed the USA we were filled with excitement. When we arrived, we were dried out from the air conditioning and exhausted from the hours of boredom in a small tube flying at breakneck speeds across a seemingly endless ocean.

As we dragged ourselves off the airplane we searched for signs of life in each other's eyes and movements. We immediately felt the hot, humid air of the tropics. The first ones to show signs of revival were Ellice and Joel. How they can retain such energy at such unexpected times is amazing. Then again at three and five years of age they could sleep quite well in the small airplane seats. They were ready to start their new life as missionary children bringing the Gospel to the world.

We worked our way through the corridors and past immigration. We entered the baggage claim area filled with local residents returning and vacationing travelers arriving. Ellice looked around and studied the many and varied faces, most of which were dark compared to her family. Her young thoughts made a leap in logic from entering a foreign airport to preaching the Gospel to China and an idea came into her head.

At the top of her lungs she started singing, "Jesus loves me, this I know."

People quickly turned to look in her direction, then to find her parents, us, to see what the ruckus was about. Since we were there to teach about Jesus she wanted to get started as soon as possible. We quieted her down just a bit and quickly searched for our numerous bags to escape the glaring eyes of other sleep deprived passengers.

Years later Ellice reminded me of that first day. She wrote me, "I don't know how much detail you are going into but I remember that first night, because Rachel Ruth took me to her car and told me that we were going to be friends forever. She was the first friend that I remember and my best friend all the way through high school."

A new life began, took shape and molded us over the years. Looking back, we wonder at God's hand working in and through our lives. At times we need to just shout out the truth and see who is listening. God's message of salvation is timeless and always appropriate, even in baggage claim.

Going Out a Winner

"Honor your father and mother," which is the first commandment with a promise: (Ephesians 6:2 WEB)

I placed the phone in the cradle and sat staring at the wall. At thirty-four I couldn't make a decision. I couldn't move! I didn't know what needed to be done next! My resources were reduced and I lacked the ability to take the next step.

It began seven years earlier. Beth and I were raising support as full time missionaries. My father, Dad, had an unexpected massive heart attack. After several months of hospital care, bypass surgery, and recovery, he returned home weaker but ready to take on the world. We were uncertain how this would impact our missionary calling. God continued to lead us overseas so we departed a year later.

In the intervening years Dad became the best correspondent and confidant I could want. Regular letters describing family history flowed from his hands. Although he owned an early computer he preferred to bang away, in the basement, at an old Royal typewriter, hour after hour. Work didn't last long because his medication and the stress disagreed with his delicate condition. With the extra time he indulged his sons with a detailed trip down memory lane.

During these years his health rose and fell. They were good years. Mom and Dad enjoyed their time together. Five years later we returned on furlough from our first assignment. Living an hour's drive from their home, we made frequent visits. Dad lavished love and affection on his grandchildren at each visit. He didn't spoil them but they knew they were special in his heart.

We enjoyed our final furlough days in their home. We relaxed and talked. The children played. When we departed it was the end of a good visit. It was time to resume the ministry.

The first week of January 1988, I worked on the island of Chuuk. Repairing a radio station, meeting new people and experiencing a new culture was a mixture of joy and exhaustion. When I returned home I needed rest.

About 2:00 am I received a call. Half-awake, I answered the telephone. My senses returned as the voice informed me he was a police officer! My mind reviewed the day's events to see if I had broken any laws. Nothing came to mind so I listened carefully. He said, "Your mother called. She cannot reach your telephone. Please call her back."

I explained the call to Beth, wandered to the living room and began to call my parents' home. I knew, before I finished dialing, what I would hear. Mom softly answered and informed me of Dad's death. She told me, "We were playing bridge. Elton (my dad) was winning. He arose to go into the other room and collapsed in the kitchen. He never woke up."

Beth sat beside me as I asked about the funeral and my brothers and hung up the telephone. I was silent for a while and then began to cry. Beth asked why I was crying now and not when I heard the news. I said, "Dad wanted to be buried in his home back in Tennessee. He just wanted to go home again." I don't know why but that touched my heart. I never lived in Dad's home but the stories of his youth, shared through his series of letters, filled my thoughts.

I wasn't sure what to do next. This was Dad. This was my best correspondent. This was the one I always counted on for a bit of advice, technical expertise or just a good long talk. He was gone. He couldn't answer the question or make suggestions on what to do next. But he went out a winner!

The simple fact that Dad was winning when the Lord called him home tickled my heart. He didn't fear death. He knew the Lord. He always enjoyed winning. Why did Mom tell me he was winning? It seemed a strange comment. Sitting 7,000 miles from their home, it was the first word God highlighted in my thoughts.

The days ahead were strenuous but the Lord made provision to strengthen my heart. As the mission helped me make emergency flight plans to Quincy I was almost cheerful. It wasn't my effort, my cheery outlook on life, it was God who lifted me up and helped me step forward one event at a time.

Over the next two weeks, in my parents' home, God worked through me to witness of His grace and love to my brothers, sister-in-law and other friends of the family. When I heard the news of Dad's death I was in no mood to be a witness. I was devastated. But God had other plans in mind. He wanted me to be a winner in this time.

God taught me about His grace and love. The Father taught me, one of his children, how to trust in His provision. My own strength failed. God's strength was all I had left. I needed this. God used this. God made me a winner in my grief. I recalled the Psalmist's words, "The moment I called out, you stepped in; you made my life large with strength." (Psalms 138:3 MSG)

I miss my father, his letters, advice and love. However, my heavenly Father is here with me, always, in every situation. It took my earthly father's death to teach me this important lesson. I want to serve the Lord with every ounce of my being. I want to go out winning . . . winning someone to Christ.

Snakes On An Island

He was a mighty hunter before the LORD; that is why it is said, "Like Nimrod, a mighty hunter before the LORD." (Genesis 10:9 NIV)

In the late 1980s one of the US news services broadcast an hour-long story about the ubiquitous snakes on Guam. These slithering creatures originally arrived after WWII in shipments of wood from the Philippines during reconstruction. With no natural predators on the island they were quick to be fruitful and multiply. By the time of the news report they outnumbered the humans on the island 2 to 1. With this astounding fact and other little bits of history the news service frightened people into thinking our home was overrun with snakes and that we lived in daily fear of being bitten.

While this generated great sympathy for our family we must admit there was little, if any, danger from the extremely persistent snakes. The most annoying problem was their propensity to climb around barriers in order to short out power lines, causing island-wide blackouts. The island power grid, which was tedious at best, responded to the little snakes' climbing abilities and plunged the island into the dark ages. The first report in local newspapers after a power outage was almost always a report of a snake in the poles, or the transformers, causing the automatic breakers to fail and thus back feed the generators and bring them to a screeching halt. When the power dominoes fell this far it was between six and ten hours before the system would come back on line.

Nevertheless we did have a couple experiences with snakes. I was working on the bench at the transmitter site. While sitting on a stool concentrating on a project, one of my mission colleagues called for my attention. Held within the pinches of a long pair of pliers was about a three-foot snake. He wasn't a happy snake. Expecting a spectacular exclamation of fear from me, my colleagues were disappointed when I just shrugged my shoulders and turned back to my work. (I used to play with snakes as a young man in Ohio.) Setting the slithering creature on the floor, they were hooting about being trapped. I calmly said, "Well, that's OK, I have work to do. However, it's going to be a real mess if the snake goes into one of the cable troughs in the building. You'll be busy all day trying to get it out." My colleagues quickly glanced at one another then lunged to recapture the snake and return him to the wild of the antenna field.

One spring I was ill for about two weeks with pneumonia. Being a victim to a long-term illness in a new culture was quite an experience. One Japanese family brought me watermelon to eat. It was supposed to help me recover quickly. A Chinese family kept insisting I need some Vick's VapoRub. Application of this smelly substance covered by pieces of tape would, as they presented it, cure everything from the common cold to a broken leg. Forgoing the local medical customs, I accepted the prescribed antibiotic and spent the majority of two weeks in bed.

Late one night I heard a noise in the kitchen. Rousing myself from a restless sleep, I wandered out to the kitchen. I left the lights off to keep from disturbing Beth or the children. When I arrived at the kitchen I didn't see anything and then heard another noise near the window over the sink. I wandered to that side of the kitchen and peered out the window to the carport, seeing no one. Then I noticed something silvery at the bottom of my field of vision. I backed up a step, looked down and saw a silver sliver of light move along the bottom of the window. Reaching over my head I pulled the switch cord on the lamp. Blinking a couple of times to adjust to the light I was surprised to find a three-foot snake on the kitchen counter with his head inspecting the inside of a crock pot. I could only assume it was in search of a late-night snack. I made a funny noise, OK a yelp, took a step back and looked for some instrument of defense.

I found a machete and poked at the snake until he wiggled through the screen over the sink and dropped to the carport outside. I grabbed a flashlight and headed out to hunt down my escaping prey. I made a loud ruckus in the trash bins, knocked over some boards and otherwise disturbed the entire neighborhood. I slashed out at the departing intruder to no avail. He was faster than my bad aim. He dropped into a drainage ditch and quickly disappeared into the boonies (an island term for wild woods) behind our home. Returning to the house, I was greeted by a sleepy family curious about the noises their sick father was making and totally unimpressed at my skirmish with a beast from the forest! So much for the great hunter!

Sometimes dangerous situations slither into the Christian life. We attack them but they slither away into the darkness. I might not be a mighty hunter like Nimrod but I hope I recognize these snakes in my life and chase them into the boonies. I thank God for his Spirit which allows me to turn on the light in my life, see the danger and then respond in God's strength to chase away the snakes. Have you seen any snakes lately?

Family Expansion

Happy is the man who has his quiver full of them. They won't be disappointed when they speak with their enemies in the gate. (Psalms 127:5 WEB)

Three children, one girl and two boys, sounded just right to Beth and me. There was just enough room in the car, just enough room in the house and there were just enough chairs around the table, including the highchair, of course. Things were starting to smooth out about the house with the new routine, learning how to cope with James' endless energy and Joel starting into Kindergarten.

God, I have discovered, does not have the same sense of completeness and timing I have. = In the fall of 1987 we discovered another Chick was under construction to expand our family from five to six. As we considered these new circumstances we decided some things needed to change. All the items which were just the right size were now one size too small. I'm starting to sound like Dr. Seuss!

The family was expanding, including Beth, who I believe looks absolutely lovely pregnant, so our home, table, car, everything needed to expand to include the pending arrival. It was with great sadness we sold our car. Not that the car was anything special, it was only a simple Toyota station wagon. But it was the first and only car we had ever owned which we purchased new from a dealer. Things just don't last forever.

To provide sufficient space for another baby and all the necessary paraphernalia, portable crib, stroller, baby seats, etc., we searched high and low for the right vehicle. That vehicle, provided by God's perfect timing, was a 1977 Volkswagen bus. Yes, bus is the right term. The steering wheel was almost horizontal and there was plenty of room to take on passengers.

Unfortunately, this bus only had two front seats and a bench in the rear. No seat belts and the center bench seat was missing. It was time for some improvisation. It's important to remember I'm not a mechanic, machinist, or any sort of auto expert. If it doesn't plug into the wall I don't know a lot about it. However, the old adage is true, "Necessity is the mother of invention."

Purchasing an additional seat for such an old car was out of the question. Our lime green, yes lime green, bus was the only VW bus on the island so parts were scarce. In truth there were maybe six VW vehicles on the island all imported by various military personnel. All parts had to be ordered via the post out of the USA. Seats were just too big for the post.

I looked around and considered the possibilities and then came upon an idea. There were school buses on Guam. They wore out. There had to be some in the junk yard. Why not get one of the old school bus seats? Sure enough, I found an old bus and convinced the owner to permit me to remove a seat for a modest price. I had to do the work but departed from the yard with a new seat for my VW bus.

Next, I needed to add a couple legs, figure out how to mount it in the bus and add seat belts. The seat belts were relatively easy. I ordered them from a company in the USA.. The seat required me to learn to weld (thanks, Rich) and then drill some holes in the floor of the bus and mount the seat. A few days later we were ready with seats for seven in our VW bus. I even took time to get the air conditioner fixed. It didn't last long but it was nice while it lasted. We dubbed our new transportation the Sweet Pickles Bus and threatened to name the new baby Moonbeam if it was a girl.

Our pending child caused me to learn a few new things. I think that's the way God works. He uses circumstances in our lives to teach us something new at just the right time. He also uses children to teach us a lot about ourselves but that is a different story.

Evan Robert Chick

"There are three things which are too amazing for me, four which I don't understand: (Proverbs 30:18 WEB)

Having children is always an adventure. After three children we were not sure what to expect with a fourth delivered on Guam. Ellice was born in the hospital bed before it was time for the delivery room. Joel actually made it to the delivery room and popped out sunny side up. James was born in the hospital room and not the delivery room because the hospital was full and we were just thrilled Beth moved from the hall to the room before he was born.

For Evan's appearance we entered Guam Memorial Hospital. The name Memorial had an ominous connotation of remembering those long gone. We prayed this would not be the case as Beth was ready for the baby to come and I struggled with my dreaded fear of hospitals, needles, medicine, blood, all those routine things of life. I always thought this was a strange fear for someone who worked in a hospital for four years. Then again, maybe that's why I have these fears!

Beth was not afraid, just ready for the baby to be born. We waited in the emergency room to be admitted. I looked around. It was interesting. I noted the dust on the instruments and the tape across the handles of the defibrillator. Fortunately, none of these were necessary as we were transferred to a room on the maternity floor.

The room was a hospital room. What else did we expect? We were the only ones in the room, making it easier for me to stay and work through the night with Beth. By early morning things were moving along at a good clip and it was TIME! The nurses came in and said they were moving Beth to the delivery room.

Beth shook her head. Nope, no movement at this time, it was too late!

"But we have to move you to the delivery room," announced the nurse.

"No way!" shouted Beth. "I'm not going anywhere and this baby is coming now!"

The nurse did her nurse's survey of the situation, looked at me as if I knew something special, and said, "You're right, you stay here." She then left and quickly returned with another nurse to continue the procedure.

Evan was born quickly in the labor room and greeted the world with a loud and strong voice. Beth was tired, ready for rest and I was ready for a good night's sleep as well. On that morning Evan became the fourth Chick child and the third Chick son. A couple days later he enjoyed his first ride in the Sweet Pickles Bus to his home in Santa Rita.

God gives us gifts in unexpected ways. Evan was a gift. His arrival method was unexpected. Praise the Lord! Solomon was amazed at four things. Me, I'm amazed at many more and birth is one of those amazing miracles of God.

Seeking the Stars

Praise him, sun and moon! Praise him, all you shining stars! (Psalms 148:3 WEB)

As a little child I often sat in the backyard and stared at the stars. One year my father provided a telescope so we could look closely at the constellations and the man in the moon. The immense magnitude of the stars stirred my soul. I was fascinated. I read science fiction novels and watched movies like "The Forbidden Planet." These all served to increase my desire to know more about the heavens and what was out there.

Dad was famous in Atlanta because of man's desire to know more about the stars. The Russians launched Sputnik to the amazement of the world. Dad carefully aligned his Ham Radio gear and captured the short signal as the satellite passed over Georgia. Because of his recording, a story and photo appeared in the Atlanta newspaper.

I was excited to watch Alan Shepherd, John Glenn and a long list of others blast off to circle the globe and explore the edges of space. It's still exciting today! My fascination with these men, and the National Aeronautics and Space Administration (NASA) continued to grow.

I remember I stayed up late to watch the first men land on the moon and hear the memorable words, "That's one small step for man, one giant leap for mankind." I wanted to be an astronaut and explore the galaxy. Unfortunately, I was soon too tall to fit within the confines of the earlier space capsules. But still my interest and study of space travel continued.

I collected pictures of astronauts, detailed drawings and specifications for the capsules and the future plans for the space program. I wrote to astronauts and collected signatures and personal information. One day God provided me an opportunity to meet one of these men of space history.

I was working as an engineer in a little radio station in Cincinnati, Ohio. I worked the late shift since I was still in high school at the time. Due to the location of the station the doors were locked in the evening and visitors were carefully announced.

As I sat drinking my cola, listening to the programs and making my log entries I was startled when the back door buzzed. I sauntered through the equipment room to the frosted door and noticed a medium height man outlined by the street lamp in the parking lot.

I stepped close to the door and questioned, "Who is it?"

"John Glenn," he replied and waited.

I thought for a couple seconds, didn't remember anything on my list of events for the evening and unceremoniously replied, "Yeah right!" I paused for dramatic effect then continued, "So, who are you really and what do you want?"

The man on the other side of the door cleared his throat and replied, "I am John Glenn here to record a political commercial."

"Sorry, but I'm not buying this, buddy," I replied with a bit of sarcasm in my voice.

"Why don't you call someone and find out?" replied the visitor from the outside of the door.

"I'll be back in a minute," I answered. I turned and walked back to my desk in the transmitter hall. I looked up the manager's phone number. I dialed and waited for an answer.

"Hello?"

"Hello, this is Bob from the station. There's some jerk outside claiming to be John Glenn. What do you want me to do? Call the police?"

"Uh-oh," the station manager replied, "didn't I leave you a note?"

"Note? What note?"

"John Glenn is coming to record political spots for his senatorial campaign. Record the spots and leave the recordings on my desk," instructed the manager.

"OK," I replied and hung up the phone.

Sheepishly I returned to the back door, ushered in Mr. Glenn and profusely apologized for treating him in such an impolite manner. We chatted about his work in the space program, a highlight for me, and I recorded his comments for political commercials. He went on to serve as Senator for Ohio for several terms.

That was my first direct interaction with the space program. My collection of photos, signatures and special documents have long since disappeared but my interest continued even to the mission field.

On Guam NASA maintained a tracking station near the southern end of the island. One day I drove over with some friends for a short tour of the small facility.

One Thanksgiving we hosted a gentleman who worked with the shuttle program. Guam served as a backup landing site for the space shuttle in case there was an emergency. The shuttle didn't divert to Guam but I learned a number of fascinating facts concerning their backup plans.

As thorough as backup plans might be they are never one hundred per cent. It was during our furlough from 1985 to 1986, while we were living in O'Fallon, Missouri, that I was once more reminded of the space program. We had just returned from a speaking trip to Kentucky where our speedometer cable broke.

I purchase the appropriate parts and spent the afternoon working under the car to install the new cable. This was necessary to make the cruise control work. Cruise control is a vital necessity with the number of miles we travel during furlough.

Several hours later, two trips to the car part store and some choice words to the designer of the car, I finally had a cable positioned for testing. I climbed into the car, started it up, cranked the air conditioning to frostbite and drove down the road. When I saw the speedometer begin to function I turned on the radio.

As I listened to some music, my sing-along was interrupted by major news. The space shuttle Challenger had just exploded during takeoff. I couldn't believe it! This had to be some sort of a joke. I remembered years before the news of the Apollo crew burned to death in the capsule. My heart went out to the families of the crew and all those involved in the details of the shuttle mission.

This was a national tragedy I never forgot. I drove home, turned on the television and watched the video of the event while listening to the ground crew try to assess the damage. None survived; it was a stark reality obvious in the film but denied in the heart.

As I worked to bring the heavenly news of the Gospel to the world I was reminded of man's fragile, unexpected life. How many people around the world die unexpectedly without understanding the Gospel message and choosing to turn to God through Christ?

Another shuttle disaster occurred a few months before I wrote this. Again, my heart went out to the crew, their families and all involved in the program. God gave us minds to overcome many of the limitations of our earthly life, including reaching out into space and to the moon.

Still, it's here on the earth God chose to send his son to provide us a way of salvation. I want to seek God's face in everything I do. Like many, I can find myself looking off to some unknown world diverting my vision from the one who saved my soul. I am excited as mankind grows, learns, discovers new things God created and reaches to the stars.

I pray I may be used of God to help others reach to the heavens through the savior on the Cross. We need a heavenly vision, with Christ as our focus, to reach the world with the good news of salvation.

Mother of Learning

Instruct a wise man, and he will be still wiser. Teach a righteous man, and he will increase in learning. (Proverbs 9:9 WEB)

Some people appear to know everything. No matter the subject at hand they seem to be experts in the details and functions of the topic. When a problem comes along they always seem to have a solution. My children accuse me of this but I know it isn't true. God has proven that over and over during my life.

When living outside your comfort zone it doesn't take long before you find yourself with a problem you don't understand. It might be a problem you quickly recognize but have never been asked for the solution. For me this applies to anything dealing with cars and car repair. I like to drive, enjoy it immensely. I love road trips and watching the countryside whisk by, revealing God's glorious handiwork.

This is great as long as the car works. Unfortunately, cars are mechanical beasts created by the imperfect hands of men. Looking carefully at the inside of the engine compartment, I'm in a quandary. I'm not sure whether the designer is a genius or schizophrenic. How they figure which wire goes to which place and which vacuum hose pulls from which nozzle is beyond my understanding. Give me a transmitter schematic diagram or modulator section and it makes perfect logical sense.

Cars and their internal combustion engines are a mystery. So, when things go wrong I'm in trouble. I never thought of Guam as a school for auto repair. The Lord had other things in mind. During our fourteen years on Guam I learned how to change brakes, universal joints, reseal an engine and replace a clutch. Repairing items such as radiators and air conditioners were included, as well as welding together a gear shift which fell off the car in the parking lot!

Rich was a great help. He actually knew how these things worked in a car and how to make repairs. If a mechanical problem appeared to stump everyone we would ask Rich to look at it. Sometimes he would say, "It can't be repaired." We would smile at one another, let an acquiescent "hummm" escape our lips and then say, "You're right, no one could fix this." That was the key phrase. It was like a bell to a Pavlov pup. Rich would take up the challenge and discover some new inventive resolution to the problem and have things running in no time.

But it wasn't fair to have Rich fix everyone's car, or dryer, or whatever. So, understanding this when I was suddenly the computer expert inundated with requests, I decided it was best to do the work myself and resort to Rich as an expert consultant. As I put my hands and back into the fray, he would more than gladly provide me with the necessary instruction to get the repair done.

He could do the task but preferred I learn how to work on my own car. He was right, it was good for me and for him. When I was really stuck he'd jump into the repair job with joy and demonstrate what needed to be done. After extracting me from the difficult situation, Rich would leave me to continue and finish the work.

Automobile repairs weren't the only learning experiences on the mission field. Through the expert guidance of colleagues, I discovered I can rebuild engines, drive tractors, operate a back hoe and even sit in a bosun's chair hanging between the wires of an antenna to help with some high wire work. The last is a mere miracle with my fear of heights! Walking where God called us provided assurance as I stepped outside my comfort zone again and again.

Comfort comes in many forms and one is storage space in the house. This requires lots of closets or storage cabinets. We didn't arrive on Guam with a large quantity of furniture. Our container held some keepsakes from our family and additional storage spaces were necessary. Furniture was available on Guam, but for a price larger than our missionary bank account could accommodate.

I checked out the spare items available at the transmitter site. I found old shipping containers from our shipment and others who arrived from the mainland. With the help of Kevin, another colleague in ministry, we started a small furniture factory. Well, maybe not real furniture but we made it useful! All the tools were available in the mission shop and long night shifts were a great time for cutting, hammering, and making a general mess when no one else was around.

We created a couple of nice entertainment cabinets complete with doors and curtains so they looked presentable. They're still being used in our home fifteen years later! Not bad for leftover shipping boxes. I was inspired by the work and actually purchased some good wood to build a couple small items for holding magazines and a doll house for Ellice.

As each necessity unfolded I surveyed my talents and knowledge to discover there was always something new to learn. In each adventure God provided the necessary skill, training and guidance through His Spirit and the Spirit-led lives of my companions in the ministry. That's the way God works in our lives. We don't know everything at one time but receive what we need at the right time.

Testing My Theology

I have hidden your word in my heart that I might not sin against you. (Psalms 119:11 WEB)

For most of our years on Guam Beth worked in the listener mail department. It was encouraging to hear her read letters from folks whose lives were redeemed and headed for eternity because they heard the word of God on the radio. This kept us close to the listeners we never saw face to face.

Occasionally the listener response department would receive a letter with detailed questions which could not be answered easily during the working days. These would be passed to different members of the staff for a more extensive biblical response. Some were directed my way by my loving wife.

When I was young and began to understand the Gospel, I realized there were many aspects of Christianity I didn't understand. This is how it works with everyone. Nobody has all the answers just because they're born again. Some who are religious have a good head start like the Apostle Paul. He knew God's word and promises but needed a little blindness to open his eyes to the truth. He had the knowledge but not the correct response or interpretation. That took time and experience.

Listeners hear God's word, respond and come to salvation! Praise the Lord! Unfortunately, they don't have instant complete theological interpretation and understanding. None of us do. This is how God works. Through fellow believers God teaches us. Through the Holy Spirit God teaches us. Through the Bible God teaches us. Only one person I know correctly understood all aspects of theology. This was Jesus as he walked among us.

When writing in response to programs, believers are honest with their questions. I remember a few choice questions which were passed my direction. One man wanted to know whether he was still permitted to have intimate relations with his wife now that he was saved. At the other end of the spectrum were new believers asking whether they should discontinue their relationship with concubines. (Yes, they still exist in many parts of the world.) Others asked questions as they came from other religions such as, "Is Jesus just a prophet or the son of God?" The questions covered a large range of topics and depths.

Working with these letters made me think back to my college years. Believe it or not, I am trained as a theologian, not an engineer. It's strange the way God uses people to work in His plans and not in our preconceptions. The occasional letter that crossed my desk was welcomed as a chance to hone my understanding of God's word. In the process of discovering truth, to answer the question of someone I don't know, I learn a lot.

Learning has always been something I enjoy. The exception is when I do something stupid or sinful and have to learn the hard way. It's more enjoyable to learn from God's word than through God's discipline. Answering questions, teaching Sunday school and even teaching at Bayview Bible Institute all taught me more than I taught others.

God works this way. He brings people into our lives with questions we thought we understood until we start to explain what we thought we understood. This process tests our theology, our faith and expands our understanding of God's love, God's grace and the work of the Holy Spirit. We might find ourselves growing when we tackle the questions that come our way.

A Rose by Any Other Name

His name endures forever. His name continues as long as the sun. Men shall be blessed by him. All nations will call him blessed. (Psalms 72:17 WEB)

William Shakespeare was a brilliant wordsmith. If we accept all his credited writings as demonstration of his abilities, then his command of the English language was beyond compare. Fortunately for William he was working in his native tongue, writing to reach people in his native land.

In radio ministry we often take programs from one language, translate them to another language and send them thousands of miles through the air. God works miracles in people's lives through these programs. Souls are saved. Believers are encouraged, believers edified and churches receive resources for ministry. Pastors are trained as programs come into their home with personal relevant instructions.

I never translate the programs myself. I only hear about the difficulties some of our program producers have while tuning the sermons to fit a culture different from the original speaker. Program lengths must be modified to provide culturally sensitive and culturally relevant examples, understood by the listener, or explanations to further illuminate a biblical point. Sometimes they work, sometimes they don't.

Many times our listeners search for English programs. In their desire to know God better, curiosity about the Gospel, or enjoyment of the music, they tune in and listen to English as their second or third or fourth language. Personally, I have difficulty understanding my native tongue much less a second, third or fourth language. As careful as the producers are there is always room for misinterpretation or just hearing it wrong.

Some of my favorite snippets of humor come from non-English listeners writing in English. Although we communicate with one another it's evident English is not their native tongue. We have received letters addressed to programs such as "Throw the Bible" (*Thru the Bible*), "Dropping Your God" (*Dropping your Guard*), and the "Wrestling Hour" (*Wesleyan Hour*). One gentleman sent us a question. He wanted to know "how to go through Chuck's window to get inside for living" (*Insight for Living* by Chuck Swindoll). Another listener wrote to say he was "rolling around with the radio one day when he found our program." Just picture him. . . on the floor, radio in hand, rolling back and forth while searching for a program.

Reading God's word is sometimes like these misinterpretations of program names. Our minds and eyes read passages but our subconscious translates it to something totally different from the written word. It takes careful study, the inspiration of the Holy Spirit, and sometimes the clear direction of a brother in Christ to straighten out our understanding. As I read or hear a listener's response I chuckle over the minor but entertaining language difficulties, then

I consider what I read in my morning devotions to see if I clearly heard the word of God.

Hidden Treasure

But we have this treasure in clay vessels, that the exceeding greatness of the power may be of God, and not from ourselves. (2 Corinthians 4:7 WEB)

When I was a young man I enjoyed watching movies about pirates. There was always a buried treasure to be found by the one-eyed, swashbuckling seafarers. I remember reading <u>Treasure Island</u> and the tales of Long John Silver and young Jim Hawkins. I think every young boy dreams of being a pirate or a cowboy. Granted, cowboys might fit better in the Christian perspective than thieving pirates, but I liked pirates.

I made pirate swords from anything long and pointy. My brothers were subject to raids when the spirit of the skull and crossed bones took over. I read about pirates and watched movies. Fortunately for my friends, I mixed pirates with a touch of Robin Hood. My collected goods were distributed to my needy friends. Granted, a button here, an empty writing pen there didn't make for much booty but to us it was treasure. I was a good pirate. Somewhere along the line I was introduced to Tom Sawyer and Huck Finn. Their American adventures along the Mississippi sparked my interest as well.

During our first furlough from Guam, between 1985 and 1986, we drove to my parent's home in Quincy, Illinois as often as possible. When my parents moved to Quincy, situated on the mighty Mississippi River, thoughts of pirates and adventure came to mind once more. The tales of Mark Twain, featuring Tom Sawyer and friends, also came to mind. Tom looked for buried treasure on more than one occasion while getting into the most unusual trouble you could imagine.

Joel was about five years old during one of these visits. My father helped raise three boys and knew boys like adventure and treasure. In preparation for one of our visits, he took a small coffee can, filled it with pirate booty, and buried it in the backyard. Using an old paper grocery sack, he created a pirate map with directions to the secret stash.

Dad called Joel close and handed him the map. "There's treasure in the backyard," he said in a quiet, secretive whisper. Joel's eyes grew wide and he scanned the room to make sure no one else overheard the exciting news. The two whispered some special words of conspiracy then headed out the back door of the house.

Several years earlier, in 1980, my parents planted a small cherry tree in the backyard in honor of Joel, their first grandson. The treasure hunt started from this historic location and ended under a bush. Joel carefully studied the map, measured out each step and ended up at the bush. Dad sat in a lawn chair, keeping a protective eye on his conspiracy to find the pirate treasure. A few minutes later Joel stood next to the suspect bush looking at his grandpa.

"Is it here?" he asked, pointing at the ground.

"I'm not sure," replied Grandpa. "Get the garden shovel from next to the house and start digging!"

Joel ran across the yard and returned with the small hand shovel. With gusto he began digging away at the base of the bush. Dirt was flying everywhere! Dad stepped over to direct his digging to the proper spot and save the bush from destruction by his eager grandson.

Suddenly Joel's shovel hit something hard. He probed it a couple of times and listened to the dirt-muted thump. Dad smiled, shifted the pipe in his mouth, knelt down next to his grandson, and together they extracted the round pirate chest from the loose dirt. Removing the plastic Folgers lid, Joel investigated each nut, bolt, piece of candy and all the treasure of the world at his fingertips.

Dad explain each treasure except the candy, which was obvious. For the remainder of the afternoon they talked of the treasure, the map, and the fun of exploration. It was good medicine for a curious little boy, a great lesson in following directions. To this day Joel keeps his treasure map in a box full of other treasured memories.

Searching God's word is sometimes like a treasure hunt. We look for nuggets of gold to enrich our lives and prepare us to walk with God faithfully. At times we find revelation easy to understand, like a treasure chest full of candy. Other times it requires the seasoned directions of someone who's been there before us to explain the path. We head out and they patiently watch our progress to provide occasional course corrections. We when reach the end, we've discovered the truth God wants to reveal in our life.

I find reading about men and women of faith exciting, instructional, and revealing. Missionary biographies are my favorite. OK, go figure, I'm a missionary so that makes sense. Others such as George Müller, R.A. Torrey, and A.W. Tozer can be discovered on my bookshelves. Sharing their walk with God helps me interpret the plan God has for my life. They've been there before.

I pray my life helps others find God's truth. It's not always a straight path. Sometimes it needs a course correction from a watchful grandpa in the faith. Other times we find ourselves feasting, in abundance, on God's clear, and free, love and grace.

High Tech Invasion

"Be still, and know that I am God. I will be exalted among the nations. I will be exalted in the earth." (Psalms 46:10 WEB)

During each of our deputations we were thrilled to use some high-tech tools. A carousel projector for slides, a cassette player for audio, and foam boards for pictures about the ministry were regular parts of sharing the ministry. We were at the cutting edge of missionary presentations . . . at least for the 1980s.

Arriving on the mission field, I used our portable typewriter to maintain communications with family, friends, and supporters in the USA. Postal mail was slow but it worked great. Evenings were regularly set aside and I would take over the dining room table. I'd place the typewriter on the table surrounded by paper, envelopes and a list of addresses. Photos were reduced to verbal descriptions as we shared our ministry. Purchasing multiple prints was too expensive.

There is a great feeling of achievement in writing a letter by hand and sharing our thoughts and God's work with others. The handwriting portion didn't work well for me. My handwriting is awful. Occasionally I write a note to myself, which I puzzle over for days to remember what it says. I kept a journal at times and find it difficult to read as I go back through the pages. The typewriter was my salvation - on the human writing a letter level, not the spiritual level.

Typewriters, unfortunately, soon became yesterday's technology in the USA and even on the mission field. In the early 1980s the personal computer began its invasion of the office and eventually the home. Our first computer was sent as a gift from a supporter in the USA. The Heathkit H-89 was a monster by today's standards and a marvel in its day. With 16 Megabytes of memory, 90 kilobyte hard sectored single-sided floppies and a built-in monitor, it was a self-contained miracle. If there was a hardware problem I could find the individual chip and replace it.

After receiving this modern device, I wrote a letter to our friend in thanks. Several months later he sent a letter asking if it was received. I replied again the computer was received and living well on my desk at home. A year later my original letter was received in their home. This was a clear sign from God something was changing our method of communication. On the other hand, it might be a clear sign from the post office that letters do occasionally get lost.

Curiosity about computers took over and I delved into the inner workings of the hardware, software and anywhere I could work on the computer. I wrote inventory software, worked with electronically generated operational manuals (previously a laborious job to keep up to date) and developed an excellent word processor for the Atari computer, written in machine language, which eventually entered our home. In short, I soon became the most knowledgeable computer user on Guam. At least, in our staff.

Knowledge can be a dangerous thing. With limited personnel, when you become an expert in one area you become the expert for the field. Within a couple of years, I was suddenly the person to call for computer problems in the mission and the missionary homes. This time saving device began to eat up the extra time I thought I had.

Learning to use the computer was a great benefit to our family. Prayer letters were more colorful with better spelling. Photos eventually made their way into regular letters. We developed a family website. Email replaced many letters and brought the world, family, and friends to my keyboard in seconds instead of weeks.

In the years that followed I became immersed in computer technology. Becoming a system administrator and software programmer, my computer skills expanded beyond our field on Guam to include other Asian offices and the home office in the USA. Special training at IBM headquarters put me in a position to help the mission deploy a new set of computing tools worldwide. (AIX Unix for those interested.)

This time saving device now consumed all my time and ministry within the mission and often at our local church and the homes of friends and acquaintances. One day I received a call from the US Customs office on Guam. They had a computer problem and were looking for an answer. When I asked whether I could see the computer to determine the problem, I was informed it was classified. They wanted an answer by some miracle of intuition. I declined their call and have been declining other intuitive requests for assistance ever since.

Computers are a way of life now and I recommend every missionary have a computer with email access. There are aspects of the device which are beneficial to the ministry and aspects which are detrimental. At times its demands control us and other times we control it.

The many trees killed thanks to cheap printers can't be good for the world. Our own nerves are often put on edge as we try to keep pace with the faster and faster computing power of the machine God allowed us to create. Once we took our time to write a letter, consider our words, and communicate with each other. Now we type quickly, hit the spell check button, and whisk our immediate thoughts around the world.

So many areas of life are like a computer. Given careful attention they can be helpful and beneficial to our walk with God. Time in reading, music, fellowship and church are great for building our understanding of God's work as it applies to our lives. Too much time reading, in music, in fellowship and even at church can have the inverse effect. There are extremes and excesses which can move a good activity into a harmful arena of life.

We must be careful, listen to the prompting of the Holy Spirit, and approach the tools and ministries of life with wisdom and careful moderation. As I sit in front of the computer writing these memories, I, too, need to "be still" and know that He is God!

Flying First Class

Like the dew of Hermon, that comes down on the hills of Zion: for there Yahweh gives the blessing, even life forevermore. (Psalms 133:3 WEB)

For years we lived in the Pacific and travel always involved a lot of airline miles. After a couple years of bouncing back and forth between the US and Guam, I had a large number of unused miles saved in my airline account. For years I felt the airline miles packages were a scam until I had a massive number waiting to be used.

One spring I was again scheduled to travel from Guam to North Carolina and back. I must admit, I'm not a lover of airline travel. The seats are too small with the headrests constantly pressing against my shoulders and providing no rest. Sitting in the shape of a pretzel for twenty hours is not my idea of fun.

With the trip pending I pulled out my air miles report and made some calculations. If I pooled my miles with the other family miles I could fly first class! I'm not talking the mediocre business class but right up front, glass dishes and all, first class.

I went to the airline office, handed them the tickets and they upgraded my cattle car, shoe horn seats for the luxury of first class. I wasn't sure what to expect but figured it had to be better than riding in the back mooing for dinner.

The travel date arrived and I boarded the plane ahead of everyone else! The flight attendant's manners were spectacular, pleasant and helpful. I didn't have to wait for takeoff to enjoy a refreshing drink or a snack. They were just waiting for me to climb aboard and indulge.

To compare the seats in first class with economy would be difficult. The cattle car contains benches with arm rests to separate the stalls. First class has cushions, foot rests, headrests (which actually reach your head) and sufficient lateral space to wiggle until you are comfortable. Thirsty? Drinks are available any time during the flight. Hungry? You have a choice of several meals served with real dishes and glass glasses.

I landed in Japan and was personally greeted by the sunny smile of an airline worker. Apparently, I was the only one in first class and the others were subject to the lesser honor of business class. Nobody greeted the business class passengers. They were on their own.

I was escorted around the crowds, through special walkways to a waiting area just for first class. There was more room for the dozen or so first class passengers than the hundreds of cattle rustling against one another two flights up. Food and drink were available and part of the package. No announcements were necessary. When it was time to board, ahead of everyone else of course, the staff tapped lightly on my shoulder and escorted me to the plane.

This treatment continued for most of the four flights to North Carolina and back. When the domestic planes were too small for a real first class cabin, the service was reduced to drinks, food and smaller seats. At least I could still board and exit ahead of the stampede.

I have never again flown first class. The strange thing about upgrading was you got extra mileage flying first class. Thus, I recovered my mileage in the one trip plus some.

Later I used the mileage to move up to business class and gave up unused mileage when I left the Pacific and participating airlines. One year, Beth and I took Ellice to visit Thailand using mileage. It was our high school graduation gift to her, a once-in-a-lifetime treat.

Computers put me on more air flights than I imagined. There were chances to see my brothers and visit my mother while in the USA. In the midst of their frustration, computers provided little gems of enjoyment and benefit. Attending training and global IT meetings in the US racked up plenty of mileage.

When the Lord puts us in a ministry we didn't expect we sometimes wonder what He is doing. There are frustrations which threaten what sanity we have left. Then He reminds us it is His work and not ours. He is in control and knows what we can and cannot do. When we are faithful to press forward God reminds us again with little gems of enjoyment and benefit.

Suffer the Little Children

But Jesus said, "Allow the little children, and don't forbid them to come to me; for to such belongs the Kingdom of Heaven." (Matthew 19:14 WEB)

God did not call Christians to suffer through the little children even though some children are insufferable. In these small bodies innocence is looking for answers to life just as adults struggle with the same questions. Working with children, sharing with them the Gospel is a delight, a challenge, a struggle and requires a person with a lot of imagination and energy.

Beth is this kind of person. She is great with children. This is probably why I like to be around our four children. She is creative, marvelous with stories, and loves making arts and crafts for our home and children's ministries. Everywhere we live she gets involved with children one way or another.

Brownies, Awana, and Vacation Bible School all benefited from her gifts and talents. Even during our furloughs she would take the opportunity to work with children. I was usually relegated to behind the scenes constructing projects before the classes.

One year we enjoyed a tee pee in the classroom. This full-size re-creation required the ceiling tiles be removed so the top would fit in the room. The children thought it was great. One young man wanted to build a fire in front of the Indian dwelling. As a deacon I didn't think this was a good idea. There were no vents for the smoke in the building.

Another year there were paper fish hanging from the ceiling as the children experienced life under the sea. Wall size paintings, on bed linens, were often used to liven up the evangelistic opportunities. If something wasn't nailed down in our home it was used for a children's ministry project.

One Guam summer it was time for Vacation Bible School. Our church held an ambitious program each year. Recruitment began just after Christmas, running right up to the day before the joyous event started. The only excuse for not participating was being off island. I would go to the beach, stand in the water and shout I was "off island" so I could go to my mission work without a guilty conscience.

Each year Beth was thrilled as the little hearts responded to the Gospel message. She would sing, teach, play and show them God's love from a heart filled with God's love. I looked forward to the last night of VBS when the children would present music and skits for their parents and anyone who wandered into the church auditorium.

One year I was laughing with the antics of the kindergarten class and humming along with the music of the first grade class. A few more skits, songs and presentations followed and then came Beth's class.

Over twenty young ones came prancing onto the platform with stick horses. They used white socks to make the horses' heads, complete with button eyes, felt tongue and twine manes. It took me a couple moments to come to a startling realization.

The morning before the presentation I dressed to go to the mission. Working in technical areas I often wore work boots and white socks. For some reason I couldn't find any clean white socks. I figured they were all in the wash until I saw them dancing in young hands across the stage. My sock drawer had become a herd of horses to the squeals and delight of Beth's class. The next year I started hiding my clothing when the subject of Vacation Bible School was broached.

Although some people view me as a grumpy person I have a grand time with children. For some reason they enjoy climbing, talking and having fun. I enjoy watching as they figure things out and seeing their eyes grow wide with wonder as they listen to a story about God's love.

Jesus called the children to him. He told us we need to be like children. We need to be innocent in our devotion. No withholding before God. Clear, clean, innocent openness. It is here He takes us into His heavenly lap, tells of the miracles of a life with Him and we find rest.

Spirit Led

You didn't choose me, but I chose you, and appointed you, that you should go and bear fruit, and that your fruit should remain; that whatever you will ask of the Father in my name, he may give it to you. (John 15:16 WEB)

As I grow older I see more and more change. I have the sneaking suspicion I was less observant as a young man. Still, while growing up my father was excellent at teaching me to observe things. Not just big things that you can't miss but the small, almost insignificant, changes.

Learning this was very important for working in a technical field. When it comes to troubleshooting problems, accuracy involves noticing small changes and then discovering why. There is a mystical gift for good troubleshooting. My father taught me how to use the gift.

Over the years I've worked with many engineers and technicians. Some were excellent at noticing the small things. Hearing the slight change in pitch from a blower, catching a scent of ozone from some failed part or noticing the telltale wisp of smoke escaping a component were second nature. Others couldn't find the problem when the transmitter was in flames before their eyes.

Following the Holy Spirit's lead is much like troubleshooting. Sometimes the direction is obvious. At other times it's noticing the small changes in life, family, work, prayer time, and studying God's word that tweak our heart to change. We each have a gift to recognize this prompting. Responding to God's call for change is important in our Christian walk.

Calling us to the mission field was a major undertaking for God. I am rather thick-headed at times and can easily choose to ignore the signs and wonders which are so obvious. Still, once we were called, we knew it and responded to that call.

A calling it is. I emphasize the calling because it was not the choice I, nor Beth, would have made. As a matter of fact, mission work was far from our thoughts and not part of our plan as a newlywed couple. And yet God prepared the way during my schooling and through the friends Beth established in Wilmore.

Reading missionary biographies, being introduced to furloughing missionaries, and being burdened for the lost were just some of the methods God used to put our feet on the right path. Because God did the calling, because God did the directing, because it was God's direction and not ours, we see things with a different perspective than some.

Granted, there are many missionaries who understand what is involved in being called by God. Others, including some missionaries on the field and some full time Christian workers, don't appear to have a clue. It appears illogical, from a human standpoint, to work outside our training.

When our work is a calling we can either obey or run. This is like Jonah and the whale. If we choose to run, there is no place we can escape God's hand or voice. If we obey, we may not immediately know the results but can trust God to accomplish His purposes.

Hearing requires listening, obedience requires following. Our problems can begin when God's calling is not to do what we feel we are trained or prepared to do! We use logic to try and avoid or ignore God's call in our lives. "Surely the Lord will want me to use my training and education to serve Him," we say when God's leading doesn't fit in our earthly plans.

According to Beth's training and education she is a physical therapist. According to my education and training I am a theologian and an engineer. When we arrived on Guam they didn't need a physical therapist or a theologian. They needed a secretary and a ditch digger. While this was not our training, God used these jobs to teach us to trust in Him. It was not a question of using our skills. It was a question of obedience to God's calling.

Through the years we haven't always been so willing to follow when called to work outside our skills and training. Still, God used us in areas we never expected. In each case God provided the skills, understanding, and abilities to accomplish his task.

As I listen to people clamor about their rights, their need to use their training and skills, I am concerned. The concept of a calling appears to have faded. I think many of God's prophets were working outside of their training and abilities. They were willing, sometimes through divine encouragement, to obey God's calling regardless of the task ahead. What are we willing to do?

Are we guided by the Spirit or are we guiding the Spirit? Cleaning toilets, mopping floors, or digging ditches for water pipes are not the normal activities for theologians, technicians or physical therapists. But God can and will work through us in these, and other areas outside our expertise, when we are willing to heed the calling and obey. I pray the Lord will remind me of this next time I kick against the calling because of my own selfish desires. I pray He'll remind me and I'll listen and obey.

Beth Remembers the Children

My little children, let's not love in word only, neither with the tongue only, but in deed and truth. (1 John 3:18 WEB)

As I, Beth, am reading all of these memories it reminds me also of wonderful things God has done and how good it is to remember His work in our lives. You have read about my working with children. Bob also writes about working in areas that you want to work in and in which you feel gifted. It made me laugh that these two stories tie together in a way Bob doesn't even remember.

Before we went to Guam I taught many ladies' Bible studies and felt this was a good match for my gifts. I didn't really like working with children and the thought of walking into a room of twenty-three or more two-year-old bundles of energy for hours sounded awful. The church asked me to teach and I started with the fifth and sixth grade girls in Pioneer Club because they were the oldest class. I had a blast because I had great girls and they were old enough to obey and behave without much work from me. Many thanks to Rebecca and Heather.

Then I was convinced to help with Vacation Bible School, so I helped people who really knew what they were doing. I watched Jacki and Kim and thought, hey when you control the kids in a loving manner it's fun to teach them. I then took on my first VBS class of four- and five-year-olds. My son, James, was in this class and about twenty-one other children. We did an ocean theme and we were a team of four with a memory verse person and a craft person and a teen for crowd control.

We decorated the room like you wouldn't believe. It was great. There was a blue carpet for seaside Bible lessons and huge dolphins swimming around. Bible verse time was at the palm tree on an island, complete with a treasure chest.

The unique part happened with our Bible story and the presentation of the Gospel. The first day I gave the lesson and presented the salvation message and the children listened and looked. The second day the same. Then, on the third day, sixteen children raised their hands when we gave the invitation! You should've seen the looks on our faces. We were stunned. All four of us sat there with our mouths open. There was this pause as we looked at each other. "What do we do now?" was written on our faces.

We quickly took each of the children aside who had raised their hands and talked and prayed with each one. They seemed to understand and were sincere and all of them prayed. Our only regret was one dear boy named Teddy who had seemed so open and wasn't there on Wednesday.

This shows how great God is and that it wasn't us that did any great work. Teddy's dad brought him in on Thursday and said, "Teddy, tell the teacher what you did yesterday." After lessons on Monday and Tuesday he talked and talked at home about the Lord and his parents led him to Christ on Wednesday while waiting in the dentist's office. I have followed some of these kids into their teens and am happy to be a tool God could use.

Bullfrogs and Butterflies

Seeing you have purified your souls in your obedience to the truth through the Spirit in sincere brotherly affection, love one another from the heart fervently: having been born again, not of corruptible seed, but of incorruptible, through the word of God, which lives and remains forever. (1 Peter 1:22 23 WEB)

All my life I enjoyed nature. I have a great love for most animals and a favorite pastime on furlough is to visit the numerous zoos across the USA. Reading about different animals, watching them crawl, creep, slither and swim has always fascinated me. Hiking in the forest, camping, sitting and watching the clouds go by are engaging activities.

My love for nature probably explains my interest in Scouting and camp outs. Several times a year my father and I would join the Scout troop and go camping. Summer or winter, it was always delightful and gave me a chance to observe the local wildlife. In the creek near our home I investigated the life span of frogs and watched the fluttering of butterflies in the forest.

Scouting was not a big option on the small island of Guam. They were there but not with the same friendship building, skill developing activities I remembered as a boy. Our children enjoyed the nature found in our neighborhood and throughout the island. Geckos, chameleons, praying mantises, snakes and numerous bugs were carefully investigated by all our children.

My favorite run-in with animals occurred during a church presentation. It was a children's musical called "Bullfrogs and Butterflies." There was an ark and our friend Dave played Noah while dressed as a pirate. The children took over the animal parts with a wide variety of costumes. It was the first big children's presentation at our church in years.

Ellice was called on to be a butterfly and Joel was cast as the green squatting bullfrog. Their responses to their parts were very different.

Ellice was thrilled to wear fluffy sleeves, a beautiful skirt and a hat with antenna. If she spun herself around the skirt would flare out like a ballerina. At each practice she carefully followed directions, learned her part, and took the whole event seriously.

Joel, although willing to participate, was not quite as excited. He almost learned his part, followed most of the directions and made a great frog all hunched down on the platform. He was fascinated with all the costumes, the ark, and the fun and excitement of so much singing and dancing.

I don't remember the whole performance. In truth I remember only a few special parts. Video tapes are a wonderful thing for resuscitating memories.

At one point, Ellice was twirling about portraying the elusive butterfly. Suddenly her little skirt came loose and fell to the ground. Quickly she picked it up and tried to tie it back on. Poor Dave, he tried to help but wasn't sure how to attach the thin fabric of the costume.

Joel, at one point, squatted down near the front of the stage. Beside him were a couple other green-clad crouching frogs. In unison they would belt out their "reedeep," then hop around the stage trying not to knock the other children off their feet.

Although they sang a number of songs I remember only one line from the theme song. It ran, "Like bullfrogs and butterflies, you got to be born again." It's amazing I remember this line. My memory isn't that good!

As Christians, God pricks out memories with simple and poignant messages. You've got to be born again! Praise the Lord all four of my children are born again. I pray daily they will lead others to God's throne of grace. I pray they will help other tadpoles and caterpillars discover they can be born again through God's grace.

Roast Pig

When one of those who sat at the table with him heard these things, he said to him, "Blessed is he who will feast in the Kingdom of God!" (Luke 14:15 WEB)

Fiestas were common on Guam. There was a long history to the island's culture, which held onto island legends and also include religious elements. Between the historical celebrations and the religious celebrations there was always a good reason to party hardy!

These celebrations were large. If necessary a second mortgage on someone's home would be used to pay for his daughter's christening or sweet sixteen birthday party. It was taboo to have a small party for selected guests. Everyone in the family was invited and all the neighbors who heard the noise were welcome to wander on over.

A central food item, along with red rice, lumpia, pancit, and short ribs, was the roast pig. Watching the preparation was akin to watching an old swashbuckling pirates and damsels movie.

The pig was killed somewhere and the carcass brought to the home. Then the pig was gutted and skewered on a long spit and placed over an open fire. For hours the spit was turned as the pig was roasted to a beautiful dark brown color. The head, tail and feet remained attached and the fur on the skin burned off over the fire.

When the meat was fully cooked the pig was un-skewered and placed on a long table with an apple in its mouth. Yes, they really did put an apple in the mouth. The family and guests gathered around the table, someone prayed a prayer and the feasting began.

The first time we went to a fiesta we were not sure how Ellice and Joel would react. I don't remember the event but I do remember there was an abundant amount of food, a constant flow of beverages, and the requisite pig gracing the center of the food table.

Fiestas were generally buffet style eating arrangements. Each person grabbed a paper plate, a knife, fork, and napkin and then piled it as high as the plate would hold. If you were really a pig, or just hungry, you could take several plates to build up a stronger food base. You would then balance the plate on one hand, eat with the other and keep track of your drink.

Ellice walked up to the table and waited until someone placed a little pork on her plate. She then selected a few other delicacies she recognized. Joel, only four at the time, walked up and stared into the eyes of the roast pig. We watched to see what he would do. Our hosts noticed his stare and waited. It was like a staring contest which we felt the pig would win.

Finally, Joel turned to our host, who was serving the pig and said, "Give me some of that pig!" Our host smiled, laughed, and cut Joel a big piece of pork, which he ate with delight. The pig might win in a staring contest but Joel had the last laugh.

We were invited to this banquet to honor a special event in the host family's life. God has also called us to a great banquet. I'm glad we attended this earthly banquet and didn't make excuses to stay away.

Sometimes we approach God's invitation, like the banquet Jesus described, and make excuses. We don't take time to enjoy the bounty of God's provision. I think it's time to remind myself I don't want to be excused from God's banquet table in Heaven. I want to enjoy the feast He will place before us, including the roast pig. I can only imagine the delicacies He will have in store for me.

A Word in Due Season

. . . so shall my word be that goes forth out of my mouth: it shall not return to me void, but it shall accomplish that which I please, and it shall prosper in the thing whereto I sent it. (Isaiah 55:11 WEB)

In the course of dealing with mail, Beth sent out a large number of pamphlets from Guam. These small pieces of Scripture and teaching wandered about the world reminding us that God's word does not return void but accomplishes His purposes. Here is a letter Beth received in response to one of these pamphlets:

Dear Friends because of Christ,

It has taken me a long time to write back to you. It was because I've been on a long journey on a ship going round the Solomon Island Seas doing fisheries work. Yes friends, there is one thing I do mostly want to share with you. During my journey I received the letter you sent and the booklet. One night as I was about to go to sleep I took the booklet and started to read.

As I read something unusual happened to me. I broke down and cried. I was crying because I was the same as the man in the booklet mocking Jesus sometimes and didn't believe in Him. As I was crying one of my workmates came into my room! I showed him the book and after looking at the parts that stuck with me most he said to me, "Today is the day of salvation, your sadness will turn to gladness." From that very night on I've become somebody new, a believer.

Now I am a new being, a life which is new to me. Jesus has changed my life and has made an example of how a young lad like me leaves his rubbish ways and becomes a new being. And now I am starting to witness to my friends, I will let you know if Christ will win some soul through me.

Sometimes we feel our work falls into the cracks between the keys of life. A tract here and there appears to be just paper to fill up someone's waste can. That special word of encouragement invokes no response. Sometimes we are tempted to think, "Why bother?"

Still, often we find God uses these words, these efforts, these struggles to touch a soul for eternity. God works in His time, not ours. He makes our faithfulness useful in touching other lives, even when we don't see the immediate results. We must not grow tired in doing good knowing that God will accomplish his purposes if we remain faithful.

Four for Furlough

My God will supply every need of yours according to his riches in glory in Christ Jesus. (Philippians 4:19 WEB)

When mission work was established many years ago, some missionaries would depart for their foreign field never to return. Others would remain on the field for twenty, thirty or more years before returning to their home land. The idea of the two, three or four-year term is a modern invention.

At times I am thankful for this modern convenience and other times find it an interruption in my ministry. Most furloughs are a blessing and a chance to see family and friends. But, in truth, sometimes they interrupt the flow of ministry, forcing a change of direction midstride. When furlough is over it is at times difficult to get back into the swing of things and pick up projects which sat idle for months.

Our furlough in 1989 was a welcome break from the fast-paced work of the mission field. We now sported four lovely children and were ready to give everyone a glance at Evan, our new "Guam baby." Mission projects were in good shape and coverage during our absence was carefully arranged.

We put together a number of plans, including an extensive travel schedule beginning in California and then on to the eastern USA. Friends we met on Guam were to be married in Pennsylvania, a trip was scheduled across a portion of Canada, and visiting supporters in Michigan was on the schedule. There were also trips to Texas, across the southern US to Florida, and back up through the midwest and Kansas City.

Contrary to many opinions furlough was and is seldom a period of rest. It did provide a break in the routine but rest was a word that seldom applied to furlough, at least for our family. However, being busy was fun. Visiting supporters, family and churches was all an encouragement to our family and we prayed we would be able to encourage those we visited. The occasional side trip along the way to see some historical monument, museum, or natural wonder was an added bonus to all the travel.

As a family of six, furloughs presented special challenges. Corralling four children through numerous airports without leaving one behind required eyes in the back of our heads. Evan took some of his first steps through the crowded passenger-strewn waiting lounge in Tokyo's Narita airport.

Once we reached our home base a logistical challenge awaited. How would we fit six people, all our luggage, display material, playpens, portable cribs and car seats into a vehicle where we would essentially live for three months? We became very creative car packers. Every nook and cranny had some shoe, toy or other essential item stuffed inside. By the end of furlough, we had the packing and unpacking down to a precise series of steps.

Each furlough, from the first through the most recent, God provided through His people a vehicle for our travel. This was quite a challenge but God provided abundantly. We never could organize such transport nor afford to rent vehicles with sufficient space. God has provided abundantly through His people.

Since we brought our children along (no one on the field wanted to keep them), our furloughs always fell during the summer months. The day after school was over we headed to the mainland and returned one or two days before school restarted. For the children our travel about the USA made for great "What I Did This Summer" stories.

With few exceptions, I remember our furloughs with great fondness. Taking our youngest son, born on the field, to visit his grandparents for the first time was a highlight. There were many tales and adventures for sharing in churches and with new found friends along the furlough trail. We enjoyed log cabins, fancy hotels, holidays for our anniversary while friends watched the children, theme parks, zoos, mountains, plains and just about every part of the USA.

Furlough is a break in the routine of the ministry work but not a break in experiencing God's provision and care each step and every mile along the way. At times we were uncertain what was coming next and excited to see what God planned and provided. Our thanks go to the many that have made our furloughs a time of encouragement and renewal and occasionally restful.

I am reminded of God's rest. Scripture speaks of this as a future event. It is definitely not furlough but God's care and supply. I look forward to our next furlough even as I think and write on the subject.

Word Limits

For in the multitude of dreams there are vanities, as well as in many words: but you must fear God. (Ecclesiastes 5:7 WEB)

Evan was an unexpected and delightful addition to our family. Of our four children, he was the only one born on the mission field. Granted, being born on Guam makes him an American citizen but it's still special, just as he is special.

As each of our children were born, we wondered what characteristics they'd develop and how God would use us to raise them for His glory. Evan began showing his verbal abilities at a young age. There's a repetitive series of events for raising children. You have a newborn baby and are excited while waiting for them to start walking and talking. When they finally reach these plateaus in their life, you spend the next few years wishing they'd sit down and be quiet.

As soon as Evan discovered he, too, had the ability to speak, he took to talking like a fish takes to water. There's a direct link between every thought which goes through his brain and the movement and sound from his lips.

According to his older brothers and sister, he was a great source of conversation even as a three and four-year-old. They'd come home from school and have difficulty sharing their tales from the day because Evan had so much to say.

I read a magazine article which discussed word limits. The author figured each person has a word limit per day, after which others need to speak. Based on their numbers and my calculations Evan exceeds his word limit before he finishes breakfast. If you figure the remainder of the day when he continues to talk and look at the average life span, he would have to be mute from the age of thirteen to compensate for the abundant number of words spoken on an average day.

We love Evan and figure he is a slow eater because he talks so much between bites. When it comes to school plays, speeches in class and sharing the Gospel, there's a benefit to a large vocabulary and unhindered speaking ability.

Compared to the volumes published by many modern preachers and teachers it's amazing to discover how few words of Jesus are recorded in Scripture. God knows just how to turn a phrase and make a point without long detailed explanations.

Evan is learning this and so am I. Maybe we should each look at how we share the Gospel and consider whether we are adding too many words to the perfect words of Christ. Apparently, Jesus didn't think that long theological explanations were necessary to point people to God. If Jesus didn't think we needed all that verbiage then why do we feel a need to inundate others with our educational prowess and extended vocabulary when the simple message of the Gospel will suffice?

There's a place for many words in this world. I pray we can carefully determine when and where they're necessary and how they may lead others to God's throne of grace. I also pray we learn when a few choice and simple words will suffice to describe God's love and grace.

Like Candy for a Baby

For who among men knows the things of a man, except the spirit of the man, which is in him? Even so, no one knows the things of God, except God's Spirit. (1 Corinthians 2:11 WEB)

The first few weeks of one of our furloughs went as planned. We shared with family, friends and churches what God accomplished through the radio ministry. It was a joy to see excited faces and answer questions about God's work. We started in Houston, headed east, then north and wrapped around back through Kansas City and down through Oklahoma, heading back to our starting point.

That furlough we enjoyed the comfort of a beautiful Oldsmobile sedan. Three in the front, three in the back and the trunk full to the brim. With cruise control and air conditioning we wandered along the highways from house to house and church to church. There were two big loops through different portions of the US planned that trip.

Toward the end of the first loop, just as we entered the northern reaches of Oklahoma City, I heard a funny noise; the engine was suddenly bogged down and I pulled to the side of the road. A sudden rush of hot air from the air conditioning ducts led me to suspect the compressor was in trouble.

I turned off the air conditioner as I rolled to a stop on the shoulder of the highway. It was hot, unbearably hot. In the few seconds between turning off the air conditioner to stopping the car the temperature in the car rose sharply. This did not bode well in the middle of summer.

Stepping to the front of the car I opened the hood. At my shout Beth pressed the air conditioner "on" button. Immediately I shouted, "Turn it off!" as I watched the belts flop wildly and heard them squeal against the frozen shaft of the compressor. The air conditioner was a dead duck and there were several hundred miles to go before we could consider repair or changing vehicles.

With the windows down, we headed south toward Texas and our next stop. It would be a long two days until we reached our friends in San Antonio. The next day we were caught in a traffic jam in Austin. It was hot, cars weren't moving and the children, not to mention Beth and me, were hot, irritable and ready for a cool breeze. The breeze didn't arise but the heat continued to rise.

Evan reached a boiling point and decided he was hungry for something. Traffic didn't permit us to pull over and enjoy a break. Evan continued to clamor for something to eat or drink. It's amazing how the combination of heat, thirst, and an upset baby can quickly get on your nerves.

In the years God provided for us to raise our children we worked to reduce the amount of sweets and other "bad" foods they ate. The only thing in the car at this time was a bag of Sweet Tarts we'd picked up somewhere along the way. Evan was only a one year old, tired, hot, hungry, thirsty and bored from sitting in the car.

Beth and I knew these were not the best items to eat in the heat. The last thing Evan needed was more energy he could not expend in the confines of the car seat. After a few minutes of his crying and complaining we relented and said, "Give him the Sweet Tarts!" It quieted him down, calmed our nerves and brought a sense of peace back to the stifling air of the car.

It's amazing how the wrong thing could produce such a good response. Beth and I knew he didn't need the candy but a cool drink and some food. Evan cried out to get what he wanted. He didn't really care what it was. He saw the candy and wanted it. After a while, we let him have it.

I think God deals with us like this sometimes. We look around and see something that looks exciting and enjoyable and cry out to get it. God knows better. He knows what we need and when we need it but we at times are too impatient to wait for His perfect will in our lives.

A few minutes later we were able to get off the highway and enjoy a nice meal in an air conditioned restaurant. Evan was too full from the Sweet Tarts to enjoy the meal. He'd filled his stomach with the pleasures of his eye, Sweet Tarts, and was unable to enjoy the good food of the restaurant.

The same happens in our spiritual life. We fill up on the lust of the eyes and when the blessing of God comes we don't have room in our hearts to rejoice. If we have a little patience, a little time of waiting for God's answer, then we'll receive what He planned for our lives. The next time we see something we just can't wait to obtain, maybe it'd be a good time to check with God about His plan and timing. We might be asking for Sweet Tarts when God has a steak dinner planned!

All in the Family

He made from one blood every nation of men to dwell on all the surface of the earth, having determined appointed seasons, and the boundaries of their dwellings, (Acts 17:26 WEB)

Before we started our second furlough, arrangements were made with our home office in New Jersey. The last time we had visited the headquarters of the mission was in 1980 when we were appointed as missionaries. Thus, our leadership felt it was time we stopped by to reintroduce ourselves to the staff. With this in mind, our second stop, after some time in California, was New Jersey. This was the land of Beth's birth and a number of her relatives!

Beth and I were married in 1974. On the day of our wedding some of her relatives from New Jersey came to join us in the celebration. Here was my chance to renew acquaintances and discover new relatives on my wife's side of the family.

Borrowing a car from someone in the mission, we navigated through the confusing streets of New Jersey to the house of Beth's Aunt Ruth. Her home was a mere fifty feet from a major highway which they called a parkway. Since it was against the law to park on the parkway I was always confused by why they called it a parkway. In this small house, filled to overflowing with memories, I was introduced to close and distant relatives living in the general vicinity.

I once commented to my children that I was experienced in dealing with cross cultural marriages. Beth was a Yankee and I was a good old southern boy. Meeting her family confirmed we were definitely from different worlds.

The conversations covered a myriad of topics. At times I felt they were speaking a different language as they recalled events of their youth and the wonders of the region of their heritage. The children were a continued source of entertainment as well as a bit of anxiety as we wondered if they would knock over a valued family treasure in the crowded house.

I'm an avid believer in Manifest Destiny. If things get crowded, then head west and find some breathing room. Aunt Ruth was delightful and the food delicious. The house was crowded, bringing dreams of wide open spaces to mind.

Once I became accustomed to the close quarters, something I would call upon years later in Europe, I was able to learn more about Beth's past and northern culture. Talking to aunts, uncles, cousins and visitors provided a great wealth of understanding and information on the family I married into.

These were great folks: loving, caring, and willing to help when and where they were able. Because of one person, Beth, we were related and a bond of friendship and care existed. I've seen similar relationships develop in the body of Christ.

When we understand God's love and grace we come to Him, through Christ, to receive salvation and the promise of eternal life. But we have eternal life with whom? It's eternal life with God. Not only is it eternal life with God but with God's people, as well.

God's people come from every walk of life you can imagine; some are even Yankees! People from every culture and government you can imagine will be represented in the eternal community. We will all be related through the one who shed His blood for us, Jesus Christ. Then we'll understand the true meaning of cross cultural and the complete relationship we have in God through Jesus.

The Statue of Ribbery

...casting all your worries on him, because he cares for you. (1 Peter 5:7 WEB)

On furlough, while enjoying the welcome of our home office in New Jersey, we filled all the rooms of the lodge. The lodge was formerly a livery stable and carefully modified to provide all the comforts of home for those away from home. There was a nice common kitchen and a collection of nice rooms with private baths. The rooms were situated on either side of a large common room which came complete with comfortable couches, chairs and a fireplace. Nice.

This was a chance to develop new friendships and renew old friendships in the midst of our mission family. As a mission family we worked together to reach the world with the Gospel. Whether we tuned transmitters, balanced the books, changed light bulbs or expounded the word of God we were related through our Savior, the one who called us to serve.

While in New Jersey we decided it was the perfect opportunity to introduce our children to New York City, the Empire State Building, the Statue of Liberty and the World Trade Center. After a couple calls we had plans set to take the train and the subway tube into the city. We would arrive and reach the city through the bottom of the World Trade Center.

Finances were a bit tight so we counted our pennies to determine whether the trip were possible. Later that day the founder and president of our mission met us as we were chatting with other missionaries in the front lobby. Hearing us discuss the cost of the trip, he pulled out a twenty-dollar bill and held it out in our direction. Feeling a bit awkward and not wanting to bother the head of the mission we politely declined and he wandered down the hall toward his office.

A few minutes later, as we headed out the door, one of the secretaries came out of the back hall and flagged us down. She handed us an envelope and said the staff took a collection to ensure we would enjoy the trip to the city and not have to worry about the costs. Again, the Lord let us know this was a family.

We thanked our colleague, took the envelope and walked toward the lodge. Looking inside the envelope, we discovered a twenty-dollar bill on the top of the pile and have a pretty good idea who made that donation. Our pride kept us from the first offering and here God made the point that He can provide if we are willing to let our family care for us.

The trip to the city was fantastic. We rode a train from the office to Hoboken. From there we rode the tube train and exited beneath the World Trade Center. Rising from the depths of the buildings to the street we were taken in by the immense size of the city and the busy streets. The children clung tightly to us as we navigated the streets and made our way toward Battery Park and the shuttle boats to the Statue of Liberty.

James was wide-eyed through the entire event. Walking in the canyon between the buildings and then finding the opening at the park, with the harbor in front, were new wonders for him. He was really excited to be visiting the Statue of Ribbery, as he called it. Time didn't allow us to walk the stairs to the crown of her head. I was a young man the last time I was in New York and remember the long stairway to the top. So we walked around the statue, enjoyed the ferry boat once more and saw the city. That was more than enough for one day.

In one day we traveled from a quiet lodge at our headquarters to New York City, the Statue of Liberty and back. I love trains so that in itself was a delight for me. God provided the transportation, the funds, and the timing, to see everything and return to the office.

Through God's family we were treated to an experience never to be repeated. When we think we are on our own God lets us know we are His and He does care enough to provide our needs and even some of our desires.

Furlough is Family Fun

Trust the LORD and live right! The land will be yours, and you will be safe. (Psalms 37:3 CEV)

During our first furlough we lived in one home for many months. I traveled regularly to meet with churches and share the ministry. Once in a while the family came along for the weekend. Later furloughs were different. Our second furlough was more realistic and a hint of coming furloughs.

With one or two exceptions, we spent our second furlough on the road. Most of our stops were for two or three days. A couple times it was four or five. After a few miles our four children, in one car, let us know that they were bored. They wanted to do something fun and exciting.

We desired to be good parents, relieve our children's boredom, and maintain our own sanity. Beth and I decided it would be good to stop regularly and have some fun. Games such as license plate alphabet didn't last long. The close quarters of the car called for more drastic measures.

I remember riding many miles with my parents. We usually had a destination in mind as well as planned stops along the way. I tried to do the same with our family. It seemed very efficient for an engineering mindset like mine and my father's. However, I do recall as a young man seeing a sign for some special location and wanting to stop. But, since it wasn't on the schedule and slowed us down, we didn't stop.

Now it was my children in the car. What would I do when they read the signs and wanted to stop? Beth and I discussed it briefly and decided we would beat them to the punch. When we saw a sign to some supposedly interesting place we would investigate. Even historical markers were on the list of possible reasons to stop for at least few minutes.

We visited Beth's parents in Florida, where the children learned about fishing. Grandpa prepared a fishing pole for each of the children and taught them how to catch, clean and eat the fish. They even learned to watch my hat float away when it was blown into the waterway.

Beth was reading the Laura Ingles Wilder series about the little house on the prairie. One of the churches we visited put us up in a log cabin beside a small lake just outside of town. The children thought we were living out part of the story.

Since there was only a small zoo on Guam, and I like zoos, we visited many zoos across the country. My favorite would be the Saint Louis Zoo. While visiting the San Antonio Zoo, Beth discovered we had monitor lizards on the island of Guam. She didn't believe me when she saw the sign although I told her we saw them on the island. After finding out they had lizards as big as herself, that ate small mammals, she wasn't sure she wanted to return.

Not everything we experienced or every place we stayed was wonderful. There were some hard times with poor housing, illness, and car problems. But overall there was much more to be thankful for than to worry about.

God works in our lives to provide the rest and refreshment we need to serve Him fully. Sometimes we don't see the benefits, sometimes we sail by the historical markers, sometimes we miss the joys along the way because we're too busy trying to get to that next place of service.

God has taught me to slow down on furlough and look around. He created a marvelous world full of faithful servants for which we are eternally thankful.

Home Improvement

But the fruit of the Spirit is love, joy, peace, patience, kindness, goodness, faithfulness, (Galatians 5:22 WEB)

Over the years I've been placed in numerous situations which required me to learn how to do something new. I was never a construction worker nor a machinist. Fortunately, my father taught me how to make normal home repairs. Growing up Dad repaired most things around the house and when he was unable my mother stepped in to keep things going forward. This instilled in me the need to attempt to repair and fix things about the house.

I use the word "attempt" because my abilities and understanding of housing construction and repair are sometimes less than adequate to achieve the desired result. In truth, sometimes the item under repair was worse when I finished than when I started. It was all part of learning my limitations and the phone number of the local plumber, handyman, or fellow missionary willing to lend a hand.

One year a retired couple came to Guam to help with fixing my mistakes, housing repairs, construction, and other types of repairs around the mission property. Roy and Agnes were delightful. Roy was great at repairing just about anything around the house or office building. It was like having grandparents on the field to enjoy the children and lend a hand where needed.

We needed a new home to have room for four children. Before our furlough there was discussion about adding another room to our house. Then another missionary family decided to move to the USA so their home became available and it had the extra room we needed.

The house was situated directly behind our old home so traveling back and forth to help Roy, when I was not on duty, was easy and convenient. I just climbed the fence and I was there. When we finally moved we dropped the fence for a few hours as colleagues helped carry our furniture from one home to the other across the backyards. But before we moved the house needed some preparation. This was right up Roy's alley.

Beth and Evan brought Roy and me coffee each morning. Evan told Roy he could sleep on the end of his new bed since he was moving out of the crib into a real bed.

A lot of the refurbishment was handled directly by Roy. The removal of old carpet, tile, and preparation to re-tile the entire house required my assistance to complete the job on time. When we pulled up the old carpet most of the house was in good shape. Holes from the furring strips needed to be filled and in two rooms we discovered old tile beneath the old carpet.

Removing the tile from the dining room was straightforward. Removing tile from Joel's new room was less than spectacular. The original tiles were installed with contact cement and did not pull off the concrete easily. For three

127

weeks Beth and I chipped away at the old tile until it was finally removed and the floor prepared for the new tiles.

One thousand, two hundred and twenty-one tiles later, Roy and I completed the new flooring. Walls painted, cracks patched, we were ready to occupy our new home. Our fellow missionaries and friends from our church arrived to help us move.

I had shift duty the day we moved so timing was critical. With a flurry of arms, trips, boxes, furniture and dodging children at play, our personal items were transferred from one home to the other. As I prepared for work there were no curtains, so I moved from place to place to be out of the way as the final items were brought over.

I departed for the transmitter site and left Beth with our friends to complete the move. Their love and care for our family was spectacular. By the time I returned home at 6:00 a.m. the next morning there were curtains and shades up so I could get some rest before starting to hang pictures and deal with other "moving in" items. Evan went to bed the first night and was sad that Roy wasn't really going to live with us; he thought the "grandpa" came with the house.

After a couple weeks we were fully settled into the new house and holding a Bible Study in the living room. At one point in the evening there were some loud noises from the boys' room. I walked back to the bedroom Evan and James shared. I stepped inside their room and my heart dropped, my blood pressure rose to astronomical heights, and anger took control.

There was James, a floor tile in one hand and a pile of tiles beside him. He had discovered the tiles could be pulled up, one by one until he revealed most of the underlying concrete foundation. I believe my parents could hear my comments back in the USA as I informed James what he was doing was wrong, with a capital "W!" I think that's when my hair turned gray.

I was not a shining example of patience and understanding. Roy and I had worked for weeks, late at night, between shifts, on hands and knees, to carefully install the one thousand, two hundred and twenty-one tiles. Each tile was hand sculptured to fit the form of the house. My children still remember that night. I'm sure our former neighbors still remember that night.

When Paul writes about the fruit of the spirit one critical word is patience. This fruit is preceded in the list by love, joy, and peace. At that moment, looking at the destruction of my hard labor, I doubt I experienced any of the other fruits much less patience with my children. Until that moment I thought things were in order.

Our home was occupied, pictures on the walls, children playing in their new rooms, friends visiting. It took only a few seconds to realize my calm was easily shattered by the world around me. I was looking at the horizontal, the work "I" had done, not at God. "I" didn't experience the fruit of the spirit because "I" tried to control things, instead of allowing God control.

I think my children have long since forgiven my outburst but I doubt they will ever forget that evening. Last time I mentioned it to the children it was remembered with humor and laughter. It was not the first nor the last outburst of my temper. Many times I've had to apologize and ask their forgiveness, not something parents enjoy doing but necessary. I also prayed for patience, joy, peace, and joy.

As Christians this is the way things work. When our eyes are fixed on the world around us we fail. When we see our accomplishments as the fruit of our own strength and our own hands we are blinded by our worldly hearts. It's only when we fix our eyes on Jesus, the author and perfecter of our faith, that we can experience the fruit of the spirit at work in our lives.

In the fruit of the spirit we experience peace and joy when the world around us appears chaotic and hopeless. As we experience the fruit of the spirit it allows us to demonstrate patience when things go against our nature. It's only when we seek God that we may walk through events, like having our hard work destroyed, without permitting the old sin nature to have its way.

Maybe, just maybe, we need to close our physical eyes occasionally to allow our spiritual eyesight to once again find the object of our longing, Jesus Christ. We can then open our physical eyes with the assurance that what we see is nothing compared to the wondrous glory we will witness for eternity. Maybe next time I might consider using contact cement.

Guam Goodies

Who satisfies your desire with good things, So that your youth is renewed like the eagle's. (Psalms 103:5 WEB)

During our years living on Guam we met many people just passing through. Some just visited friends for a day or two and others were stationed there with the military or their business for a couple of years. Their different reactions to the island were interesting.

Some folks stationed on the military bases only left the familiar confines of their compound as a last resort. Church was often a last resort. Thus, some of these folks attended our church and we got to know them a little better.

Those who lived in a compound, on a military base, or secluded from the rest of the island had few, if any, good things to say about the island. They didn't experience the wonders of the island but remained safe and secure in their familiar surroundings. The folks who took the time and effort to venture out, explore the island, meet the people, and get involved, discovered a wealth of fun and many fascinating aspects about Guam and the people.

Not everything on Guam was good in those years. Telephone dialing seldom reached the intended person. I had a theory. Somewhere in the main telephone exchange was a random number generator. As a call would pass through the exchange, the dialed number would be used as a seed to generate a random number to some unknown home where you would be connected. The most common phrase heard when answering the phone was, "Who's this?"

Power outages were the norm. Outages were expected following typhoons. Unfortunately, the power company was beset by a heavy dose of nepotism. Workers were often assigned tasks because of their relationship to Uncle Joe and not based on their ability to maintain the massive generators. One summer the power went off just before the Liberation Day parade that's in July. We figured we'd go to the parade, return home and the power would be back. NOT! Of the eight generators (yes, we knew how many, where they were, and what they were named), they forgot to put oil in six of them, causing them to come to a screaming halt. For months we enjoyed the power being turned on occasionally, not off. Power would be turned on at the house two or three times a day for an hour or two at a time.

Water shortages were expected once or twice a year during the dry season. We would wait for the heavy rains, the reservoir would refill and life would return to normal. During one long power problem the need for electricity overtook the need for water. Residents stole the generators from the water pumps to power their homes and left much of the island without water. We also operated a small generator at our home so the children could complete their homework using a light bulb instead of a candle.

130

All of these experiences - water outages, power outages, typhoons, random telephone calls - made life unique, interesting and sometimes down right annoying. However, there were many things which were down right fun.

One year my father sent the children a pup tent. As a young boy I went camping many times with my father. Pup tents were the way to go when you were trekking through the Appalachian Mountains or paddling a canoe in Canada. Now it was time to camp with my children on a tropical island.

Several times we ventured to the northern tip of Guam to camp with friends. All of these were great experiences for the entire family. We discovered the night flights of fruit bats, what sea creatures came out in the dusk and how often the security guard roamed the beach looking for trouble.

The beach was a common meeting ground. Often we'd go to the beach, fire up the grill and enjoy steaks or burgers in the open air. The children, not to mention Beth and I, would snorkel, hide in the shade in the middle of the day and pick fresh fruit from the local trees for snacks. Friends from the mission and church would meet us at the beach for an afternoon of fun in the sun.

One afternoon on the beach the children were swimming and building sand castles. Beth and I were relaxed in a pair of beach chairs under the shade of an ironwood tree. Actually, Beth was just beyond the shade in the sun enjoying the rays and I was hiding from the ultraviolet menace. I looked up and down the beach, watching our children enjoying themselves and looked at my gorgeous wife. With a relaxed sigh I said to Beth, "Some days, dear, it is tough suffering on the mission field for the Lord." We both laughed then went to the shore to enjoy the water.

Cookouts with short ribs, burgers and chicken, camping on the beach, snorkeling and swimming were a delightful gift from the Lord on our small island. When the power failed there was usually a breeze on the shore. When the water ceased to flow in our home there was plenty available in the ocean. When the typhoons blew over the trees, God grew another forest.

Taking time to explore the island, meet the people and gawk at God's beautiful creation was well worth the effort. Getting involved with the local schools was also a delight for the entire family.

Throughout the years we had children in five different schools. One year we had four children in four different schools. This was a logistical nightmare when it came to parent teacher night!

In elementary school our children experienced the Guam culture including riding the ubiquitous carabao, eating coconut candy and the many local fruits. By the time Ellice was in high school they were part of the local Chamorro culture. Through their involvement opportunities arose to share the Gospel.

Ellice discovered the wonder of bands and instruments. The Oceanview High School band was no match for many of the slick and polished bands I remember in the USA, but they had a big heart. Ellice's talent with a flute and piccolo earned her a spot on the all island honor band and a chance to play at the governor's mansion

The mission was also a source of activities beyond the daily work of the ministry. As a staff we were a close-knit family working toward the same goal of proclaiming the Gospel using our technical abilities. Not everything was work, work, work; sometimes there were opportunities for fun and fellowship.

More than once we held costume parties to celebrate anything from holidays to missionaries coming and going from the field. One evening we were seriously in search of a murderer in our midst. Clues were planted throughout the office building implicating one of the members of the staff in a dastardly deed. It took more than an hour for each team to find the bits and pieces and pin the blame on someone.

There was a heritage night, complete with costumes. Another costume night referenced favorite fictional characters. Beth and I chose Running Deer and Falling Rock, the famous pair of Indians often seen, as indicated by the signs, along so many US highways.

Christmas on the beach, staff socials, cookouts, camping, typhoons, all were part of the interesting goodies on Guam. The work of the ministry required long, hard and tiring hours. Striving to bring the salvation message to people we never saw was difficult at times. Living far from family and friends added stress and sometimes a desire to be back on the mainland.

God knew these struggles and knew our needs. God provided an alternate family for fun, learning, fellowship, and encouragement. Our children were cared for, educated and experienced events in their lives many people can never imagine. God cares for his people in ways we could never imagine.

Visitors

Our friends, you yourselves know that our visit to you was not a failure. (1 Thessalonians 2:1 GNB)

Living on an island far from anywhere had advantages and disadvantages. One advantage was a lack of visitors. One disadvantage was a lack of visitors. Family, friends, pastors, and tourists, with the exception of the Japanese tourists, seldom considered flying to a small island they could barely locate in a National Geographic world atlas.

In December of 1990 Beth's parents decided it was time to see just what we were doing out in the Pacific. Their grandchildren were growing up and they wanted to experience island life in the tropics. Plans were made, tickets purchased, accommodations in a local hotel reserved and bags packed. We were ready as well. Our home was in order; the children were excited that Grandma and Grandpa would be with us for Christmas. Things just couldn't look better.

Then four days before Christmas, on December 21st, Typhoon Russ made its dramatic visit to Guam. The island power went out. Water became scarce. Severe damage was inflicted on the mission transmitter site. We scrambled to work during daylight hours to repair antennas and transmitters and restore the Gospel programming quickly. Things weren't looking so good.

Programs prepared for Christmas broadcasts lay unused in the control room. All the able-bodied staff worked with us in the mud and heat to gather the pieces of equipment spread across the property and into the neighboring countryside.

Two days after the typhoon Beth, the children and I were at the airport to pick up Grandma and Grandpa. It was Sunday. They arrived on an island struggling to restore basic services. As a staff, we interrupted our repair work to worship the Lord and celebrate His provision through the storm. With all the damage across the island not a single life was lost.

Beth's parents were introduced to the realities of island and post storm life. They sought the quiet of the hotel in the evenings. It was sure quiet. No power to the hotel. Situated on the beach they listened to the quiet lapping of waves each evening.

For the first few days of their stay I worked at the transmitter site to help restore the broadcasts. Not only were the antennas and transmitters damaged but our emergency generator also failed and needed repair. I, along with my colleagues, was called upon to do things we never did before. All of this was to get the Gospel message back on the air.

In the months following the storm we received numerous letters from listeners praying for us because they knew something was wrong to prevent the airing of the programs. Programming resumed the 26th of December.

As I worked Beth and the children enjoyed fun times with her parents. The generator at our home kept the fans providing a cool breeze and the food preserved in the fridge. When things were desperate we'd visit Denny's. They had electricity and air conditioning!

Air conditioning is important after a typhoon. When the storm completes its damage to the island and departs, it takes all the associated weather and clouds with it. So, after supersaturating the island for several days the sky became clear, the sun came out and we lived in a tropical sauna. No breezes to counteract the heat and humidity except what was created by the generator-powered ceiling fans. No fresh water to cool off since the electricity was out, stopping the water pumps from filling the pipes with fresh water for our homes.

Beth took her parents on a drive around the island. Everywhere they turned the evidence of the storm's destruction was visible. Many homes lost their roofs and their Christmas trees were now part of their yard decorations. Some lost everything and others only suffered minor damage. Beth and her parents were heartbroken as they witnessed people picking up pieces of their homes to start over.

While the lack of electricity and water was annoying, Beth's parents experienced it in full each evening. The pair was experiencing reduced sight in their old age. They couldn't see things in their room or read by the insignificant candle light. The day before their departure from Guam the power was restored. However, by then they were accustomed to the evening darkness.

Two visitors came at Christmas; one we wanted to come, the other uninvited. With Beth's parents we enjoyed the visit in spite of the weather and living conditions. Our family fellowship was delightful and the children were thrilled to have their grandparents about for the holidays. Russ, on the other hand, wasn't invited but crashed the party anyway. Despite his attempts to hinder the ministry it was only stalled for a few days and then the word of God continued to reach into the Far East.

One visitor without the other would never have created the memories and excitement we experienced that December. In fact, one visitor, Beth's parents, enhanced the unexpected arrival of the other, Typhoon Russ. Their visit provided an encouragement in the midst of extra work, under uncomfortable conditions. God's timing was perfect.

Sometimes, when I think things are just not going right, God surprises me with little gifts of encouragement. Our Lord encouraged us in the midst of what many might consider a catastrophe. When we stop and listen to what the Lord is saying, when we look at what the Lord has provided we find He can bring success to what we cannot. We, as His servants, need to listen, watch and learn.

Water Baptism

Go, and make disciples of all nations, baptizing them in the name of the Father and of the Son and of the Holy Spirit, (Matthew 28:19 WEB)

Baptism is a subject which can divide churches from one another. Every church has something to say on interpreting the meaning, method and application of baptism. I don't like to debate issues such as baptism. I don't like to debate many religious issues because religion cannot bring salvation. Religion is a set of rules, created by man, to define the confines of their faith in human terms easier to understand. My concern is whether someone has turned to God through the saving grace of the cross and entered into the heavenly family for eternity.

As parents this was a heart concern. We desired each of our children to understand our faith, God's grace and the salvation offered from the cross. To see our children cleansed by the blood of Christ and know we will be with them for eternity was a major concern.

For years we dedicated our lives to serving God and brought this message of salvation to a lost world. It was just as important to see the lost world within our own home and ensure they, too, heard the Gospel message.

I fear, and sometimes this fear is confirmed, we spend so much time concentrating on reaching the world that our global vision doesn't include our own home. I'm reminded of Paul writing to Timothy when he says, "But if anyone doesn't provide for his own, and especially his own household, he has denied the faith, and is worse than an unbeliever." (1 Timothy 5:8 WEB) We read testimonies of pastors and Christian workers discovering, after many years of fruitful service, they've neglected their own families. I wish I could say I was always properly balanced between family and ministry, but I can't.

Sometimes I got so involved in a project that home became a place to eat, sleep and have my laundry done. The longer I spent in ministry, the older I got, the more I recognized the need to give as much attention to the spiritual growth and relationship of my family as I gave to reaching others with the Gospel. At times I was successful. Other times, I was not.

After twenty plus years of overseas ministry I was thrilled to know all my children came to the Lord's throne of grace. Each of our children gave their lives to the Lord. Each of our children were baptized.

On Guam baptisms were held in the ocean. We said we had the largest baptistery in the world. Several times a year, since it was always warm, our church held baptism services after the Sunday services.

We'd gather together outside the church and form a caravan of trucks, cars and vans to drive to hotel row and find parking near Tumon Bay. With a portable sound system each candidate would share their testimony with the church and any interested beach combers. When the testimonies were

135

complete, the pastor, and those to be baptized, entered the water and the ceremony commenced.

Wind surfers, snorkelers, sun bathers, and other tourists watched and wondered. We were ready with tracts to hand out and willing to talk with anyone interested in the Gospel being brought to life in the baptism. More than once a curious bystander saw the baptism then came to church and the Lord led them to salvation. The circle was completed as they returned to the same beach to be baptized as a witness to another bystander.

In Vienna baptisms were a bit different. Since our church rented space at the YMCA we didn't have a baptistery. During the summer, since it was cold in winter, a baptism would be scheduled on a beach at the Alte Donau (Old Danube). This was a big event.

Food was prepared and brought to the beach and a large table covered with numerous delicacies from the variety of countries represented in our church. We gathered, ate, sang and the candidates shared their testimonies. When others at the beach noticed the food table they were invited to join in the celebration. This was a chance to minister to people who might never step foot in our church services.

Singing and testimonies complete, we gathered at the river, no pun intended, and each person was baptized. Between baptisms we sang a rousing chorus of celebration. People gathered from all along the beach to see what was happening and ask questions.

One year, a man who had witnessed the baptism the previous year came and spoke with our elders. In the intervening year he, too, gave his life to Christ and desired baptism. After an interview on the beach he joined others from our church to celebrate his new life in Christ.

In the ocean, in a river, in a baptistery, a pool or a bath tub (yes, we have seen that, as well), each of these people were willing to proclaim to the world their faith in Christ. I grew up watching people baptized in the safe confines of the church. This is definitely an encouragement to the body of believers.

On the mission field I was introduced to public baptism. This was an encouragement and witness to the dying. Watching our children be baptized was an encouragement to us as parents.

Instead of arguing over the methods maybe it's time we concentrate on the witness of baptism to the world around us. With a little attention to this detail we might lead others to God's throne and need more baptisms. I'm just wondering . . .

Teaching and Training

The things which you have heard from me among many witnesses, commit the same to faithful men, who will be able to teach others also. (2 Timothy 2:2 WEB)

I love to teach. I prefer to teach through the Scriptures, exposition, but sometimes need to teach on a topic. Digging deep into God's word to unlock the mystery and majesty of our Creator's love has no end. Each time I open God's word, even for a casual reading, I find some new revelation to apply to my life and ministry.

Others have told me this is one of my spiritual gifts. When the opportunity arises, I dive in and learn more personally than I ever share in a classroom. I believe if someone wants to know and understand God's word they need to teach. To explain a discovery clearly to someone else we must understand it carefully and clearly.

For years I taught Sunday school and the occasional home Bible study. I preached when I could. Each time I found myself immersed in more of the wonder of God than I could imagine as His word sprang to life. Most of the time, I taught as a simple ministry in the church. The Lord blessed me with good classes and great participation.

One year the church established the Bayview Bible Institute, which lasted for three years. I was recruited as one of the teachers. My subject was New Testament Greek. I enjoyed the challenge as well as refreshing my understanding of the language. There were four students in my class and they enjoyed themselves and did well.

As a missionary I was not permitted to accept pay. I could volunteer all I wanted. I didn't want to be divided in my purpose and goal. So, what could be done?

My solution was for them to give me a piece of software I couldn't afford to purchase and we would call it even. The mission agreed, the Bayview Bible Institute agreed and I was ready to write the great American novel on my little notebook. I've written many things since then but no great American novel.

I continue to enjoy teaching when the opportunity arises. At times I wish that was my central ministry. God has a different plan but allows me to exercise this gift now and again to further His kingdom in this world.

There are courses on discovering our spiritual gifts. Books abound on discovering God's gift in our life and how to apply it to minister. But, I think God gives us gifts to meet the needs of our present ministry and not to establish a new ministry. God doesn't give us the gift we need and send us in search of a ministry. He places us in a ministry and then gives us the gift we need, when we need it.

Although I enjoy the gift of teaching God hasn't called me to full time teaching but to minister as an engineer in global missions. I praise the Lord for guiding me in this ministry. It wasn't my talents and abilities that permitted me to do the work but His gift and guidance each and every day.

God teaches and trains me daily. When I allow Him to guide my choices and His ministry I can be assured I'm in His will. When I insist on using the "gift" I think I have then I can easily find myself outside of God's will.

I must remind myself that my perception of what I can do best is not God's perception. His is divine; mine is marred by my human nature. My desire is not pure and heavenly directed. His is always in line with reaching the world with His love and grace.

I think, just maybe, I should listen to Him, not myself, and then I'll discover the wonder of walking His path and the joy of accomplishing the purpose for which I'm called.

Fun in the Familiar

There is nothing better for a man than that he should eat and drink, and make his soul enjoy good in his labor. This also I saw, that it is from the hand of God. (Ecclesiastes 2:24 WEB)

Not everything in life is intended for serious contemplation and study. I think this is why I enjoy so many of Solomon's writings in Ecclesiastes. I have no intention of going to his extents in experimentation but I do enjoy the simple things of life. Living on a small island, there were opportunities to make simple things memories.

For vacations we would usually stay at home and have fun. Things like patching the cracks in the walls, power washing and painting the roof were very popular holiday activities. Going somewhere from Guam was usually out of the question due to the high cost of airfare. Still fun events abounded throughout the routine activities of the week.

On Wednesday evenings we busied ourselves with church activities. For a number of years, I directed the church choir and other years provided musical direction for the Pioneer Clubs. Beth was involved as a singer in the choir or as a teacher in the Pioneer Clubs. The children came along to enjoy the fun events of the clubs and a midweek break from homework.

When the evening's events were completed we headed home along Marine Drive. It was the only way home. With one main road circling the island our options for different routes were very limited. I think I could have driven the route blindfolded, it was so well worn. I never tried.

Along the way we passed the government buildings, beaches, restaurants and in the late 1980s they opened a 7-eleven as part of a local gas station. Invariably, or with careful attention to timing, we were in need of additional fuel as we passed the 7-eleven. I would pull up to the pump, Beth and the children would head into the store and I joined them when the tank was full.

The political status of 7-eleven has risen and fallen over the years. Some like the shop and others feel it's to be avoided. However, they were the proud owners of an Icee Machine. This cup full of flavored sugar water was just the ticket after a long evening of singing or playing or studying. Selecting from the available flavors, which changed each week depending on the shipment arriving on the island, we would each wait for a chance to fill our cups to the brim.

Icees, or slushies in some places of the world, are a culinary delight. All that sweetness surrounding your favorite flavor could quench the thirst of a camel in the middle of the desert. If you weren't careful you would drink too fast and get "brain freeze." This painful experience was avoided by drinking slowly after the first onset and provided a source of laughter as others watched your reaction.

Icees were cheap, refreshing and contained nothing of nutritional or long-lasting value. Sometimes we need a little nothing to liven up our evenings and give us delight. In the early 1990s we were visiting my mother's home when I remembered another empty delight: lightening bugs.

Growing up in Georgia I was well aware of these marvels of luminescence. My brothers and I must have captured hundreds when we were young. We'd put them in a glass jar and take them to our room for the night. When they stopped flashing, the jar would receive a vigorous shake to liven them up once more. By morning they would be let loose, if they survived.

Sitting on the back porch of my mom's house, Ellice and Joel came up and pointed out in the dusk towards the trees. "What are those flashing lights?" they asked with wide eyes. I explained they were lightning bugs and remembered the delight I had in catching them in a jar.

Into the house I went to raid my mother's cabinets for empty jars. Grandmas always have the right accouterments for the fun and games of grandchildren. Sure enough there were four jars with lids, just waiting to experience the thrill of the hunt.

After a few instructions and a little training, the four hunters took up the challenge to capture the brilliant little creatures. I helped Evan catch a few as his little hands had problems coordinating the big jar with the lid and keeping his eye on the bug. Within minutes four glowing jars were set like trophies across the back porch railing.

We enjoyed studying them for a while as the children asked questions like, "How do they do that?" I created fictitious answers such as, "They are actually miniature dragons from the fairy kingdom and their lights are small internal flames." They didn't believe me but enjoyed the story.

Other fun adventures were part of living on the mission field and back in our homeland. They were each little treasures, learning experiences, encouragements in our lives. A moment here or there and then each was remembered long after the day they were discovered.

God uses the routine, the common things of life to teach us. In the wonder of lightening bugs, the "brain freeze" of a slushy or the strange appearance of starfish we discover bits and pieces of His marvelous creation. It's not always the spectacular we remember but often the quiet voice of God speaking to our hearts, when we take time to listen.

Scratch Golf

Cease from anger, and forsake wrath. Don't fret, it leads only to evildoing. (Psalms 37:8 WEB)

I like to enjoy life. I like staying home with my family; even if we just sit, talk or read in the same place I enjoy it. I enjoy a good meal with friends, chatting about the day, about life and about how God is working. I enjoy games of all sorts with just about anyone if there's a chance to laugh, relax and no one takes the outcome seriously.

I enjoy the outdoors including golf; the carts, the talking and the interesting things which can occur on the links. One time, while golfing with my father-in-law, I hit the ball into the rough. When I looked for the ball I was greeted by an alligator guarding his new-found treasure. I let him keep it.

I remember playing golf with my father many times but one time in particular. We were behind another foursome, taking our time and enjoying the beautiful weather. Three of the four men playing ahead of us appeared to be having a great time. The fourth man was losing his cool hole by hole.

By the time we reached the 18th hole the man was furious with his progress. They chipped on the green and motioned for us to tee off. We took our first stroke and sauntered down the fairway toward the green. As we drew closer we watched the first three men putt. Finally, the fourth man took a stroke and missed the cup. He took another and another before he dropped the ball in the hole and let out a few expletives.

He turned toward the lake beside the green and he tossed his ball in the water. With tensed shoulders and a running barrage of comments he walked to the edge of the green and picked up his bag, cart and all, walked to the other side of the green and heaved it into the lake. As the ripples spread across the small lake, the man turned and stomped across the green toward the club house. His friends stepped back to clear the way then followed him toward the parking lot.

Dad and I chipped onto the green. As I was lining up my shot Dad caught my attention. The angry golfer stomped toward the green. We stepped aside as he apologized for interrupting our shot and crossed the fine cut grass.

He marched across the green, down through the rough and right into the lake. Soon he was splashing around looking for his golf bag. We figured he had second thoughts about tossing his good clubs into the lake.

He splashed around for a couple of minutes until his hands located the waterlogged bag and cart. With disgust on his face he lifted the bag until the top of the bag poked out of the water. He reached around the bag, opened a zipped pouch on one side and extracted his car keys. He dropped the bag back into the lake and stomped across the green, with apologies for the interruption, and headed toward the parking lot and his car. Dad and I chuckled, finished the hole and headed home. Golf is a game of control. This man lost his.

I wish I could say I've never behaved like our wet golfer. Unfortunately, my temper has always been a bit of a problem. Sometimes, I remain calm and cool in the face of things going wrong and other times I lose it, to my own shame.

I could laugh at this man's predicament. I could also feel his inner turmoil. I don't know his relationship to God. I do know mine. If not for the presence, strength and guidance of the Holy Spirit I might spend more time in anger than joy.

God continues to teach me. Sometimes I get an "A" in class and other times I don't want God to give me my report card. Like my parents, he already knows, long before I have the courage to fess up and reveal my shortcoming.

Parenting Codes

He didn't allow him, but said to him, "Go to your house, to your friends, and tell them what great things the Lord has done for you, and how he had mercy on you." (Mark 5:19 WEB)

In all my studies about parenting I've yet to find Morse Code listed as a vital tool. When children are small you can talk about anything and they don't understand. After a few years they understand so you resort to spelling. But, what do you do when they learn to spell? Use Morse code, of course!

I remember hearing my dad use Morse Code to communicate with fellow amateur radio operators around the world. From the time I was old enough to descend the stairs to our basement in Georgia I remember the lilting sound of dots and dashes. This was long before computers, internet access and the ubiquitous email. This was when a mobile telephone filled the trunk of your car and let you sport a long whip antenna attached to your bumper. SMS and cellular phones were the things of science fiction movies.

As soon as my brothers and I learned to spell our parents resorted to Morse Code. In the middle of a dinner conversation the shouts and whoops of three boys would be interrupted as Dad would dah-di-da his message to mother, who would reply with the appropriate di-dah-dit. This kept my brothers and I at bay for a number of years as we struggled to learn letters and words in regular English. Visitors thought our parents were a bit loony when they began making beeping noises at one another during a meal.

Eventually, we all learned code in the interests of self-preservation. It was nice to again know what was going on at the dinner table and around the house. After many years of procrastination, I finally took my amateur radio examination and earned my "ticket." My communication with the world expanded beyond the telephone to other nations, without international calling charges.

My children, on the other hand, never succumbed to the desire to develop a good fist (a HAM radio term for sending smooth code). There's something magical about communicating with people from around the globe. Using Morse Code is more romantic than making a phone call or sending an email. It takes a bit of skill, preparation and you never know who will answer your CQ. You meet some interesting people when you open yourself to chat with anyone "out there."

One of the first additions to our home on Guam was a radio tower. It was attached to the rear of our house with a tri-band beam mounted on a rotor topping the steel structure. I was ready to talk to the world.

I had more opportunities to share my faith as this international hobby brought the diverse cultures of the world into my life. My bedroom closet was full of equipment and I would often be found chatting with someone across the globe late at night.

One morning I connected my transceiver to one of the huge curtain antennas at the transmitter site. In minutes I was chatting with folks throughout Europe. They commented on my magnificent signal considering the five watts of power I was dribbling into the antenna. When I explained the details of the antenna system they were amazed.

Simple language, common terms and a little bit of power brought people to my door and allowed me to visit their homes. Too often we use special codes, known only to those in the know, when attempting to share the message of salvation to friends and neighbors.

God's message of salvation is simple. Our sharing of God's work in our lives should be simple. Maybe then we can communicate better and bring others to God's doorstep. We don't want to hide our messages in code but make them available to anyone who might hear. God's plan of salvation is simple. Likewise sharing about our faith too should be simple and clear.

Chewing

"All things are lawful for me," but not all things are profitable. "All things are lawful for me," but not all things build up. (1 Corinthians 10:23 WEB)

When we first arrived on Guam the number of fast food restaurants was limited. The ubiquitous McDonald's were spotted about the north half of the island. The children loved that sight.

I wasn't so thrilled, even though I'd grown up with a great love for fast food. Restaurants such as White Castle and Krystal make my heart flutter with excitement. I'm not sure if that is joy over the food or an arterial reaction to the blood clotting fat in the meal. Regardless, I've always enjoyed such fine eating establishments and occasionally sneak a bite even in the face of my present dietary restrictions.

McDonald's was as close as we got when we arrived in the tropics. With careful research, known as driving around the island, we eventually discovered a Pizza Hut way up in the north. A couple years later we were thrilled when they opened a second shop close to our home.

When the spirit of fast food, mixed with the grain of available cash, moved, Beth and I would stop by Pizza Hut for lunch. One time, while Ellice was in school, we took Joel along to enjoy the treat.

We selected a booth by the window with a view toward the main road. Joel took a seat beside me as we ordered our pizza and drinks. Joel played while Beth and I chatted about the week's events and our upcoming schedules.

After a few minutes Joel decided he'd have more fun sitting by Mommy. So, with the usual shifting of our legs Joel descended beneath the table and arose again beside Beth. We continued our conversation as the waitress brought our drinks.

Out of the side of my vision I saw Joel coloring on the placemat and chewing on some appetizer. At least I thought it was an appetizer. Glancing about the table for the crackers he appeared to enjoy I couldn't find them. I wanted a little something to chew on while waiting for the cook to finish the pizzas. I asked Beth if she gave him some gum and she said, "No." We stared at each other a moment then turned toward Joel.

Looking at Joel I asked, "What are your chewing, Joel?"

"Gum," he replied without looking up as he continued to fill the paper before him with color.

"Gum," I mused, "where did you get it?"

"From under here," he said, without concern, as he pointed under the table.

Needless to say, Beth and I had Joel spit out the gum. We then instructed Joel in no uncertain terms never to take it from under a table again. We promptly lost our appetite! Our son was passing by the attractive collection of colored temptations on his way from Dad's side to Mom's side. In the joy of his colorful discovery he partook of the offering and enjoyed himself for a while. He wasn't aware of the potential danger.

Sin has a way of entering the Christian life as we casually saunter by temptation out of the sight of others. The appearance is good and no one is looking. We take a bit and off we go . . . until we get caught.

We were glad to catch Joel and provide proper instruction for the future before something tragic happened. He survived his short episode as we sometimes survive our tripping into sinful situations. If he had asked before he partook of the secret temptation he could have saved himself some trouble. As believers we can save ourselves some trouble if we pause and take time to ask before we start chewing on the wrong thing in our walk with God.

What Did You Say?

Yahweh said, "Behold, they are one people, and they have all one language; and this is what they begin to do. Now nothing will be withheld from them, which they intend to do. Come, let's go down, and there confuse their language, that they may not understand one another's speech." (Genesis 11:6 7 WEB)

One of the advantages of serving as an audio consultant is the occasional opportunity to visit other studios to provide advice. I serviced equipment in Hong Kong a couple of times. One visit to Hong Kong was scheduled to coincide with the need for consultation on a new studio under construction in Kao Shiung, Taiwan.

The first flight was from Guam to Hong Kong. There I used two days to align and maintain a number of reel to reel recorders and other studio equipment. (These were the days before digital audio.) This kept me busy with little extra time to see the town. The most I was able to see was when we, my colleagues and myself, went to find something to eat. One of my friends lived in Hong Kong for many years and knew the Chinese language, Mandarin, quite well.

One evening we went for dinner in a restaurant which served a number of American delicacies, including the infamous hamburger. At times, when I'm traveling, I appreciate an item I can usually identify and know won't cause my stomach to object. Adventure in food is OK when close to home, but when traveling it can be a disaster. So, this evening I ordered a hamburger.

Our conversation included the events of the day and news from our families. After a few minutes I was rewarded with a nice-looking burger and fries. Just what I like. Poking through the condiments on the table I could not find mustard, one of the basic ingredients for a good burger. When the waitress returned I attempted to request this spice for my sandwich to no avail. She didn't understand English. Bill, my friend fluent in Chinese, made the attempt. He used a number of words, descriptions, phrases and gestures until the waitress appeared to understand and departed on the hunt. A few minutes later she returned with soy sauce, ketchup and something we have not been able to identify to this day. I ate my burger with only ketchup.

The third day I prepared for the flight to Taiwan. Everything was arranged and the director's brother was to meet me at the airport. His big concern was whether his brother could find me in the crowd. I didn't think that was a problem. I was in the last row of a 747 taking off toward the city of Hong Kong. Anyone who has flown into or out of the old airport understands the steep climb necessary to prevent crashing into the tall buildings. The tail of the plane, where I was sitting, dropped like a roller coaster and scared the daylights out of me!

147

An hour later I landed in Taiwan. As I departed the plane and walked across the tarmac the idea of being found in the crowd became humorous. I was the only western, white, foreigner on the airplane! I stuck out like a pole, literally, head and shoulders above all the remaining passengers. It wasn't a problem for Andrew (his westernized name) to spot me coming through immigration. One small bag of test equipment and a taller than normal foreigner.

After a quick tour of the small town we came to the building where the new office and studio were under construction. The studio was on the fifth floor with one wall bordering the elevator shaft, creating a number of noise problems. When we added in the need for air conditioning to keep from suffocating the workers, we decided it was a large project which needed some rework. There were old walls to remove, new walls to build and rooms inside of rooms to be constructed as a sound barrier. My job was only to make recommendations on the construction and materials.

After surveying the room, making some sketches and lists, we headed to the ground floor for some lunch. Andrew is Chinese. He was born and raised in Hong Kong. When the waitress handed us menus in the southern Taiwanese dialect I was at a loss. The pictures, which didn't look very appetizing, didn't help me interpret the menu. I turned to my native speaking colleague and asked him to order something for both of us. He promptly entered into a ten-minute conversation with the waitress. They pointed at the menu, discussed and described items, pointed some more and eventually she made a note on her pad and departed.

I turned to Andrew and asked, "So, what are we having for lunch?"

"I have no idea," was his unexpected response. "Her accent is so different and the dialect so far removed from Taipei I can't understand what she's saying. It will be an adventure!"

Adventure was true. I'm not sure what I ate but it tasted OK, went down, and stayed down. That's always a blessing when traveling. A couple of hours later I was on my way back to Hong Kong to catch a connecting flight back to my home on Guam.

More than once I've encountered language difficulties in the course of our ministry. Currently living in a land with a native language other than English is a challenge. I'm reminded, over and over, of the need for people from every tongue and nation to be proclaiming the Gospel to people in their home land. God may use us in a language we've learned. However, there is none so eloquent to reach another as one raised in the same language. Let's praise God for lifting up workers in every language and nation on earth and watch Him accomplish his purpose of bringing the Gospel to the world.

Choir of Angels

I will be glad and rejoice in you. I will sing praise to your name, O Most High. (Psalms 9:2 WEB)

Music has and continues to be a major part of my life, our family and our ministry. The right melody, the choice poetic rendering, the appropriate tempo can move a person's thoughts toward God in a way ten thousand words will never accomplish.

One year Beth and I put together a small ensemble of missionary colleagues for the Christmas holiday season. Using parts of a cantata we assembled a presentation of songs to worship God and proclaim the incarnation of Jesus to any who would listen.

Church was one place to share this musical message. One evening we shared our few pieces with the congregation in preparation for a time of communion and remembrance of Jesus' work in our lives. Another less conventional presentation took place at the governor's mansion. The governor at the time was a Christian and permitted a number of religious events.

One of these was a Christmas gathering at the official mansion overlooking the Philippine Sea. Christmas gatherings were not unusual. They were held each year. However, allowing an "evangelical", non-Catholic group was outside the norm. We gathered for the festivities and shared God's love and salvation through song with the dignitaries and invited guests.

Christmas wasn't only a time for special music and ensembles but it was a time for church choirs to gather and present the annual cantata! Our church, Bayview, was no exception. For months I directed the choir through rehearsal after rehearsal to reach the point I thought we were ready for a public hearing.

Cantatas are interesting pieces of work. In most churches, ours included, everyone practices for months to be prepared. Then, one fine Sunday morning or evening, or maybe on Christmas Eve, the presentation is made before the congregation. An hour later it's finished, not to be repeated. The works of months of preparation are poured into one hour of concentrated ministry to proclaim the wonder of God to those present.

During this concentrated presentation things can become rather tense for the choir on the platform, the accompanist, and the director. Regardless of careful preparation things can, and will, go wrong.

I love to see my choir smiling while they sing. In fact, I believe they sound better when they're smiling and enjoying the music they're singing. If it becomes too laborious then it becomes a task and not praise to God.

Since the director faces away from the congregation there are opportunities to do things only the choir can witness. I like to put on a big smile and poke my cheeks with my fingers to get the choir on the verge of laughter. It helps to get everyone relaxed and ready. One year I borrowed a Christmas tree pin with little lights. I pinned it to my shirt. Unknown to the congregation I turned it on just before the choir sang. They sounded happy and cheerful that year.

Another year I purchased a bowtie with flashing lights which became a regular part of my Christmas attire, especially for the church choir. Not all activities to get the choir's attention come from the director. Sometimes the music, if pre-recorded, can glitch or someone can forget the melody to their solo. I figure, if you start right and end right what happens in the middle can be forgiven by the congregation.

One Christmas this was tested to the max. We were performing one of my favorite cantatas with a marvelous missionary message woven into the arrival of our Savior in Bethlehem. The choir was pumped up. We knew the music, the intros, the exits and the cut offs. Everyone was smiling and the music began to play.

Things went well. My son was operating the sound system and knew my hand signals. Ellice was one of my altos while Beth was busy with the sopranos singing their hearts out for the Lord.

Ellice was an old hand with church musicals and presentations. Starting when she was about four she took every opportunity to sing, dance or act her way across the platform. She has an excellent voice, and a very outgoing personality which is important in any musical or play. Singing a Christmas cantata after singing in the youth choir, the school choir, and singing with mom and dad was routine.

About half way into the cantata I noticed Ellice looked a bit pale. Sure enough, near the end of the song she swayed one way, then the other, and then . . . collapsed on the floor.

Normally this type of activity will stop things immediately. My choir, bless their wonderful hearts, looked at me, watched me direct and keep time and completed the song we were singing with an amazing crescendo.

I motioned for Joel to stop the music and then looked at Dr. Vince. He was one of my tenors and also the family doctor. He and Beth helped Ellice through the side door into the small classroom just off the platform. The choir faced the director. I lifted my hands in preparation and Joel started the music once more.

We sang the next piece right on cue. A few minutes into the song Dr. Vince came back and resumed his position in the tenors smiling to indicate everything was just fine. Ellice was just a bit too nervous and it was a hot night.

The choir sang the remainder of the cantata with renewed energy and careful attention to detail. The final piece was as spectacular and moving as any other Christmas cantata I remember. When the cantata was over most people forgot about Ellice's swan dive. We finished well and that was important.

I'm reminded of Paul's words in 2 Timothy 2:12. "If we endure, we will also reign with him. If we deny him, He also will deny us." We make mistakes along the way to our heavenly kingdom. However, it's not every step along the way which counts but the direction we're heading and how we end the race. Paul reminds us to run to receive the prize. If we stumble, we need to get up, brush ourselves off, take a bearing on the direction of the goal line and enter the race once more. In this eternal race there's more than one winner. All who finish well will win an eternal prize in God's new heaven and earth.

A Mountain Top Experience

After he had sent the multitudes away, he went up into the mountain by himself to pray. When evening had come, he was there alone. (Matthew 14:23 WEB)

If you stand on the highest peak of Guam you're probably on the tallest mountain in the world. Granted, Guam doesn't rise above Mount Everest until you go to the roots of the island at the bottom of the Marianas Trench. The trench reaches a depth of 36,000 feet. Mount Everest could be dropped into the trench and still be over a mile below sea level. When you add the depth to the height, Guam is a pretty tall island.

Being afraid of heights, and therefore not an avid mountain climber, I wanted to feel I was standing on the top of the world. So one rainy day, as a family, we headed to Mount Lamlam. We didn't plan our trip to coincide with the rain but planning around the rain on Guam wasn't easy. There are two seasons on Guam, wet and dry. So why not go in the dry season? You need to understand the actual difference between these seasons. It rains in the rainy season. It rains a lot in the rainy season, up to thirty inches a month. In the dry season it still rains, just not as much. Regardless of the season it rains just about every day on Guam, at least for a few minutes.

Pressing forward with our plans, undaunted by the rain, we drove south into the mountainous region of the island. In contrast to the many quick showers which keep the humidity high, this was a long shower ensuring everything was soaked, especially the dirt. Our friend Kevin joined the expedition. All the necessary equipment was in the car as we parked near the start of the trail. Water bottles, hats, . . . that's about all that was needed.

Donning our hats and gathering the water bottles we headed up the trail toward the summit. The same trail is used each Easter season by the local church. Priests, the faithful, and observers, trudge upward, stopping to remember the walk of Jesus to the cross. Our goal was not spiritual but mental. I wanted to say I climbed to the top of the highest mountain in the world!

With each upward step the rain continued to soak the ground and make our footing slippery. Ellice and Joel thought it was great to be out in the rain. Beth smiled, Kevin laughed, and I tried not to get water in the camera lens. Thirty minutes later we were at the top.

There before our eyes stood three crosses. The largest was concrete and sported an official plaque of dedication. The others were wooden. These were brought up each year at Easter and planted at the top. Older crosses were removed to ensure there was always room for one more. As we considered the imposing concrete cross, the sun made an appearance to liven up the day and dry off our soaked spirits, shoes, hats, clothes and lens cap.

I stood on the peak of the tallest mountain in the world and looked around. I looked east. I looked west. I looked south and I looked north. What did I see? Water! In every direction we could see beyond the boundaries of our little island to the vast ocean beyond. Until that moment I didn't realize how "confining" Guam might appear to many people. It felt much smaller when I could see each line of the coast.

There I was, 1332 feet above sea level, and about 700 feet above the road where our car was parked. To the west was the Philippine Sea and Ceti Bay. To the north I could just make out the profile of Rota, an island smaller than Guam. To the east and south was water, the water of the Pacific Ocean.

After a few more minutes of enjoying the passing sunshine, and worrying about the children falling over the edge, we started our descent. We had conquered the mountain top. It was there, and we made it to the top.

Beth, Kevin, Ellice, and Joel began their trek down the trail and I lingered at the top for a few minutes. In that few moments alone on top of the mountain I could understand the desire of the Lord to meditate at such an altitude. Here above the world it was quiet. Here away from the noise of day it was easy to find peace and concentrate on God.

Rousing myself from my spiritual moment, I began the descent of the trail. I soon discovered there was no longer dirt on the trail but slippery, slimy, and slushy mud. The children were attempting to not slide or get too dirty. I watched for a moment before a stroke of genius came to mind. Some people might say I just suffered a small stroke.

With a smile on my face I sat down in the mud then lifted my shoes out of the mire and started sliding down the mountain on my backside. In no time Ellice, Joel, and even Kevin were enjoying this slimy mode of transportation provided by nature. When we reached the car we were laughing, muddy, and ready to head home. I think it took a week to get all the mud out of the car.

My mountain top experience was fun and revealing. Our home was bound by the physical space available above the surrounding waters. This limited our travel and our daily life. Our spiritual life contained no boundaries.

Guam provided a perfect location to reach the Far East with the Gospel message. From another mountain side, Mount Schroeder, programs reached into remote regions where lives were changed by God's message of redemption. They were not limited by the island shoreline.

Sometimes it takes a trip to the top of the mountain to realize God's work in our life and the limitless nature of the Spirit working within us. As we live in the valley let's seek the mountain top vista and recognize the height, depth and breadth of God's care in our life.

Animal Adventures

"Tell the daughter of Zion, Behold, your King comes to you, Humble, and riding on a donkey, On a colt, the foal of a donkey." (Matthew 21:5 WEB)

I like most animals. During my formative years we enjoyed the wonders and the chores of having a dog in our home. Throughout my life I have provided food and shelter to various dogs, cats, snakes, fish, hamsters and mice. Moving to the mission field you experience another set of animals. Sometimes we get along fine, as I did with our cat, Popcorn.

Why Popcorn? When she was a kitten she liked to sit in my lap and eat popcorn from the bowl. The name sort of stuck. Popcorn also sported a hook tail. It was supposed to be a type of cat but we thought it looked funny. The end of her tail curled around in a sharp hook, like the letter "J." Occasionally it would become entangled on various things about the house.

One Christmas season Popcorn was hiding under the Christmas tree waiting for a victim to stroll by unsuspectingly. I was the victim. As I passed the decorated tree out she sprang. There was a rustle of pine needles, a shivering of ornaments and a look of amazement on her face. As Popcorn's body cleared the lower branches on a trajectory for my leg I noticed the fine green chord caught in her tail. She had hooked the Christmas light wiring and it was securely hooked to the tree. Crash, boom, bang, down came the cat, short of my leg, followed by the Christmas tree, which I caught in my arms.

Popcorn's antics were a source of entertainment to the family. She was a constant companion for Evan when James started school. When Evan went up the hall, along went Popcorn. When Evan went down the hall, Popcorn followed. When Evan took a bath, Popcorn sat on the back of the toilet watching like a guard.

Other creatures from the island had less than friendly relationships with our family. Joel remembers one day when Beth was working on the laundry. Our washer and dryer were outside on the covered porch. Joel writes:

"One day Mom and I went outside to do the laundry. When she looked into the sink she found a nest of gnats who are carriers of dengue fever. She screamed and ran to grab a can of bug spray. With much screaming, smashing and swatting Mom eliminated the nest. Satisfied with the results, she went back to the laundry.

"Reaching into the washer, Mom pulled out a towel and saw a lizard. Screaming once more the towel hit the floor and she ran into the house looking for me. Even staying home with chicken pox I had to eliminate the lizard.

"I walked out to the washer and looked for the little lizard. I found a foot-long chameleon, freshly washed, sitting in the machine. I laughed so hard I could barely control myself. Removing the lizard from the washer in a towel,

I went inside to show my prize to Mom. She screamed and Evan was excited and wanted to touch it. We let it go, squeaky clean and ready for a new life.

"Walking back into the kitchen I tossed the towel on the counter. Later I walked out to find Mom cleaning the counter with the lizard towel and I screamed, Mom screamed and the towel hit the floor. I would call this day a real scream!"

Lizards were not the only creatures on Guam to entertain our family. A host of geckos, carabao, snakes and miscellaneous flying insects were part of our daily routine. Joel remembered another incident:

"Has your car ever been chased by a dog? My mom has had more excitement in her life which, as always, made some fun for me. Some days Mom takes James to H.S. Truman Elementary School and then Evan and his friend Deborah to J.P. Torres Elementary School in Santa Rita. Finally, she takes Neil and me to Piti Middle School on her way to mail day at the mission. On these days she takes a road less traveled. Several times we've enjoyed watching a carabao family foraging on the edge of the jungle. The mom, dad and teenage carabao were fascinating to watch.

"One week it wasn't quite as much fun when the teenage (a mere 400 pounds) carabao lowered his head and started chasing the van. Mom yelled and tried to avoid the lumbering beast. Like a roller coaster the van went up and down the twisting road with the beast hot on her heels. Finally, the Toyota out ran the weary water buffalo and Mom continued to the mission. She doesn't like to take that route from school to the mission anymore."

And I'm not immune from the impact of critters in our home. Joel reminded me:

"This summer, as the rainy season began, a cricket found its way into a door frame in my parents' bedroom. After two nights of non-stop serenading, my dad reached his limit. Around midnight he decided to kill the cricket. He moved furniture and all sorts of stuff around until he found the critter. Finally, he gassed the varmint, silencing his chirping. When Mom got up to do something my dad said, 'Watch out for the . . .' THUMP... 'desk?' From that night on, my family and I have called him Dances with Crickets."

We still have pets in our home. When we departed from the tropics the massive number of insects and small creatures we encountered was reduced but occasionally bugs can be found in our home. Animals are found throughout the Bible. Some are food, some beasts of burden, some talk, but all have a purpose and part in God's plan.

When I think of the donkey Jesus rode into Jerusalem I'm amazed. This common beast was God's choice to demonstrate Jesus' triumphal entry into the Holy City. I'm sure the donkey had no idea what was to happen and wondered at the glorious reception as he carried his sacred rider into the city. He was available, God called and he did his job carrying something on his back. The same thing he was destined to do throughout life.

How often do we miss God's blessing when we're called to do our routine work? We buck and bray and complain about the burden. God knows better and carefully determines our burdens and our calling. We need to respond with willingness and wait to see God's glory revealed. Just remember what Jesus said.

"For my yoke is easy, and my burden is light." (Matthew 11:30 WEB)

Water World

The moon and stars to rule by night; For his loving kindness endures forever: (Psalms 136:9 WEB)

Like many special events in life, the camp out was a planned time of enjoyment and family togetherness. The idealistic pictures of children at play on the beach and the family frolicking in the water for the day were forefront in our minds as we prepared for the weekend. Extra vacation days were approved and the food menu was carefully planned to ensure nutritional balance with the right amount of plain, but good, camp food. All the tents, sleeping bags, quilts, pillows, swimsuits, plates, stoves, flashlights, and toilet paper were inventoried and stacked with care throughout the living room and dining room.

The big day, Friday, arrived. Most of the day was filled with thunderstorms and rain which delayed the start of our adventure. That was OK; we could go Saturday and sleep through to Sunday morning. So, on Friday the family cooked out at the nearby Pizza Hut followed by a nature walk through "Free Willy 2" at the Naval Station Theater. The afternoon was lots of fun. We arrived home late and everyone went to bed to be prepared for the next day.

Saturday morning came along as the sun poked its rays through the scattered cloud covering. Everyone climbed into their cars. With all the gear we didn't fit into one car anymore. Forty-five minutes later we arrived at the gate to Anderson Air Force Base. It seemed to me all the best beaches on Guam were on the military bases. Passes were issued and we drove to the beach. The view to the beach was spectacular as we drove down the road through the break in the cliff. The ocean was spread out like a beautiful quilt a couple of hundred feet below us. The waves crashed against the reef and even the island of Rota was visible in the distance looking like a thick fog on the horizon.

As soon as we arrived at the campsite the boys headed for the sand, bound and determined to be covered with the gritty particles until we headed home the next day. Their plans were momentarily interrupted when we forced them to help unload the van and the car. An awning was put together over our lawn chairs and the portable grill set up for cooking a scrumptious lunch of hot dogs with chips of course.

For the remainder of the afternoon we ate, played in the sand and water and sat in beach chairs relaxing. What a true delight! The time to just sit and chat was wonderful. Jay and I took the time to talk about several areas which were often pushed to the background by the tyranny of the urgent. No telephones, no radios and due to the clouds, no one else on the beach, except the lifeguard. I think "refreshing" would be the appropriate word for the afternoon, refreshing for body, mind, and soul. Late in the afternoon it

157

appeared occasional sprinkles were the worst we would see so we pitched the tents and laid out the bedding for the night.

I need to stop here and state why we enjoyed camping at Terrague beach. This beach, on the north end of the island, was known for the continuous breezes which made camping cool and comfortable in the tropics. As dinner was consumed and the darkness fell we discovered that night would be different. The palm branches ceased frolicking in the wind and hung like limp wash rags. So far so good; there were temporary respites from the doldrums as a breeze would rift its way through the campsite.

Bed time arrived and we all crawled into our tents. The unfortunate thing about tents is they tend to block the breeze with the mosquito netting. After some shuffling around on the mattresses, which felt like sleeping on pregnant balloons, I resigned myself to a warm night's sleep. A little later in the evening a breeze arose, followed by rain. With my head at the window and my feet at the door, I began to get wet at both ends. It was time to zip the tent closed. OK, it was a little warmer but still tolerable. Then the rain came harder and, just as I was dozing off, SPLAT! a drop of water hit me in the face. Then splat, splat, splat… I began to feel I had entered a B grade kung foo movie complete with water torture! It was time to move the mattresses once more.

Beth slept off and on as I awoke and shifted and went back to sleep. It got to the point as another leak was formed that we began to laugh and wonder if we would wake our sleeping neighbors. We learned early the next morning the children in their matching tent experienced similar late night difficulties. At one point, Evan complained to Joel he was cold. When he reached over to check, he found his blanket was soaked and he was lying in a puddle. It was four children snuggling together in the middle of a leaking tent during a late night tropical rain storm. Now that is a mental picture if there ever was one!

We enjoyed the entire weekend, water and all. We looked at this not as a problem weekend but a "BONDING" weekend for the family. As nations are brought together in times of distress so the Chick family draws closer together in times of hot tropical rain storms.

Breakfast was delightful with Boy Scout sandwiches (a specialty of mine) and more time for the boys to build sand castles. When we arrived home later that morning, everyone fell fast asleep until midafternoon. It took a couple days to dry out and put away all the soggy camping equipment. We couldn't wait for another chance to go camping. Who knows the depth of family bonding this can bring about!

God made the stars and moon for the nighttime. He also made the rain and wind. I slept in a cold, wet, sleeping bag, under God's stars and moon and remembered, "His love endures forever!"

Here to There

Come now, you who say, "Today or tomorrow let's go into this city, and spend a year there, and trade, and get gain." Whereas you don't know what your life will be like tomorrow. For what is your life? For you are a vapor, that appears for a little time, and then vanishes away. For you ought to say, "If the Lord wills, we will both live, and do this or that." (James 4:13 15 WEB)

The first time I climbed aboard an airplane I was married, in my twenties, and headed to my best friend's wedding in Ohio. I flew from Jacksonville, Florida and returned to the small, miniscule airport in Gainesville, Florida where the airplane barely had enough room to stop. I was excited and scared all rolled into one.

My second flight was to Guam. There was a big difference. After a few years on the mission field, with trips here and there about the Pacific, I became a seasoned traveler. While my height didn't quite fall in the standard for airline seats I could easily enter a state of the living dead and become a zombie from one end of a flight to the other. Other than the food few things bothered my ability to drift off to another world during a flight.

In the 1990s I had the opportunity to help at our offices in Sri Lanka. This was not a normal flight. Not by any means!

The first leg of the flight was not direct to Taipei but via Saipan. After checking in on Guam I headed past the first ticket gate to the gangway for the plane I was told was at Gate 4. As I approached the airplane ramp the attendant in the hall said, "Oh no, your gate is over here," and directed everyone from Gate 4 to the door for Gate 3 and everyone for the Manila flight to Gate 4. Gate 3 went outside down the stairs and across the tarmac to the waiting 727. Gate 4 was a regular gangway connected to another Boeing 727 preparing to depart. As I and the other passengers began to ascend the stairs to the waiting aircraft a man came out and said, "This is the wrong plane; you want to be on that plane," pointing to the plane docked at Gate 4. We all shuffled back across the tarmac and up the outside stairs of Gate 4 (the stairs reserved for ground crew.) As we approached the top of the stairs, a similarly confused set of passengers were exiting the same gate attempting to descend the outside stairs of Gate 4 to reach the aircraft sitting in the Gate 3 location. Needless to say, it was interesting watching the passengers shuffle between both planes until everyone was on the correct flight.

Finally, they pushed the plane away from the gate and we waited, and we waited, and we waited. As the rustle of discontent began to rise in the cabin we heard a message over the speakers. I don't think the engineer knew he was connected to the speakers when he commented, "Just call the tower and have them to pull us back into the gate. Then call maintenance to see what they can do." I was curious to say the least and I watched as a flight attendant opened the cockpit door and whispered to the flight crew to tell them the intercom was coming out over the speakers. The look on the flight crew's face was great. Immediately there was a "click" as the intercom speaker was turned off. A couple of minutes later they informed us we had to go back because they couldn't start the engines.

We finally left after the maintenance crew brought out a jump starter, fired the engines up, and sent us on our way. We arrived in Taipei about an hour behind schedule. The flight via Saipan to Taipei was uneventful until I got off the plane. I was the only white 6-foot plus passenger on the plane. The airline personnel on the ground knew they had to do something with me. I just didn't fit into the crowd! After a lot of discussion, which I couldn't understand, they relieved me of my passport and tickets, deposited me in a transit lounge and left me without any explanation. With five minutes to spare before my next flight boarded, the airline personnel returned with my precious documents and a boarding pass for the remainder of the trip.

I'm not a fan of airport terminals. I've been in some very poor and extremely uncomfortable airport terminals around the world. Some were mere grass huts while others so massive they contained their own subway systems.

When I arrived in Singapore I enjoyed what I consider the best airport I've ever seen. As a transient passenger I was treated well with all the conveniences I needed. Even a meal at the airport restaurant was reasonably priced, something US airports need to consider. As I walked around to kill three hours of boredom I thought to myself, "Where was this terminal when I was carting four small children all over the globe?"

We were boarding the plane to depart. Everyone was checked in at the gate waiting for the bus to corral us to the waiting aircraft. As we stood up to walk to the bus the lady carefully announced we were headed for Bombay. This created quite a stir until someone at the counter corrected the error with the proper destination.

I did fairly well for someone who doesn't like to fly. I survived until the last couple hours on the final leg to Colombo. At that point, it was hot, I was tired (being about 3:00 a.m. my time) and I couldn't straighten my aching knee. I made it to the ground without accosting any flight attendants then spent forty-five minutes waiting for immigration to pass everyone through their routine. The hour drive to the office and the guest apartment was exciting with the unique Sri Lankan driving technique. It reminded me of Bangkok and Thai driving methods. Our driver was cool as a cucumber when a cycle without any lights would appear unexpectedly before our front bumper or a truck on the side of the road decided it was time to move and chose our lane while we were still occupying the same space.

Jesus did a lot of traveling during his earthly ministry. He walked everywhere. I think he would have still walked even if there were airplanes, buses and cars. When you walk you meet new folks, talk about life and see how they live. It's from these visual interactions Jesus drew some of the parables with the most impact. On a plane you hunker down in your seat and try to endure the long flight.

Studies over the last couple decades indicate we're moving fast. We're moving so fast we can't keep up with modern technology and the demands it makes on our lives. Stress increases, worry increases and our ability to cope with life decreases. It seems to me, we need to return to walking and talking so we can understand, relate, and celebrate God's presence on a personal basis. Maybe I can book passage on a cargo ship for my next furlough from Europe!

Church Services & Beggars

For such men are false apostles, deceitful workers, masquerading as Christ's apostles. And no wonder, for even Satan masquerades as an angel of light. It is no great thing therefore if his ministers also masquerade as servants of righteousness, whose end will be according to their works. (2 Corinthians 11:13 15 WEB)

When I travel to new lands I enjoy meeting the believers and, when possible, attending local church services. Occasionally, I've been asked to share from God's word at the last minute. I believe there are three things a missionary should always be ready to do on a moment's notice. When called upon a missionary should be ready to preach, pray or die. I try to be ready for the first two at all times. The last one, well, that's not my favorite but I'm ready.

In Colombo, Sri Lanka I was privileged to attend church with some of our local staff. Church was fascinating. This was my first interaction with a Dutch Reformed Church. The pastor was Sinhala and spoke with an often over dramatized Indian accent. It was Vacation Bible School Sunday. April was a holiday month in Sri Lanka and I was treated to a series of songs and Bible verses by the local children. It was great. The songs the children presented were very familiar songs from fifteen years earlier. I asked our staff about this and learned it was very difficult and slow to acquire VBS and Sunday School materials. The children were excited and their eyes wide with the joy of their songs and dances. The adults joined in the fun with the up and down songs and many of the hand motions.

The church building was located in the center of a public school compound. Originally the school belonged to the church until all schools were nationalized. Most of the three- story buildings looked beautiful from the outside. The classrooms sported wire mesh windows, no glass, no electricity and from what I could tell, no running water. It would be a rather dark learning experience on a cloudy day. I understood why the expatriate staff sent their children to boarding school or home schooled them in Sri Lanka.

In the evening I attended another Dutch Reformed Church across town. Their pastor was away for the evening so the fellow from the morning church came to present the word of God. The service began with three guitars, an organ and an electric bass player leading the congregation in praise choruses. It was a rousing time of singing and praising the Lord. This lasted almost thirty minutes before the final song which accompanied the collection. Instead of fixing everyone's mind on the collection or a special music presentation they jumped into another lively chorus while passing the bag through the aisles. If you didn't pay close attention you didn't know they were gathering the offering.

The church building was similar to the church I visited in the morning. The exception was their preparation for the possibility that their school would be acquired by the government. They separated the school buildings from the church buildings and built a wall to provide a definite separation between the two. Thus, if and when the government acquired the school, they were left with the church, fellowship hall and a nice green lawn not overrun by the government school officials.

After the service I met my first beggar. Beggars are the ubiquitous landmarks of a nation that's been struggling to unite for more than thirty years. A young fellow, nicely dressed, approached me while I was standing in the walled church yard. I figured he was from the church interested in the foreign visitor. He then proceeded to describe his local home, hungry grandmother, and equally hungry stomach. Not having any local currency, and having been equally warned of the often fictitious stories I refused the man and turned to depart. His tenacity, with which these professional beggars pursue their mark, was suddenly evident. He followed me to the car and started to climb inside, insisting I should help his starving stomach. When my colleagues arrived, he departed quickly and disappeared outside the compound walls.

Lest you think I'm the ugly American savagely ignoring the plight of the local people, be assured this fellow was not hungry, nor destitute. The local pastor and many of the local people kept track of these frauds to turn them away regularly.

There are "real" beggars in the country. These are people living as outcasts from society and solely on hand outs. It's considered good form to give them a rupee or two to help alleviate their plight. Many are cripples from the years of war. In contrast the professional beggars are not outcasts but choose to solicit their income rather than join the work force.

Distinguishing between the real and the false beggar is difficult for a visitor such as me. As an outsider I couldn't distinguish between those who made false claims and those who were in real need. I needed to rely on those who worked within the country and knew the culture to guide me clearly. The same problem exists in the church today.

Many people in church are redeemed, seeking God's face and allowing the Spirit to work in and through them. Others are actors, charlatans who know the proper makeup, activities and phrases so they look and sound believable. When new believers enter God's family they're often accosted and entreated by the charlatans in our midst to partake of ungodly activities.

As we walk with the Lord we need to provide guidance, especially to those new in our midst, so they won't be carried away by the deceptions of men. We must help them distinguish between the false gospel of the world and the true Gospel of Jesus Christ. In order to do this our own hearts must not long for the world but be set on God.

Rats!

These are they which are unclean to you among the creeping things that creep on the earth: the weasel, the rat, any kind of great lizard, . . . (Leviticus 11:29 WEB)

After we arrived on Guam and established our home, we explored the island. Sometimes a colleague with years of experience on the island would accompany us and tell us what was what. Other times, we were on our own to explore and discover.

Once I drove around Agana Park and noticed a large animal sitting next to a picnic table enjoying the leftover bits from a forgotten meal. A few seconds later I realized it was a rat, a big rat. He was so big he could sit on his haunches and still reach the top of the table. This was not a creature I wanted to meet in the middle of the night.

Outside of this unusually large rat there were a number of other rodents out and about on the island. Twice I was unfortunate enough to encounter them one on one. The first was in our home.

My morning routine included waking up, taking a shower, eating something and heading to the office. The children were usually up and getting ready for school or already out the door and on their way before I moved. That was a routine morning.

I rolled out of bed and headed for our small bathroom and shower. Half-awake I removed my clothing and stepped into the shower stall. Routine took over as I turned on the water and pulled the curtain closed behind me. In my early morning daze, I noticed something out of the corner of my eye.

Glancing about I expected to find a hand towel on the floor of the shower. This hand towel moved, just a little, but enough to wake me quickly from my half slumber state. It was a rat! Not a big rat but a rat in my shower none the less.

I knew this was always a possibility. These nocturnal creatures often live in the sewers. When searching for food they sometimes crawl up the drain pipes to a house and swim the short distance through the toilet trap into the house. This was supposed to happen in other homes, not mine!

Alert, wide eyed and ready for action, my mind went into overdrive and quickly deduced it was time to exit the shower as fast as possible. Backing away from the frightened creature I exited the bathroom, closed the door and put on my robe.

Beth was surprised when I walked briskly to the living room and demanded, "Where's the cat?"

"There," replied Beth, wondering why I wanted the cat so early in the morning.

I grabbed the petite feline and made a beeline for the back bathroom. I opened the door slightly, tossed the cat inside, slammed the door, and left the diminutive cat to do her job, catch and kill the rat. The casual observer might have noticed the rat and the cat were about the same size!

I proceeded to gather my clothes and dress for the day. I wandered into the living room and looked for some missing piece of clothing. Suddenly the cat sprinted past my legs under the couch and out of sight. She was definitely the weaker vessel in this battle.

Beth continued to eye me as I wandered back to the bedroom and found the bathroom door open and the shower stall empty. The rat was out! Where? I didn't know. Donning the remainder of my clothing I sauntered back to the living room.

Curiosity taking control, Beth asked, "What was that all about?"

"There was a rat in the shower," I reported as if it was the evening weather report.

"Where's the rat now?" she asked with a quizzical look on her face.

"I don't know," I said with a tilt to my head. "The cat knocked the bathroom door open and the rat escaped into the bedroom." I put my keys in my pocket, gathered my office papers and prepared for the day's ministry.

"So what are you going to do about it?" she asked. Her attention was diverted momentarily by the vision of the cat poking her nose from under the couch watching for her new enemy.

"I'm going to work," I announced. "When the children get home from school they can catch the rat. The creature will hide in the dark somewhere all day so you don't have to worry."

"You're going to do what?" Beth asked incredulously.

"I'm going to work. My ride will be here shortly, I can't find the rat without Joel and Ellice's help so there's nothing to be done this morning."

Beth wasn't sure. Her look told me I was skating on thin ice and the cracks were beginning to form under my blades. Before we could continue the conversation, I heard Ray honk the horn and quickly scooted out the door and headed to the office.

Beth continues to remind me I was no knight in shining armor that day. I left her to deal with the diminutive dragon hiding in the cave of our closet in the bedroom. I found out later she did laundry, cleaned house, and kept the bedroom door closed until the children returned home from school.

When Joel came home Beth commissioned him to find, catch and dispose of the intruder. He found his friend David and they went on the hunt. Using a special blanket, reserved for those who didn't feel well, they bagged their quarry.

When I returned home, Joel met me at the gate, excited with his accomplishment. He guided me across the carport and pointed to a bucket covered by a piece of wood. Inside was the deceased rodent. Curious, I asked, "How did you kill it?"

"We gassed it," replied Joel, proud of his work.

"With what?" I asked.

"With RAID," he responded pointing to the empty can beside the death bucket.

I looked once more in the bucket to see the dying creature twitching its legs twice before collapsing in death. It wasn't a pretty sight but I was glad the vermin was dead.

When the day was done the rat was in a bag in the trash and out of his misery, I was in the dog house for leaving the rat in our house and Joel was the hero of the day. Something tells me I didn't handle that situation as well as I could have. Maybe that's why God classifies rats as unclean.

Squalor Housing

For we brought nothing into the world, and we certainly can't carry anything out. But having food and clothing, we will be content with that. (1 Timothy 6:7 8 WEB)

My family wasn't rich. At least we weren't as rich as folks like Howard Hughes or Bill Gates. On the other hand, we weren't poor either. While my parents hailed from the hills of Tennessee I was raised in the more cultural areas of big cities like Atlanta and Cincinnati. During those years I never knew hunger although I thought I would starve some evenings waiting for dinner to be served.

I read stories and heard news about poor people around the world living in cramped conditions. Occasionally I would see a "homeless" person in the city. Most of my life that glimpse was as close as I came to the poor and homeless. Then God put us out on a little island in the Pacific.

There were very few poor people on the island. I'm talking about the folks who have no home, no income and beg for food daily. Then I visited other areas of the world. My view of the poor and homeless changed forever. I remember riding back to my room after church in Sri Lanka.

After church I rode to the B's home through some of the most pitiful squalor housing I could've imagined. Along one street, if the pot holed, narrow cart path could be called a street, there were houses literally one next to the other. When I was young I would've said they were "stuck" on each other, physically.

The wall of one home was the wall of the next home. Each was a single room about the size of the van, sometimes slightly larger and often smaller. This room was home for the entire family. This might include the extended family with children, grandchildren, and grandparents sharing the same piece of floor each evening, sleeping side by side. There were no facilities in the small room.

All bathing, eating, and cooking was done on the street. A local stand pipe on the street was everyone's shower or kitchen sink. Many of those people were proud because they owned their room. They felt that at least they owned something. Those houses had no water, bathrooms or electricity. Home after home was illuminated by the orange glow of a single candle in the center of the floor.

As strange as it might seem there was the occasional flicker of a television coming through the doorway of a few homes. Battery powered televisions were the pride of the few who had scrimped sufficiently to enjoy this treat. They still lived in their one room house without water or electricity other than a battery they charged at work during the day.

The Sri Lankan people I met were amazingly content with their life. It was what they knew and expected. When things for a family improved they were happy as well. Paul reminded Timothy to enjoy the simplicity of having his needs met. Food and clothing should be sufficient. (1 Timothy 6:8)

I think many people have scratched this verse from their copy of the Bible. I find myself guilty as well. When was the last time we were encouraged to be satisfied with where we were? The world today, and often times the church, says we should always want more, better, and fancier stuff. We should want better stories to tell about our lives, more spiritual trophies to share with one another.

I think I need to look about my home, be satisfied with God's provision and stop looking over the fence to someone else's fields. Maybe I can write this verse back where it belongs.

Take Cover

Keep me as the apple of your eye; Hide me under the shadow of your wings, (Psalms 17:8 WEB)

Many times I found the best place to have fun was hard to reach. On Guam some of the best beaches were secluded away on military bases, requiring special permission to visit. Guam did sport Fina Lake in the center of the island. A great place to fish, I understand. Like many other nice spots, Fina Lake was snuggled into the center of a military base, the Naval Magazine.

Fina Lake was unique. It was the only lake on the island. It was also a manmade lake to keep water supplies flowing between the rainy seasons. The lake was built by the military after WW II. With its central location and surrounding mountains, it was secluded and quiet. The location was so secluded the US government felt it was a good place to hide weapons of all sorts. Well, maybe not hide but at least keep them away from the general populace.

So the Naval Magazine was constructed surrounding the lake in the central portion of the island. There was one road in, one road out. Since the facility was generally bereft of people the local carabao population felt it was a great place to rebuild their numbers. After many years in what they must have considered their own resort, their numbers increased and the largest herd was located within the guarded gates and double fences of the Magazine.

No ordinary soldier was commissioned to guard such military power. The Magazine was guarded by a group of Marines. With three boys at home this was a triple threat: a lake, a herd of carabao and Marines with cool-looking weapons.

A friend of ours at church was the former commander for the Marines on the facility so he offered us a tour and a visit to the lake. After we passed through security and an inspection of our vehicles we entered the facility. Some of the soldiers provided an impressive demonstration of the Marines' ability to lock and load on command.

The lake was beautiful and several local workers enjoyed fishing. We meandered through the small roads in search of the elusive carabao. On the far side of the base we found them casually munching on some grass and ignoring our intrusion.

We saw all the attractions and began our journey back to the front gate. Our Marine friend was slightly confused by the unmarked roads. Eventually we drove beside an interior fence that surrounded a massive and secure-looking building.

As we moved slowly along the outskirts of the enclosure we noticed soldiers on the roof with binoculars marking our progress carefully. Next there were more soldiers running across the roof manning several gun emplacements. We were suspicious this was not the right place to be enjoying a Sunday afternoon drive.

As we approached the end of the secured enclosure, several vans drove around the corner and stopped in front of our two vans. Soldiers poured out of the vans, big guns in hand, fanned out across the road, took up prone positions, pointed their guns at us and we all heard the numerous clicks as safeties were turned OFF! We were definitely in the wrong place at wrong time.

Their commander walked toward our vehicles. Our Marine escort climbed out of his vehicle with his hands up to meet the commander and our children dove for the floor out of sight. While we listened to the children whimper from the floor and wondered what the inside of a military prison would look like, the two Marines chatted for a while. Suddenly the commander started laughing. He shouted to the vigilant troops, who clicked the safeties back ON much to our relief. We were released, passed out the front gates and never considered visiting the lake again.

I'm reminded of many saints who find themselves suddenly in the wrong place at the wrong time. Serving the Lord, enjoying His grace and guidance and then glancing up to see the world around them aiming their weapons toward them.

We were under the protection of our Marine friend and his connections. As saints we are under the caring wings of the Almighty. If we stare too long at the opposition we'll dive for the floor and whimper in fear. When we feel the comfort of our heavenly father we relax, wait, and watch as He handles the situation and makes the path clear.

If we're going to hide, let's hide under the shadow of God's wings. There we'll find comfort and strength no matter what lies ahead.

Taming of the Shrew

But nobody can tame the tongue. It is a restless evil, full of deadly poison. (James 3:8 WEB)

In high school I was required to read Shakespeare's plays. Shakespeare was wonderful with words, both soothing and searing. I don't remember any of the plots except for "Romeo and Juliet" because they made a movie out of it. I am a very visual learner.

I always liked the title "Taming of the Shrew" but thought it was something akin to Mutual of Omaha's Wild Kingdom show. At one point in life I wanted to be a zoo keeper but my yard wasn't large enough for the cages, elephants, and giraffes. I like giraffes. Then I needed to get a job and became an engineer.

Engineers are meticulous people. They like everything in order, categorized, quantified and sanitized. When looking over a piece of equipment, each minute detail is recognized by the trained eye. By just walking into the room a well-trained engineer can sense problems before the normal operator knows something is remotely amiss.

With these skills at hand I entered the restroom at the transmitter site one day. My eyes noticed the soap by the sink was scratched. My mind ignored it as useless information. Preparing to make use of the facility I heard a noise. Quickly I looked toward the top of the toilet tank. With bubbles popping on his lips a soap-chewing shrew smiled a greeting.

I backed out of the room, closed the door and announced loudly, "There's a small rat on the toilet!"

George opened the door a crack and peeked in to confirm it was a small rodent. Closing the door, he quantified and clarified it as a shrew. George was an expert on small creatures and a pretty good engineer as well.

I assessed the situation and decided reinforcements were in order. After I called the rest of the crew, Ken and Rich came running into the transmitter hall. I explained the situation and we put our heads together to devise a plan of attack. When we stopped rubbing the bumps on our heads from smacking our foreheads against one another, we started to think.

Four adults, each close to six feet tall or taller, educated, serving God on the mission field, were trying to figure out how to eradicate the life of one four-inch shrew in the restroom. None of the technical manuals available contained anything about how to deal with small animals in large buildings terrifying God's servants. It was a matter of prayer.

We bowed our heads and Rich noticed a large insulated electrician's glove on the counter. That was the ticket. Smack the little beast into animal heaven. We were not about to have the message of salvation curtailed by a short-tailed varmint. The great white hunters were ready to bag their quarry.

I poised the glove rakishly over my shoulder, ready for the attack. Rich and Ken crouched down to stand guard and prevent the monster from escaping. George cautiously opened the door, entered and scared the shrew out the door into the hall, interrupting the varmint's dinner of Safeguard soap.

Corralled by my two colleagues, the shrieking shrew turned my direction and made a run for freedom. *Wham!* Down came the heavy leather glove on the sinister shrew. The blow was too much and the miniscule mouse plopped back to the floor, unconscious.

We gathered around, ensured our quarry wasn't moving, and congratulated one another on a job well done. Before he moved his four feet and regained consciousness our visitor was unceremoniously cast into the forest near the building. I'm sure he told his four-footed friends never to go up against four engineers just to snack on soap. It was time to get back to the message of the Gospel.

I'm reminded of that small organ called the tongue. It's usually hidden, always active and very difficult to tame. I've spent my entire life trying to tame that roaring beast, sometimes successfully but often with failure. James talks a lot about the damage a few words can inflict.

Maybe I need to put a glove in my mouth from time to time to keep it in check. When it revives it may be a little gentler and in its proper place.

Hide and Seek

It will happen, while my glory passes by, that I will put you in a cleft of the rock, and will cover you with my hand until I have passed by; then I will take away my hand, and you will see my back; but my face shall not be seen."
(Exodus 33:22 23 WEB)

I was the youngest of three brothers. As children we enjoyed the normal games of childhood. There was "Ghost in the Graveyard," "Freeze Tag," and the ever popular "Hide and Go Seek." I usually lost. I was suspicious my brothers would gang up on me and report my position to one another and ensure I was always "it."

I wasn't looking forward to a life of always being "it," so I accepted the Lord's call to the mission field and left the country. For more than thirty years my brothers and I have been playing hide and seek with each other around the globe.

I'm no longer found hiding under my parents' bed or sitting in the closet on my brother's stinky shoes. These days they just type in my email address and let the wonders of the internet find me. I know I've been found when I hear, "You've Got Mail" oozing from my computer speakers.

We share with one another the current events in our life while Mom provides regular parental advice between messages. Unfortunately, there are some events which go beyond her expertise. Playing hide and seek with an octopus is one of those.

Snorkeling is a great hobby. Of course, you don't see much if you practice in the local pond. A nice tropical beach, plenty of sunshine to burn your back and a picnic lunch waiting on the beach are the perfect ticket.

We were enjoying the beauty, warmth, and relaxation of Agat beach. Protected from sharks by the coral reef I donned my goggles, plugged a snorkel into my mouth and floated away from shore. The coral reef is home to a plethora of beauty in multi-colored fish, artistic formations and miniature sandscapes created by the currents.

Caution must always be applied when snorkeling. The clown fish are very protective of their realm and will nip at your toes, fins and fingers to drive you away. Sea Urchins anchor themselves in the crags of the coral and cause good news, bad news stings. The good news is you won't die; the bad news is the pain might make you wish you would die.

One afternoon I was surprised to find a small octopus seeking refuge amid the rocks. My first instinct was to scream but swallowing sea water isn't fun. My second idea was to swim like mad for shore but I figured the octopus was faster than my little fins.

While staring wide eyed through my foggy goggles, I realized the baseball sized multi-legged glob of jelly was just as scared of me as I was of it. I moved

173

closer and it scrunched tighter into the rocks. I backed off a little and it oozed out enough to see me over the rock. Up and down, in and out, we played our little game until I returned to the shore.

I was excited with my discovery and playing hide and seek with the octopus. I'm sure Moses was thrilled to be hidden in the cleft of the rock when God strolled between the pieces of offering. He couldn't pop out of the rock because God protected him with a loving hand. There were things he wasn't permitted to see for his own good.

The octopus was interested in watching me to know what I'd do next. His concern was for his own safety in the face of a creature many times his size. Moses was interested in seeing God's hand work with the children of Israel. He was satisfied to see God's back and enjoy the protection of God's hand. Are we satisfied with God's revelation in our life or do we want to push aside the hand and try to see more than we should?

Sometimes we hide in closets and under beds to play a game with those trying to find us. God hides us in the cleft of the rock to let us know He is present, caring for us and leading the way. He doesn't need to find us. He knows right where we are.

Trying to sneak a peek at my brothers would almost always make me "it" because I gave away my hiding place. God is always "it" in the Christian life. Like Moses we need to take comfort and courage with what God chooses to reveal. It's here we know God is leading, God is providing and God will reveal all we need to know: no more, no less.

Monitor Lizard

"'These are they which are unclean to you among the creeping things that creep on the earth: the weasel, the rat, any kind of great lizard, the gecko, and the monitor lizard, the wall lizard, the skink, and the chameleon. (Leviticus 11:29 30 WEB)

"Boys will be boys." That's what my mother would say when I was growing up. As the baby in a family of three sons I was at a distinct disadvantage. While my brothers were interested in sports, rock and sock'em, I was into music, poetry and reading.

One thing we held in common was a love for the outdoors. This is something my wife reminds me of now that I spend so much time indoors with this computer. As boys we enjoyed playing with various curious creatures we found. Sometimes the bugs, worms, snakes and rodents we captured were happy to spend time with three curious boys. Other times, well, we won't talk about those times.

Small creatures are very common in the tropics. Large creatures are also common. When we left Guam, there were twice as many snakes on the island as people. This isn't a good ratio to put in the tourist brochures. Along with the ubiquitous snakes, Guam sported wild dog packs, carabao herds and the komodo dragon or monitor lizard.

I read about these three- to five-foot creatures with toxic breath and saw one in the Guam zoo. Zoo might not be a good word. Ten animals in someone's backyard with a ticket booth in the driveway don't quite match the wonders of the Saint Louis Zoo. The monitor lizard is a leathery creature that eats small mammals and generally steers clear of people. With the large wild dog population on the island I was sure they were well fed.

One day we strolled along Tanguisson Beach and wandered into the boonies (island slang for jungle). The massive growth of a tropical jungle is fascinating. Beth was wandering ahead when I heard her call out. I jogged ahead and found her pointing at a log across the trail.

"I think we can just step over the log, dear, you're not that short," I commented and continued along the trail.

"Not the log, what's on the log!" she shouted and pointed again at the moss-covered decaying trunk.

"COOL!" I exclaimed after I recognized the five-foot monitor lizard relaxing in the shade.

Beth quickly turned to exit the boonies while I stepped forward for a better look. The lumbering lizard caught a glimpse of my movement and high tailed it off the log into the dense undergrowth. I gave pursuit but to no avail. The creature crawled faster than I could navigate the dense foliage.

Armed with the most toxic mouth in the animal kingdom the komodo dragon recognized I was too large for even his appetite. That was the first, last and only time I saw the lounging lizard in the wild. He was smart. Although I meant no harm he knew when to turn tail and run.

Timothy writes about our flight from evil. He reminds us, "But you, man of God, flee these things, and follow after righteousness, godliness, faith, love, patience, and gentleness." (1 Timothy 6:11 WEB)

Sometimes we think we can stand even when the Scriptures remind us to be careful lest we fall. We might learn from small creatures. There is a time to stand, and a time to flee.

Bragging Rights

But if any widow has children or grandchildren, let them learn first to show piety towards their own family, and to repay their parents, for this is acceptable in the sight of God. (1 Timothy 5:4 WEB)

My work with computers has definitely impacted my life. Learning command lines, file formats, software and hardware were just the tip of the iceberg. Discovering things like bugs, crashes and the innate ability of a machine to make one rip roaring mad came with time. There's a human quality in a computer. They usually do what you tell them but sometimes they take on a mind of their own. This reminds me of raising children.

Computers provided a number of excuses to fly to the USA for meetings, training and development. On these trips I often took an extra day or two to visit my mother in Tennessee. One summer other members of my family arrived at the same time. My brother and his wife were visiting from Asia. My other brother and his son were visiting from California. It was a mini family reunion. The only ones missing were my wife and children. They were back on Guam and missing all the family fun.

My brothers and I may be older and gray but we're still boys. To demonstrate our maturity, we'd sit about the living room and talk about life, love, and the meaning of the universe. We had all the answers, just ask us. Eventually the conversation would escalate to a competition.

I remember John stating, while changing the subject completely and starting the challenge, "I can bench press 200 pounds." He glanced from chair to chair waiting for the rebuttal.

"Yeah, well, I can build a notebook computer from tin foil and old plastic toys," responded Steve, calling on his technical background.

"Oh yeah," countered John, moving to the edge of his seat. "I can build a beam antenna from tinker toys and erector set parts."

This banter continued back and forth for several minutes as I silently considered my entry into the fray. This was no simple battle of words. This was a life and death struggle for filial superiority. As my mind worked through a series of exaggerated boasts, I considered how to end this verbal banter with a crushing blow.

I cleared my throat. My brothers paused and looked my direction. Here sat their little brother. Here was the poetry reading, music playing, baby of the family attempting to enter the holy ground of verbal one-up-pence. I paused, in a polite southern manner, made eye contact and launched my attack.

"I maintain thirty computers, two servers, two networks." So far they were not impressed. "Living on a tropical island I can go to the beach any day of the year." A slight nod of their heads but the barricades of pride weren't breached. "And . . . I have four children, and . . . I am taller than either of you!" I turned to look toward our mom, Grandmother, and proud ancestor of my brood.

No response, just a look in their eyes conceding to my taller stature and larger family. The victory was complete. Single handedly I conquered their claims with statements only a mother could appreciate. Since it was Mom's house that was the winning blow. Four grandchildren, what more could she want?

In truth, there was another grandchild to grace our family in the years ahead. However, at that time I was at the head of the pack. The battle won even if only temporarily, the victory assured for the moment, it was time to move on to more important things - food!

Mom's house was small and the kitchen was the favorite meeting place. My Filipina sister-in-law made great lumpia, my favorite Asian delicacy. To sit, eat and discuss family life is one of the great pleasures of being in a parent's home.

Fixing faucets, shutters, and trimming trees are a delight when we have the chance to be home and helpful to Mom once more. Since we're spread across the globe this doesn't happen often but we enjoy every chance to get together, boast, share and laugh with one another and see who gets the upper hand.

I'm reminded of the banquet table set in Heaven. Think about it. An eternal chance to sit, laugh, share, boast, (well maybe not in Heaven), and fellowship with the Father, Son and Holy Spirit!

We can make our claims and our accomplishments in the world known and then smile as we counter each other's claims. Then, from his seat at the table, the Lord will clear His throat. We'll all turn to watch and wait. After a short pause, a good southern tradition, He'll make one statement.

"I gave my life as your ransom for you."

We'll remain silent.

Searching for the Lost Pond

"Again, the Kingdom of Heaven is like a treasure hidden in the field, which a man found, and hid. In his joy, he goes and sells all that he has, and buys that field." (Matthew 13:44 WEB)

The longer you live in a place the more you hear the tales, mysteries and mystical history surrounding the land and the people. Guam was full of such stories. The local tales explained the creation of the island, their local mermaid, and why little children should stay away from the jungle.

One item often mentioned by island natives was the Lost Pond. Everyone seemed to know where it was located except us. I figured it must not be too lost if it was the topic of such repeated conversation. I asked some folks where it was but they didn't know. Maybe it was lost. A wandering pond, lost in the jungle, amazing.

When I was young I wandered my stomping grounds with friends in search of new and exciting places. Many times we'd jump into an inviting stream or small pond to escape the summer heat. Between the mud, leeches and other creatures we found in the water it's amazing none of us became ill. The lure of a lost pond on an island in the Pacific was too much to ignore; I had to find it.

I finally located the secret directions to the pond. I'd say where but that's a secret. It was time to explore and see what we'd find. Swimsuits, shorts, sandals, hats, children and towels ready we left home in search for the Lost Pond.

Parking near one of the power plants, Beth and I walked up the beach for so many paces, turned right and followed the small trail so many paces, then turned left around the old stump and went deeper and deeper into the jungle. We were like pirates as we searched for hidden treasure. Perhaps some scallywags from a previous century used the pond to hide their hoard of gold.

Hot, sweaty and ready for a rest we stepped around another stand of trees to see the pond nestled in the jungle. The water was smooth as glass, silent and still. It was inviting in the hot tropical summer heat. An old rope hung from the branches of an overhanging tree, the only evidence that earlier explorers were successful in their ability to follow directions.

Tossing aside my hat, removing my sandals and shorts I scampered over the tree roots and took hold of the inviting rope. Of course I first used a stick to ensure the water was deep enough so that no one would get hurt. A couple tugs to test the rope and I was ready. I knew after a short swing I would experience this new delight.

I climbed back from the water's edge, part way up the tree for a better take off. I shouted to Beth and started my Tarzan swing out and over the water. Johnny Weissmuller, eat your heart out! I made an arc, I just cleared the roots,

179

swung up over the water, reached a peak above the center of the pond and let go.

I shouted in triumph as I plummeted toward the inviting water. Just as my toes made contact my mind was thrown into panic mode. The day was hot. I was sweaty from my trek. The water . . . well the water was ice cold! I plunged beneath the water and turned into one large goose bump. Down through the icy water I hurled until my feet touched the sandy bottom. As fast as possible I pushed off, eyes wide open, to find the surface of the water and a desire for heat.

I gasped for breath as I shot out of the water. I fell back in and began to swim like an Olympian toward the shoreline. Beth started to laugh uncontrollably as I shot out of the water. She watched as I clasped my arms around my chest and danced around trying to use some of the tropical heat readily available in the jungle.

"A little cold, dear?" Beth asked with a chuckle in her voice.

"N . .n . .n . .n . .no, d. . .d . .d . .dear, th . .th . .the water's fine!" I shouted back.

The water wasn't actually icy cold but it felt like it after the heat and the humidity of the jungle. The pond itself was fed from a fresh water spring so it was cooler than the ocean nearby. After a while we became accustomed to the cold and enjoyed the pond. It was refreshing. It was like liquid air conditioning in the tropics.

I discovered my watch fell off in the pond and was lost. That might be why they call it the Lost Pond. It was too deep and murky to find anything so I figured there are plenty of lost watches and other trinkets lining the bottom like a hidden pirate's treasure.

We enjoyed a few more plunges into the pond before we headed back to the beach and the warmth of the ocean. After we baked on the beach and splashed about in the waves we headed back to our car and our home.

Jesus talked about finding things which were lost. He talked about the widow's coin, the lost sheep of Israel, the prodigal son, you and me. Whenever they are found there is great rejoicing by the searcher. When we are found by Jesus there is great rejoicing in Heaven.

Beth and I rejoiced to find the cool, jungle-shrouded pond and relax in its refreshing waters. Just think of the rejoicing in Heaven when one lost sheep comes into the fold of God. Do we remember the refreshment of God's Holy Spirit to our souls when we turned to God for salvation?

It will be beyond our wildest dreams to rejoice with God in Heaven for eternity! How wonderful to be found.

Tasting Tea

I am the vine. You are the branches. He who remains in me, and I in him, the same bears much fruit, for apart from me you can do nothing. (John 15:5 WEB)

Although my parents drank coffee I avoided that delicacy for many years. Finally, at twenty years of age I took my first sip and it was awful. I was working in a hospital in Florida and entered the world of coffee as a reaction to the stress. My work with often terminally ill children was counteracted by the effects of the caffeine.

Although I continue to enjoy my daily coffee I've also developed a love for tea. According to popular belief it's better for you. I'm sure my British colleagues would argue it's God's gift for afternoon tea time. I'm not interested in the health issue just good taste. I appreciate the wonders of Viennese coffee as well as a wide variety of teas.

During a visit to Sri Lanka, there was some spare time between projects. With my eyes closed to the dangers of the fast driving, crowded roads and suicidal tendencies of motorists we rode from Colombo to the village of Kandy. We enjoyed a leisurely lunch in the cooler climate with a wonderful view and then we headed back down the mountain toward Colombo. Along the way we decided it would be fun to visit a tea farm.

I'm not sure if they call it a farm or factory but it was along the way. Earlier we'd passed the gates to the factory as the workers, hundreds of them, arrived on foot. Many were elderly women, some young men, some dressed in business attire while others arrived in country clothes.

We entered the gates, passed the guardhouse and stopped by the central preparation building. The tour was straightforward, beginning in the drying room, then the rolling (cutting) room, the roasting room and finally the separating room.

Fresh leaves only from the top of the bush were picked each day by the ladies. They were then deposited in the drying rack, along with anything else that happened to jump in their basket. There, forced air dried the leaves until they were ready for processing. Once dried the leaves were gathered from the drying bin, tossed on the floor and shoved through a trap door to the floor below.

On the lower floor the leaves went through a series of rolling machines designed to separate them by size and value. Each machine rolled the leaves and dumped the separated piles on the floor. The leaves were scooped up in shovels and tossed onto the roasting machine. When the roasting was complete they were once more deposited on the floor.

The final separation process again dumped the results in piles on the concrete floor. From there the prepared tea was shoveled into bags for packaging and sale. It's interesting to note the staff members tending this process, mostly women, wandered about the factory in bare feet. I suppose they didn't want the tea leaves spoiled by their shoes!

We exited the factory and stopped by the little in-house shop. In various bins they had tea available from $10 to $500 per kilo. I purchased a small amount of the cheap stuff, took it back to Guam and brewed it up. With my first sip the hair on my head, what little there was, stood on end, it was so strong!

I found the process fascinating, simple and almost primitive. With the exception of the giant rolling machines, most of the labor was done by hand. A friend in Austria read a report on the contents found in tea bags, including grasshopper legs, and still he continued to enjoy the brew. I was a little dubious at first, then figured I couldn't see all the foot prints, the leftover grasshopper legs, or other articles collected from the bushes. Maybe that's why so much tea is hidden in little packets.

I looked back at my life and thought, "This is how God prepares us." God rolls us to separate the wheat from the chaff. This process is repeated again and again to prepare us to minister for Him. Those who listen to our testimony, sermons, Bible studies, don't know all the times we've fallen on the floor after God pruned our life. It doesn't matter. What matters is the final product. After we fall God picks us up and prepares us for the next step in our walk with Him.

When we begin to concentrate on the areas in life where we've failed we become crippled. Like pausing to drink tea after watching it fall on the foot-trodden floor over and over again, we sometimes spend too much time looking back and not forward to the Lord.

I am reminded of what Paul wrote to the Philippians, "Brothers, I don't regard myself as yet having taken hold, but one thing I do. Forgetting the things which are behind, and stretching forward to the things which are before, I press on toward the goal for the prize of the high calling of God in Christ Jesus." (Philippians 3:13 14 WEB)

Let's look forward to eternity in Heaven with the Lord. That's what matters in the end, not the past. There will be wonder in walking with the Lord in the new Heaven and Earth knowing the rolling process is over. Now that will be a good cup of tea.

Elephant Orphanage

. . .even we ourselves groan within ourselves, waiting for adoption, the redemption of our body. (Romans 8:23 WEB)

Tarzan was my hero. At least he was when I was young. I didn't miss an opportunity to watch Johnny Weissmuller, along with others, swing through the trees, shout "ahh-ee-ahh," then save the jungle people or rescue the damsel in distress with the help of his animal friends. "Me Tarzan, you Jane," was one of my earlier sentences.

When I was old enough to enjoy the forest around our home I was a Tarzan wannabe. At first I searched the trees around our house for vines to swing my way through the foliage. All I found were vine wannabes cluttering up the undergrowth. I guess forests in Ohio just don't have the necessary vines for jungle rescues.

Once, I tied a rope to a high branch to practice my swing and jungle yell. With nowhere to swing to it was short lived excitement. I just couldn't figure out this jungle transportation mode. Then I remembered the elephants. When there were no vines Tarzan resorted to the lumbering elephant's sturdy service.

In the jungle there were no jeeps, no taxi cabs or buses, only beautiful, big, gray, trumpeting elephants. These lumbering beasts fascinated me. When a colleague suggested we visit an elephant orphanage in Sri Lanka I jumped at the opportunity. I practiced shouting, "umgawa!"

The Pinnawela Elephant Orphanage is one of a kind. As the only elephant orphanage in the world, they are proud of the ministrations and love they provide to these gargantuan beasts.

Most of the residents are young and many require bottle feeding. They'd take a three gallon jug, add a nozzle and pour it down the youngster's throat. Bath time was a daily ritual. Herded to the local stream each elephant was carefully scrubbed, using a car brush on a long stick, to ensure good skin and freedom from pesky bugs.

As they grew they were prepared for work on the island. On Sri Lanka, as well as in other parts of the world, the elephant continues to serve an important role. A good working elephant is a prized possession, especially by farmers.

The handlers, nurses and caretakers ensured each orphan was properly cared for and loved. Occasionally they would ride atop the older elephants and demonstrate their abilities to tourists like myself. There were no Tarzan imitators attempting to save the world from the invading safaris or treasure hunters. There were only elephant caretakers who watched out for the welfare of the lost and forgotten.

Without the love and care of the Pinnawela staff these gentle creatures would soon perish in the wild. Their parents were lost or dead. Each elephant was named, brought into the household and nurtured for a productive life.

I've never been an orphan, at least not in this world. I was born into a loving and wonderful family with mother, father and brothers. However, in the eternal, spiritual world, I was born an orphan. No father, no mother, no relatives just lost and alone in human wisdom, without a purpose.

Without the love and care of God I would have remained an eternal spiritual orphan. However, God has adopted me. John reminds us, "But as many as received him, to them he gave the right to become God's children, to those who believe in his name: who were born not of blood, nor of the will of the flesh, nor of the will of man, but of God." (John 1:12 13 WEB)

Not only am I one of God's children but I've been given a name! I'm an overcomer in God's family and will receive a special name, from God's heart to me, a name for me alone (Revelation 2:17). I'm no longer a spiritual orphan but a child with a new name in an eternal household! What more could I want?

I look forward to eternity. I look forward to hearing my special name from God. I look forward to swinging from cloud to cloud shouting, "ahh-ee-ahh," knowing everything is in order in God's kingdom.

Udon Thani

Come, let's go down, and there confuse their language, that they may not understand one another's speech." (Genesis 11:7 WEB)

By the time I departed for the mission field, my experience with bus travel boiled down to a couple city bus trips and one trip from Gainesville to Jacksonville, Florida during my college days. During my trip from Gainesville to Jacksonville, a whopping 2-hour drive, I sat bored watching the flat Florida countryside roll along. Not fully understanding the bus route I pestered the driver to let me off at a corner near my parent's home. He was a bit annoyed but figured putting me off the bus was better than listening to me.

I thought Guam might have a bus system I could use to go to and from the office. Guam was, and is, a small island with tour buses. These were small buses which took the predominately Japanese tourists from place to place. The local residents never rode the bus. They drove everywhere. I thought I was destined to be bus impaired for life. This was until Beth and I visited Thailand.

My brother worked for Voice of America at a station in Thailand. My travels across the Pacific qualified me for some free tickets. With a destination, free tickets and a book titled, "How To Visit Thailand on $10 a Week," we were ready for the adventure. We made reservations, withstood the eight-hour layover in Narita, Japan and arrived in Bangkok for our holiday.

Beth and I enjoyed a couple days in a mission home while touring bits and pieces of Bangkok. Finally we went to the bus station to book a ticket to Udon Thani. The ticket agent spoke just enough English to sell us two tickets. When I asked which bus was the right bus, his English skills suddenly evaporated.

We walked through the maze of buses and realized interpreting the language was going to be difficult. The Thai language uses a form of Sanskrit. To us it appeared like scribbles on the sign. We carefully looked at our tickets and held them up to compare them to the bus signs and figured we found our transportation. We took a chance and asked the driver, "Udon Thani?" He smiled, shook his head and we climbed aboard.

We were in God's hands because no one on the bus spoke English. The bus attendants used hand signals to inform us when it was meal time, toilet time and sleep time. The attendant passed out the bagged meals, collected the remains and left us to enjoy the rest ride.

We sat on an unknown bus, traveled throughout the night on an eight-hour drive, in an unknown land, with an unknown language and an unknown destination. This made it a little difficult to sleep. I doubt it had to do with folding my six-foot plus body in a seat designed for a five-foot Thai.

As morning dawned and the sun provided a spectacular array of color the bus entered a city. It was about the right time so we thought this was the place. I stepped up to our road attendant and asked, "Udon Thani?"

"No," she replied with a frown on her face.

"Not Udon Thani?" I inquired.

"Udon Thani," she replied and smiled.

This conversation went back and forth a couple times before the bus pulled over to allow some of the passengers to depart. Beth and I took the chance, departed the bus and collected our suitcases.

The local travelers disappeared into the morning mist and left us on the side of the road as the bus departed. One Sam low (sic) driver came to offer a ride, at a price of course, but we didn't know where to go. (A Sam low is like a rickshaw with a bicycle on the front.) All the shops were closed, the signs looked like scribbles and we were in an unknown town in the middle of nowhere.

As we contemplated our situation one of the shops opened its security gate. The owner came out, dumped something into the street and began to retreat behind the gate. We approached, almost scared the man to death, and used sign language to see if there was a phone available. After a few minutes of flapping our arms around like lunatics, attempting to demonstrate the universal sign language for, "I need a phone, I don't know where I am," he smiled and let us step into the shop.

In the center of an otherwise empty room sat a chair with a telephone on the seat. I dug through my wallet for my brother's number and dialed.

"Hello," came the groggy voice of my brother so early in the morning.

"Hi John, it's me!" I replied with a thrill of joy in my voice.

"Me who?" John asked. It had been a long time since our last phone conversation.

"Your brother Bob. Beth and I are in town, I think, and need to be picked up."

"That's today?" he asked.

"Yep, we are at the bus stop."

"Which one?"

"The bus stop from Bangkok."

"There are five bus stops in the city. Which one are you at?"

"I haven't a clue," I answered. I began to wonder what we were doing in this strange place.

"Any signs around to tell you where you are? Perhaps a shop or something?"

"You've got to be kidding! They all look like chicken scratch to me. Let me look outside once more." I set down the handset and poked my head out the door to find some distinguishing landmark. Returning to the phone I said, "There's a sign across the street with a horse on the front."

"There's a lot of those in town as well," my brother replied. "Just hang tight and we'll drive around until we find you."

"Ok, see ya."

When I expressed my thanks to the shop keeper and returned to the street I gave Beth a detailed report on the conversation. We were apparently in the right town, but John had no clue where to find us. We sat on our bags and waited.

Within ten minutes a Jeep rolled up in front and we were greeted with John and Jeanne's smiling faces. What a relief to be back with someone we knew, who spoke our language, and who would bring us to safety.

Our vacation was great. We ate dinner by the Mekong River, visited the transmission site, and caught up on years of separation. It was well worth the trip. I'd do it again in a heartbeat except my brother doesn't live there anymore.

Attempting to communicate with the bus personnel, the Sam low drivers and the shop keeper reminded me of the Tower of Babel. Getting things to work well was difficult. I didn't understand them and they sure didn't understand me. God's plan to confuse the languages was a job well done. We weren't accomplishing much by speaking gibberish to one another.

Sometimes when we share the Gospel it sounds like a foreign language. We use big words, church words, and theological words to express simple ideas of God's love and salvation. After the demon possessed man was healed he wanted to follow Jesus. Our Lord sent him back to his home, not with theological proclamations but with a simple testimony, "Go to your house, to your friends, and tell them what great things the Lord has done for you, and how he had mercy on you." (Mark 5:19 WEB)

How well do we communicate? Are we refugees from the Tower of Babel or are we messengers and ambassadors for Christ? Maybe it's time to ride a bus into the country and learn the simple life and the simple language of a personal testimony. What great thing has the Lord done for you . . . in twenty words or less?

Coconut Trees

Where there is no counsel, plans fail; But in a multitude of counselors they are established. (Proverbs 15:22 WEB)

After moving into a new home on Guam I made a survey of the yard and realized that the coconut trees were a problem. If you consider a ten-pound coconut falling thirty feet onto a five-year- old head, as a parent you begin to shiver thinking about the consequences.

The coconut trees had to go. They posed a serious health threat to our growing family. Holding our six-month-old, James, in my arms, I counted two looming disasters towering over our concrete bunker we called home. It was time for action.

We engineers like to plan things, use the appropriate instruments and consider all the ramifications of a project. I gathered my fellow male colleagues one sunny Saturday afternoon to tackle the problem. This was a man's job. Women were only there as spectators and to bandage wounds in case of disaster.

I looked over the situation, considered the options and then I had it all figured out. Mark brought the chain saw, Ray brought some ladders, Rich, George and a couple others handed out hard hats and provided the muscle.

The first tree was partially cut midway up the trunk. A rope was attached. With our flexing muscles impressing the girls, we heaved and heaved until the top toppled to the ground. Cutting down the rest of the trunk was simple. We surveyed our successful work, turned, and considered the taller of the two trees.

Climbing a ladder, tied to the tree at the twenty-foot level, Mark pulled the chain saw to life and worked around the hearty trunk to "top" the tree. When he was almost through the tree he climbed down and we once again heaved with the rope to pull the top off the tree. It came crashing down, partially buried in the lawn. Coconut trees are very, very, verrrryyyyy heavy!

A rope was tied to the top of the remaining trunk. We gathered just outside the fence area, ready to pull the tree safely away from the house. Sputtering with a vicious appetite to devour wood, the chain saw was applied to the base of the trunk.

We heaved, our muscles bulged, the women were impressed, the chain saw cut, things were going just as I had planned. Did I fail to mention this was all my plan? Yes, I was the successful engineer planning the project all by myself.

The tree began to tilt, the chain saw dug deeper into the watery pulp, success was imminent. My moment of glory was at hand. In slow motion the tree began to fall away from the house under the insistent tug of the rope.

As the tree began its plummet to earth my heart soared in pride. My planning was perfect. Then, in even slower motion, I realized I missed one small, very small but very important, point. The tree was going to clear the house and that was good. Unfortunately, it was headed directly toward the front fence.

Squeezing my eyes almost shut, scrunching up my shoulders, there was nothing left to do but wait the pending destruction of my fence. *Sproing . . .the tree toppled, the fence bent, the job was done. I just stood and stared. Not at the successfully fallen tree but the big dent in my front fence.

I planned perfectly. I gave careful directions. My friends followed my advice. Unfortunately, it was only my advice and I missed a very important point. A point which would remind me of my limitation every time I walked out the front door of our home and eyed the bent condition of the front fence.

Solomon was a wise man when he wrote about multiple counselors. There's a lot to be said about asking for advice. The problem with asking for advice is we don't like to admit we don't know something. Solomon understood this point as well.

When we don't ask advice, whether from God or our colleagues, our plans might fail. When we seek advice, when we seek the Lord's direction, our plans are established. There is success.

Over the years I've learned the wonderful advantage of good counselors, co-workers and expert advice. I still launch out on my own occasionally and usually fall flat on my face.

It's good to seek advice, direction, and help from God and others. When we combine God's revelation in our life and his revelation to us through others we'll succeed. A missionary once pointed out that any project started by God will never fail but many projects started by man for God lie in dust. That is one counselor I need to seek every time, especially if something might be damaged like my poor fence.

Giving Directions

He said to them, "To you is given the mystery of the Kingdom of God, but to those who are outside, all things are done in parables, that 'seeing they may see, and not perceive; and hearing they may hear, and not understand; lest perhaps they should turn again, and their sins should be forgiven them'"
(Mark 4:11 12 WEB)

Twice I was privileged to visit the island nation of Sri Lanka. Each time I worked with computer systems. I provided installation and training for the new System Administrator. The system was integrated in our global networking. While the computer work was interesting what I remember most were some of the side trips and, on the second trip, my arrival at the airport.

My first trip was routine. I arrived, went through immigration and customs, then met my colleagues outside the security area. No problem. About a year later I returned to Sri Lanka to move the system to a new office and upgrade some software. Normal arrangements were made including my arrival time and date. The plane arrived at the airport, I went through immigration and customs and exited to the waiting area outside of security.

The place was full of busy people coming and going with all the routine hustle and bustle of an airport. I'd seen this many times before. However, after about twenty minutes I found myself alone in the large arrivals room. The only other folks were employees waiting for customers in the different vendor windows. No sign of my colleagues or friends, no notes, no messages, just a big empty room and me. I figured they were delayed by traffic so I waited another twenty minutes.

I started to worry someone made an error with the dates and times. I walked up to one of the car rental booths and was inundated by a long speech about their cars in a language I didn't understand. Just before I signed my life away he realized I wasn't there to rent a car. His speech, unintelligible as it was to me, was very impressive. I think he could have sold snow cones to Eskimos. I put down the pen as the salesman looked on with a disappointed frown. I pointed to the telephone.

Using international sign language, I'm an expert at pointing, jumping up and down, and making a fool out of myself until I'm understood. I signaled I wanted to use the telephone. No way, if I wanted to make a call it was going to cost me. I think he wanted some compensation for not renting a car.

I exchanged some money, at an exorbitant rate, to the local currency. It was almost midnight and the salesman was ready to leave and go home. With a few coins I called the number of a colleague and prayed someone would be home. A sleepy voice answered the telephone. I identified myself and asked if someone was coming to meet me.

She was suddenly awake. Her husband and another missionary drove to the airport over three hours ago and should be waiting. I let her know I was the only one left in the airport waiting room and the vendors were anxious to see this foreigner depart so they could close shop.

"Did you take the blue bus?" she asked as if it was a routine question.

"What blue bus?" I replied. I felt as if I just stepped onto another planet in the conversation.

"You know, the one they told you about in the e mail."

"I didn't receive any instructions in e-mail about the airport or a blue bus."

"How about a fax?"

"No fax."

"Uh-oh . . . ." she responded and there was a short silence. "You need to take the blue bus to the pickup area. Go out the front door, with your bags, and walk the quarter mile to the curb where the shuttle bus will take you to the pickup area, which is about five miles from the airport."

It seems that the security issues at the airport had changed with the increase in bombs around the capital city. No one picking up or dropping off passengers was permitted within five miles of the actual terminal. There were concrete barricades between the road and the building to prevent suicide bombers from driving trucks loaded with explosives into the crowded terminal.

With the new information in hand I was the last passenger on the last bus to the pickup area. Five more minutes and I would've been stranded at the airport until the morning bus run eight hours later. Praise the Lord for the great timing of the telephone call and the patience of my fellow missionaries to wait for their unprepared visitor to arrive at the right place.

When Paul started going on his missionary trips he was excited about God's mystery. He would arrive in a new town and his message was as new and revelatory as discovering I needed to find a blue bus. My blue bus took me to a gravel parking lot and the comfort of friends and colleagues. God's mystery takes us to His kingdom and the comfort of our savior for eternity.

I was overjoyed to discover the bus was still there to take me on my way to safety. I remembered a greater joy. I discovered the revelation of God's mystery and my travel plans were both laid out for me in Heaven and eternity. Sometimes we forget to tell someone how to find the bus. Other times we forget to tell them how to discover God's mystery and the Gospel of salvation. In both cases we leave someone stranded.

Next time someone asks directions, or travels to meet us, maybe we should consider what directions they need; along with the bus route they need to know the narrow road to eternity. I pray I don't forget to include God's mystery revealed with any travel instructions.

Swiss Army Ax

Let us therefore draw near with boldness to the throne of grace, that we may receive mercy, and may find grace for help in time of need. (Hebrews 4:16 WEB)

I have mixed feelings about weddings. Not really about my wedding but about attending other people's weddings. They are usually lovely affairs, the food is good and the pastor seldom preaches a long sermon. With the focus on the bride and groom people are happy when weddings start and the celebration begins.

One furlough we were invited to the wedding of a short-term missionary and a former Navy man. We knew the two young people from their time on Guam. The wedding was held in Pittsburgh, Pennsylvania. Having never visited this city of steel we thought it would be fun to see the city and enjoy the celebration with our two friends.

We drove along the Pennsylvania turnpike, entered the city of Three Rivers Stadium and located our accommodations at a wonderful Red Roof Inn. The groom's parents and other members of the wedding party enjoyed the same hotel. We found our friends and looked forward to the ceremony.

On Friday evening I took Joel to a baseball game. Guam doesn't have a professional team so this was a new and exciting experience. The closest Guam came was Little League. Hot dogs from the roaming vendors, a warm night, cold drinks and a good scoring game made the evening memorable.

Close to midnight we returned to the hotel. Beth, baby Evan and I were in one room. Ellice, Joel and James were in another room. They weren't adjoining rooms so all visitation involved going outside to get between the rooms. The game was good, the night was warm and we all looked forward to a good night's sleep.

The next morning, we arose and began preparations for the wedding. Beth and Ellice were participating in the wedding with silk dresses and matching shoes. I called the room next door to ensure Ellice, Joel and James were starting to get ready while Beth and I prepared in our room. They were awake, excited and getting ready for the big event.

Finally, I stepped out our door to go next door and help our children with their final preparations. I knocked on the door, Ellice peeked from behind the curtains and then I heard her working with the lock and door knob. I tried the door and it was still locked. Knocking on the window I told Ellice to turn the knob to unlock the door. I heard the movement of the knob and tried the door again; it was still locked.

It was obvious the dead bolt was dead. Turn, turn, and turn again; Ellice was unable, even with Joel's expert assistance, to unlock the dead bolt. Beth

192

came from our room and tried to get in the children's room. No good - our children were locked in a hotel room with a broken door.

I went to the hotel office and explained the situation to the attendant and then returned to the broken door to try and find a solution. I explained to Ellice and Joel in a loud voice through the window the hotel was working on the problem and should fix it soon.

Just as I finished shouting through the window the young lady from the office arrived and said, "I called the maintenance man and he will come as soon as he can."

"How long will that take?" I asked as a concerned parent with three small children locked in a hotel room.

"At least an hour or more," she replied sheepishly.

I looked at my watch, remembered the time of the wedding and replied, "That won't work. Our children are locked in the room and the wedding starts in less than an hour so they need to get out."

The young lady looked at me helplessly.

"What will it be?" I asked her.

"What do you mean?" she queried, looking uncertain.

"The window or the door lock?" I responded.

"Huh," she replied and her eyes opened wide as she understood my question.

"I can either smash in the window or break the lock on the door to get them out. Which do you prefer?" I gave her a few seconds to consider the options.

"I don't know," she answered, looking around for unfound help.

"OK, it's the lock then," I replied and whipped my Swiss Army Knife from my pocket. I went to work on the lock with minimal results and started to reconsider the window option.

Suddenly, the groom's father walked up and asked about the problem. I explained the situation and he walked off around the corner. I continued to work, ineffectively, on the door lock with my little knife.

After a couple minutes the groom's father returned carrying a fire ax from the hallway. "Let me give it a try," he said and positioned the ax near the door lock.

Wham, wham, wham, he smashed at the locking mechanism until the outer cover came loose. That was just the ticket. Again wielding my Swiss Army Knife, I built upon the work of the Swiss Army Ax to remove the lock cover, poke into the lock mechanism and release the lock and free our children.

It was a joyous reunion, perfect timing for the wedding and the start of a fun day. By the time we returned to the room the door was repaired and the next morning held no more surprises.

Unexpected problems come into our lives at the most unusual times. In Psalm 46 we are reminded that God provides us help in the present when troubles come. Sometimes that help comes from the everyday people God places in our lives. The groom's father was a present help in time of trouble. He was God's instrument that morning.

It's times like this when I stop and think of the help God has provided throughout my life and ministry. The times are beyond counting and a fountain of blessing to my soul. God wields his Swiss Army Angel, Knife, Ax or whatever tool is necessary to care for His children. We need to stop and thank those folks God uses in our life to provide present help in times of trouble. Who knows, maybe we will be God's Swiss Army Angel in someone else's time of trouble.

Searching for Magnum P.I.

The heavens declare the glory of God. The expanse shows his handiwork.
(Psalms 19:1 WEB)

At the end of our first furlough we were tired and ready to return to the mission field for some needed rest. All the travel, the speaking engagements, the birth of our son James, and the pressures of raising support took their toll. Whatever pressure there was on the mission field, it was nothing compared to the pressure of furlough and being constantly on display from house to house and church to church.

As we prepared our bags, shipped our container, and closed our US affairs, we looked forward to heading back to our home on Guam. In the midst of preparation we received a note from the home office. We had received a gift. Someone, who we were never able to identify, provided funds for us to spend two days in Hawaii on our way back to Guam so we could rest and relax.

We were amazed! This was an unexpected joy. We completed our packing, spent a week visiting my parents and headed west to the romantic island. Unfortunately, I opened a hot radiator and received first degree burns to my arm three days before our flight. Ellice, while playing in the park, fell from a jungle gym, broke her arm and sported a nice white cast two days before our flight.

Bandaged, wearing a cast and seeking safety we sat back on the plane and looked forward to seeing a bit of Oahu Island. The flight was uneventful. We arrived, checked our extra bags into a storage facility at the airport and rented a car for two days of exploration.

Most people when they visit Hawaii spend a lot of time at the beach. With a six-month-old baby, Daddy in bandages, and a daughter in a cast, this was not one of our options. We could see the beach beckoning from our hotel room. A walk along the beach was as close as we would come during this visit.

So, in the interest of having fun we started a search. The television program "Magnum P.I." was popular at the time so we decided to tour the island and look for the mansion used in filming the show. We've spend a lot of time on holidays looking for bits and pieces of shows or movies we've watched.

In the morning we piled into the car, squeezed our bags in the trunk and headed around the island. Literally, we drove around the shore road of the island. Each little neighborhood was the chance to diverge from the beaten path in search for the ever-elusive Magnum Mansion.

We stopped by Diamond Head and went inside the dormant volcanic funnel. We watched paragliders gracefully sail from the cliffs on the eastern shore. Pineapple fields were an interesting and new sight. Toward the center of the island we were fascinated with the rugged mountains, lush vegetation, and beautiful waterfalls. There were surfers anywhere a wave was present. The island was teeming with life and vacationers.

In all our driving we eventually forgot our quest and never found the television mansion. On the contrary we discovered some of the wonders of God's magnificent creation on a small piece of rock in the middle of the ocean. From the pineapple-filled plains to the tropical forest covered mountains God's attention to details was evident.

Even though man created beautiful and ugly buildings and cities in the midst of the beauty, the beauty stood out none the less. We were searching for the imaginary in the midst of reality. It wasn't the glamour of a world-famous vacation spot, the marvel of surfer dudes riding the curl, or the finding of a television set that caught our attention that day.

That day on a small island we were impressed once more at God's creation. God's glory was declared by the beauty of this small bump in the midst of the mighty ocean. I'm amazed. Some folks can look at the world around, see the minute details of creation, the beauty of carefully sculptured mountains or the fine weaving of a leaf and not see God at work.

Sometimes, I get so caught up trying to find something man created that I miss the bigger picture. At those times I'm likely to miss the obvious things around me. Burned arms and broken wings forced us to slow down, use our eyes to see, enjoy, and be impressed by God's work.

By awesome deeds of righteousness, you answer us, God of our salvation. You who are the hope of all the ends of the earth, Of those who are far away on the sea; Who by his power forms the mountains, Having armed yourself with strength; Who stills the roaring of the seas, The roaring of their waves, And the turmoil of the nations. They also who dwell in faraway places are afraid at your wonders. You call the morning's dawn and the evening with songs of joy. You visit the earth, and water it. You greatly enrich it. The river of God is full of water. You provide them grain, for so you have ordained it. You drench its furrows. You level its ridges. You soften it with showers. You bless it with a crop. You crown the year with your bounty. Your carts overflow with abundance. The wilderness grasslands overflow. The hills are clothed with gladness. The pastures are covered with flocks. The valleys also are clothed with grain. They shout for joy! They also sing. (Psalms 65:5 13 WEB)

Out with the Old, in with the New

Therefore if anyone is in Christ, he is a new creation. The old things have passed away. Behold, all things have become new. (2 Corinthians 5:17 WEB)

One of the hallmarks of a good engineer is his ability to keep a piece of equipment running forever! Well, at least as long as the engineer thinks it's worth fixing. Unlike modern devices, such as personal computers, CD Players, DVD players, etc., many pieces of radio equipment have operated for thirty, forty or fifty years.

With the simplicity of the earlier designs it was easier to determine which part was faulty. As the years wore by the problem became finding spare parts. This was a growing problem for the AM station on Guam. KTWG sported a classic transmitter.

Even in the harsh island conditions the transmitter usually operated well. Occasionally a component would fail, usually the few modern solid-state parts, be replaced and the programs would again bless the people on the island. Time marched on, parts became harder to find, and repairs became more frequent until one dark night when it gave up.

After working on the transmitter for a couple of days the prognosis was dark. Finally, I declared it dead, permanently dead. The costs for the necessary parts, even if they were available, were more than the value of the transmitter. Our station went dark. Thankfully it would only be dark for a little while.

After a shuffle of funds and communication with a transmitter manufacturer, the process was underway for the emergency purchase of a replacement transmitter. It would take at least two weeks to ship the unit to the island.

During the two weeks we worked to remove the old transmitter from its concrete bunker under the parking lot. When it was originally installed the walls were not in place so it was easy. Removing it was a bit more difficult.

Heavy components were removed from the chassis. Environmentally hazardous material was transported to the proper disposal authorities. With lots of huffing and puffing, pushing and shoving, twisting and turning the remaining skeleton was removed from the building.

The room was cleared, cables were prepared, wiring was updated and we waited for the new transmitter to arrive. It was to be a modern solid-state wonder! No more old tubes to replace, no more large oil transformers. This was a miracle of technology coming to our little island.

The unit arrived and we went to work to get it into the building. It was smaller than the old transmitter but still a tight fit through the doorway. It took more huffing, puffing, pushing and shoving to get the unit into the building.

It was finally in place. The muscle men of the mission went about their normal routines while the engineers went to work connecting all the wires, gadgets and controls. It was a big job and we were in a hurry. We wanted to be back on the air!

Rich, Ray and I poked, prodded, tested, tweaked and worked through the night to finish the project. Finally, in the early hours of the morning, we were ready to begin.

I strolled across the parking lot to the main building. The three of us climbed the stairs to the main studio room. We looked at each other, smiled and pressed the button.

Lights flickered, meters moved, our hearts skipped a beat and we were back on the air. I sat down at the control console, played a station's ID then selected my favorite song and pressed "play."

Our work was rewarded as we heard music coming from the receiver. It was a long road and lots of work to hear those sweet sounds wafting over the airwaves once more. We smiled, gave a toast with our coffee cups and called the morning operator to return to work.

I'm reminded of a song titled "New Lives for Old." It is a great song about how change is brought about in us when Christ becomes Lord of our lives. We don't need new parts; we are a new creation, top to bottom.

The old transmitter could never be fixed; it was filled with old, rotting and dead components. Our life without Christ is not fixed at salvation. It, too, is filled with old rotting components of the sinful nature. Instead, Christ gives us a new life. We are a new creation. We are ready to be put into service.

Too many times we try to fix the old when it is just not worth fixing. Sometimes we keep the old parts and try to fit them into the new man. This doesn't work any better than putting an old tube in a new solid-state transmitter.

It's time I stopped stockpiling my old parts and started paying attention to the new man Christ has created. Only then can I discover how He will use me to broadcast His message of salvation to those around me. Thank God we are not repaired but NEW!

Just Hanging Around

...but those who wait for Yahweh shall renew their strength; they shall mount up with wings as eagles; they shall run, and not be weary; they shall walk, and not faint. (Isaiah 40:31 WEB)

When Beth and I were newlyweds we loved to visit new places during weekends and holidays. Even after forty plus years we enjoy visiting a new spot and experiencing a new adventure. One Saturday, right after we were married, we visited Natural Bridge State Park in Eastern Kentucky.

These bridges are arches of stone carved out by the wind and rain over centuries. They are staggering in size and breathtaking in their natural beauty. In the course of our visit we hiked to the top. People stood about the edges, without guard rails, and enjoyed the view.

I centered myself on the land bridge, glanced about frantically, and looked for a quick excuse to get off. I don't like heights. Beth thought it was funny as she skipped about and enjoyed the various views with the other tourists. My heart leaped in fear when anyone, especially my dear wife, stepped near the precipice of death. We didn't stay on top very long.

Although I don't like heights, I overcame my fear on occasion. Sometimes it was because of the need and other times because of the dare. In high school I worked one summer in Colorado for Young Life. On a free day we climbed the face of Silver Cliff. About half way up I made the mistake of looking down. I froze where I was. It took a lot of will power, and coaxing from my friends, to move onward and reach the top. At the precipice I discovered a nice trail down the backside and wondered why we risked our lives on the rock face. But I could say I did it!

When I was young, I remember reading about heights in Isaiah. The prophet spoke about soaring like an eagle. All I could think of was the height above the ground and the possibility of falling, hard, to the earth. I was leaning on my own understanding, not the Lord's.

The Lord often calls us to stretch our limits as missionaries. With antennas reaching three hundred feet into the corrosive tropical sky there was always a need for maintenance. One day the Lord called me to stretch my trust in Him by helping with tower work.

I studied the bosons' chair. It was carefully cabled to the pulley at the top of the tower and anchored back on the ground by a jeep. I shook my head at the thought of swinging so high in the breeze. What was I thinking? In a moment of temporary insanity, I actually volunteered to help with the work. I suppose I didn't dare say no. Oh the terrors inflicted by a false sense of self pride!

Strapped and buckled with a hard hat in place, I was slowly hoisted up the side of the tower to help apply primer to the structure. We were repainting the eight masts, a long and laborious manual job.

Once aloft, casting sound reason to the wind, I again looked down. Whoa! Beneath my feet was air. My faith in the strength of the rope was increasing by each foot I rose above the ground. As my heart slowed to a normal pace I began to enjoy the bird's eye view of the island.

What looked confusing on the ground took on the appearance of order from a different perspective. During breaks from slopping primer on the metal surfaces, I studied the shoreline, the neighboring island of Cocos, and even the construction of the curtain antenna.

In the years that followed I again took more opportunities to climb into the bosons' seat and help with the necessary repair or maintenance. There was freedom in hanging high above the ground. There was freedom in conquering a long-time fear. I am still afraid of heights and continue to be reticent to be in high places but the Lord provided strength to teach me something new each time I rose above the solid ground.

As a Christian I am often rooted deep in my perspective of the world, my life and those around me. Sometimes the Lord pushes me to new heights so I learn to view the world and those around me with a new perspective.

At times fear binds me. It's then God places a new challenge, a new opportunity in my path to teach me to trust in Him. Once I allow God to overcome my fear I can see things from a new and better perspective. It's good to trust in the Lord and not rely on our own understanding. I'm ready to soar high above the earth like an eagle with God's hand. Are your ready to soar?

Why I Hate to Repair Cars

...being confident of this very thing, that he who began a good work in you will complete it until the day of Jesus Christ. (Philippians 1:6 WEB)

I love my children. I always have. I always will. However, they do, at times, strike fear into my heart. Teaching them to drive was one of those times. Don't get me wrong, they are all, so far, good drivers and I trust them. I even let them drive my car un-chaperoned. When they came back from a night out with friends, I resisted the urge to run outside and do a visual inspection for scratches or smudges. Then again, my cars are usually very old and well-worn so finding minor damage is difficult.

When Ellice was in high school she survived my driving lessons and expert parallel parking tips. She passed her test, smiled for the camera and received her first driving license. She was proud as could be.

It wasn't long before the urge to own her own car took over and she started saving her pennies and looking here and there for something cheap, less than $1000, reliable and cool-looking. The Lord prepared the way. A neighbor she knew from one of her baby-sitting jobs was ready to sell a car, cheap.

Ellice discussed the issue and had me come to make a manly inspection. I kicked the tires, looked through the windows and even opened the hood to ensure there was an engine inside. To convince the sellers I was a car expert I started the car and revved up the engine. Yep, it was a car and the motor ran. That was the extent of my expertise.

She bought the car and beamed with pride. Her first set of wheels. Freedom was within the grasp of her key chain and the world was before her. After a few months my nerves calmed down when she would roar off to meet friends or attend a play practice.

A few days after the purchase, we discovered the car had cooling problems, a major issue in the tropics. The original owners informed us they replaced the radiator, the hoses and even the blower without a resolution to the problem. On level ground things were OK. However, any uphill climb and the temperature gauge would usually rise faster than the hill. It was such a problem they reduced the price of the car to almost nothing just to get it out of their carport.

I looked at the radiator, the hoses and the fan, everything was where it should be and no water leaks were visible. It didn't make sense. If the auto shop couldn't fix this what made me think I could fix it? My engineering mindset just wouldn't let this go. Engineers can fix anything!

I kept looking, scratching my head and saying "hmm" now and again as if some revelation was passing through my head. Joel was my faithful assistant, as clueless as I was. Finally, I leaned over the radiator and looked into the engine compartment while Joel started the motor. Suddenly, like a revelation, an idea came into my head.

I signaled for Joel to stop the engine. When it was quiet I walked into the house and returned with a small piece of scrap paper. Joel looked at me funny but enjoyed sitting behind the wheel with keys in his hand so he said nothing. I signaled to start the engine once more.

Tearing the corner from the piece of paper I dropped it into the engine compartment. *Whoosh*, it disappeared into the radiator fan. I dropped another piece of paper, which quickly was sucked into the radiator fan. The fan was working. The problem was solved. The fan was blowing the wrong direction!

Joel turned off the engine and I had him crawl under the front of the car. Following my instructions, he located the wiring to the fan, reversed the wires and we did another scientific paper dropping test. This time the paper was blown back onto the engine. A short drive, up the nearby hill, proved the problem was solved and Ellice no longer experienced overheating of her car.

A couple weeks later we received a call from Ellice. The car had died. It wouldn't start. I drove out and with the help of friends we towed it back to the house. I called on another friend who really did know about cars. He told me the timing belt was broken, all the valves were bent and needed to be replaced.

Ordering parts from the USA, reading manuals on car repair, and asking assistance from anyone with two hands, I embarked on the valve replacement and engine rebuilding. Two months later with bruised knuckles, grease covered clothes and lots of assistance from my neighbors, we had the car going once more.

It started, but it didn't run well. It ran rough. I looked through the books, tried this and that but nothing helped. Finally, I asked my mechanic friend for some help. He was great for advice and always willing to help anyone who at least put some effort into their own work first.

He poked, prodded and took a test drive. Then he reached through the bundle of hoses and cables and pushed a loose hose onto a connector. Now things ran perfectly. I was happy, my friend was happy and my daughter was delighted.

The car worked so well we drove it to church a couple weeks later. Then the noise started. I attempted to get the car home but it died along the way. The timing belt had come lose and bent all the valves again! This time it was caused by not tightening one bolt just right.

We sold the car, as is, to some folks desperate to fix up anything to drive. Ellice went off to college. A year later the police called about an abandoned car in my name. The folks who bought the car had fixed it, driven it and abandoned it when the tag expired without transferring the title from my name.

I traded the car to the tow yard to cover the storage fees which were due. They weren't sure at first but figured they could sell it and come out ahead.

They did. I didn't want to see the car again. A lot of time and work went into fixing the car but in the end all our fixes turned out to be temporary.

When I fix things in my life they don't stay fixed for long. I am glad to know God is a better mechanic than I am. When it comes to working on my life, what He fixes He fixes for good! I'm looking forward to eternity. No car repairs, no lingering cancer, all our tears will be wiped away. The master mechanic will complete the work He has started in me, permanently, for eternity!

My First Castle

For he shall not often reflect on the days of his life; because God occupies him with the joy of his heart. (Ecclesiastes 5:20 WEB)

Growing up in the USA I enjoyed reading about foreign lands. In particular I was fascinated with Europe and castles. Knights, dragons, kings, queens and even serfs garnered my interest and curiosity. However, I never figured I would never have a chance to visit, much less live in, Europe. I was wrong. My first experience in Europe was the result of a test run to meet my prospective new supervisor and consider a transfer from Guam to the continent.

After thirteen years in the tropics the thought of spending three weeks in the cold north brought shivers to my heart. I was scheduled to fly to Vienna and from there help with an installation project in Central Asia. The staff in Austria told me winter was arriving so I might need warm clothes.

I purchased some warm boots from Wal-Mart, and dug through my closet for long sleeved shirts and a jacket. None were found. I brought my plight to my colleagues. Fortunately, a recent arrival on the island offered his jacket to keep me warm and another offered a couple long sleeved shirts.

A hodgepodge of clothes filled my suitcase as I headed through the USA to Europe for a new experience. Dropped into Austria, knowing only two words of German, I was on my own the first day to forage for food and get my bearings. Since I arrived on Saturday and everything closed at noon I had plenty of time to wander through the little town of Perchtoldsdorf.

Wandering by a 14th century church and tower, from the time of a Turkish invasion, and visiting the local park was relaxing. I was too uncertain to venture into the local restaurants. Without an understanding of food names, numbers or even civil greetings I kept to myself and ate some pretzels from a local shop.

The next day a couple from the mission picked me up at the hotel and took me to church. I was treated to an English church service. Lunch in their apartment was followed by another walk about Perchtoldsdorf.

The streets, buildings and sights were something right out of a history book or a travel documentary. Everything looked old. Everything was old! In fact, most of the impressive structures dated back before the US was even a fledgling colony of England.

Next, we drove a few kilometers to the area of Mödling. Winding our way on the edge of town, we entered a park surrounding my first castle. There before my eyes was a dream come true. It was my first sight of Liechtenstein Castle.

It was spectacular! Built on top of a rock outcropping and rising majestically, it sported turrets, stone balconies and guard towers. My imagination ran wild. I never thought I would visit anything like this in my life, much less look forward to living nearby.

I walked about the walls, touching them now and again to be sure it wasn't a dream. Eric thought I was a bit touched myself. Since it was late in the year the castle was closed to visitors. After moving to Austria, I learned most castles were closed from November until Easter because of the winter season. But that day it didn't matter because the castle was there, I could touch it, I could conjure up tales of knights, ladies and battles. I could stand and look out over the valley below as many others did years before I arrived.

From the base of the castle we had a beautiful view of the Vienna valley. Later, after we moved to an apartment nearby, I would enter the castle, climb to the highest turret and enjoy an even larger view of the plains to the east and the Vienna Woods to the west.

My collection of photos of the castle has grown over the years. My wife and I affectionately refer to it as "our" castle. Living only five minutes away from "our" castle, we enjoy taking our guests for a visit. Over the years we've visited many castles in Austria and surrounding countries.

Each time I visit a new castle I am again amazed at the uniqueness of the individual structures. Reading the history of the rulers, owners, and peasants fascinates me with each new castle. Each new story reveals some way these magnificent structures played a part in my life by shaping history.

Unfortunately, I can't say the same eagerness always existed when I opened the word of God. It should have. Each biblical visit revealed some new facet of God and His work in my life. Every page opened new visions of eternity and God's grace. When I take time to look, consider and appreciate God's revelation, I am always amazed.

Now, when I read of God's care and interaction with His creation, if I am tempted to rush to get through with the passage I stop and think. What is new, what is fascinating, how does it relate to my life or those I know personally or the world in general? Then as God speaks through the word I am encouraged, strengthened and brought closer to the throne of grace.

Maybe we all need to visit a castle or two, or some other place which fascinates us and encourages our imagination. Then, our minds can reflect on the reality of God's word and the work of the Spirit in our lives today.

Preaching in Central Asia

For as the rain comes down and the snow from the sky, and doesn't return there, but waters the earth, and makes it bring forth and bud, and gives seed to the sower and bread to the eater; so shall my word be that goes forth out of my mouth: it shall not return to me void, but it shall accomplish that which I please, and it shall prosper in the thing I sent it to do. (Isaiah 55:10 11 WEB)

When Beth and I sought the Lord's direction for our life we were amazed to be led into missionary work. I was working as an engineer. Wires, buttons and equipment filled my working day. We thought God would use us in preaching and teaching. I'm glad God goes by His understanding and not mine.

Because God called us to work in a technical missionary ministry, opportunities opened to visit and work in many countries around the world. One year in the late fall I flew from the tropical sea level warmth of Guam to the mile-high cold of Central Asia. I borrowed coats, sweaters, thick socks and anything to keep warm. For a week the team worked on satellite downlinks and transmitters and lived in an unheated house on a beautiful and cold lake.

At night I wore my coat over my clothes and climbed into an insulated winter sleeping bag carefully placed under at least three blankets. An electric heater was strategically located on either side of the bed to help me survive the cold nights.

On the weekend for a break, we visited the capital city. Sunday was a unique and very enjoyable day. We started the day attending the local church. We sat on the front row. A local helper attempted to translate from the row behind us. Since she was not a Christian it was a struggle for her to translate some of the terms and concepts she was hearing. It was a good time for her to hear the Gospel message presented by the first speaker. The music was delightful and the people sang with the fullness of their hearts.

The church was located in an old cinema which formerly showed pornographic films, and seated about 500 people. Unexpectedly, we discovered we were part of the morning message. We were whisked up to the platform. One look over the sea of faces in the dimly lit room was enough to break your heart.

In this city of used to have and want to have again, there was little for encouragement. Parks abounded throughout the city and were in disarray with many abandoned. People lived from day to day in houses which had water in the evening and power in the day light hours. The only heat was provided by small electric heaters or hot plates. It was a constant struggle just to survive.

In the front row alone were the worn old faces of the elderly, the timid faces of the children and the curious and questioning faces of the young adults.

These were the faces you saw in the side streets of a movie like "Dr. Zhivago." Each woman wore a shawl over her head and lifted her eyes toward Heaven as they sang praises to God. The men stood to give way to the older women or sat with their spouses. The place was packed. It was standing room only.

The reception was overwhelming. Here in this different land with little to make life bearable were people praising the Lord for His love and care. We saw a warmth on the faces and a desire for close fellowship was evident despite the language barrier.

Then without warning I was asked to share with the church. I thought to myself, I have no common ground with these people. How can I relate to them? I don't understand their life, their country or their culture. What I knew, what they might be seeking, was the grace of God. So I shared the only thing I knew we might have in common. I shared the simple Gospel message. The people listened quietly to the translation.

I finished speaking and sat down. The pastor walked over and said, "You cannot sit down. You are not finished. You need to give an altar call."

I was there as an engineer, I thought, not in any pastoral role; this was not in my job description! What did I know about altar calls? I stood and hesitantly walked to the podium and presented the opportunity for seekers to come forward.

I was amazed as the platform was flooded. Hearts sought escape from spiritual darkness. It was an amazing time. I could see the Lord working throughout the congregation. The presence of the Spirit was evident.

As we departed a little later in the service the pastor called for new believers to come forward. There were a number of others headed for the front of the auditorium as we departed the building. Praise the Lord for such a valiant group of believers seeking to serve Him each day in a land opposed to God and their faith in God.

We returned to the cold house on the lake but my heart remained in that dilapidated old theater where God's Spirit was moving. I couldn't believe it. God was using me, an engineer, to proclaim a message of salvation. The Holy Spirit was moving in that congregation and I was a useful tool in God's hand.

It's easy to leave the Gospel message to those trained as evangelists and preachers. They know the right words, phrases and techniques to touch people's hearts. We may be great engineers, cooks, housewives but preaching is the work of preachers. At least I used to think that.

I realize again, it isn't the flowers in our speech or our linguistic abilities. It is the power of God's word which reaches into people's hearts for eternity. God's word does not return void. We need to be sure it is shared, even when we don't feel qualified, and let God accomplish His purposes.

The Magic Flute

See the birds of the sky, that they don't sow, neither do they reap, nor gather into barns. Your heavenly Father feeds them. Aren't you of much more value than they? (Matthew 6:26 WEB)

After many discussions with Beth about going to the opera, I finally agreed. My reticent attitude hinged not on opera but on attending via the "standing room only" option. I don't usually jump at the opportunity to stand for five or six hours, but it is cheaper.

The day of the opera, I enjoyed the trip on public transport from our home in the country into the city. Eventually I met Beth, and a friend who worked at the school, outside the Vienna State Opera House. We entered a long hall, not quite the first in line, and sat on the floor. On the floor you say! Oh, yes, we had a two hour wait in line to be almost first in line to purchase standing room only tickets. It's quite the process. Careful planning was required to ensure you had a great piece of land for your feet and hindquarters.

First, you arrived three hours prior to the start time of the opera. You sat on the floor, read books, played cards, talked, slept, whatever passed the time and distracted your mind from that awful pain that developed from sitting on a hard floor for so long. During the wait the opera house stationed a brute force along the hallway to be sure no one tried to cut to the front of the line. Even if your friends were up front you had to stay where you were or be escorted to the end of the line. On this particular evening, one of our guards looked like Al Jolson, little mustache included. The other gentleman looked like he was there when they built the opera house. He reminded me of Tim Conway, with his aged shuffle and thick glasses. He shuffled, but he was quick and you didn't dare try to jockey for a better position in line. Finally, about an hour before the performance, they opened the flood gates and allowed the waiting line to trickle through to the ticket window.

Once through the first set of doors, another garrison of uniformed opera thugs ensured you remained in an orderly line to purchase your cheap tickets. You could pay 3.50 Euro to stand on the main floor area just under the Emperor's Box, or be real cheap and pay 2.00 Euro to stand on the fourth floor with the pigeons and albatrosses. As a generous husband and big spender, I purchased the 3.50 Euro tickets and we quickly moved to another line.

There were two lines for the main floor and people jogged back and forth, hoping for a better position in line. Fortunately, the diminutive female opera police ensured everyone went to the end of whichever line they finally selected. About forty-five minutes before the performance the flood gates were opened and additional security was installed to be sure everyone walked up the stairs in pairs to the standing place. We were in the third row on the right side.

This was a great place. We were just above the main floor and just below the best box in the house, the Emperor's Box. Carefully tying our scarves to the banister in front of our claimed space we were then free to find the WC (a.k.a. toilet) or sit on the floor in anticipation of a world-renowned performance. From our locale we had Austrians to the left, Mexicans behind, French in front and Americans alongside the French. I was at the end so I could lean against the wall. Praise the Lord for small favors.

We were there to watch The Magic Flute by Mozart. It was the first opera written in German and immensely popular around the world. I had been a fan of this opera for years but never enjoyed a live performance. Since we attended a German opera in a German-speaking opera house the entire performance was in German. Go figure!

To overcome the language difficulties, since it is more difficult to understand a foreign language being sung versus spoken, the opera house was very ingenious. At each seat or standing position was a small display screen. The screen provided, in German or English, the text of the songs and dialog as the opera unfolded. Since I'm not too short, and the screen was somewhere in my midsection, I was constantly looking up then down then up then down to match the activity with the text. It was fun! Really! I might have looked ridiculous bobbing my head up and down like a dog in the back window of a car, but I was glad I went.

Don't tell Beth or she will want to go to all the operas! About two and a half hours into the performance my legs were starting to scream for a place to sit. With endurance and will, not to mention leaning on the rail, bumping the people in front and behind me, plus a little hip-hop dance from foot to foot I made it to the end, including the six times the cast came out for applause. It was late, we were tired, hungry, and ready to sit anywhere!

Exiting the opera house, we crossed under the street to Merado's Restaurant for some dinner. I don't usually eat at 10:20 pm but with no lunch or dinner I was ready for food, drink and the unimaginable comfort of sitting. (OK, I forgot to eat lunch and we missed dinner sitting on the marble floor waiting for standing tickets so it was my fault. I was trying for the sympathy vote here.)

After our meal we rode the subway, reached our car, drove home and walked in our front door as the local church bells chimed midnight. All in all, it was a great day; I was even willing to consider another opera, even standing. First, I would check for tickets which include a seat! For five years I had avoided the opera. It just didn't sound fun to stand for so many hours. When we finally went, I was glad I did.

The Lord wants me to trust Him and take a step in faith. I look at what I perceive the situation to be and keep my feet firmly planted. Then finally, sometimes after a long period of procrastination, I take that fateful step. It's then I discover the wonder of what God has in store. It's never what I imagined. It's always better!

Sometimes, even after long periods of procrastination, we need to put our feet into motion. We need to take that step of faith we know God has been prodding us to take, and discover the wonders of His grace and plan. Until we do, we will never hear the beautiful music He has orchestrated just for us.

When was the last time you visited the opera?

How is Your Salt Content?

Oh, taste and see that the LORD is good! Blessed is the man who takes refuge in him! (Psalms 34:8 ESV)

I'm a good southern boy. I grew up eating fried chicken, corn on the cob and other marvelous dishes which I can no longer enjoy. Occasionally, on furlough, I'll indulge my senses with a good southern meal. I then have to repent and go back on a strict diet to recover. But some things in life are worth the consequences.

A major ingredient in southern cooking, and other regional favorites, is salt. Small white grains of natural preservative and flavor enhancements are added throughout the preparation of a meal. If you do a quick query on the internet it will reveal that salt is a big subject with millions of hits.

Historically salt was used for seasoning, as a preservative, and for money. If your land contained a large salt deposit you were rich! The Salt Institute, yes there is such an organization, provides reams of information on the history and usefulness of salt.

In Salzburg, Austria, I visited a large salt mine with my boys, James and Evan. Donning white coveralls, we boarded a special train that took us deep into the mountain side. It was like sitting on an overgrown sausage rumbling down railroad tracks. We walked through tunnel after tunnel. The lights came on as we entered a section and went off behind us. When we went down to lower levels we used the wooden slides enjoyed by miners. We picked up some pretty good speed sliding deeper into the mountain.

It was the seemingly endless tunnels which fascinated us. When the lights went off, which they did after a warning for a demonstration, we saw nothing. Not even a faint outline was visible in the pitch black. We could touch our faces and still not see our hands. What is amazing is that people have spent their entire lives in and around these tunnels. For hundreds of years society was built around these mines as a source of personal and commercial salt extraction and thus wealth.

All I wanted to do was get out of the tunnels. I couldn't imagine the constant darkness and damp cold the workers must have endured. Working in a small space illuminated by a single oil lamp had to be difficult. All of this, just to add a little spice to someone's life.

Salt also plays an important function in the Middle East. When two people make a pact by eating salt together they are bound for life. Throughout the world salt is used for medicinal purposes as well. In Scripture we see babies bathed in salt (Ezekiel 16:4). The pools of Jericho were cleansed by salt (2 Kings 2:20). Even a wayward wife was turned into salt (Genesis 19:26).

Scripture tells us we are the salt of the earth. Jesus said, "Let me tell you why you are here. You're here to be salt seasoning that brings out the God flavors of this earth. If you lose your saltiness, how will people taste godliness? You've lost your usefulness and will end up in the garbage." (Matthew 5:13 MSG) When I remember my mother telling me, "It only takes a pinch," she was proclaiming a culinary and spiritual application.

A pinch of salt while cooking works its way through the dish, enhancing the flavor. It's important to understand how much salt is in a pinch. It's a very precise cooking measurement which is learned by intuition and experience. I learned about cooking and salt from my mother, which is probably why I'm not a good cook.

My mother would scoop up three fingers worth of salt and poise her hand over the dish. Then she would wiggle her fingers against one another as the grains of salt descended to the food until just the right amount was distributed. The rest was tossed away. Too little and the flavor would be bland. Too much and the dish would be too salty and totally ruined.

Watching people eat, and their use of salt, can be interesting. Some never use salt. Some douse their entire meal in salt before they even taste the food. Others apply so much salt that it is all they can taste. Each person has their own habits and ability to consume quantities of salt.

As a pinch of physical salt seasons a meal, a pinch of spiritual salt in the world works through lives, pointing people to the Savior. Evangelism is like pinching salt into the world. Think about the Salt Shaker Christian's impact on those around him.

There are the salt pinchers. They hold the message of salvation between their fingers and carefully apply it, grain by grain, until the right amount makes a person's heart open to God. Next there are the salt misers. These Christians keep their faith so close at hand it never falls from their fingers on the world around them. Their salt bottle stays closed and they are glad to know they have a plentiful supply, never realizing that it's wasted. Then there are those at the other extreme in the salt sprayers. These overzealous believers toss about their beliefs at, and on, everything around them. Although it may sound spiritual and good, often it smothers the other person and drives them away with a bad taste in their mouth.

The salt of the Gospel message needs to be pinched out, grain by grain, or teaspoon by teaspoon, to meet the situation at hand. It shouldn't be kept in the jar, or under a bushel (that sounds like a good parable), because then it's useless to anyone other than the one who owns it. It shouldn't be dumped by the bucketful either; that suffocates the person. Instead we need to look at each situation, each person, wiggle our fingers together and carefully distribute the right amount of spiritual salt.

I'm a missionary. I'm supposed to be distributing salt. But, how are my contents being distributed? As individuals, how do you season the world around you? Are you a pincher, or a miser, or a sprayer? Or, has your salt lost its flavor?

When salt is old and no longer salty it's a problem. "For everyone will be salted with fire, and every sacrifice will be seasoned with salt. Salt is good, but if the salt has lost its saltiness, with what will you season it? Have salt in yourselves, and be at peace with one another." (Mark 9:49 50 WEB)

Believers are grains of salt mined by the Lord to season the world with His love and grace. We are an offering (Ephesians 5:2) and offerings must have salt to be acceptable (Lev 2:13).

How salty are you today? Do you season the world with God's presence in your life? When people meet you are they encouraged with the enhanced flavor of God in your life? Or, do they find you just as bland as the rest of the world?

Let us taste of the Lord and see that He is good (Psalm 34:8). Let us think first so our speech is seasoned with salt (Col 4:6), just the right amount. Let us season the world with God's presence in our lives!

Best Laid Plans

The heart of man plans his way, but the LORD establishes his steps. (Proverbs 16:9 ESV)

Planning ministry trips can be a long process involving a number of staff members. Thursday morning arrived as we completed gathering equipment and supplies for our trip to Central Asia. Just after lunch the purchase of additional suitcases provided the final packing cartons for our expedition. Four days of scouring stores and interpreting technical specifications resulted in most of the test equipment we required for the unknown ahead.

Two cars, five men, eleven suitcases, four carry-on bags and no tickets arrived at the airport around 1530 in time to see the planned flight depart for Paris. The autobahn traffic was horrendous and impeded out efforts on all fronts. Praise the Lord, a later flight was available which would bring us to Paris before our connecting flight departed, . . . so we thought.

Our arrival in Paris was two hours later than we planned. To ensure the satellite equipment and down-link were on the Central Asian airline flight one colleague ran ahead to purchase tickets and pay shipping costs. Passport control was painstakingly slow, consuming a precious thirty minutes in our forty-five-minute time window. Another fifteen minutes was lost retrieving our bags.

It was a circus. Our departing flight was in a different terminal. We dragged the bags to the curb and waited for the next shuttle bus. It arrived, the doors opened and we started carefully placing our bags into the back of the bus. The bus driver, a fine French gentleman, started yelling at us to hurry up. He had a schedule to keep. Suddenly, we were tossing our cases in a heap.

We made numerous stops to allow other passengers to reach their destinations. Finally, we arrived at the proper terminal. Before the doors were open and the bus came to a complete stop the friendly driver made sure we knew he was in a hurry. Once more we tossed the bags. This time they landed in the roadway and were still bouncing as the bus roared away from the terminal.

We loaded up luggage carts, ran for the gate, and discovered our colleague anxiously awaiting our arrival. Tickets were in hand and the plane was waiting for us to board.

The counter personnel gaped at our luggage carts piled high with bags. They began rushing us toward the departure gate. We ran toward the moving walkway when *wham*, our carts hit the rails on either side of the walkway. Carts were not permitted. We quickly pulled the posts from the ground to let our carts through.

Two buildings later we reached passport control and customs. Additional customs paperwork, much to the dismay of the airport crew attempting to get the flight in the air, was required before we could board and load our luggage.

Just past customs we arrived at security. I plopped the first bag into the X-ray machine and watched it wedge itself sideways in the small opening. The machine was not designed for large bags. In popped the smaller pieces to the delight of the French technicians. The larger bags were a problem.

One of the officers motioned to bring the big bags to a table behind the X-ray machine. *Great,* I thought, *we can have a quick visual inspection and be on our way.* I keyed in the combinations and opened the cases. The inspectors began to extract each piece of electronic equipment. One by one they placed each piece on the S-ray belt for scanning.

I was required to unpack, scan and repack, cautiously, the test equipment so it would not be damaged during the flight. What took me two weeks to carefully pack was crammed into the cases in five minutes.

Finally, we boarded the Soviet made aircraft under the scrutiny of waiting and disgruntled passengers. Eventually we were provided with claim tickets for the luggage, boarding passes and left the ground in a deafening roar.

The plane was enormous. The seat pockets contained no documentation or information. People piled luggage and other articles in, between, and under seats, which made a number of them unavailable for actually sitting. Interestingly the seats folded forward. Since no one was in front of me I could fold the seat forward and stretch out my legs. There was a nominal safety demonstration in a foreign language and broken English.

Much to our delight they served dinner on the plane, which was not too bad. Vodka and wine passed back and forth in almost every row and the passengers smoked incessantly. They were enjoying themselves.

We were on our way. God provided, in a unique and unexpected way. What were the results? The work was accomplished, the word of God proclaimed from another location. But I think there was more to this than expanding the ministry.

I avoid talking about and especially praying about patience. Sometimes, against my better judgment, God decides it is time to learn a little more patience. This was one of those times.

Graduation

But we have this treasure in jars of clay, to show that the surpassing power belongs to God and not to us. (2 Corinthians 4:7 ESV)

In 1972 I spent an evening in the Cincinnati Music Hall. Growing up I visited this imposing facility numerous times to enjoy presentations by such greats as Pete Fountain, Peter, Paul and Mary, Van Cliburn, Carlos Montoya, Vladimir Horowitz, the Cincinnati Symphony and others. A lot of memories were tied to this one location and another was born that warm June evening.

As the last combined Greenhills and Forest Park High School class to graduate, we were also the largest class to ever graduate from Greenhills High School. Our school couldn't hold the largest graduating student body, their parents and friends. The school administration was pressed to consider alternatives. So the music hall, with all its history and magnificence, was rented and prepared.

I was one of more than 500 students gathered in the basement, caps and gowns carefully arranged for the ceremony. In spite of the valiant efforts by the principals to herd us into one room, we scattered like roaches when the light turns on to explore the underbelly of the auditorium.

Eventually we were rounded up and lined up in alphabetical order. It was our time of recognition. It was time to fill the bleachers set up on the platform with a mosaic of green and white caps and gowns. It was time to receive our diplomas and start the next step in life. We were thrilled to cross the same platform previously hosting such a long list of famous people. I'm not sure what was more exciting, receiving my diploma or walking the boards of the rich and famous.

From the front row to the third floor balcony, parents and friends celebrated with us. Normal people gathered to celebrate great possibilities. Each hoped their son or daughter would grow to become someone great who would impact the world. Bright eyes and smiles beamed from the student body as we considered the seemingly limitless opportunities which lay before us. Time would reveal all.

Thirty-two years later I sat with the parents and friends of the largest graduating class of Vienna Christian School. The school couldn't hold such a large gathering of parents and friends so we rented a local church auditorium.

Twenty-three students gathered together in the simple room to celebrate a new step in life. This time my second son, James, was to graduate with honors. When the principal handed him the honor chords, he didn't know what they were or what to do with them. None of us - mom, dad, or friends - expected to see this academic honor bestowed. A fellow student saw the chords in his hand and said, "James, put those back! They're not yours!"

Not only did James display his honor chords but he also shared his testimony as part of the ceremony. Christians, Muslims, and Hindus heard the message of the Gospel working in our young son's life. Normal people gathered to celebrate great possibilities. Each of us hoped our son or daughter would grow up to become someone great would impact the world. Their eyes gleamed and lips grew into large smiles as they considered the seemingly limitless opportunities which lay before them.

Me, I prayed for James; not that he would complete the speech without disaster but that he would remain true to the Lord and Savior he just proclaimed was part of his life. Sharing with his class, the faculty of the school, and others, my jar of clay was opening the Gospel to people in need. James wasn't just a normal person but a child of God taking the next step in life.

God's surpassing power is amazing. Never did I imagine as I strolled across the stage in Cincinnati where God would place me more than thirty years later. Here, in a foreign land, I was watching my own son graduate from high school. He was a normal person, using normal skills to proclaim the Gospel message to the world.

At times I'm reminded God doesn't reveal everything in our life until it's necessary. Think of where you were, where you are, and what God has done in between. You'll be amazed. We're just normal people, using normal skills to bring the Gospel message to the world.

Musicals

The LORD is my strength and my shield; in him my heart trusts, and I am helped; my heart exults, and with my song I give thanks to him. (Psalms 28:7 ESV)

As early as I can remember I listened to music, sang music, and enjoyed music. I married a beautiful lady who also loves music and singing. It's no wonder a love for music also developed in our children.

Ellice, our firstborn bundle of joy, started singing when she exited the womb and hasn't stopped since. She sang in the crib, sang in the tub, sang when we traveled, sang in church, sang in the shower, and still sings whenever the chance or a momentary silence provides an opportunity.

In high school Ellice was involved with a theater group on Guam. This collection of students from schools across the island presented a number of excellent musicals including "Camelot," "A Christmas Carol" and others. The best students from each school worked on their musical abilities and prepared for the big opening day.

Ellice said she had a singing part in "A Christmas Carol." She was part of the chorus. She said it was not a big lead but she was a part in many scenes throughout the musical. Beth and I purchased tickets and headed to opening night.

You can imagine the surprise on our faces and the flutter in our hearts when a young lady began a long solo. It took about two notes to recognize the voice and know Ellice had hoodwinked her parents.

She was part of the chorus to be sure but also had a major piece as part of the plot. Singing about bedclothes and parsing out the dead Scrooge's things, she delighted us and the audience with her talent. Humility is a great Christian virtue. That evening we were humbled at God's gift in our daughter. At the same time, we were proud of her abilities and rolled these feelings into one set of emotions.

Over the years our family listened to many musicals and sang along with one another and the tape, CD or record (yes, we had all those things are one time or another). We would spend an entire day interspersing songs from different musicals into the events of the day.

We would start the morning singing "Oh, What a Beautiful Morning" to wake one another. A news program might bring out the chorus to "Everything's Up to Date in Kansas City." Talking about boyfriends and girlfriends might spark a rousing rendition of "Matchmaker." Singing as a family has always been a delight.

I don't have the chance to hear her much these days. She is grown, teaching school, raising children and singing for a church in another country. When we do get together you can be guaranteed there will be at least one songfest as a family.

It's amazing how many people remember the songs in musicals. When you start singing part of "Sunrise, Sunset" someone is bound to join in the refrain. Our hearts and souls respond in a miraculous way to the musical melodies of the world.

Starting with Moses and Israel singing "The horse and its rider He has thrown into the sea," we have been singing praises to God ever since. We may argue over "acceptable" music but cannot deny the ability of music to teach, admonish and encourage us as believers.

Ellice astonished us with her solo. I still remember the stage, the song, and all the events of that night. God astonishes me regularly with a melody, a psalm, a musical song that grabs my heart and brings me closer to Him. I remember these moments.

When was the last time God amazed you with a touch of music? What musical score do you remember best? Is "Oklahoma" easier to remember than your favorite hymn or chorus? Maybe it's time to rekindle the work of music in your soul and give God thanks through music.

Father and Sons

And a harvest of righteousness is sown in peace by those who make peace.
(James 3:18 ESV)

Since I was able to crawl I made my way through the cables, cabinets and equipment of radio and television stations. I probably knew more about electricity before I started kindergarten than most people ever learned in their life. Granted, this was not a particularly useful skill in elementary school, but it kept me from biting the electrical cord and those shocking results.

Needless to say, some of my children acquired an interest in electronics and especially audio. Joel was the first to discover the wonder of mixing audio in the church for a good sound. Working with Dad, aka me, he discovered what he could and could not do with the available equipment.

It didn't take him long to notice the sheepish singers and boost their microphone a little more than the accompaniment. Getting the right mixture so instrument and voice could be heard was always a challenge.

On the other end of the spectrum was the confident, loud singer. They always wanted the monitors and speakers blaring as loud as possible to help ensure permanent hearing loss for themselves and the audience. Floor monitors directed at the singer are wonderful devices. Lowering the volume to the congregation while boosting the floor monitor would give the singer a sense that they were blasting away at their captive audience while the audience was spared hearing damage and could enjoy the music without pain.

Working with a group was even more fun. Joel learned quickly to turn down, and sometimes off, the microphone of that one individual who was swaying back and forth in spiritual sync while singing in another world and another key. Their voice would fade in and out as their mouth passed across the microphone in time with the music.

For years we worked together. Joel was always behind the mixing board. I was sometimes helping him. Sometimes I was providing the music and became the victim of his mixing decisions. Either way it was an exercise in making peace between the musician, the preacher, the choir and those listening in the congregation.

There was also a time of peace when we worked together on special audio projects. More than once we worked the sound board together for church or special programs at the boys' school in Austria. For several years Joel helped our church in Vienna mix the sound in our small and noisy meeting hall.

When Joel went off the college, James stepped in and picked up the ministry. It was fun watching him keep the peace between the musicians and the congregation. One time he turned off his mom's microphone. When she asked why he said, "Trust me. It was better off not letting people hear what you were singing."

220

OK, so maybe there wasn't always peace at home. I have the sneaking suspicion he often turned my microphone off but just didn't say anything. There was that one Sunday when I had a stuffy nose, and sounded like a walrus with his head buried in the sand.

It's times like these, working with my children, that I remember and cherish. God allowed us to work together, to be at peace with one another, usually. As father and son we carefully sculptured audio to help others worship and praise God through song.

What events remind you of God's peace working in your life? Mine are with family and friends. God's calm hand helps us work together.

Hike in the Woods

For you are my rock and my fortress; and for your name's sake you lead me and guide me; (Psalms 31:3 ESV)

During high school I participated in a week-long hike of the Appalachian Trail. I was young. The mountains were beautiful and the rattle snakes abundant. That week-long hike was a once-in-a-lifetime experience not to be equaled. Sometimes I thought I got close.

On Sunday afternoon, while on a church retreat, we decided to enjoy a hike in the forest surrounding the little village of Baden. A castle ruin near the retreat site beckoned for a visit. I, and a few others, decided to pay it a visit.

Our Austrian friend took the lead. He was an accomplished outdoorsman, native to the land and all around a nice guy. We started our hike to the castle. Our trail blazing guide said it was only twenty minutes away.

An hour later we discovered there were many paths through the forest not clearly marked on the trail map. The landmarks appeared to be taking the day off. Turning the map round and round, trying to figure which way was which, our intrepid leader said, "Maybe it's this way," and pointed to another trail heading into the deep dark forest.

In spite of being lost, in a foreign land, in the deep dark forest with a confused guide, the day was beautiful and cool. The conversation was delightful and jokes abounded.

We looked like an international hiking club. A mixture of Nigerian, German, Austrian, Filipino and American explored the wild together. These were good friends to be with when lost in the forest on a sunny day.

We were so far off the beaten path we figured we would soon cross the border into Slovakia. Despite our guide's claim to understand the trail map, we doubted his abilities after the first hour. However, we trudged onward, upward, downward and around many a bend in the trail. After almost two hours we finally arrived at Rauhenstein.

The castle sat on one side of a mountain pass. Across the valley sat another castle. The two were situated to guard the pass and defend the valley from attack.

We figured our next trip to the area we'd hike up to the other castle and take more pictures. Maybe by then I'd learn how to read the trail map myself. If I'm going to get lost, I want to lead the way.

In the end we arrived at a great spiritual revelation. Never accept a seasoned outdoorsman as your guide through the Wiener Wald . . . even with a map in hand!

As a Christian I try to lead others as they follow the narrow way. Sometimes I read the map well. Sometimes I take a wrong turn. Fortunately,

Jesus is a better guide and never takes me down the wrong trail when I follow Him.

Coconuts

...each one's work will become manifest, for the Day will disclose it, because it will be revealed by fire, and the fire will test what sort of work each one has done. (1 Corinthians 3:13 ESV)

I never liked coconuts. Growing up I could taste coconut buried in almost any mixture of food. It made my taste buds scream in disgust. I could always discover the secret ingredient no matter how hard the cook tried to cover the flavor with other ingredients.

On Guam coconuts were everywhere. We removed the trees from our yard so the heavy seeds wouldn't whack our children on the head. A ten-pound coconut does considerable damage when falling thirty feet onto a child's head. This is another reason to dislike coconut.

Then while visiting Pohnpei I enjoyed cool fresh coconut milk. A native man climbed the tree and lopped off the coconut so it fell to the ground. After he climbed down he then whacked off the top with his machete and offered it as a refreshing drink. I'm not sure whether it really tasted good or I was that thirsty. I'm still not convinced it is a viable food source.

I once saw a coconut in a US grocery store. It was a brown, round, furry, hard seed. When I experienced a whole coconut on Guam, I discovered it's originally packed in a strong green fiber covering. Getting the cover off is much more difficult than opening the seed. Still, this is another reason to leave coconuts on the tree.

My family, on the other hand, loves coconut. In elementary school Ellice and Joel learned how to make coconut candy. They claim it's a sweet and delicious treat. I'm not convinced. Since they ate everything on the way home from school, they had nothing to offer as proof of their wild claims.

It sounds like a simple process to make coconut candy. First you take a machete, the size of my young son, and whack the top off the coconut and split the seed. A good islander can open a coconut in seconds. I tried opening only the seed once. Hours later, after using a drill, a saw and an axe, I finally had a small hole in the tough seed.

Next you scrape the white meat out of the seed using a small stool with a dangerous looking projection on the front. Sit on the stool, twirl the seed around the sharp pointed thing and watch the white meat fall into the bowl on the ground. This is a skill everyone should learn. Why? Because some people actually like coconut.

Finally, you boil the meat in a pot over a wood flame, mix in some other stuff and then you have hot, supposedly delicious, candy. My children like it. My wife likes it. I suppose there is no accounting for taste. Given a choice, I wouldn't choose a coconut.

It's also difficult to understand why God would choose me to be one of His children. Like a coconut I have a strong fiber husk surrounding a hard, internal seed. It just isn't easy to get inside. But God has whacked away the husk and lopped off the top of the seed to work with the valuable meat inside.

He scrapes out the essential parts, boils it in the fire of his Holy Spirit and produces something good. I don't understand it but I'm thankful He's a good cook. If a coconut had feelings, I'm sure it wouldn't enjoy the process of being made into candy.

We don't enjoy the process as God works in our lives to turn us into useful children. He breaks us open, scrapes out the good and discards the useless. When He has cooked us just long enough we become useful instruments, valuable sweets in His hands. I still don't like coconut.

The Shelf

I will remember the deeds of the LORD; yes, I will remember your wonders of old. (Psalms 77:11 ESV)

There is a shelf in our dining room. It first appeared in our second mission house on Guam. It's a simple Shaker design made from pine and stained some shade of brown. Since its first appearance it has moved from mission house to mission house. Although it's just a shelf it holds a special significance in our home.

I built the shelf on Guam. I am not a cabinet maker but this was carefully crafted. As carefully as this amateur can craft any cabinetry. It isn't perfect, it isn't spectacular. In fact it's rather plain. About four feet long, it provides space to set things and pegs underneath on which to hang things.

You might wonder why I built this shelf? I built the shelf because Beth asked me to build the shelf and I'm a good obedient husband. It was also cheaper to build than to buy! Why did she want the shelf? To put things on, of course!

It's important to understand that not just anything was to adorn The Shelf. This was to become a sacred place, a reminder, an Ebenezer for our transplanted family. We were no longer in the land of our ancestors. Now we were living as strangers in a strange land.

Through the years, and more than once, we revealed some childhood memory to our children. We wanted them to identify with us and us with them. They would sit with perplexed looks on their faces as we talked about Fourth of July holidays, Thanksgiving feasts and gathering the extended family at Christmas time. These were foreign concepts to them. Just the thought of snow boggled their minds while we lived on a tropical island.

Our children grew up on a small island that seemed light years away from the quiet little towns where Beth and I grew up. Our boys also enjoyed a number of years in Austria, a far cry from the red clay of Georgia I remembered as a child, or the forested fields of New York state from Beth's youth.

We wanted our children to understand something of their homeland while living on foreign soil. Beth, the ingenious person she is, used The Shelf as a reminder, a marker stone for our family. Throughout the year it'd be redecorated according to the holidays, or special events of our motherland, which we wanted to be our children's motherland.

In the spring there were Easter eggs and daisies perched on The Shelf to remind us of the missing seasons and our Savior's sacrifice. In July the red, white and blue would adorn The Shelf with other patriotic memorabilia of the USA. November would find a cornucopia, turkeys and pilgrims looking down from The Shelf over our dining room table. There were decorations for New

Years, Christmas, Saint Patrick's Day and other holidays we remembered and our children never experienced.

They didn't experience them the way Beth and I remembered them. But, they did experience them as we celebrated in our little home in a foreign land with a visual reminder on The Shelf. When I wanted a reminder of the land of my youth I just glanced up from my meal and surveyed The Shelf, and smiled.

It's nice to have a reminder of things easily missed in the rush of day to day ministry. God does the same thing. He reminds me through circumstances, friends, family and the beauty outside my window that I have an eternal homeland. I'm looking forward to that land.

Austria, where we lived when I wrote this, was not my home and when I forgot my homeland I lost something of who I was. The world is not my eternal home and when I lose sight of Heaven I lose something of who I am and who I will become. When I need a reminder I glance up, see God's wonder around me and smile. How do you keep touch with your homeland?

Lighthouses

You are the light of the world. A city located on a hill can't be hidden. (Matthew 5:14 WEB)

I remember watching an old monster movie with a lighthouse. "The Day of the Triffids" was a classic. A meteor shower blinded anyone who was outside watching the beauty of the lights in the sky and turned simple plants into giant, walking, noisy, man-eating plants. Beth was never interested in man-eating plants so she never saw this particular lighthouse. I think she missed an important aspect of life and might want to check the contents of her flower pots for giant man-eating plants.

Other lighthouses, unlike the one in the movie, were not ignored by my lovely bride. I'm not sure where Beth's fascination with lighthouses originated but she enjoys pictures and paintings of and especially visiting lighthouses. She talks about the lighthouses in New England, where she grew up. When I was growing up the closest I came to a lighthouse was holding up a flashlight on the side of a lake to catch my friends' attention.

Our son Joel would tease his mother about lighthouses. He called them big flashlights. When we did visit a lighthouse, he went around asking where they put the Duracell. He never found them even when he looked in the basement.

I must admit I do admire lighthouses. They are stately, imposing, and cool-looking. Standing at the top of the lighthouse commands a magnificent view of the surrounding land and sea, which makes sense due to their purpose in life. I can imagine myself standing on the walkway, spyglass in hand, wind and rain whipping through my long hair (what little hair is left), with scraggly beard searching the horizon for a ship in danger. Beth has been known to hug a lighthouse in her excitement.

The lighthouse is an old device used by sailors to find safe harbor, a warning against the shoals and a comfort to know where they are along the coast. The first lighthouse is mentioned around 1200 BC in Homer's Greek epic poem "The Iliad."

Every lighthouse looks different and its beacon flashes a unique pattern. They are listed in "The Light List" so sailors know where they are by the characteristic of each lighthouse's glow. Only once did I see a lighthouse in operation. I don't stay up after dark too often.

On our honeymoon we stayed on Sanibel Island. Late in the evening I watched the beacon at the southern end of the island sweep across the Gulf of Mexico at regular intervals. There was a soothing comfort in its piercing sweep of the water.

I believe it takes a lot of work for the lighthouse keeper to maintain such a strong and clear illumination. If the Fresnel lens is dirty the lamp is useless.

The lens must be checked, cleaned and maintained at regular intervals. The power house needs to be kept fueled and the fog horns in working order.

In Philippians, Paul reminds believers to live a life worthy of the Gospel. When we do this we are a beacon to the world around. We announce to those who heed God's beacon there is a safe harbor. To those who ignore the beacon and head for the reef we are proof of disaster on the horizon.

Are we a beacon of hope or is our lamp dusty and useless? Maybe it's time to clean the lens, increase the power and be a guide to a perishing world.

Riding the Rails

And let the peace of God rule in your hearts, to which also you were called in one body; and be thankful. (Colossians 3:15 WEB)

I never lived in a really big city. Some think that Cincinnati is a big city but it's nothing like New York, Chicago or Los Angeles. Big cities have subways. Subways have always fascinated me. I find there is something about riding in a hole in the ground through endless tunnels that's exciting. Cincinnati started a subway system once but it was never finished. The tunnels poke out of the hills here and there but no trains run through the bowels of the earth filled with anxious commuters.

Once, Beth and I rode in a train across Florida. It was less than exciting. There were no bandits on horseback robbing the train. There wasn't even a rush down some mountain tracks without brakes. Then again, Florida is rather flat and a little too east for western bandits.

It wasn't until we moved to Europe that I was able to enjoy the full wonders of public transportation and especially riding in a train. To me there is something romantic, like a children's story, about trains and riding the rails.

I once aspired to be a hobo. I was young and it looked exciting to jump a moving train headed to some unknown place with no responsibilities, no money, and no future. As soon as I met a real hobo and discovered it wasn't exciting but filthy, smelly and dangerous, I decided I was better off riding trains as a rich or middle-class man. Besides, my parents told me not to play near the railroad tracks.

In Europe I never rode a train as a rich man, but I didn't go as a hobo either. I was one of millions of European passengers getting from one place to another. Taking the train was almost a daily event. My children rode a train to and from school every day. I was in train heaven.

Several times I traveled on an overnight train through the mountains to and from Monte Carlo, Monaco. It was fascinating. I slept in a small room. Rocking back and forth to the sway of the tracks was actually restful. Riding through village after village, along the Mediterranean Coast, watching the houses and fields rush by the window was fun.

It didn't take long to discover train tracks do not go through the beauty spots of the city. In fact, most train tracks go through industrial areas. Many stations are underground, out of the way, and many stations are just a slab of concrete in the middle of nowhere.

One of the greatest joys was watching the people on the trains. I watched many people board and exit trains throughout Europe. Some were laughing, some serious but most looked lost. They knew where they were headed, what train to ride but their faces hinted at a lack of purpose.

Once in a while I would catch sight of someone with a smile of peace on their face. Occasionally I would talk with other riders of the rails. Those with peace in their faces were walking with Christ. The rest were avoiding God or thought He was some piece of crystal or a guru from a mountain top.

Beth was approached by a stranger on one train. The lady walked up and started a conversation. Eventually she asked if Beth was a Christian. When Beth said yes, the lady replied, "I knew it, by the look on your face."

What's the look on your face? I must admit mine isn't always beaming with the glory and peace of God. Beth, on the other hand, is famous for her smile and beautiful face. When I stop thinking about my destination or which train to take my face changes its appearance.

We are called to be imitators of Christ. I don't think Jesus would ride the rails with a lost or abandoned look on His face. When I set my eyes on the Lord, not myself, I, too, can ride the rails of life with a look of peace.

The Chickwrights

May He grant you your heart's desire, and fulfill all your counsel. (Psalms 20:4 WEB)

Life in our home was like living on the Ponderosa. Just call us the Chickwrights. The advantages which I have include a wife, still alive, and a daughter to even out the antics of my three sons. (That sounds like a good title for a TV series.)

As I wrote this we lived in a flat which overlooked the plains of Burgenland to the East, Vienna to the north and the Vienna Woods to the West. Our children rode the trails to and from Vienna (Virginia City) undertaking adventure after adventure. Meanwhile, I kept the home front, with my marvelous wife, and dispensed wisdom and expert directions as situations arose and fell. I'm a Pa, proud of his family.

One year we were traveling through Nevada and I hijacked the scheduled plan to divert us to visit the original Ponderosa. First we stopped in Virginia City to stomp the wooden walkways and relive the past. Next it was on to the Ponderosa.

I was thrilled. My children thought I was nuts. I remember when I was young and our family watched the colorful peacock fanning its tail on TV before the beginning of each program. Then we watched as Pa, Little Joe, Hoss and Adam rode across the plains ready to stand for justice against the evil forces of the world. I didn't want to miss a single episode.

We parked our car, paid the entrance fee and sauntered up the hill to the most famous ranch in history. There I was. I was finally standing before a log cabin I knew as well as my own home. I was in memory heaven. My television world was brought to life. To enhance my excitement, they were filming a new "Return to the Ponderosa" episode that day. What more could I ask for?

It was one of my dreams come true. Famous and not so famous stars walked the dusty streets. Occasionally someone would shout for quiet as they filmed another segment of the pending show. In all the excitement I discovered some very important facts.

First, the Ponderosa is indeed located beside Lake Tahoe. Second, the burning map, which introduced each episode, was correct, even though north was on the left and not the top of the map! But, that is where reality ended.

Virginia City(the movie version, not the real one) sat right behind the Cartwright homestead. It was much smaller than I remember from the show. The homestead itself was a deception. The sprawling two story cabin was in truth a one room cabin. The extensions and upper floors were fake. They were created by the mechanics of Hollywood special effects.

A lot of Christians are like movie sets. Outside they appear to be larger than life capturing our attention. When we draw close to look inside the doors

232

we discover something is missing. The inside is hollow, useless. It only exists in the imagination.

In Luke 6 Jesus tells us the good things come from inside, from the heart. On the other hand, evil things come from the same place. What people see in me as they open the doors reflects my walk with God. Do they see good things or evil? I pray they see God things.

Fast Food

The next day, he saw Jesus coming to him, and said, "Behold, the Lamb of God, who takes away the sin of the world! (John 1:29 WEB)

I remember my first visit to White Castle as a little boy. This paragon of good food and fine dining set my standard of cuisine excellence for a lifetime. When I was older, I was introduced to the world wide favorite, McDonald's. Say what you will about their dietary presentation, I like the place and apparently so do millions of other people. My life is filled with fast food and I'm not complaining. I'm enjoying the experience.

Fast food makes any dietitian shudder with fear but it has its uses. When you have two minutes between trains, it can keep you from starvation. A car full of boisterous children can quickly be quieted by a stop at the drive thru. And, traveling missionaries can eat without the fear of ingesting a case of Montezuma's Revenge.

I remember eating at McDonald's in Russia, Sri Lanka, Guam, Hong Kong, Japan, Korea and a mess of European countries. (Some European countries are a mess but that is not the point.) Other countries, unfortunately, don't support such modern conveniences, at least nothing I recognize. One exception was my work in Central Asia.

After arriving and gathering all our equipment and then loading the vehicles, we drove from the city where the airport was located to another city in the mountains. What would normally be a one-and-a-half-hour drive took more than two hours, including a stop for a bite to eat at a roadside BBQ. This was the Central Asian version of fast food.

The outdoor BBQ kitchen was located on what used to be a building site on the side of the road. All that was left was the concrete flooring which made room for parking. The kitchen stove consisted of a tin tray with wood burning at one end. When an order was placed, the pieces of lamb were stuck on a long metal spit and laid across the tin box with hot coals from the fire pushed below to start the cooking. It didn't take long to cook the meat and the heat from the fire helped warm up my cold hands.

When we wanted more, the proprietor reached into the trunk of his car and extracted more pieces of meat for the next spit. I watched as small pieces of rust fell from the dilapidated vehicle trunk lid into the box of freshly butchered meat. I suppose this was part of the unique seasoning.

It was a particularly tasty meal served on flat, paper thin bread. As the cook prepared our afternoon snack we stood in a heavy breeze between snow-covered mountains. My Guam blood wasn't happy with the situation and I was already bundled up with a sweater, two shirts, several pairs of socks, coat and gloves. I reminded myself God called me there.

Sometimes people approach the Lamb of God like selecting items in a fast food restaurant. We order a piece here to cure that grumbling in the stomach. We order a bit there to give us a little strength as we hurry to another event. It might keep us alive but we won't develop properly, any more than eating fast food for a lifetime will provide all the necessary nutrients.

I like what it says in The Message, "An intelligent person is always eager to take in more truth; fools feed on fast food fads and fancies." (Proverbs 15:14) Are we grabbing for fads and fancies? It may be time to grow strong on the good food of God's word.

"Every Scripture is God breathed and profitable for teaching, for reproof, for correction, and for instruction in righteousness, that the man of God may be complete, thoroughly equipped for every good work." (2 Timothy 3:16 17 WEB)

Sand Castles

How precious to me are your thoughts, God! How vast is the sum of them! If I would count them, they are more in number than the sand. When I wake up, I am still with you. (Psalms 139:17 18 WEB)

I learned to swim when I was in kindergarten. My family was living in New Orleans at the time. Three sailors living in the apartment complex where we lived took it upon themselves to teach my brothers and me this vital necessity of life. I remember my first lesson vividly.

Standing beside the kidney shaped pool, they told me to hold my breath and move my arms and legs. I nodded as I looked up at their husky faces. In one swift motion they grabbed my arms and legs and tossed me high in the air. They summarily plopped me in the middle of the deep end of the pool.

I had followed their instructions to the letter. As my head slid beneath the water I held my breath and furiously waved my arms and legs. I looked great! There I was, lying on the bottom of the pool executing what I thought was a perfect stroke. After a few seconds my instructors dove into the pool grabbed under my arms and whisked me up to the side where I sputtered and spit chlorine from my lungs.

One fellow asked, "Are you OK?" Unthinking, I gasped, "Sure!" Before I knew what was happening I was pulled from the side and again tossed into the air to plop once more into the pool. This routine was repeated over and over until I eventually learned to swim.

Once I had learned to swim, I discovered the beach. Playing in the rolling waves was lots of fun. Years later I was living on Guam where we had plenty of beaches. There were plenty of chances to swim and also plenty of sand. The only problem with the beaches was the sand. It was everywhere.

Sand is great for squishing between your toes. Strolling along the sandy beach in the late evening with your honey is very romantic. Camping in the sand lets you custom form your bedding. But when there are waves and sand then there is sand in the shorts. I hate sand in my shorts.

Splashing in the waves is great. Walking from the surf with your swimsuit hanging around your knees and full of sand is both embarrassing and uncomfortable. We spent a lot of time at the beach with our children. I spent a lot of time walking funny and rinsing sand from my shorts. I guess girls don't mind the sand. Beth never complained about sand in her suit.

Sand is useful for other things besides providing ballast for my swimsuit. It cleans things, cushions things, looks great in a fish tank and you can build with it. With the right mixture of sand and tide you have the perfect place to build a sand castle. I started building when I was young and passed my skills on to my children. We built many a magnificent structure in the sand.

Our castles included the requisite moat, walls and towers. This was just the beginning. Adding pieces of drift wood, there were draw bridges. Tunnels were carefully dug to provide escape routes for besieged residents. If there was enough daylight, we would include all the interior features: chairs, tables, toilets. The ultimate was the dungeon. You couldn't see the dungeon, because it was underneath our five-story castle, but we knew it was there and held evil criminals.

We always built our castles near the high-tide mark so we could watch their destruction. I'm not sure why that was so much fun. Perhaps it's a guy thing. Since there was more sand than we could count it didn't matter when the castle dissolved in the tide. We just gathered the sand back up and started over.

Scripture says if we can count the grains of sand we will count God's people. I tried that once. When I ran out of toes and fingers I figured God had a lot of people to watch over. I have enough trouble just watching over my small family.

But according to the psalmist God has more thoughts about me than there are grains of sand on the shore. There are lots of shores in the world filled with lots of sand, not to mention all those deserts. I find comfort when I realize God never runs out of thoughts about His children.

Potter's Clay

But we have this treasure in clay vessels, that the exceeding greatness of the power may be of God, and not from ourselves. (2 Corinthians 4:7 WEB)

My wife loves pottery. She has a special love for terracotta pieces. When she brings up the subject, I tell her terracotta is just a fancy word for clay. Beth is always on the prowl for a new perfect piece of pottery. Some she buys to decorate our home and other pieces are put to practical use in the kitchen and sometimes she collects them to give for gifts.

I tried to make a vase once in art class. That was a disaster. The final result looked more like The Blob from a B grade monster movie. So I turned to music. There is no physical evidence when I make a mess from a good song.

While I couldn't twirl clay into a pot, I did visit a pottery factory in Slovakia. One Friday afternoon some of our staff took a trip up to Modra. Nestled in a small country village, the factory produced exquisite pottery.

The factory traced the ceramic work back to somewhere in the 1400s. It was steeped deep in traditions. A video showed us the history of ceramics in Modra then we toured the factory.

Everything was done by hand; no mass-produced pottery came from this place. In one side of the building you had the potters. These folks spent three years in school learning how to properly mold the clay on the potter's wheel. The precision with which each item was created was amazing.

There was a display of ceramics in the lobby. One held the students' creative works of art. In school they learned all the techniques and processes. For graduation each student was permitted to create whatever piece they felt expressed their own imagination, their creative work of art. Once in the factory they would only create pieces according to tradition. These were artisans caught in a world of conformity.

On the other side of the building were the painters. Each piece was hand painted. Colors, patterns and styles were limited to factory traditions. During business hours there was no place for creative juices to flow. This was a time to remember the past and recreate it again and again and again.

God, on the other hand, is not limited to tradition. There are no mass-produced products in God's kingdom. Walk down the street and witness the marvelous creativity and variety of God's handiwork. We look different. We talk, walk and live different. And yet we are the work of the same craftsman.

We are the product of God's hand. Carefully molded, colorfully adorned and perfectly shaped to worship Him. We are not the traditional work resulting from a mere three years schooling. We are a product of the eternal that created the universe.

After our shape is set and our adornments affixed we are fired in God's furnace. It's here, in the day-to-day life with God, we are strengthened into tools to be wielded by God's hand in the world.

Paul reminds us that as clay vessels we hold the treasure of God's Son to share with the world around us. God uses us as we were made to reach the world around us. What is your shape, color or size? How is God using your perfect shape in the world?

Black Cow

...and you shall teach them diligently to your children, and shall talk of them when you sit in your house, and when you walk by the way, and when you lie down, and when you rise up. (Deuteronomy 6:7 WEB)

Atlanta, Georgia is a great place to grow up. Alongside many other auspicious historical events, I figure Atlanta is best known as the home of Coca-Cola Corporation. Everything else in the city's history pales by comparison. At least that was how I was raised. My family held a great devotion to this sparkling, thirst-quenching concoction.

My brothers and I were born, bred and taught early the marvelous wonders of an ice-cold Coke. I figure we were teenagers before we heard of any other soft drink, as we called them. Pepsi was considered a dirty word in our home and just the mention of it would get our mouth washed out with soap. We had very clean mouths in Georgia.

We learned early the important and varied uses for a Coca-Cola. If you fill your mouth and then shake your head back and forth it will fizzle wildly. The growing internal pressure will eventually be released through your nose with a wild shout of excitement, and a disgusting dribble down your face. Pour a small amount, you don't want to waste it, on the porch, and it'll attract a passel of bugs to examine and collect. Even the critters from our yard had sense enough to know a good thing when it appeared.

One day, when it was hot and my brothers and I were sweaty, Dad introduced us to the miracle of a float. For the uninitiated, a float combines the sweet delight of a coke with the cool refreshment of vanilla ice cream. Some non-purists might venture to use other flavors of ice cream, or even consider using a different soft drink; perish the thought! Mixing the appropriate two, Coca-Cola and vanilla ice cream, in a glass produces a marvelous drink. There is a long-standing debate. Which comes first, the ice cream or the Coke? I'm sure this serious issue will continue to be debated through the ages. I'm sure, when we get to Heaven, God will tell us the Coca-Cola goes in first and settle the question once and for all.

As my own children grew I feared that I might fail them as a father. I never instructed them in the proper technique for making a cool float on a hot summer afternoon. This became overwhelmingly evident when our youngest, Evan, was about five years old.

We were on furlough visiting some folks in San Antonio, Texas. The summer was hot, our schedule was full, and the children spent their afternoons with the family where we were staying. Visits to the bowling alley, another new experience, and the local pool kept the children busy while my wife, Beth, and I shared our ministry with the missions committee and at different meetings around town. As the story goes, relayed to us by our children, our hostess offered Evan a Black Cow.

Evan wasn't sure what a Black Cow was, outside of the four-footed bovine, but jumped at the offer when he learned it included ice cream and root beer. Let me make this clear; I don't condone root beer for making a float. The use of this foreign substance is totally contrary to my pledge of allegiance to the state of Georgia and the Coca-Cola Corporation. However, these folks were Texans, and Texans have some peculiar ideas about things.

This fine lady carefully filled a glass with root beer while Evan watched with his brown eyes wide in anticipation. The ice cream was retrieved from the freezer and opened. The excitement rose as Evan watched her find her ice cream scoop and dig into the cool, delicious-looking, white ice cream. At least they had the decency to use vanilla ice cream in Texas. A large portion was scooped from the container and then *whoosh*, dropped into the glass of root beer. The white lump floated at the top as a brown foam rose from the quickly cooled root beer.

Evan was aghast with a mixture of disappointment and disgust. How could someone destroy good ice cream by putting it into a glass of root beer? He started crying. As a matter of fact, he was still crying when we returned home a few hours later. It took a while to reduce his noise to a simple whimper. At bed time he drifted off into a fitful, ice cream concerned sleep.

Years later Evan commented on the horror he experienced when a good scoop of ice cream was destroyed by drowning it in a glass of root beer. He was sixteen then and the scar remained. Some things in life are just too horrific to forget.

Since that raucous day I've tried to teach him other unique things before he's caught unaware. Chocolate syrup on toast for breakfast, Boy Scout sandwiches (a combination where the bacon is cooked inside the egg), and oatmeal on toast have become part of his dietary experience. It's very important for us to teach our children the good things of life, things they can pass on to the next generation with pride.

God told the Israelites to teach their children His statutes. God didn't want anyone confused or traumatized by the unexpected. Without proper preparation I'm sure little Jakob would have been aghast at the Passover meal. "What do you mean no leaven in the bread? I wanted a fluffy cinnamon roll with dinner!"

I try to teach my children God's statutes as they grow. They can learn to live with a food oversight. A spiritual oversight is more devastating. As believers, what piece of God's wisdom have we failed to pass on to our children? When God drops a beautiful scoop of divine calling into a glass of routine life we want our children to shout with joy, not recoil in disgust.

28 Steps

But sanctify the Lord God in your hearts; and always be ready to give an answer to everyone who asks you a reason concerning the hope that is in you, with humility and fear: (1 Peter 3:15 WEB)

"I have a headache," I said to my wife Beth.

"No!" she responded without looking up from her work.

"I'm tired?" I purported.

"Too bad!" she replied unsympathetically.

"Someone needs to stay home. The boys are sick!" I attempted with a Cheshire grin.

"We are only two doors away! Whatever the excuse it won't work. You're going!" she said, looking up. Her eyes said it all. The discussion was over. I was going.

It was an annual event. Our neighbors invited us to their Christmas party along with a number of other friends. We knew some of the folks. Others were strangers. All of them spoke German. Only a few of them spoke English. Those who spoke English didn't do so well.

For me this was part of the issue. I was not excited about several hours mumbling through my poor language skills with strangers. Besides the language, the food was usually strange and often unidentifiable. There was always a lot of fish stuff and I don't like seafood. I'm a meat and potatoes man. Good southern fried cooking was my preference.

But, regardless of the cuisine, language or additional creative efforts I applied in an effort to stay home, no excuse satisfied Beth to save me from the ordeal. With slouched shoulders I bathed, dressed, curved my lips in a coerced smile and shuffled the long walk to our neighbor's flat. Step, step, step, I walked down the stairs like a condemned criminal.

You need to understand. I liked my neighbors. I liked their friends. I like to get together with folks. But, I don't like crowds and I don't like being put off balance by not being able to understand most of the conversation. We finally arrived at their door, knocked, smiled, said hello and entered. Beth was thrilled. She likes large parties and busy get together times.

Inside, fighting against my party pooper attitude, the festive air began to cheer my spirits. But they were quickly dampened as a barrage of unintelligible words were cast in my direction. I'm sure it was some human language but to me it sounded like nonsense. Occasionally, I would capture a single word I understood but too few to construct a complete sentence.

I found a comfortable chair at the table and settled in for the evening. I would smile, nod my head when someone spoke to me and make it appear I knew what was happening.

Food and drink flowed about the table from hand to mouth as the evening wore on. Locating a couple of recognizable morsels, not from the ocean, I kept my mouth sufficiently occupied to reduce conversation to the six words in my German vocabulary.

Beth, the more adventuresome linguist, was delighted with the short conversations she held. What a marvelous help-mate God provided. I just smiled and nodded my head . . . a lot! I'm sure I imitated one of those dogs in the rear window of a car.

Unexpectedly the view from my rear window on the evening changed. Susan, sitting to my right, turned to me and said, "We know you and trust you. You broadcast religious programs. Tell me the difference between what you teach and believe and what we believe in our church."

With all the intellectual presence I could muster I stared blankly back at her and said, "Wie bitte?" (Loosely translated, "Huh?") Not suave and polished but an honest reaction to an open window of opportunity God dropped in my lap. This was not what I expected of the evening.

I have a saying which deals with the unexpected. A Christian should be ready to preach, pray or die at a moment's notice. I have my preferences on which of these three I would like to do and not do, but I try to be ready, nonetheless, for all three. God was checking up on me. How would I deal with an obvious opportunity regardless of the language or delicacies present? God has a tendency to test our resolutions in the most unexpected ways. It was time for me to put up or shut up.

We took up the challenge. For the next two hours, together Beth and I used the opportunity to explain the Gospel, faith, and the grace of God. Stumbling over the pronunciation of some words, mumbling those we weren't sure about, and working through the gaps in our vocabulary turned an otherwise straightforward conversation into a mental marathon. When we reached the end, we were out of words and exhausted. God worked through us to bring His word into their lives.

Struggling back up all twenty-eight stairs to our flat, we returned home, ready for a good night's rest. Doors were opened. Opportunities created. Hearts pointed in the right direction including mine. It just goes to prove God can, and will, at times, use us in spite of ourselves.

How to Create World Peace

"Don't think that I came to send peace on the earth. I didn't come to send peace, but a sword. For I came to set a man at odds against his father, and a daughter against her mother, and a daughter in law against her mother in law. A man's foes will be those of his own household." (Matthew 10:34 36 WEB)

Over the years I've visited many countries that experienced the ravages of war. This opened doors to homes and offices where I could sit and chat about God, the world and why I was there. This led to a personal revelation which I think can turn the tide of world peace. All the unrest, the discontent and fighting can be resolved with the proper application of furniture. Yes, I wrote furniture.

Just think, when our furniture is uncomfortable we go outside and commiserate with other uncomfortable people. In the United States we experienced one divisive war. Contrary to most history books it wasn't over slavery, taxes or philosophical differences. It was because a group of guys were forced outside due to the lack of a La-Z-Boy. Standing around the streets, feeling miserable, they started talking.

"Life is lousy," said one guy, as he rubbed his hindquarters to relieve the pain of a wooden bench.

"Yeah, something needs to be done," retorted another guy twitching his shoulders awakened from a restless nap on a short rope bed.

"What can we do?" asked the third guy, trying to remove the crick from his neck which was caused when he attempted to stretch out on a log couch.

"It must be those guys in the north," claimed the first guy as he scrunched his face into an angry frown.

"Hey, I'm from the north," responded the second guy. "It isn't my fault you're miserable."

"It must be," interjected guy number three. "Why else would all those northerners move to Florida? They brought the lousy life with them!"

All the while none of them recognized the common factor in their misery: uncomfortable furniture. So, the arguments continued, war broke out, and fighting started.

Since then we have learned how to make a comfortable reclining lounge chair. They have been sold across the nation and internal wars have ceased. Guys are no longer forced to wander the streets because they can't find a comfortable chair at home. The reclining, cushioned, swivel chair with sole access to the remote control has solved our internal discontent and brought peace to millions of homes.

Just think what this revelation could do for world peace. Ship billions of comfortable La-Z-Boy chairs to war torn countries and get all those guys back in their houses where they can relax. The evidence is obvious.

People all over the world are trying to enter the United States. You may think it is for political reasons or financial reasons. NOT! They want to experience the pure joy and relaxation of a comfortable Barco lounger. I have sampled chairs across Europe, Africa and Asia. There isn't a comfortable one in the whole lot.

Christians clamor for world peace. Pastors preach about peace. Politicians and sociologist tell us if we are nice to one another we will establish peace around the globe. NOT!

Jesus tells us in Luke 12:51, "Do you think that I have come to give peace in the earth? I tell you, no, but rather division." (WEB) The Gospel message divides the world. People accept or reject God and His grace. If Jesus tells us the message of salvation divides why do we stand amazed at the world's reaction?

Faith is the final ticket to real world peace. It is faith in Jesus' redemption which brings rest to our souls. In Hebrews 4:9 we read, "There remains therefore a Sabbath rest for the people of God." (WEB)

Furniture may relieve some of the world's troubles but not all. While I don't expect things to improve in the world I do look forward to that perfect rest, that perfect peace, that world of peace, when Jesus returns and God creates a new Heaven and a new earth. Then, and only then, we will discover what it is like to live in a world of peace and see our Savior face to face.

Date Line

This is the boldness which we have toward him, that, if we ask anything according to his will, he listens to us. And if we know that he listens to us, whatever we ask, we know that we have the petitions which we have asked of him. (1 John 5:14-15 WEB)

I was married before I took my first airline flight. It was quite an experience. Actually both the marriage and first air flight were eye openers. I flew from Florida to Ohio to my best friend's wedding to be the best man. That first take off was almost more than my heart could take. I was shaking in my seat once my stomach returned to its proper position. When I returned to Florida I landed at a tiny airport with a runway just long enough for the plane to stop inches before the surrounding fence touched the nose of the plane.

In the following decades I flew around the globe more than once. Air travel has become normal, routine and mostly boring. Our children have become seasoned travelers, offering assistance to adults who are experiencing their first flights. It is fun to watch a 12-year-old offer comfort to a geriatric passenger and explain, with proper hand motions, how to use the life jacket and emergency exits. But they were not always seasoned travelers.

When our son, Evan, was about five we flew from Guam to the United States. By this time airplanes were modernized and displayed a map which constantly updated to show our current location. The little video airplane moved slowly across the screen from island to island struggling to reach the west coast of the US. As we crossed over the middle of the Pacific Ocean, Evan watched as the screen showed our plane approaching a dark crooked line spanning from north to south.

"What's that line, Daddy?" he inquired as he pointed to the screen. I shook myself awake from my travel-induced coma and looked at the screen. I couldn't see anything. Then I remembered to put my glasses back on. Through the dim lighting of the cabin I quickly recognized the International Date Line on the video screen.

"That's the dateline," I quietly replied, trying not to disturb the other snoring passengers. I assumed the conversation was over and closed my eyes to drift off to a numbed state of boredom.

"What's that crooked part?" Evan continued ignoring my closed eyelids. I peeked out and had a thought. A thought, somewhere between lala-land and reality, is sometimes dangerous.

"Well," I said, pausing to rub my chin like some wise sage, "that's where a pilot made a mistake. You see, normally we fly really high and so we fly right over the dateline. If you watch out the window carefully you will see it go by when we fly over." His brown eyes opened wide in amazement. So, I started to reel in my willing son's imagination.

"One day a pilot wasn't paying attention and was flying too low. His wheels suddenly were caught on the line and he dragged it for miles before he pulled lose. That's why they make the planes fly higher now so the line doesn't get damaged," I stated with an air of authority.

Evan looked at me. He looked at the map where our plane was approaching the line. He looked out the window. He looked back at me and said, "Oh!" I smiled, closed my eyes, and once more attempted to get my six-foot plus body comfortable in a seat designed for midgets.

For the next hour Evan's eyes darted between the active flight map and the window. He scrunched up his eyes, peered into the darkness and tried, with all his heart, to catch a glimpse of the dateline. He was captivated by his misguided understanding of reality. As he grew up he eventually learned all about maps and imaginary lines.

I suppose as a father it wasn't fair to take advantage of my son's naivete. But, after the first ten hours of travel in a thirty-hour journey, I was glad to keep him quiet for a few minutes.

Fortunately, God is not like me. Regardless of when and why; He is willing to listen to my questions, my requests, my praises, and give me an honest answer. I wonder if Jesus ever used the sad modern art of sarcasm? I doubt it.

I have fun with my children. I'm sure Joseph had fun with Jesus. Creative stories are an integral part of our family. But, when it comes to God there are no stories. I have no wish to keep my children silent or distracted from learning about God and faith. Instead, in love, I try to speak the truth so they can grow up in Christ.

There is no place for creative distraction when sharing God's truth with others. We must be clear. God loves us. God sent his Son. Jesus died for us. He rose again. There is only one way to Heaven and eternity. Enough said!

Tiny People

For nothing is concealed except to be revealed, and nothing hidden except to come to light. (Mark 4:22 HCSB)

Perspective is a wonderful thing. With the proper perspective you can understand much of the world around you. For years Beth has attempted to change my perspective on many issues. It gets harder as you get older.

On the other hand, children hold no preconceived perceptions about the world. They always look at things differently until they learn. Beth was reminded of this as our flight approached the island of Oahu. Evan sat by the window with wide eyed wonder, taking in all the sights.

Watching the approach of the tiny piece of land consumed his attention. He wasn't sure it was big enough for our large 747 to land. When we finally flew over the land he realized we would fit but another concern peaked his interest. Carefully observing life below, he finally turned to Beth with a puzzled look.

"Mommy?" he asked.

"Yes?"

"Are those real people and cars down there?" he asked and pointed out the window to the highway and beach below.

"Yes, they are," she replied, confident of her understanding of reality.

"Oh no!" he said, eyes growing wider and leaning closer to the window. "How are we gonna play with those tiny people without steppin' on them?" he asked in all seriousness.

Beth looked out the window. She knew all about perspective and distance. She knew the cars were full size. She knew the people were like everyone else. But Evan was still learning.

He had no concept of distance and its impact on perceived size. What he saw was real. If it looked only one finger long it was only one finger long. What looked like play cars to him were just that and he had to be careful not to step on them.

Sometimes we read or hear a passage of Scripture and our eyes get wide with concern. "How can this be true?" we wonder. Everything seems suddenly out of place and confused. We aren't sure how to step forward without stepping on problems. It's then we turn to God in prayer or talk with another believer about our dilemma.

Suddenly we find God providing the answer to our question. Our perspective is expanded to include the revelation of another mystery. God reveals something new to help us in our walk on earth. There is always something new to learn.

"They'll get bigger when we land so we won't step on them," Beth told Evan. They watched the cars and people grow as the plane approached the landing strip. Evan was quiet until we stepped off the plane and he understood the people were not really tiny. He had a new perspective. His perception of the world changed.

We hear the truth, a new revelation, a new mystery, and how God explains it. Then we step forward, wide-eyed, and experience God's wisdom once more. When we are willing to have our perceptions changed by God's word we grow and learn. When we think we know it all, we stagnate.

When was the last time we were sitting wide-eyed reading through God's word in amazement? Our perspective on the world and God may need some changing, some growing.

Fire Alarms

God, you know my foolishness. My sins aren't hidden from you. (Psalms 69:5 WEB)

I grew up a normal American boy. I liked baseball, hot dogs and fire engines. All those bright, shiny red vehicles made my eyes glaze over in wonder. "Emergency" was one of my favorite programs and the sound of a siren starts my mouth watering in excitement.

Feuerwehr is the German/Austrian word for fire station. Our first apartment in Austria was located at the opposite side of a parking lot from the Gießhübl Feuerwehr. The station sported a tall tower with the siren right at the top. This elevation was perfect for calling the volunteers to resolve the latest emergency. It was also the same height as our dining room window. Every Saturday at noon we were reminded of its presence. It was loud, ear shattering and we couldn't miss it even with the windows closed.

Whenever they sounded the alarm we enjoyed watching events unfold. As a volunteer fire department, the men came running from their homes up and down the hill to bring out the trucks and ambulance. On several occasions we had our thoughts jarred as the loud horn began its call to arms.

One week I was in Bratislava for some mission work. When I returned home the family filled me in on the evening's events. Late that evening the fire alarm sounded. It startled the family from their activities. Being curious, Beth and Joel went out on the balcony and watched the men arrive and the trucks drive out of the Feuerwehr.

Instead of heading down the street, the trucks came around the back of the Feuerwehr and into our parking lot. They bounded off the vehicles and headed up the stairs in our building, axes in hand, helmets wagging on their heads.

A few seconds later there was a resounding knock on the apartment door. When Beth and Joel opened the door, they were greeted by firemen with glow-in-the-dark hats and appropriate jackets, looking for a fire.

Apparently, someone had seen the flame from the citronella candles on our balcony and thought there was a fire in our apartment. Beth showed them the candle after they gestured that they were looking for a burning residence. Speaking no English, the firemen looked at the candle, shrugged their shoulders and turned to leave. Other firemen saw the cause of the commotion and laughed at the situation.

We can now confirm the Feuerwehr in Gießhübl works quite well and responds quickly to calls for action. They also appear to be nice fellows and were understanding of the mix-up.

Sometimes we jump to conclusions. Even as Christians, we see a small flame, make a wild assumption and call out the theological fire department to squelch the flames. The results can be devastating as spiritual doors are battered down by well-meaning believers.

God knows. He doesn't jump to conclusions. When He sends out the fire department there are flames to be quenched. When His convicting spirit points to a sin in our life in need of attention we can't point to a misunderstanding.

We love to watch firemen rushing to some disaster. Sometimes the disaster is in our own life. Next time we hear the fire alarm maybe it would be a good time to pray for those experiencing some disaster and evaluate our own heart to be sure there are no wildfires in our own soul.

Rock Garden

For you are my rock and my fortress, therefore for your name's sake lead me and guide me. (Psalms 31:3 WEB)

One of the joys of growing up is the wonder and excitement of everything in the world. Sunrise is a miracle to behold. Sunset a beauty to enjoy. Each blade of grass and twig contains a hidden story in its discovery by a little boy or girl. Every bug, worm, or other slimy creature is fascinating. Just the discovery that things grow and change is a mind-blowing experience.

Children don't understand everything that happens and sometimes jump to wrong conclusions. Often, we, as good parents, enjoy the humor of our children's innocence. We laugh at their naive mistakes and the unspoiled freshness of their view on life. Me, I'm a practical joker from the word go. Just ask my children, they'll give plenty of examples of Dad's strange sense of humor. Add this to the simplistic outlook a child has on life and you have a formula for comedy.

I came home one day and our young son, Evan, was gathering five rocks into our carport. I sat on a bench, opened a book to read, and watched. He organized them carefully and then dashed behind the house. A few moments later he returned with a bucket of water sloshing from side to side and proceeded to douse the five smooth stones and much of the carport. His face showed his apt attention to the process. He ensured each rock received the appropriate amount of water until the overflow flooded off the concrete into the yard.

"What are you doing, Evan?" I asked as I looked over the top of my book.

"Watering the rocks," he replied without looking up from his project. He stepped around them slowly, checking that each stone was soaked.

"Why?" I wondered aloud.

"So they will grow!" replied Evan. He looked up at me, now that his watering was complete, and smiled.

I just nodded my head, twitched my eye and said, "OK."

Evan was convinced rocks, like trees and flowers, would grow when given enough water. We lived on a tropical island. Things grew with a flourish everywhere he looked, thanks to the daily rain showers. The rain fell and he watched the trees and grass grow taller while flowers bloomed. Each time Dad cut the grass, more rocks appeared to grow up from the ground to bend the lawn mower blade. It rained every day and more houses appeared in the neighborhood. Flawed logic, sure, but simple logic based on simple observation.

That evening I started a week on the late shift. The evening broadcasts kept me at the transmitter site until around 3:00 in the morning. Before I headed home I looked around the transmitter site and found five nice rocks a little bigger than the ones Evan "planted" on the carport.

When I arrived home I carefully tossed the original rocks out of the yard and replaced them with the larger stones. Later I rose early just to see Evan's reaction when he walked out of the house.

He looked at the rocks. His big brown eyes became bigger and browner. He walked around his rocks and smiled. Quickly he ran behind the house, retrieved the bucket and proceeded to water his growing rock garden and the carport.

This went on for almost a week. By the fourth or fifth day I was bringing boulders home in my car. They were getting too heavy to cart home each morning, my back was killing me, and fortunately my night shift schedule was coming to an end.

Each morning Evan inspected his rock garden. Another bucket of water was applied. He showed his new garden to everyone who visited. He carefully explained the daily watering process and how quickly they grew. They all looked at Beth or me to see if our son was bonkers. We just smiled and put a finger to our lips to keep quiet.

Finally, the rocks stopped growing. My back had reached its limit. A couple days later he asked why his boulders we no longer growing. I finally explained that rocks don't grow. I was playing a trick on him. He looked at me funny for a few minutes then started laughing.

I am reminded of another rock, one that is unchanging and a firm foundation. Unlike Evan's rocks in his garden the rock of our salvation is the same yesterday, today and tomorrow. No tricks, no substitutions, just the real thing. Believers whose lives are watered by the truth of God's word grow and build upon that sure foundation for eternity.

Evan was building his hopes on a changing stone. Eventually it would fail. As a young man he now builds his life on the solid rock. No fear of failure, no misconceptions, just faith in the sure foundation of Jesus Christ. Where are you building today? Is your foundation a tumbling stone or the solid rock?

The Wrong Bus

For the Son of Man came to save that which was lost. (Matthew 18:11 WEB)

My first experience riding a bus was in middle school. We didn't live too far from the school and I could walk there in almost the same amount of time it took to wait for the bus, make all the others stops, and then unload at the school's front porch. Not exciting by any means but it was a first experience with a school bus or a bus of any kind.

Forty years later my next experience with buses was wide ranging as I undertook the public transport systems of Europe. In most European cities you can get about quite well on buses, street cars and other inter-city vehicles. You soon learn the critical bus routes and numbers for your routine trips. My experience included street cars, trains, subways as well as the ubiquitous bus.

One of my colleagues, Harry, was visiting our office in Slovakia one day so I offered to show him the city. Harry is an interesting character. He is the only man I know who would alphabetize his spice rack and remember the position of every item on his desk. He's married now and discovering a whole new world of changes. His routines have changed but order is still important.

There was only one electric bus which started at a station one block from our office and ended at a stop one block from the city shopping center. The electric bus was predictable, reliable and always followed the same route. It was the only bus I ever rode and I knew it well. Get on at one end, get off at the other. No need to read the local language or know what stops were peppered along the way.

We purchased tickets, boarded the bus and started riding along. I explained some of the sites along the way. Everything was going according to plan. Then it happened. The bus turned right when it was supposed to turn left.

Perplexed, I stopped my commentary and stared out the window. The view was taking on a shape I didn't know.

"What's wrong?" asked Harry.

"Well," I started slowly, "the bus is going the wrong way."

"What?" Harry responded with a little concern in his voice. "Where are we headed?"

"That's the problem. I don't know," was all I could answer. We watched the streets and buildings rush by and waited in hopes of spotting something familiar.

Finally, the bus pulled into a major train station and everyone got off. We took this as our clue that we were at the end of the line. I looked about and figured we were about one kilometer from where we should be. With determination, and no way to read the other bus schedules, we walked toward town.

254

After some unexpected morning exercise, we eventually reached the city center, enjoyed some sightseeing and shopping and then contemplated our return. I wasn't sure how to get back since my favorite electric bus was going to the wrong place. We walked to a street corner and looked about for any helpful indication. I still didn't know the local language or even the local name where the office was located.

Then I glanced across the street. There, waiting for a bus, was another colleague from the office. She lived in the city and knew the system well. We were saved! Laughing at our predicament, she guided us to another bus with instructions for a safe return to the office. It was perfect timing, at the perfect place, for two wandering souls.

That's also how God works in our lives when we open our eyes and look around. Sometimes we find ourselves dropped in unfamiliar surroundings; we don't understand the language and we want to go home. God watches over our every step. The Holy Spirit guides day by day.

Next time you are wandering open your eyes. Look for the Father. He is there, just waiting to put us on the right bus, train, streetcar or subway back home.

Swiss Alps

He puts forth his hand on the flinty rock, and he overturns the mountains by the roots. (Job 28:9 WEB)

Everyone knows Heidi. She's that famous Swiss girl epitomized in story and portrayed by many a cute young actress. When we first visited Switzerland I thought I would be on the lookout for Heidi and Peter. I figured they were living somewhere up on the mountain in a beautiful little chalet. When I finally spotted an elderly couple, rocking on their porch, I thought, "Heidi didn't age well."

During our trip we shared a small cottage with another family. High up on the mountainside, each morning we would revel in the spectacular view from our windows of the surrounding mountain ranges. We relaxed, walked the many trails, played games, sang songs and enjoyed ourselves.

For several days my wife, Beth, and her friend Clarice kept talking about climbing the final 600 meters behind the cabin to the peak. I figured 1700 meters was high enough, why bother with the last few hundred? We surveyed the sharp incline and thought it might be too much.

"We can go this way," Beth said, pointing to one section on the right.

"Too steep," I replied. They tried, then returned and agreed it was indeed too steep.

"We can go that way," offered Clarice, pointing to the left.

"Still too steep," I answered after a brief look. They tried and then returned and agreed it was indeed too steep.

About the third day Beth noticed the cows half way up the mountain. She figured if Swiss cows could climb it then American ladies could conquer the imposing sight. Next thing I knew the two of them, along with the older children, were headed across the pasture to reach the summit. Phil and I waved goodbye, kept the youngest with us, shook our heads, and wondered if we would ever see them again.

They reached the cows and stopped to rest. Clarice and her daughters were suddenly disturbed. Although they were from Texas they had never experienced cows at such close quarters. When the beasts inspected their packs, canteens and snacks, things were a little crazy. Beth and the boys shooed the bell-clanging cows away and the journey continued.

We watched them weave back and forth up the mountain, looking for the right trail. From cow level up, hands and feet worked together to make progress. Eventually they became little dots approaching the summit. They made it. They rose above our doubts and conquered the peak. They disappeared over the top and we waited for their return.

At the top one of the young ladies looked down the sharp, steep wall they had just climbed. She was at the top of the world. She had conquered the challenging mountain face. All she needed to do was descend and share her achievement with the rest of the family. Then fear took hold. With tears she flatly refused to descend.

Eventually, our son Joel discovered a trail around the back of the mountain. They worked their way around the peak, down the trail, onto a road, and back to our cabin. The conquering heroes had returned. They had only a few injuries along the way to add excitement and color to their tale. The young lady taken with fear at the summit was glad to be back on flat, secure and familiar ground.

Christians experience valleys and mountains. Sometimes we try routes which are too steep. At times we find just the right trail. We struggle. We deal with the unexpected along the way. Then reach the goal.

We reach the goal, look back, and wonder how we made it to the end. Fear takes hold and the next step is too difficult to undertake. We look up, see our Father calling, survey the terrain and undertake the challenge. God guides, strengthens and protects as we weave our way to the wonder of His majesty.

Knots in a Kite's Tail

Let us therefore draw near with boldness to the throne of grace, that we may receive mercy, and may find grace for help in time of need. (Hebrews 4:16 WEB)

I used to love flying kites. If I'm given the time, a good breeze, a paper kite, and plenty of string it still sounds great. I'd carefully tie some old rags to the tip of the kite with knots here and there to provide stability. A high-flying kite with knots in its tail is a beautiful thing to see. There's comfort and relaxation in tugging on the string to keep it aloft. I remember many days spending hours keeping a kite aloft on a stiff breeze. Behind the elementary school was a perfect field for the launch site.

Launching a kite takes a bit of experience, lots of running and just the right friend. Since I was often the pilot I would hold the spindle of string so it sat in my hand and the string spooled out between my fingers. My partner would hold the kite over his head. I'd walk about ten feet away, leaving a little slack in the string and then we would get set. On my signal we both ran the same direction until my friend tossed the kite in the air. I'd tug on the string to keep it taut and spool out the leader foot by foot as the kite rose in the sky.

On a good day we could let out over a hundred feet of string and keep the kite flying high the whole day. If the breeze was really good, we'd take another spindle of string and tie it to the end of the first then watch our kite slowly rise into the stratosphere. At least it looked that high to us. This was our version of the space program.

At one time I'd tie a message in one of the knots on the kite's tail. The message contained a dream or wish I wanted to see come true. I figured it might bring my desire just one step closer to God and Heaven. Silly, maybe, but as a child it was fun.

As an adult visiting Central Asia, I was reminded of knots in the kite's tail. I visited a monastery nestled at the end of a long canyon in the mountains. There, chiseled into the face of the cliff, was a 12th century offering of praise and worship to God. There were some outlying buildings and a church but the most impressive were the chapels and homes dug into the solid rock.

The complex dated back to the 4th century. In the main chamber I experienced the beautiful acoustics. One voice would fill the room like a choir fills a church. The face of the cliff was decorated by many crosses carefully carved into the stones. According to legend, the spear which pierced Christ's side was brought here.

Outside the church there were trees filled with handkerchiefs. I saw these in other places around the country. Here it was like a sea of colored hankies blanketing the local vegetation. I had to ask whether there was a cold epidemic or some other explanation for the strips of cloth fluttering in the breeze.

I was told they represented the dreams and prayers of the faithful who came to visit this and other churches around the nation. Like burning candles to make your special request known to the almighty, these strips of cloth were physical expressions of needs and desires. I found it rather spooky myself.

Then I remembered my childhood dreams flying in the wind on the tail of a kite. I didn't understand how God heard my prayers. It wasn't the piece of paper carefully tied in a knot but my heart reaching to the throne which resounded in the ears of God.

In the church today, I see and hear people bargaining with God. They want to put a strip of cloth on some spiritual tree or fly some note in the tail of a mystical kite to feel they are heard in Heaven. It's like a bargain. I'll do this, or hang that hankie here, if God will do this or that. It seems we can't fathom the love of God toward us. We think His love is conditioned by our actions.

The writer to the Hebrews reminds us we can come with boldness before God's throne. No tricks, no candles, no bargains, just open the door. It's the offering of Jesus on the cross which paves the way into the heavenly throne room.

Are we bargaining with God today? Are we offering useless tokens when the entrance before the throne is already open? Jesus stands ready as our High Priest to intercede for us. We can lift up the needs of our hearts knowing God hears, knowing He will show us grace in our time of need. Let's pray without conditions. Let's trust God to answer because of His love for us.

Night Watchman

Watch and pray, that you don't enter into temptation. The spirit indeed is willing, but the flesh is weak. (Matthew 26:41 WEB)

Beth and I were married more than thirty years ago. It's great! Unfortunately, many of our anniversary dates fell on travel dates coming back from furlough. It's hard to get romantic at 35,000 feet in a seat designed for midgets with 500 other people contributing their germs to the captive oxygen. Sharing a meal of plastic packaged "whatever," while the flight attendant bangs into your shoulder with the cart, puts a damper on the celebration.

Often we celebrated a little later than the actual date. August 31st is the real date. For our twenty-fifth anniversary we planned a trip to Rothenburg ob der Tauber in Germany. I found a little bed & breakfast inside the walled village next to one of the many famous gates. It was just Beth and me, no children, for a weekend of celebration and sightseeing. Hot diggity dog!

When we surfaced to wander around the city, we were fascinated with the history and beauty. In the evening we walked down the main street and there he stood in the middle of the road, the night watchman, dressed in a hooded black cloak and carrying a lantern. He caught our attention!

He wasn't there to dispense some strange ancient justice. He was a tour guide for the evening watch. Fortunately, we found the night watchman who spoke English. For the next thirty minutes we wandered in and out of the city walls listening to the tales of the city and its defenses.

The night watchman had a job. He was to watch the gates at night to ensure no enemy would enter undetected. I'm sometimes a little slow but I think that is where he got his name. Tales of boiling pitch sending attackers fleeing in pain filled our heads with horrid images. Special doors, too small to walk through upright, pitted the gate's wood and iron structure. These were used so infiltrators had to stoop and enter the city, making them vulnerable.

The night watchman was to watch and then send up the alarm when something went wrong. He wasn't a warrior but an alarm. He was to check to ensure things were in order then remain vigilant, looking for signs of intrusion.

As the night watchman continued his slow cadence through the city I thought about the fortress of my own soul, this temple God has taken as His residence. I thought of the Holy Spirit standing guard to send up a warning when I chose poorly. Was I listening? I thought of the gates to my heart. Were they flung open wide to the world or carefully braced, allowing only the pure to enter?

If Rothenburg constantly maintained a night watchman but failed to heed his cries of invasion the city would fall quickly. In the same way, if we are saved we have the presence of the Holy Spirit to lead and guide. What good is the Spirit if we don't listen?

It might be time to check the gates, survey the walls and see if our defenses against the devil are in place and secure. A heedful heart will be ready when the Spirit cries out a warning. Then, braced and ready, we will be able to stand firm and be watchful. We will no longer submit to the yoke of slavery. We will stand against the schemes of the enemy.

Woody Woodpecker

"Be still, and know that I am God. I will be exalted among the nations, I will be exalted in the earth!" (Psalms 46:10 ESV)

Do you remember the old cartoon "The Woody Woodpecker Show?" That was back in the 1950s and 60s. I remember watching the old cartoons. Walter Lance was the creator, designer, writer and artist. Woody was an annoyingly persistent woodpecker causing trouble everywhere he went. I loved the show. I would sit on the floor of our Georgia home in my Saturday morning PJs and laugh over and over at the obnoxious woodpecker. My fascination with the show might explain some of my personality quirks. For years it was in black and white. Then magically, one Saturday morning, it was in color! That was cool.

Many years later I was on my way to our mission office in Perchtoldsdorf, Austria. Normally I rode the 0730 bus filled with noisy, active school children. I was reminded of Woody's loud voice and penchant for pranks. The elementary and middle schools (what I would call them) were near the office so I walked by them each day. I enjoyed watching the children relate to one another. The shy, the charismatic, the clown, they all bumped and jostled their way from bus, to sidewalk, through the park, to the school.

But this day was different. It was a holiday week in Austria. No school children on the bus. Just me, one grumpy bus driver, and a couple old ladies going out to shop. I forgot my MP3 player at home so I couldn't drown out the bus noise as we jostled our way down the hill, through the vineyards toward the little town where my office sat.

I got off the bus, sans children, at the normal stop and headed through the park. Did I mention there was a beautiful park near our office? There was. I liked to walk from the bus stop, through the park, past the school and down the hill to the office. It was a nice walk that took about six minutes. Usually I watched the children interact on the bus and walk through the park. Not this day. It was quiet and there was plenty of room on the sidewalk. No little boys climbing through the bushes or girls whispering secrets to one another. Just a beautiful, warm clear sky morning. Ho hum.

As I came up the hill from the bus stop, I heard a *bang, bang, bang*. There was a pause and then *bang, bang, bang*. The repetitive clamor reminded me of something. I listened intently for a while and then remembered. One furlough we visited friends in California. Their house was riddled with small holes from the numerous woodpeckers in their area. Our friends weren't fond of these beautiful birds.

I listened again. *Bang, bang, bang*, pause . . . *bang, bang, bang*, pause. . . over and over like a machine. I walked slowly, searching the trees and cocking my head to the side trying to find Woody. Finally, I found the tree and spotted the little fellow, way up high, hard at work looking for his breakfast. It was fascinating to watch. His head was a brilliant red, and he had a white chest with spots and black wings.

He would bang away at the tree then pause and listen for the rustle of some juicy, tasty grub. I stood there for a long time watching him work. Industrious, oblivious to the world around, concentrating on the task at hand, he chiseled his way into the tree trunk. He knew there was a treasure trove of succulent delights waiting to be slurped out by his lengthy tongue. He just needed enough persistence until the tree would give way and then he could enjoy the fruit of his labor.

The persistent widow Jesus mentioned in a parable in Luke came to mind. The widow asked and asked and apparently stopped now and again to listen for an answer. That judge wasn't about to give up and give in. But she kept banging away, asking then waiting, asking then waiting. He persistence won the day. Eventually she received what was needed. The judge didn't want to be worn to a frazzle.

I wonder how often we do this in prayer, persist in asking because we need an answer and can't let the issue drop. That's a good procedure. But, how often do we stop to listen for an answer? I know some people who talk so much it's funny. They rattle on, endlessly, without pausing for a breath and intersperse questions along the way. The problem is they never pause long enough to listen for an answer.

I think I do that in prayer at times as well. I ask, ask, ask, wrestle with God looking for an answer I know needs to come. But then I realize I'm exhausted from asking and never pausing long enough to listen. I can't hear the answer if I don't listen.

God isn't quite like the judge. He doesn't respond because we annoy him. God responds because he loves us and wants to help us. I've beat my head against the wall at times until I'm dizzy. When I finally stop I discover God has already provided an answer. I couldn't see it because my eyesight was blurred from the constant motion of whacking my head against the wall.

The Psalmist reminds us to "Be still and know that I am God." (Psalm 46:10) In an active world people see stillness as a weakness. Christians seem to think busyness about God's work is the sign of a true and faithful believer. Jesus took time away. He stepped out of the mainstream of his ministry to refresh himself with the Father. I'm sure he and his Father had some great conversations.

As a Christian stillness is necessary to listen, to hear what God is saying. Just like the woodpecker, we need to bang away with our needs and requests. And, like the woodpecker, we need to pause, now and then, to listen for a reply.

Are we listening today?

Fireworks Symphony

There were lightnings, sounds, and thunders; and there was a great earthquake, such as was not since there were men on the earth, so great an earthquake, so mighty. (Revelation 11:19 WEB)

I was always fascinated with fireworks and the beautiful display of colors and patterns. Growing up in Greenhills, Ohio we attended the annual Fourth of July fireworks display. We sat on the grassy hill at the front of the local lodge across from an open field. For hours we sat, ate sandwiches and waited until it was dark enough to start the show.

Skyrockets, spinning wheels, and roman candles filled the sky with colors and patterns and plenty of booms. Each ear shattering thunder clap was accompanied by *oohs* and *aahs*. The grand finale was always the Niagara Falls wall of white sparks. When the last watery spark fell to the ground the show was over for another year. Mom and Dad packed us into the car for the five-minute ride across town to our home.

Over the years I witnessed fireworks in many countries. Some were spectacular, some mediocre. On furlough we often attended the Fourth of July celebrations with the requisite fireworks. But none of these compared to a show I witnessed in Monte Carlo.

Within weeks of our arrival in Europe I was whisked off on a trip to visit satellite downlink sites and our station in Monte Carlo. Within hours I drove through the Alps, Germany, Italy and France to reach Monaco. There are 130 tunnels (I counted them) between Milano, Italy and Monaco.

It was July and warm. In the evenings we stretched our legs and walked the busy streets and alleys of Monte Carlo. I discovered this was fireworks season. Each year different countries presented a synchronized show of fireworks and music to compete for some prize.

Promptly at 9:45 PM the show began. We stood along the rail looking out over the marina. At the entrance to the marina two lighthouses framed the opening in the sea wall. The fireworks were sent from both sides of the watery gateway with the Mediterranean Sea as a dark backdrop.

There were selections from Schubert, Beethoven, Mozart and even a couple contemporary instrumentals. Each was accented by the resounding boom of the fireworks. There were seven selections altogether. Each round would begin with roman candles or twirling sparklers near the base of the sea wall. The size, color and grandeur of the display would rise with the music and in altitude to punctuate each round with a spectacular light display. At times there was more illumination from the fireworks than the normal street lighting. This went on for quite some time and I thought, "The boys would love this!" I haven't seen such fireworks anywhere else in my life. I thought Disney World did a top-notch job until now.

I'm reminded of the earth-shattering descriptions in Revelation. After the seventh bowl God declares, "It is done!" Lightening fills the sky, thunder rolls and we'll witness fireworks to make Monte Carlo and Disney World pale in comparison.

I'm excited when there's a chance to see fireworks. Even more I'm excited to see God's redemption of the world. Then my dream fireworks will have a purpose. It's good to enjoy fireworks but we must keep our hearts attuned to the eternal fireworks which declare the finished work of redemption in the world. Amen. Come, Lord Jesus!

265

Vicarious

...and saying, "The time is fulfilled, and the Kingdom of God is at hand! Repent, and believe in the Good News." (Mark 1:15 WEB)

I once read a devotion to our staff in Vienna. It's important to first note most of the people in the room spoke English as a second, third, fourth or umpteenth language. Some had excellent English vocabularies, some were still struggling with the basics of the language.

One of the words in the devotional was vicarious which elicited quirky looks from my fellow colleagues. I read the devotion and when asked, explained the word meant simply, "to be a substitute for someone else." One of the North American colleagues gave me a quirky look and commented, "I think it means more than that."

This started me thinking, "Do I really know the meaning of the word?" So I went looking. Here's what I found and some thoughts on using such words, especially in a foreign language setting.

According to a World Book definition:

Vicarious: (1) done or suffered for others, (2) felt by sharing in the experience of another, (3) taking the place of another, (4) the substitution of one person for another.

As a side note the etymology of the word comes from the Latin *vicar*, which is a substitute.

The same definition is confirmed through several online sources and in numerous dictionaries I consulted. So saying that "vicarious" means doing something on behalf of someone else was actually a good definition to simplify the word for non-native English speaking staff members.

The word is often used by theologians in describing the substitutionary death of Jesus on our behalf. It's such a unique word it sounds like it has its roots in some theological conclave of overly educated seminary students. Then again theologians are notorious for confusing the chasteness of God's revelation. By applying multisyllabic, obscure words which confound the masses they ensure their prestige as closer to God because they can pronounce and wield such literary extensions. Just think about words like *propitiation* which have oozed their way into our speech as believers thanks to the 17th century King's English. In truth many believers have no concept of what the word means or its implications. (Propitiation: a conciliatory offering to God.) (Conciliatory: From reconcile, to regain friendship or trust by appropriate or pleasant behavior.)

Ah, but all this is just fun with words and demonstrates the great expanse and flexibility of the English language. It's no wonder people don't understand how to translate into their own language when our language is often bedimmed by frequently misapplied terminology in the religious realm.

I guess I'm simplistic. I try and sometimes I succeed in using the right language skills for the right situation. Other times I find people staring at me as if I sprouted a third eye. Highfalutin words are great, in the proper context. I have to remind myself the message is important, not my ability to wax eloquently and adorning my speech with big words just to garner attention.

Jesus used simple examples, the common tongue to proclaim a simple message, "Repent for the Kingdom of Heaven is at hand." What more needs to be promulgated?

Baroness

On his robe and on his thigh he has a name written, King of kings and Lord of lords. (Revelation 19:16 ESV)

I, Beth, went for a walk in the woods one day and found something unusual. Did you ever think you would go out your front door and meet a baroness? Well I certainly never thought I would really meet a baroness in the woods. Maybe a bear and I've seen deer and jack rabbits and martens and wild boar...but a baroness? That was something I never thought would happen, but it did. I often walked in our woods around Gießhübl. In truth, I walked every day that I could. I took this as a gift from God. I found peace and blessing in the woods. I found this a wonderful place to pray and talk with God. I also found this was a good place to walk and talk with my neighbors.

I walked on Mondays with a fellow missionary. We walked about 5 km in wind, rain, fog, snow or sleet . . . well maybe not sleet. We talked and encouraged one another and shared about our weekend past and the week to come. We worked with the same mission and could share many details and understand what each other brought up as a topic. The rest of my walks during the week were more spontaneous. My neighbor, two flights down in the apartment building, was from Malta and married to an Austrian. They had three children close to our sons James and Evan's ages and the kids were actually friends.

When we first moved to Gießhübl she was my help and good neighbor. She spoke English and German and often provided help dealing with living in a foreign land. During some tough times she experienced with her health and her daughter's health I was able to be there for her and we became good friends.

Often, when the weather was nice, she would yell from her balcony, "We go for walk?" We went hunting for flowers. We exercised and talked. We sat on top of the Salatberg and rested in the beauty of our surroundings. She knew everyone in the community from the little Catholic church they attended. The church had a new priest no one was very fond of.

So, she told me about our neighbors and asked questions about me, my life and my faith. Her son came to know our Savior but she still had many questions. She introduced me to the Bürgermeister, and the doctor, and the town nut. We also met up with other friends and neighbors and walked and talked with them. I sometimes had friends from Vienna up and we also walked in my woods.

I saw many wonders. I saw the beauty of the Vienna Woods. I saw the wild flowers, the trees, the herbs, spices and nuts that grew just up the hill from our flat. I saw and heard the birds and some wildlife. During the fall with the leaves changing and in the spring with flowers blooming there was an explosion of color and wonder filled my eyes. I loved the woods in the winter, too, when it became a sparkly fairy land.

One day it became a place of surprise as we walked and talked and suddenly my neighbor stopped and said hello to someone coming from the other direction. She introduced me and I saw an elderly lady; very refined, aristocratic and friendly. We spoke in German briefly and then went on our opposite ways. I, of course, asked for more information and was told this was truly a baroness and the mother of one of our neighbors. She came from the area near Graz where she lived in her castle. I felt maybe I had wandered into a fairyland myself and the baroness wasn't real but part of a book I had read or a tale I had heard.

I am a child of the King of Kings and not overly impressed with royalty here on earth. But, I am impressed over and over with my God who surprises me with the life I have been called to lead as a missionary and the tough times and the blessings he sends my way. Who knows, maybe next I will be invited to tea with a princess!

The Narrow Path

"For the gate is small and the way is narrow that leads to life, and there are few who find it." (Matthew 7:14 NASB)

Once in a while, Beth and I had the chance to show off the streets and landmarks of Vienna. After our arrival we enjoyed wandering the streets and small byways to discover hidden parts of that fascinating city. The history, stories of wars, rulers, plagues and Christianity were fascinating.

One day we once again wore our feet to a frazzle. A visitor from the USA wanted to fill a couple hours with a tour of the city before heading off to the airport. Camera in hand we started in the center, at Stephansdom, and worked our way out, across and around the center of the city. Along the Graben, up Kohlmarkt, through the Hofburg, by the Parliament and Rathaus, we explained each building and what history we could remember.

Tourists lined the streets and flashed photos of bits and pieces of history and studied their maps carefully. You can usually tell if Americans are nearby. They have a tendency to be very boisterous and excited about the sights, sounds and smells they experience. After you've lived there for a while you start telling your visitors to shush, or talk softly.

At the archaeological ruins we overhead some Americans trying to figure which way to go. I offered to help and explained how to traverse the winding streets to their destination. I'm sure everyone in the square could hear their questions and their shouts of thanks when they walked off into the distance.

A little tired and hungry we worked our way over for lunch at a cozy restaurant with an entertaining corner view and good food. The cushioned seats provided a respite for our tired feet and a refreshing meal. The German speaking waitress, from Russia, served us in record time. I went back later and found the restaurant out of business.

Ready to tackle a little more of the city we wove our way through the narrow passage by the Greek Church. Up the stairs is an ornate church beside one of the historic restaurants of the city. Mark Twain loved to visit Vienna and frequented this out-of-the-way eatery. If you don't know the city you can walk all around and never know it's there with all its delicacies. We ate there once. Mark Twain wasn't there but the food was good.

It's the same way with life. We search here and there to find something of value. We read the rambling theology of men and women. We trudge along the highway, lined with tomes dedicated to explaining God's message to the world, and miss the narrow country road. We're looking for a highway with big signs and lights. What we need is a narrow passage with a simple sign: salvation.

Many visitors crisscross Vienna and fail to discover that historic restaurant and church. An abundant number of feet have been wearied without noticing beautiful artwork and statues hidden away in the narrow passages. When we visited these areas we didn't see many tourists but we enjoyed the beauty. The beauty of Vienna wasn't found on Kärntner Straße, with the modern facades and stores, but in the small alleys and passageways.

Salvation is a gift of God's grace to a world in need. It's not found in the popular theology of the day but in the narrow words of Scripture. It's here we read Job's confession of understanding and repentance. It's the Shepherd we discover in a small Psalm of comfort. It was in the narrow cells of a prison that a guard discovered the wonder of faith and praise.

We try to be broad-minded but the message is narrow-minded. We want to be all encompassing but those who understand are few. It's a contradiction. God wants all men to be saved but only a small number will come. It's the grace of God, the call of a father to his children, that single recognizable voice, which reaches our heart and brings us home.

Let's stop trying to make a foot path into a highway. Preach the word clearly, the narrow message, so those who are searching will find the path. Only a guide who has already discovered the path can show others the way.

Another Time

And He who sits on the throne said, "Behold, I am making all things new."
And He said, "Write, for these words are faithful and true." (Revelation 21:5
NASB)

International agencies often lend a hand to one another. Think about it: we are all working toward the same goal. As a global body we demonstrate to the world our unity when they see one agency working hand in hand with another. Because of this interaction of expertise, I had the chance to visit some interesting sites. Whether I was the best choice is always debatable but I enjoyed the travel and new places.

One year a fellow colleague and I spent several days on the island of Chuk. For history buffs it used to be called Truck, even though there were only a few roads and more horse carts than semis. There we helped diagnose and repair the transmitter for a local radio station. We stayed with coworkers on the island. It was great to meet folks from another part of the world with the same type of work. As a result of getting to know one another my colleague invited a certain young lady to spend a few days on Guam.

My colleague was a man; I'll call him Fred. Fred's visitor was a woman; I'll call her Sue. As a single Fred couldn't have Sue staying in his home so my wife and I offered our home. Fred picked Sue up at the airport, showed here the sites of the island and arrived at our home thirty minutes later. It's a small island; there's not much to see.

As a nursing student from Yap Sue was excited to visit another island. She was delightful and fascinated by everything she saw. Growing up on the tiny island of Yap she had no idea of the culture and convenience of our large modern island.

We talked, got to know one another better and enjoyed our first meal together. After dinner our children loaded the dish washer. That's why we have children, to load the dishwasher. Sue had never seen a dishwasher. The intricate frames for holding the dishes, the soap, the noises it made while working amazed her. She was sad there wasn't a window in the front so she could watch and see what was happening inside.

Our refrigerator was another unique experience. They have refrigerators on Yap but they operate by propane. The power company doesn't extend to the smaller villages. These gas-powered coolers were run only two or three days a year for special events. Regular cold drinks, ice cream, and leftovers were the exception, not the rule.

Everything Sue saw and experienced was a new enchantment. Everything was exhilarating and eye-opening. It was as if she stepped into the present from another time. She took nothing for granted. Each new machine, each new taste, garnered her intense scrutiny. Like a little child discovering the world she discovered a world new to her. She laughed, smiled and enjoyed life.

When I was first saved I was like Sue. Everything fascinated me and received my full attention. I wanted to know God more and more each day. Each verse I read opened a new revelation, making me laugh, smile and enjoy life. What happened?

It took me a while but I finally figured it out. I had begun to take things for granted. God was loving, gracious, forgiving, and caring but that became the norm, expected. The excitement was gone. My heart and mind began to harden like an artifact buried for centuries. You could recognize it, understand its function, but it didn't live.

But, once God's word, through the encouragement of family and close friends, caught my attention once more, the petrifaction of my soul began to soften. Life slowly returned and the vastness of God's grace once more opened my eyes to the wonder of it all. There was still a long way to go before I could regain the awe of those first days as a believer. Many hard spots needed to be chiseled away but the pain and difficulty were worth it to draw closer to God.

What do we take for granted today? Our family? Our spouse? Our ministry? Maybe God? Too much familiarity often makes us forget the awe of God's work in our life. Paul reminds us we are a new creation. We need to renew our view of the miraculous.

God took us as sinners and through faith alone made us his children for eternity. Eternity where? Eternity in a new Heaven and a new earth. A new Jerusalem where we can walk in God's presence and discover all things new, day by day, not in another time, but for all time.

Lost Things

"I permitted Myself to be sought by those who did not ask for Me; I permitted Myself to be found by those who did not seek Me. I said, 'Here am I, here am I,' To a nation which did not call on My name." (Isaiah 65:1 NASB)

Have you ever lost something? I have; many things. Have you ever, years later, found something you thought was long lost and gone? I have, usually when I'm packing to move to a new home. Fortunately, moving doesn't happen too often.

It starts like this: I'm not looking for any item in particular, just going through things, when something catches my attention. I stop and look closely at the newfound treasure. Actually it's something old, something lost a long time ago, usually something I didn't remember I had. Sometimes it's a delight and I rejoice. Sometimes it's nothing and is promptly tossed in the bin. And sometimes, it's a reminder, stirring emotions I thought were long gone.

A couple months ago I was organizing my library. I have a couple friends who are professional librarians. They would be aghast at the lack of the Dewey Decimal system in my library. I don't use numbers and often the titles are upside down. My standard librarian skill involves putting the books wherever there is space. This served me well for years but finally, in order to find things, I had to create some sort of organization.

I simply alphabetized the books, my apologies to Mr. Dewey, and found a couple volumes I needed to re-read and some I had never read. I set them aside to work through them at a later date. I always keep a stack of books waiting to fill that elusive spare time. A few weeks later I took one off the top of the stack. I rifled through the pages. Suddenly I found an old boarding pass ferreted away between the pages. I yanked it out, like removing advertising from a new magazine, ready to toss it in the bin. Then I stopped and read the faded printing. Unexpectedly I was flooded with memories.

The faded printing read January 20, 1988. That was the flight date. Northwest flight 004 from Chicago to Narita, Japan. It was a fifteen-hour flight cramped into seat 23G. Economy class, affectionately known as the cattle car, provided my 500 mph seat. This was the second of three legs to return to the mission field. I was returning from my father's funeral. I remember the flight was long, cramped and lonely. I was trying to reorder my life at 35,000 feet.

"Living Above the Level of Mediocrity" was the book title where I found the boarding pass. I was reading the book when I heard the news and took the flight back the USA for the funeral. It was a gift I received just weeks before at Christmas. I took it along, knowing full well I wouldn't read on the airplane and probably not find time to read at my parent's home. With chapter titles such as, "Standing Firm When Discouraged" and "Standing Tall When Tested," it was perfect timing. I never finished reading the book.

Seventeen years later my thoughts returned to that January as I held and read the fading data on the colorful boarding pass. Sometimes, it takes a simple reminder to recall cherished things we miss. Regular letters from home, sharing my dad's thoughts, occasional phone calls just to keep in touch, long chats when we visited on furlough, all these came to mind and I missed them. They were part of my life and me. I held the paper in my hand and smiled. There was joy in finding the boarding pass.

As members of the human race, we're born and some things are already lost. We're lost in sin we inherited from our forefathers who inherited it from their forefathers, ad infinitum. In our scurrying about in darkness God was lost to us. But God changed all that. Light came into the darkness and God allowed Himself to be found. Oh the joy in finding the God of grace.

When we repented and received God's gracious gift of salvation, we remembered cherished things we missed. Reading God's letters sharing His thoughts, hearing Him as He responds to our prayers, long conversations when He reveals His love for us, all these are found in that priceless gift of faith. Oh the depth of joy in the finding.

After I found the boarding pass, I was more alert to see what else might be hiding in an unfrequented binding. Sorting through old boxes I looked carefully to discover that unobtrusive slip of paper, that small memento, that special rock picked up along the way. I started flipping through the pages of other books I hadn't opened in years. I was hunting for another memory, sad or happy, it didn't matter. It was the reminder I wanted to find.

There are photos adorning our walls as reminders of people and places and events. I like to stand and stare while I remember and relive things long gone. But, it's often the small, unexpected, tucked away treasure we find, by accident, that brings the greatest joy and most touching memory.

Gallivanting through Scripture keeps us mindful of God's precepts, God's grace and God's plan for our redemption. But, it's often in that one verse, seen over and over, that we unexpectedly find a treasure we didn't realize was there. While looking for a specific passage we stop and unintentionally read another verse along the way. The words suddenly jump out at us to remind us of God's work in our life and how precious our relationship is with Him.

Sometimes we need to slow down and look more carefully. We need to turn the page unhurriedly. We need to ensure our goal doesn't distract us from the treasure along the roadside. Next time we read God's letters to us, will we hurry to reach the end or, take our time and see if a new nugget of wonder will make itself found. I once was lost but now I'm found! I'm glad God didn't rush by but stopped to find me, hold me in his hands and smile.

Music Hall

Then David spoke to the chiefs of the Levites to appoint their relatives the singers, with instruments of music, harps, lyres, loud sounding cymbals, to raise sounds of joy. (1 Chronicles 15:16 NASB)

I think I started singing when I came out of the womb. At the time it sounded like singing to me and screaming to my parents. By the time I was five I started taking piano lessons. At about eleven I conned a neighbor into teaching me how to play the guitar. He was a professional guitar player with a black and white television. We had color. The bargain was, he taught me a lesson each week and we let him watch his favorite television show, Star Trek, in color. I think it was a good bargain. Since then I've taken every opportunity to sing, play and enjoy the wonders of music.

I'm not alone in my quest for the soul swaying strains of that perfect blend of harmony and melody. In Germany, King Ludwig II, the fairy-tale king, built a marvelous castle named Neuschwanstein. It's rumored the castle in Disneyland was based on Ludwig's masterpiece. I've seen both and Disneyland is not quite the same.

Sitting atop Jugend, replacing the ruins of two previous castles, Neuschwanstein's structure is spectacular. Walking through the front gates is like walking into a fairy-tale castle. Unlike other fortresses designed by men of war, Neuschwanstein was designed by an opera stage designer. It's romantic-looking but incomplete. Ludwig was arrested before the final stages of construction and died shortly afterward in dubious circumstances.

People travel from around the globe to visit this imposing site and so, along with close friends, we joined the throng of tourists. It was a dream holiday for a castle lover such as myself. With our friends we toured the interior, room by room.

Each lavishly decorated room captured our interest and ignited our imagination. Electricity, central heat and other modern ideas came to life in this Old World fortress. In the middle of our tour we were ushered into the Singer's Hall. The tour guide expounded eloquently with praises for its superb construction and audio acoustic quality.

We gawked at the precision construction punctuated by beautifully painted panels depicting scenes from the legend of Grail King Parsival, the father of Lohengrin. Phil, my friend, and I looked at each other and had the same thought: *let's sing!* We inhaled, stood up straight, and opened our mouths, ready to bring forth a beautiful song. Our wives, on the other hand, looked a bit concerned as they recognized a dangerous look of mischief in our expressions. Before they could say anything, or undergo the embarrassment of our singing in the middle of a tour, we caught the look of fear in their eyes, our senses took over, and we closed our mouths and exhaled slowly. We remained quiet and could hear the smallest noise. Each breath, each step, each syllable spoken was heard clearly anywhere in the room. It was magnificent.

God created music as a glorious means of praise and worship. With all the hoopla and bantering about musical styles, instruments and tempo, we forget God put music into our hearts to praise Him. Musicians and singers were appointed for the tabernacle and continued their magnificent ministrations in the temple. We appoint singers in our churches. During the course of a day we often break into choruses and songs. As we walk through the Christian life, melodies of praise rise up to lighten our step and draw us closer to God's side.

Our praise reaches God's ears as he sits in the perfect throne room of heaven. No earthly engineer could hope to approach the spectacular acoustical precision surrounding God's faultless ears. The beauty of Heaven's throne room makes our most precious paintings appear as childish scrawls. The most carefully engineered auditorium on earth can't compare with the perfect sound of God's children as their songs of praise reverberate in heaven.

As we sing, even those of us without earthly musical perfection, God hears every breath, every beat of our heart, every syllable of our song of worship. They are perfect to His ears. They fill His heavenly heart with joy. They reach his throne as an offering of fragrant aroma. This is the joy of lifting our voices to praise our creator, our strength, our God!

Still, when we are silent, God can hear every footstep we make, every thump of our heart, every ache which cries out to Him. It's a different melody but the perfection of His throne room turns it into beautiful music in His ears.

Next time I'm silent I'll let my heart sing to the Lord in Heaven. I'll let the footsteps of my life bring a melody to God's heart. I'll know He's listening. It'll be worth it all.

Next time I'm in a beautiful place, inspired to sing and moved with God's presence I don't think I'll hesitate. I'll open my mouth and sing my Lord's praises. Let those around me think I'm strange. What does that matter if God is praised, if He is worshiped, if His name is lifted in the miracle of music before His throne? It will be worth it all.

Lock and Load

"For nothing is hidden that will not become evident, nor anything secret that will not be known and come to light." (Luke 8:17 NASB)

One advantage of living on a small island with an extensive military presence was the chance to tour the impressive vessels. With three energetic boys, there was always an interest in the latest demonstration of power sailing into the harbor. When a ship dropped its gangplank, we were there waiting to be piped aboard.

Some ships were more impressive than others but each held its own unique features. As the boys and I strolled the decks and explored the belly and superstructure of each steel behemoth we tried to imagine life on board. Of course, we always glamorized it as fun, exciting, saving the world and being seen as heroes wherever we sailed.

We imagined flying freedom missions from the decks of aircraft carriers. Sending an enemy to the bottom of the sea would be our mission while touring a submarine. Storming a beach to free a nation from tyranny became our goal on troop carriers. Serving the thankful needs of our comrades in arms gave us joy while looking over the machinery of a tender.

One day we toured a guided missile frigate. The man in charge of the three-story launch platform spoke excitedly about its capabilities. "I can lock and load a missile in ten seconds," he declared with a gleam in his eyes and pride in his voice. Immediately he manipulated the controls, spinning the mount to demonstrate its flexibility and speed, no missiles of course.

The expected question soon arose from someone in the crowd, "Are these nuclear missiles?"

Immediately our guide's appearance became staunch and empty faced as he repeated by rote, "I can neither confirm nor deny the nuclear capabilities of this vessel." He waited a while as everyone nodded their heads and mumbled a chorus of "umm." The capabilities of the vessel were well known but could not be discussed.

We like to keep secrets. We want to surprise people with our abilities. On the other hand, we don't want people to know our deepest secrets. We're afraid of their response if they knew what we really thought or what we might do.

Jesus addressed this tendency and told us without mincing words there is nothing which will remain hidden. This is a sobering thought when I take an inventory of my own thoughts and activities. I would like to say, "I can neither confirm nor deny the sinful capabilities of this vessel." My capabilities are well known but carefully hidden. How they are used may be hidden from the world but not from God.

Jesus also reminded us that our words decry the intent of our heart. Good speaks good, bad speaks bad. Sometimes we can hide what is inside by carefully weighing our words. While the sailor sidestepped the issue of weapons, we knew even from his veiled response the immense destructive power safely stored in the belly of the ship.

The same is true for us as Christians. We can try to hide, try to veil the truth but it reveals itself even in our carefully crafted speech. Now, before we are called to action, is the time to clear out the destructive contents of our heart. Only through the revelation of the Holy Spirit can we see ourselves properly to know where to start and all that is hidden within.

"But I, GOD, search the heart and examine the mind. I get to the heart of the human. I get to the root of things. I treat them as they really are, not as they pretend to be." (Jeremiah 17:10 MSG)

Sunday on the Mountain

Therefore, we will not fear, though the earth should change And though the mountains slip into the heart of the sea; Though its waters roar and foam, Though the mountains quake at its swelling pride. Selah. (Psalms 46:2-3 NASB)

"I sing the mighty power of God, that made the mountains rise." High on the side of a mountain in Switzerland the morning activity was slow. The weather was iffy but gave the hint of improving later in the day. Our two families were enjoying a holiday of fresh air, mountains, flowers and fellowship. It was our first trip to Switzerland. The children staggered their way down the stairs from their loft bedrooms to the larger living room.

After a breakfast of French Toast, prepared by Phil's caring hands, we contemplated worshiping the Lord of salvation. Sunday morning had dawned and our hearts were ready to approach God's throne of grace. However, a little cleaning was a must.

I led the way outside for the boys to undergo a cleansing with water. The cabin was provided with water collected from a stream flowing down the mountain. There was no hot water. There was no electricity to heat the water. The hose hanging from the back of the cabin provided clear and cold mountain spring water. The emphasis here was on the cold. Just the process of washing the hair on our heads created a frostbite headache. Rinsing out the soap was an exercise in steady nerves, fast reflexes and pain. My poor hands hurt for about an hour after the refreshing adventure. With a little coaxing the boys were willing to brave the water and removed a layer or two of grime.

The girls were the smart ones. They cordoned off the kitchen where they had access to the wood burning stove. We brought in buckets of water which they turned into hot water. With their luxurious hot water and a little privacy, they prepared themselves for the day. The boys remained sequestered in the living room for the duration until the ladies emerged, happy and clean. We all agreed that hot water would be the best addition to this gift of a mountain cabin from God. Now that we were all clean it was time for some cleansing by the word.

During the bath time, except when I was freezing in the water, Phil and I enjoyed worshiping the Lord with song. I played the guitar for songs I knew and Phil played for those he knew. We moved from one song to the next through the chorus book I brought on the trip. When everyone was clean and present Phil suggested we allow the children and youth to provide the morning message.

Beginning with our youngest Evan, and working our way up in age, each shared a verse or passage and then their thoughts on the content. We were encouraged. Here were young people freely sharing what God had taught them from His word. Our hearts were also encouraged by the words they shared. It was an uplifting time for all of us. Their insight into God and His love for them was more than we expected. I guess they did learn something at home and in Bible class.

Next, we each shared a prayer request or two from our hearts. These were requests for ministry to or for others. Everyone was willing to open their hearts and desires before God and the family. Finally, we spent a time in intercessory prayer for these and other items which came to mind. You learn a lot about others and family when they pray for things important to them. You discover their dreams, their fears and their loves.

I believe this is a great way to worship the Lord of our salvation. There's no need to impress someone with Sunday dress. No theological exposition of impressive schooling. Only hearts, touched and molded by God, seeking to know God and praise His name. I must admit I felt as though I had worshiped God more closely and faithfully that morning than all the Sundays of the previous year.

I think we should each take an occasional Sunday morning, afternoon or evening to worship God with close family and friends. There is a close fellowship, a sharing from the heart, a bond which only exists in close family and small quarters. The facade of public worship is stripped away in the familiarity of family. We are not tempted to impress those who already know us. There we can feel free, accepted, and open to worship God without psychoanalysis by a congregation.

We don't want to forsake gathering together to encourage and strengthen one another through corporate worship and prayer. We are called to this in Scripture. I've spent years studying corporate worship and love times of blessing, singing praises, shouting hallelujah and lifting up God's name with the body of Christ. But, sometimes we gain more strength and encouragement in a small body of Christians.

Sometimes Jesus drew away only with his disciples. There was a time for the crowds and a time for family. It was in those close gatherings the disciples received most of their training. Maybe we need to draw away, sometimes, with the disciples in our own family. Does your family need to grow and know each other better? There is no better place to learn than before God's throne in praise, prayer and worship.

Cultural Differences

To the weak I became as weak, that I might gain the weak. I have become all things to all men, that I may by all means save some. Now I do this for the sake of the Good News, that I may be a joint partaker of it. (1 Corinthians 9:22 23 WEB)

Every time I visit a new country I experience a new culture. Some are very similar to my American heritage. Others are so vastly different that verbal descriptions cannot convey the uniqueness which only experience could realize. Living in Europe, we mixed with a plethora of cultures almost daily. Our church was a global melting pot of believers from across the globe. This unique worship environment held together, in spite of the broad range of cultures, because of the grace of God alone.

One culture I found greatly different was the Middle Eastern mixture of cultures. This became evident one day when one of our Middle Eastern men asked to speak with Beth. First you must remember God allowed us to minister to a number of young teachers from the Christian school the boys attended. As surrogate parents we were often closely tied to them in the eyes of others.

This young man had observed a lovely young teacher for a number of weeks. In full honesty he wanted Beth, as a mother figure, to arrange a marriage! There was even a discussion of gifts, perhaps camels and goats, to pay the price to acquire his bride. This wasn't a joke. This wasn't on hidden camera. This was a young man, enamored with a young lady, following the procedures he was taught throughout his life. This was how it was done in his culture.

Needless to say, Beth turned down the offer and kindly let the young man know that this wasn't how things were done in the young lady's American culture. The young lady's response, when Beth called her and told her about the proposal, was a long, loud scream searing the phone lines. In the following weeks I, along with some elders and translators from the church, met and counseled this young man, and others from his homeland, on cultural differences.

When I remembered this event, I laughed and thought of the culture which is part of me. Sometimes I'm understood and other times I must appear as unusual to others as this bartering for a bride appeared to me. In between stands the common ground of our faith in Christ. The young man, and his fellow countrymen, continued to attend our church and understood their cultural upbringing may not be proper in their new homeland. Still our relationship in Christ bound us together to worship and glorify God week after week.

Sometimes Scripture isn't what we interpret it to mean because of our cultural background. There are times when understanding the biblical cultural settings helps us know God better. The same is true when working in other countries and with other nationalities. Understanding the cultural differences is critical to a clear understanding of the efficaciousness of the Gospel message.

We may not comb our hair the same way, deal with family relationships the same way, or even drive on the same side of the road. In Christ we are one family. There are absolutes in Christianity and there is freedom. Paul knew this when he wrote that he became weak for the weak, and became all things that some might be saved. His godly absolutes were not tossed aside but His culture was second hand to the importance of proclaiming the saving message of the Gospel.

We need to understand what is our culture and what is our salvation. These two should not be mixed up. One is an earthly boundary the other is a heavenly offering. May we always proclaim the heavenly, that others will understand God's salvation.

Exotic Dancers

From that city many of the Samaritans believed in him because of the word of the woman, who testified, "He told me everything that I did." (John 4:39 WEB)

If you attend a church named Bayview you expect a grand view. That was true on Guam. Situated at the top of a cliff, overlooking Agana Bay, we loved the view from the church grounds. Below the cliff, Marine Drive connected the north and south sections of the island and separated the cliff from the sandy beach. On a clear day, which was almost any day without a typhoon, you could see for miles out over the Philippine Sea. Fishing boats would rise and fall on the swells of the sea. Jet Skiers churning the water, and snorkelers studying the reef, would pepper the azure water near the shore. Children played in the sand while parents, stretched out on folding lounge chairs, took respite in the shadow of statuesque coconut trees.

On the cliff side of the road, stone steps wound their way up the cliff to the church. A small sign at the bottom proudly bore out the name Bayview Baptist Church.

Occasionally, the sun and sea worshipers found their way up the stairs to our Sunday services. One Sunday morning a bikini-clad young lady plopped herself in a pew behind our family. A fishnet shawl was all she had against the cool of the air conditioning in the church. We said hello, the service started and the service ended. We turned to talk but she was out the door like a shot before we had the chance for a more formal greeting. This was normal at Bayview. Now and again you could look across the congregation to find a visitor, decked out in swimming attire, trying not to look conspicuous.

Another time, during the evening service, a nicely dressed young lady, no bikini, sat behind us with her baby. Let's call her Rachael. My wife, Beth, felt the Lord encourage her to talk with the young lady. When the service ended we were delighted to find Rachael was in no hurry to leave. So, after church she talked with Beth. Over the next few days they talked again and again. She, the visitor not my wife, was an exotic dancer, a mother of two and without a husband. This was new for us. Exotic dance clubs were not on our agenda. We didn't know what to expect. It was in the Lord's hands to lead and guide as Beth continued to talk and share her faith with Rachael. Praise the Lord, in the days ahead God touched Rachael's heart and she gave her life to Christ.

The excitement of Rachael's new-found faith was evident. Soon she was sharing the gospel with her friends.

Rachael sought to follow the Lord with every facet of her life. She married the father of her children. She found a new job. Soon, her friends started coming to church to see what happened to their fellow dancer. They couldn't believe a group of religious nuts could be more interesting than their life at the dance clubs.

Most Sundays I took time, as folks entered for services, to look around the congregation and see who was there. As friends entered I would wave a greeting and make note of first time visitors to greet after the service.

One sunny Sunday morning I looked up and down the pew. I paused, shook my head to make sure my vision was clear, and looked again. I found myself, and my children, in the middle of a covey of exotic dancers on the second row of the church. Let me say not all their attire was what you would normally find in a Baptist Church! Come to think of it, I'm not sure you would find some of their outfits in any church. But, they were there. Their curiosity, and love for their former dancing companion, made them take a daring step and enter a church.

The service started. Songs were sung. Prayers were prayed and a sermon was preached. The service ended they greeted us kindly and walked out the door. They had heard the word of God. Over the next few weeks some responded, some did not.

In the days ahead, Beth developed a ministry with several of the women. Now and again I found myself enjoying coffee with Beth in a little shop when one of her new friends would join us. Invariably someone else would enter the shop and recognize Beth's friend due to her former occupation. I wonder what they thought about us sitting there, sipping coffee and talking? It was a small island with a big gossip vine.

I'm reminded of Jesus meeting the Samaritan woman at the well. Her past was, shall we say, less than spectacular. She was amazed at the open-minded Jew sharing a message of salvation. She heard, she questioned, and she accepted the Lord's salvation. She was so excited that she had to share her faith with other Samaritans.

I wonder what the other Samaritans thought when the woman from the well sat and talked about Jesus? Sipping a Samaritan cappuccino in a little shop, she would share how Jesus changed her life. I'm sure they remembered her former lifestyle and listened dubiously to try and understand what made such a difference in her life. Some would understand, some would not. Jesus changed her life forever. In their eyes her past colored their present view. They couldn't see past her to the wonder of God's grace. In her eyes life was new, the past was out of sight.

Jesus forgives. Jesus changes lives. Maybe we have a past we would like to forget but people remember. Maybe we know someone with a sordid past who now is a member of God's family. At times we let our memories disrupt our relationships with one another. We have a hard time removing the person from the past. But at the cross the two separate.

At the cross we become new creatures, new people, new children of a gracious and loving God. It is a comfort to know God has taken our sins away for eternity. Next time our head reminds us of someone's past, let's put it in the past. Let's share the grace God showed to us with them. Some may respond, some may not. But, God still forgives for eternity.

Take A Look Around

For while we were still weak, at the right time Christ died for the ungodly (Romans 5:6 ESV)

I have a notebook computer with wireless. So do many of my colleagues. They are always asking how to connect to the internet while they are waiting in different airports. When I tell them, "I don't know," they look at me, perplexed. You see, I don't use my computer much while I'm actively traveling.

Sure, I use it when I reach my destination; that's part of my ministry. But along the way, sitting in an airport, waiting at the train station, there are much better things to do. Since I seldom travel in the USA I'm not tempted by obscenely large, tasty, messy, and hot cinnamon rolls as I walk through airports. Train stations tend to be sparse. On many platforms you are fortunate to have a roof over your head while you wait.

What do I do? I watch the people. I'm sure my behavior has provided a wealth of humor and entertainment to others, especially if things are running slow and I'm in a hurry. But that is another story.

People are why I got into the ministry. You might think God is why I am in the ministry. Sure, God called me to the ministry but why? Because of people! We missionaries love to spread the Gospel. Give use a ten second break in the conversation and we'll slip a bit of religion into any conversation. The trick is figuring out what to slip in, when, and how much.

Sometimes the Lord drops a conversation in our lap. I was in the Zurich airport waiting in the check-in counter queue (translation: that's a line to most Americans) when this young lady of Asian heritage stepped up behind me. She asked me a question about how the quick check-in computers worked, and whether she could use it; I said I didn't know. Never used one. (OK, I'm a practical travel application-impaired geek!) We chatted a few more minutes, discussing why we were in Switzerland. She was a student learning German and I a computer geek helping out a colleague. After discussing who I work for she blurted out that she too was a Christian from California (yes, there are real Christians in California). I was called to the counter and never saw her again. Talking with strangers in an airport can be fun. You learn interesting things.

But sometimes, not talking with people at the airport is just as much fun. My trip began with a flight from Vienna to Geneva. But, as it happens, the flight from Vienna was late for departure. Maybe not late for departure as much as late for arrival since we passengers were waiting for a plane to arrive. My name may be Chick but flapping my arms wildly still doesn't do much except clear a few seats on either side of where I'm sitting.

So, sitting in the mostly empty waiting room - it was a small plane - I watched the people. Then my imagination began to wonder about them. Where were they from? Where were they headed, beyond Geneva? Was it business or holiday (translation: vacation to most Americans) travel? Or, was there something else hidden about their presence? I wonder. . .

I surveyed the room and started taking notes discretely on a pad of paper in my lap in plain sight. To the right a row of stainless steel chairs lined the windows to the road outside. A rather large older man decided thirty minutes' delay was just sufficient for a nap. He took off his jacket, stretched out on the chairs and quickly filled the room with his raucous snoring. He looked like a small mountain with his white-shirted belly rising high above the green metal seats. At least he made me feel better thinking if I took a nap it would only look like a rolling hill and not the Matterhorn. He must be headed home from a busy trip, ready for rest and relaxation.

Two rows away, on my left (I was sitting against a wall), was another middle-aged business man making a phone call. (I always wondered what is middle age? People talk about fifty being middle age but I don't know a lot of people who live to be one hundred.) He flipped out his phone, sat on the edge of his seat and waited for an answer. When it came we all knew. He talked so loud he could eliminate the telephone and still be heard at his destination. Some gobbledygook about a sports meeting and how thankful he was for the person on the other end of the phone and their help. I wasn't not eavesdropping; he was shouting his conversation to the entire holding pen. Then he asked the real question. Isn't it amazing how compliments at the beginning of a phone call are a secret code letting you know something more important is coming? He wanted to know the money was applied to the right place. Ah, money, the blood which courses through the veins of every business.

I was distracted from the rest of the conversation when an older Spanish couple stepped between me and my view of the telephone shouter. The lady plopped down and stood her rolling pack upright. The man shuffled in, dragging his left foot. Apparently either age, injury or disease had taken its toll on the man's physical abilities. She shouted at him to sit here, put his bag there and stop taking so long. It seemed his vision was also poor. We all discovered this. When he needed the toilet (translation: bathroom to most Americans) she pointed across the hall and sent him off with his shuffle. He turned left, right and couldn't find the WC. She sat in her seat and shouted, "Not that way! Over there! The big yellow sign! No, the other way! Can't you see the sign? You're going the wrong way! Can't you see anything?" and then finally got up and pointed him in the right direction with a final comment, "You open your eyes when you want to, why not now?" I wondered how those two kept traveling together. Then, I'm amazed. They were back, looking at a

288

magazine and laughing together. Love is blind as they say. He might not have found the WC, which he did to all our relief, but he had found his love.

Across the room was a Duty Free shop. All these years of travel and I've never purchased anything from a Duty Free shop. Of course, I never purchase anything of a big value to warrant duty when I land. A young lady sat at the counter, all in red, a bored look on her face. She sat, and sat, and sat, and no one even browsed the trinkets and travel ware she had to sell. Two hours later she had only one shopper briefly glance at a package of something. At one point she rearranged a display. A little while later she rearranged it again, back the way it was. How did she deal with a such a lack of contact all day? That would drive me crazy.

An Asian couple sat in the corner, stone faced and quiet. Finally, he moved and looked through the stamps in his passport. The excitement never ends. As boarding time approached, people got restless and started pacing about the room. That helped . . . I'm sure.

Me, I read my book for a while. It was a book all about the wonders of living and staying in a small town. I miss the small town where I grew up. It was a place where everybody knew everyone. We went to school together, church together (there were divisions between Baptists, Lutherans, Methodist, Catholics and others, but only on Sunday morning), held parades around the town square, and all frequented the same grocery store, pharmacy, and ice cream shop.

I've enjoyed my world travels. The Lord has sent me places I never imagined. Like on this day, Geneva, Switzerland. The ministry impact was great. I wouldn't trade it. But, I wondered if the deepest impact was when people minister close to home, person to person, where everyone knows everyone.

Many turn to Christ hearing a message on the radio. But somehow I feel those that stick, grow and reproduce believers, are those who learned by watching and living in proximity (a techie word) to faithful believers, when there are faithful believers nearby. For others, it's more difficult.

Now I'm not saying I'm the best example of faithfulness. I've had my bad days, hours, and decades. But I learned. Maybe someone can see what I learned and save themselves the anguish. But then again, we have a tendency to want to make our own mistakes in some utopian belief we can do it better. NOT!

Let's become real people, with real problems, and real discussions. Let's NOT hide our need, our faults, in Christianized language, for fear of what other believers might think.

Consider the people I just described. Are they saints or ain'ts? God died for each. Some may know God and some not. But we struggle, saints and ain'ts, through the same life, at the same airports, watched by the same people.

Boys Will Be Boys

And Jesus increased in wisdom and stature, and in favor with God and men. (Luke 2:52 WEB)

I think boys, compared to girls, are the least likely to ever grow up. Girls, on the one hand, start playing house and other grown up stuff early in life. Boys, on the other hand, just want to play, jump, run, scream, chase, break, toss and inflict themselves on the world around them. And as they grow older, they want to impress the girls with their ability to play, jump, run, scream, chase, break, toss and inflict themselves on the world around them. Most boys are pretty good at this approach to life. I know, I was one of them.

I also think boys are the same across all ages, cultures, and continents. Someone once said, "Give a boy a stick, a string, and a mud hole and he will be busy all day." One of my favorite hobbies is watching children play. I've done this on several continents, in multiple cultures and countries. Girls play with dolls, pretend they're mommies, look cute, sweet and innocent. They bake cookies and offer gifts to others. Boys are never so docile. They take their stick and smack the other boys and girls around them. Then, laughing, they run through the closest mud hole in their best pants. Finally, they use their string to creep up and capture some unsuspecting lizard to make it a pet. It may only be three inches long but it is a dragon in their mind.

It doesn't take much to spark the imagination of a young boy. Growing up with two older brothers, I was seldom at a loss for some lame brain idea to pass the day. While my brothers often broke things, usually themselves, I was a bit more cautious and survived youth with fewer scars and nothing broken. I took my share of risks. But I always watched my brothers make the mistake and then I tried to avoid them . . . the mistakes, not my brothers. I'm very grateful they paved the way, with their sweat and blood, so I could emerge from childhood with stories to tell and all limbs intact.

One morning, it was warm, the sun was shining and it seemed as if spring might actually arrive. I stepped onto our balcony to survey my kingdom. To most people it looked like the parking lot of an apartment complex. But, to my mind, it was my royal kingdom stretching across the plains of Burgenland to the foreign borders of Slovakia and Hungary. As I took another sip of my royal coffee - there was a crown on the package of coffee grounds I used- I looked down into my asphalt garden and spied an interloper. There, coming from the upper grounds, was a young man with a broken scooter. The handle was missing so it looked more like a skateboard than a modern scooter. I watched carefully to see if he intended to break any of the laws of the land. As the ruling monarch this was my responsibility.

The little ruffian rolled to a stop in front of a massive oak tree. There were two such trees which flanked the entrance to my royal palace. I lived on the top floor and had the best view and the most stairs. When my children were younger I tried to get them to carry me up the stairs, like good sons should do for their monarch. They weren't interested and even made some less than royal remarks. So much for absolute authority, and my aging knees.

The young man put one foot on the pavement to stop his rolling and slowly raised his eyes to survey the imposing tree in his path. I could almost hear his mind clanking away, devising some lame brain scheme that involved a tree, his youthful skills, recklessness, and a broken scooter.

He stood for a moment, giving me time to sip more of my royal blend. His head tilted to the left, then to the right. He placed his hands firmly on his waist, revealing his sheer determination. The tree was something to be conquered; a castle wall to be breached, a tower to demand a view of the surrounding region. The top was in his sights.

This epitome of youth, striving to prove his manhood, stepped up to the trunk, stretched an arm to either side, placed one foot on the wood and jumped. Three or four times, with different grips and alternating feet, he attempted to shinny up the tree. Alas, the girth of the plant was more than his eight-year-old arms could handle. He stepped back, surveyed the tree once more and his eyes sparkled with another idea.

Standing about three feet tall it was obvious, to me, there was no way for him to reach the first branch jutting out about fifteen feet above the ground. But boys are boys. Everything is there to be conquered, jumped on, chased, tossed or inflicted with their presence. He was not going to give up easily to this immobile protrusion from the soil.

He picked up the broken scooter and placed it against the tree. Sideways as first, which did little to increase his vertical advantage. Then he turned it on the end, adding another foot or more to his height. He placed one foot on the upper edge, flung his arms wide in anticipation and launched himself at the tree once more.

He bounced off the wood onto his backside and found himself lying on the ground looking into the outstretched arms of his foe. That must have hurt! I struggled not to laugh and spoil the moment. Now boys are reckless, adventuresome and often foolhardy, but, they do eventually learn from their mistakes, which they call valiant attempts.

It took a few more tries, leaving his face print on the bark, before the light dawned. It just wasn't going to happen today. With resolute determination to come back, maybe when he was older and taller, he put the scooter back on the ground, planted one foot in the center and pushed off up the hill. There had to be a mud hole around somewhere to soothe his spirits.

As I stepped inside for another royal cup of java, I thought of the many times I hopelessly attempted some grand scheme in life. It was the adventure, the possibility of success, which drove me onward.

We do the same thing in our Christian walk. We see something we want to conquer and go at it with all our might. God looks down, chuckles and watches as we struggle and learn. He knows what it's like.

When He was incarnate, as a young boy, he learned about climbing trees, skipping rocks on a lake and finding a mud puddle to play in. He understands our desire to shinny up a tree too big for our scrawny arms. His memory is perfect. So His Holy Spirit is here, beside us, cheering us on. He then reaches over and teaches us something new. He shows us our strengths and our weaknesses and we eventually learn. Even those who are still young boys at heart.

A Bit Ashamed

Come now, you who say, "Today or tomorrow let's go into this city, and spend a year there, trade, and make a profit." (James 4:23 WEB)

Yesterday I had everything planned. Our son, Evan, is one of the lead roles in the spring musical, "Seven Brides for Seven Brothers." I was recruited to manage the sound system needs. It's one of those good relationship efforts between the mission and the school. Besides, I enjoy it and it gives me a chance to see the play multiple times without buying a ticket! Of course, my able-bodied assistant, set designer and wife, Beth, must be with me otherwise I couldn't slide the potentiometer up and down properly.

I put things in order at the office, told the folks in the office I was off for the afternoon and headed to the car. Along the way I picked up a wooden ladder, another prop for the play, some shoes for Evan, and high tech pink noise generator and spectrum analyzer to adjust the sound system to the room characteristics. It really impresses the high school students when you make a loud noise in the speakers while walking about the room with a funny looking device making measurements.

I drove through the beautiful city of Perchtoldsdorf, onto the Autobahn, through the interchange onto the main highway north. There it started. Traffic was creeping along. For thirty minutes I sat, I rolled a few feet, I sat, I rolled a few feet. Five hundred meters in 30 minutes. This was ridiculous. I was going to be late. It was all planned. The tests, the equipment, the timing. It was only two in the afternoon! What was the problem?

For the first fifteen or twenty minutes I listened to the radio. The traffic report informed me there was a traffic jam, as if I couldn't figure that out. Then I started to fidget, and my halo slipped as I started to get mad at the traffic jam. I felt I had a little justification. I don't know about you but I always feel justified. I'm wrong but at the time I think I am right.

Eventually my forward crawl came to a halt. People started getting out of their cars and standing on the side of the road. It was totally stopped. I climbed out to enjoy the sun and regain my composure and try to re-affix my halo at the proper slant. It was then I noticed, about ten cars ahead of me, a helicopter. I didn't hear it arrive because of the traffic noise. This was a major accident. Someone was so seriously injured a helicopter was called to whisk them off to the hospital.

About twenty minutes later I watched the bright yellow helicopter take off toward a hospital. Within a minute I was in my vehicle and back on my way. The road ahead was clear after such a long stoppage.

As I drove away I felt convicted. I was concerned about what I wanted, where I needed to be and how the world around me was impeding my progress. The traffic made me angry at the thought I might not arrive in time.

But, in the middle of the highway someone was in trouble. Someone was seriously injured. Someone needed help and all I could do was think of why I was late.

This someone is one of the people our ministry seeks to reach. He, or she, is a person for whom Christ died. He, or she, is someone in need of salvation like me, like you, like all of mankind. Instead of being concerned for their well-being I was concerned about my frustration. I'm sorry, Lord. My eyes were on the goal, not the one who called me to the goal.

Next time I'm stuck in traffic, or the next time you're stuck in traffic, it might be good to consider who is at the front of the line. Injured or just slow they are in need of a savior. And, I still arrived on time!

News Aficionados

If anyone speaks, let it be as it were the very words of God. If anyone serves, let it be as of the strength which God supplies, that in all things God may be glorified through Jesus Christ, to whom belong the glory and the dominion forever and ever. Amen. (1 Peter 4:11 WEB)

I left the mainland for Asia and then Europe over thirty years ago. It's been one adventure after another. I've seen things I never imagined. I've visited places I never thought I'd visit. Gallivanting here and there you develop a whole new outlook on the world.

My small-town view of the world expanded as I met other cultures, learned other languages, and choked down strange, unknown foods. Another strange transformation began to take place. I'm sure it's part of my character but I discovered it watching my wife. She has developed into a news aficionado over the years.

What is a news aficionado? It's someone with an expanded worldview. Growing up we were both content with local news sources. The local paper, local radio, local TV all brought us the top, earth-shattering, important news events from our town and the world. At least we thought it was from the world.

I'm not a newsaholic like my wife. She could watch news almost all day, read the paper, go to news online and be very content. I'm overloaded after reading the headlines when my browser opens each morning. But whether with a lot or little news we both have been impacted with an expanded worldview.

We didn't realize this until we were back in our homeland after years overseas. We turned on the TV, no cable, and tuned into the local stations. Four channels seemed enough for our meager needs. The hour came, the banners were displayed, the staff were introduced and the news began.

Floods in a local neighborhood, crime in the local neighborhood, corruption in the local neighborhood, weather and coming events all were centered on the local region. One or two stories gave lip service to news and events from other regions of the state. One or two mentions were made of something from another country. We tried news from all four stations. The same. The world didn't exist, except in small drops, outside the local area.

We were starving to hear about other world-shattering events. The local stations weren't going to satisfy that need. We then turned to newspapers.

We walked to the nearby newsstand. Five papers. There were four local and one "international" paper which mostly contained US news and events. I'm beginning to understand why we had such a small view of the world as we grow up.

I must admit I don't trust news people any further than I can throw them. Everyone reporting news, no matter what culture, language, nationality, political party, or faith reports news with their own slant. But at least it gives us something to work with to see what is happening in the world. It gives us a glimpse into how God's creation is getting along without Him.

I don't mean God is gone. I mean most of the world ignores God and tries to do things on their own. In our Bible Belt society, at least where I grew up, we often have a poor perception of the great dichotomy between the nations and God.

Folks around the world are not filling churches, singing praise songs, and wearing the latest fashions on Sunday morning. In most lands, there aren't churches on every other corner vying for the tallest steeple and most impressive facade.

Call me a news aficionado. I called my wife a news aficionado. She didn't like it at first but I think she's warming up to the idea that it isn't such a bad trait after all. I want to know the needs and conditions where I live. I also want to know what is happening in the world. Not to analyze the methods or motives of world leaders but to see the needs.

Once I know the needs I can pray effectively. Once I know the needs I can minister, where I live, effectively. Once I look beyond the horizon of my front porch, or the borders of my city limits, I understand more why Jesus said to the Galileans, "Come to me, all you who are weary and burdened, and I will give you rest. Take my yoke on you and learn from me, because I am gentle and humble in heart, and you will find rest for your souls. For my yoke is easy to bear, and my load is not hard to carry." (Matthew 11:28-30 NET.)

Jesus lifted my burdens and placed his yoke on my shoulders. I understand, once more, why God called us to minister to the nations. I feel Jesus' compassion to bring the message of salvation to the world. I pray that we, as Christians, take the time to expand our vision, learn more of the need in God's world and do what we can.

Pray always. Go if we are called. Give as we are inspired. Teach our children. Learn from his word, the Holy Spirit and others. Do your work, whatever it may be, to the glory of God that his name is praised in the streets. Not just here, in our own backyard, but also with a vision for the world.

Sno-Castle

How sweet are your promises to my taste, more than honey to my mouth!
(Psalm 119:103 WEB)

When I was a child I loved to eat snow cones. First, a paper cone or cup was filled to the brim with shaved ice. Next a scoop of shaved ice was plopped on top for a beautiful round summit. Finally, fruit flavored sugar syrup was pumped all over the ice to add color and flavor. It didn't take much to make but I loved it as a treat.

I'm not supposed to eat all that sugar stuff anymore but will occasionally indulge my sweet tooth. On one furlough, one of our supporting churches provided us a house for several months. It was a great time to refresh our spirits, rest and collect our thoughts. (I always thought that phrase sounded like thoughts were scattered on the floor.) Lots of time was available for prayer and seeking God's continued direction.

I just can't pray or reflect eighteen hours a day. (I do sleep about eight hours a day and take no credit for my mental attitude while I'm oblivious to the world.) There were breaks for meals, reading, talking with my wife and the occasional visitor. You don't get many visitors when no one knows where you're living.

Sometimes, I'd take a break, sit on the front stoop (for the younger reader, that's a front porch step), and watch cars whiz past. It was a short street but some folks can get up quite a head of steam. Following the course of a car down the street my attention was drawn to a lot, just catty-cornered across the intersection from the church.

In this triangular parking lot formed by three cross streets sat a white, container-sized building. The top was decorated with a castle parapet facade and displayed the name Sno-Castle. Each side had a window for serving customers shaved ice in a paper cone.

I've visited a few castles while living in Europe. Last count it was around 300+, including the occasional palace. None were as small, nor as popular, as this little stand dedicated to the delight and fruity flavor of shaved ice.

It took a couple days to learn the box was only open in the afternoon and evening. I guess I could've walked up and read the sign, but that was too easy. It seemed so desolate sitting there throughout the morning, empty of people and forlorn in the small parking lot. But once the young ladies showed up, flipped the signs from closed to open, then the place came alive.

The drooling began as you walked up and read the menu. Like other cold confectionery shops you expected a wide variety of snow cones and ice cream. Nope, no such offering. They had Real Flavored Snow and that was the whole menu. Over 120 flavors with some special names. That was an entire summer of experimentation and sweet joy.

You could start with the Prince size then work up through the Queen and King size. One Wednesday, after prayer meeting, Beth and I wandered over for our first treat. Young and old sat around the lot, on the guard rail, leaning against their cars and enjoyed the rainbow of colored ice. Children smiled and dribbled, adults smiled and slurped. Dress wasn't important, culture wasn't important, background wasn't important, only the delicious, cold ice melting as it slid down their throats to cool them from the inside out.

We read through many of the flavors, some printed, some handwritten on the wall. I found banana, my favorite. Beth was more literate as she made her way to kiwi and strawberry. They would mix any flavors, two in the initial price, you wanted to try. You placed your order and waited.

The ice was ground in a machine you could hear working just out of sight. Your mouth started to water with anticipation. The cone was filled and that first bit of flavor was sloshed on the ice. Next, a funnel of ice was plopped on to make a pointy mountaintop. More syrup was poured to finish the construction. If you ordered two flavors they put them on opposite sides of the cone adding to the visual delight. Then they stuck in a spoon, and you were ready to enjoy.

That first taste of refreshing coolness with delightful fruit flavor was marvelous. You worked through the mountain top into the cone. One feature of snow cones is the demonstration that gravity works. Much of the syrup oozes its way through the shaved ice to collect and over saturate the ice at the bottom of the cone. Working past the peak into the bowl, the sensational flavor increases as you go deeper.

Eating snow cones reminds me of growing in Christ. You take that first taste and wow, what a delight. But wait, as you dig deeper the delight increases more and more. Some folks eat the top of a snow cone and toss away the bottom. They don't know what they're missing. Some Christians skim the surface of their faith and fail to dig deep. They miss the overpowering wonder found only in the depths of the Christian life.

The Psalmist understood when he wrote, "O taste and see that the LORD is good; How blessed is the man who takes refuge in Him!" (Psalms 34:8 NASB) How deep are we tasting of the Lord's wonder?

What Is It?

For our citizenship is in heaven, from where we also wait for a Savior, the
Lord Jesus Christ; (Philippians 3:20)

It seems the last child to leave home signals our last chance for success as parents. They are old enough to make their own decisions. Sometimes, unexpectedly, they will ask our opinion before making a choice. More often than not, they will forge ahead, making a combination of good and bad choices. We live at a distance and observe what we can. Living on another continent makes observation a little more difficult.

We went through three departures, but there was always someone still at home. Then came the fourth, Evan, the last fledgling to leave the Chick nest. That last year of high school was filled with special events, new experiences, and growth for our youngest son. There were days we wondered if we would make it to the end, other days we knew it would be spectacular.

At graduation the end was near. He was class president. He earned the highest spiritual award for the school. Applause, smiles, and camera flashes filled the evening along with celebration and food. Three days later we were on a plane to the USA. Evan was on a journey to another world, another life, a foreign land.

At graduation one of the American teachers gave Evan a present. He smiled, said thank you, then studied the paper in his hands. A couple minutes later he was showing it to me, eyes wide with curiosity.

"What's this, Dad?"

"A check," I replied.

"What do I do with it?" he asked. He didn't know. He had never seen a check. They don't use checks in Europe, just debit cards and cash. He knew it represented money because of the dollar sign next to the numbers. I chuckled.

"Give it to me," I said. "We'll take care of this in the US. I'll show you how to use it, and a lot of other stuff when we get there." He said thanks, left the check in my hand and bounded off to be with his fellow graduates and friends.

I looked at the check. A gift of love from one of his teachers. It symbolized the many aspects of his homeland he didn't understand. It was his homeland, but he had never lived there. This was going to be a great adventure. I wondered if we taught him right while he was growing up. That's a question that will be answered in the years ahead.

As I tucked the check away in my wallet, I was reminded of Heaven. This earth is not our home. We long for a heavenly home, an eternal home. We can read about Heaven, all the neat things John describes, the mansions Jesus talked about. Then we scratch our heads and hold out our hands to God asking,

"What is this, Dad?" We've never lived there but we look forward to arriving on its shores one day.

The imagery is spectacular and confusing. We've imagined it, troubled ourselves over the descriptions and made it what we imagined. But the reality, when we finally arrive, will far outshine our meager mental picture. Still, this side of our flight to eternity we have questions.

We turn to God and ask, "What's this, Father?"

"It's my love and grace," He replies.

"On the cross?" we ask.

"Yes, my son," He replies.

That one word suddenly becomes clear and we ask, "Son? I'm part of the heavenly family?"

"Yes, I have adopted you. Everything I have is yours." God smiles, tucks away our questions and waits.

Since Evan setup his little apartment he has learned many things about his homeland. He calls us regularly to ask questions ranging from cooking instructions to government regulations. It's nice to know we're still needed. It won't last forever.

As a Christian I approach the Father with my questions. How do I do this? What's that? And sometimes I apply what I learned earlier to a new situation. Sometimes I get it right, other times, wrong. God likes to hear from us. It's nice to know He is needed.

Sometimes I forget God is there, waiting, ready to answer my questions, ready to give me guidance, ready to prepare me for my eternal mansion. I think of my son. He didn't know about where he was going. He hadn't been there, but I had.

God knows where we are going. He knows the streets, the mansions, the wonders we anticipate with awe. We just need to take the time and ask, "What is this, Father?" and know we'll receive a perfect answer.

Turkey in the Wild

Finally then, brethren, we request and exhort you in the Lord Jesus, that as you received from us instruction as to how you ought to walk and please God (just as you actually do walk), that you excel still more. (1 Thessalonians 4:1 NASB)

"I've got a question for you," my brother said. We were standing behind his house in California, beneath the beautiful oak trees, looking into the valley below. We hadn't seen each other in two years. Knowing my brother, this could be a loaded question.

"OK," I said, "shoot."

"Can turkeys fly?" he asked as he gazed at the gnarly branches of the trees.

It wasn't the type of question I was expecting. No questions about the family, our children, or living overseas. Just a question about turkeys. Definitely different.

I thought back to my classes in ornithology and replied with confidence, "For short distances. They can't sustain a long flight."

"Wow, most people don't even know that," he said, duly impressed. Maybe not quite as impressed as I would hope but surprised I knew that small fact. Sometimes those odd courses I took come in handy.

That was about all I knew about turkeys. I remembered Benjamin Franklin wanted the wild turkey for our national bird. I'd never seen a wild turkey but remembered chasing turkeys in my uncle's yard many eons ago.

Steve explained an interesting habit about turkeys. About dusk turkeys wandered into the oak tress behind the house. Because they are virtually defenseless they needed a safe place to spend the night. So, they flew up to a low branch on a tree then worked their way upwards to a spot safe from predators. Did you know this? I didn't.

Later we were on the deck of the house as the sun began to dip below the mountains. Sure enough, up the little trail came a flock of four turkeys. They wandered along, picking nuts and other goodies from the grass as they made their way to the oak trees.

Mama was the first to jog a couple steps, flap her large wings and flutter up to the bottom branch. After she established balanced footing she worked her way up the branch away from the earth below. The rest of the turkeys poked around, tilted their heads this way and that, and considered where they would roost for the evening.

Finally the next turkey walked up the hill a bit, turned, and calculated the distance with a discerning eye. Jogging downhill to gain speed the wings flared out, flapped and carried the poult to another branch in the tree. This brilliant turkey figured a little elevation would reduce the distance to the branch. Soon, the remaining turkeys would wing their way to a safe sleeping perch.

Beth and I were fascinated. On what we might consider a precarious perch, these bulbous birds were planning a night in snug safety. They knew what they needed and were putting it into effect at the right time and the right place. There wasn't a turkey summit to discuss the ramifications of branch safety over ground assault.

Unfortunately, I must admit I'm not always as smart as a turkey. I've been called a turkey for sure. There are things I know I should do and things I know I shouldn't do. At times I get these two backwards. Like Paul I sometimes find myself doing what I shouldn't and not doing what I should.

There are times I'm sitting on the ground, late into the night, looking up at the safe perch on the branch. I know I should follow the Lord's guidance, obey His commands, seek His kingdom with all my heart. Jesus told me God cares even for the sparrows and the few remaining hairs on my head. He will take care of my needs when I fly up into the safety of His arms. But, there I sit on the ground.

When a turkey acts independent of his teaching and training he makes a good target. Staying rooted on the ground when the safety of the tree beckons, the turkey makes himself a midnight snack for some scavenger. The same thing happens to me as a Christian. When I stay rooted in the earthly part of myself I am open to attack from the passing scavengers of Satan's hordes. If I rest in the safety of God's word and what He teaches me, I am safe.

Where will I spend my time? On the ground, or in the air? I have this urge to spread my wings, take a few steps for momentum, and fly to the safety of my Father's arms. What about you?

A Guy Thing

I have no greater joy than this, to hear of my children walking in the truth.
(3 John 1:4 NASB)

Growing up near Cincinnati, Ohio we were just a hop, skip and a jump from the Wright-Patterson Air Force Museum. Three boys would join forces with a father who was once in the Air Force and visit this paragon of devotion to aircraft development and history.

We were duly impressed with the massive planes parked outside on the old airfield. We would walk around the variety of planes, helicopters and other flying machines. We would touch, climb in, drool and dream of flying unhindered through the heavens. None of us ever became pilots. We've flown all over the world but others piloted the planes.

Recently I took a trip back to the museum. Since all my boys were working I convinced Beth to come along. She is a loving and understanding wife. She just didn't understand what she was getting into.

We arrived to find the old air field, once covered with planes, replaced by a series of massive quonset huts. The museum was still free but now modernized with air-conditioning. Some of the rustic adventure of sweating with the oldies was replaced with fancy displays, restrooms and maps. I can be a wimp at times and love air-conditioning when it's hot outside. It was hot that day and I was thankful for the upgrade.

Starting with the Wright Brothers we wandered through six buildings filled with winged machines. The variety, a mixture of real, test, and future planes, was staggering. From the small one-man planes to the massive B52 and Superfortress, I was having a grand time. I took lots of photos and tried to sound like I knew something about the different models, their history and purpose.

This is a guy thing, I think. When it comes to planes, cars and all that is mechanical we feel we have to demonstrate our proficiency and knowledge on the subject. Unfortunately, I'm not very good when it comes to planes and cars.

I never was a car fanatic. Other guys will shout, "Wow!" and point to some sleek-looking car driving down the highway. This is usually followed by a description of the make, model and year. By the time I realize they are talking about a car it's long gone. To maintain the bravado I nod my head and say, "Wow."

I liked planes because they were cool-looking but couldn't tell one from another without the appropriate name plate. I loved building model planes as I was growing up. They would line the shelves in my room and hang on strings from the ceiling. I had to look at the boxes to figure out which one was which.

It didn't take long for Beth to realize I was often guessing, or down right fabricating, my extensive knowledge on aeronautics. She knew it was a guy thing and would surreptitiously walk past the placard so I could glance at the name and spout some authoritative insight on the plane's form and function. I wasn't very convincing. She wasn't that subtle.

She made it through five buildings before she commented on being tired. I didn't want to admit it, but they were starting to all look alike. My feet were tired too. And I was getting hungry. But it was a guy thing, I had to see everything! We persevered, a godly virtue I understand, and made it to the end.

Over the years I've met many missionaries and pastors. It's a pastor thing but you have to have an answer to all theological questions. It's also a missionary thing. We have difficulty admitting we just don't know everything about God and His world. We use human logic, peppered with good sounding verses, to justify, explain or cast aside some of the questions sent our way.

It's like standing in front of the X3 and someone says, "Cool!" You feel the urge to expound your limitless knowledge to help them rise above their lowly understanding. If you happen to know something, great. If you don't know anything, you make it up. Or, if you don't want to express your creative thinking you exhale heavily, shake your head and walk away like everyone should know. After a while you get pretty good at sounding like you know what you're talking about.

Sometimes, we, as Christians, feel the pressure to perform. A believer is looking up to our spiritual wisdom, our years of experience, our great knowledge of Scripture, to help them answer their question. How we perform, how we respond, how we live our life before others, tells a lot about our own walk with God.

When that "guy" thing comes into play we sometimes piece together the few verses we know to make a logical sounding answer. We play to the crowd of one. Truth may or may not have anything to do with the answer, but it sounds good, including the verses we quote!

When we're honest, another godly virtue, we give only the answers we know are true. We don't try to rebuild our theology on the spot, to be a modern sage. If we don't know the answer, we admit it and help our brother or sister to find the answer. Truth has everything to do with our response. It has everything to do with what others see in our life.

As we drove away from the museum I had to admit to my wife I really didn't know much about the various planes. I think they're cool looking. I've never studied their purpose or history. She smiled at me and said, "I know." She's a smart lady. After we reached home I looked up some stuff on the internet. I'm still not an expert.

When we realize and admit our spiritual limitations we can openly tell others we don't know. If that verse doesn't come to mind, we don't need to struggle to make it up. We can say we don't know and then join the discovery. We help someone. We help ourselves. We grow in Christ together. Who are you helping?

Lords of the Flies

For our citizenship is in heaven, from which also we eagerly wait for a Savior, the Lord Jesus Christ; (Philippians 3:20 NASB)

Furloughs are a mixed blessing for missionaries. Beth and I returned from a long, blessed, fun, tiring, calm, and exciting time in our homeland. We prayed that we were an encouragement and blessing to everyone we met on furlough.

We returned to a foreign land. It always took time to reorient our thoughts, cultural responses and language. A few days' rest was helpful after the busy, filled work schedule of furloughs. Preaching, teaching, sharing, answering questions, living out of a suitcase, all were fun but tiring.

We dragged our overweight bags up the fifty-nine stairs, through the doorway and plopped them in the living room. "Whew, home at last," I thought. Our colleagues brought a few foodstuffs and we were more than ready to settle back into the ministry.

A shower, nap and snack later we were awake enough to look around the apartment. Four months away, with only one short visitor in our apartment, and things didn't look quite right. A cloud seemed to settle over most of the windows. We stepped closer and the cloud moved. It was alive! They were flies! Hundreds of them were on the windows. Hundreds of them were dead on the window sills. Hundreds of them were dead on the floors. We were now Lords of the Flies. This was not something we aspired to in life.

We vacuumed, we washed, we swept - yes, I know how to use a vacuum - and still there were more. We had to make a bus trip to town where we miraculously found the right bags for our overfull vacuum cleaner. Our neighbor attempted to tackle the problem while we were gone with her vacuum and bug spray. The evidence of genocide streaked down the inside of the windows and had to be cleaned off. Her own vacuum filled twice to keep the piles from growing.

We were not alone. The plague, reminiscent of Egypt, had infested most of the flats in our building. In a land without screens, the insects found ready access to our living quarters. The ingenious ones found ways to climb between the double paned glass in the windows and now lay with their dead feet pointing heavenward. Now I know how the Egyptians felt that fateful day while Moses pled for the freedom of the Israelites. Clean, suck, dismantle the window, clean suck, reassemble the window, it went on for days.

During a break from fly gathering, I enjoyed fixing the clothes washer since everything needed washing. Then it was time to fix the vacuum after a large spark flew from the electric cord, a sure sign that something was amiss. The vacuum repaired, with a shorter cord, it was back to sucking up bugs and cleaning house.

306

Three days later we put plants back on the window sills for decorations and not as miniature cemeteries. I started a fire, using wood from an old shelf and waterbed I demolished, sat across from my lovely wife and relaxed. Everything was almost in order. Then we started discussing the work necessary to move when a smaller apartment was available. . . . that was another story waiting to unfold.

We often think of coming home as the answer to difficulties. Someone once said, "You can't go home again." I guess he experienced a fly farm in his life. Returning to the past never provides the results we imagine. The preacher once wrote, "Do not say, 'Why is it that the former days were better than these?' For it is not from wisdom that you ask about this." (Ecclesiastes 7:10 NASB) That preacher is one smart man.

Our family, our churches, our friends were all different when we returned to our homeland for furlough. The folks at home think returning is simple and easy. But it isn't. It takes a lot of work to put things back in order. Most missionaries discover this after their first furlough.

We look forward to the comfort of our apartment after furlough; our shower, our bed, our stuff. But it takes a lot of work to put things back in order. We're reminded of this after each furlough.

But this isn't our home. Our homeland is not our home. Our home is in Heaven and we anxiously await the day we'll enter the door of that special mansion Jesus prepared. After all these years I'm sure it'll make Buckingham Palace look like a shanty. No flies to kill or suck up in a vacuum. Everything will be prepared and ready. There we can finally find rest.

Next time you come home and things just aren't in order, remember, this is not your home! Remember an eternal fly-free home is ready and waiting our arrival.

Sixty Years

According to the grace of God which was given to me, as a wise master builder I laid a foundation, and another builds on it. But let each man be careful how he builds on it. (1 Corinthians 3:10 WEB)

It's a privilege. That's what I told myself. They're good friends. We've known them since we moved to their country. We've watched their children grow up. They helped us understand what was happening in our new land. They translated while we struggled to learn the language. We laughed together, shared, and enjoyed the amicable relationship of neighbors sharing an apartment building and even closer, sharing the same stairwell.

I stood staring at the invitation thinking these thoughts and smiling. I nodded my head, like a rear window mannequin, as I considered my reply. Not only were we accepted by the family, but we would also meet other friends, colleagues, relatives, if we accepted the invitation. It was a birthday party celebrating sixty years. It would be a big event in a close family and friends setting. The venue: a local Heuriger, the place everyone goes to meet anyone in a comfortable setting. The problem: strangers speaking a language I still felt I wasn't good at speaking. The solution: I accepted the invitation, much to the delight of our friend's daughter, who was standing in our doorway with the invitation list in hand.

That Friday was a busy day at the office. The building was stuffed to overflowing with visitors and board members from around the globe. I scurried about to put things in order so I could leave a little early for the party. There was just enough time to take the bus home, climb the stairs to our apartment and leave my bag before the deadline. We scurried across the street to the restaurant, up the stairs, through the tables to the secluded back room. We were the second couple to arrive.

My original hope, to sit next to the few folks we knew understood English, was quickly dashed. We met colleagues from his work, where he taught school, neighbors, and family members not versed in the wonders of the English language. My wife, Beth, selected a table in the corner near an outside door. Inconspicuous was her thought. Soon a couple from our apartment building slid around the table to join us in the corner.

We offered the appropriate greetings and introductions, although we already knew each other's names. That's part of the culture. As more people came in they stepped from table to table, offering their hands, names and greetings to everyone who arrived before them. At times it gets rather confusing. The only ones to enter and sit without proffering greetings were the local Duke and Duchess. Although no one in the country officially holds their titles, everyone knows who is who.

It took an hour for most folks to arrive, greet one another and find a comfortable spot in the room. Between greetings we talked with our neighbors. We discussed everything from their work and family to the sinking foundations of houses built over old mining shafts in the area. Finally, the guest of honor was led into the room, blindfolded. We lit our sparklers, stood up, cheered and sang "Happy Birthday" as the blindfold came off. Interestingly we sang in English. Go figure.

We ate. We talked. It was loud. It was friendly. It was fun. Three young folks decided our table was safe and joined us. I thought it might be fun to talk with them, get a younger local view of things. But they didn't talk to anyone. They barely talked to each other. Then I saw them. Those little white ear plugs with the sliver of cable running to their pockets. They used music to drown out the conversation. Maybe I should get one of those. Then people wouldn't hear my poor language skills, they'd just think I was rude. Then again, maybe not.

The funny thing about talking with our neighbors was that we had known them, vaguely, for over nine years. We walked past their door, on the ground floor, every time we went to or from our apartment. We knew about their new home in the country. We knew which cars they drove. We knew their first names. We knew about their son who lives somewhere else and occasionally comes for a visit. We knew a lot about them. But we didn't know them. Not until that evening.

They were most gracious to work through our limited vocabulary and poor grammar skills. We laughed at each other's jokes, a difficult aspect of cross cultural situations, and shared about our personal lives. It was a chance to get to know them. At one point they invited us to their weekend slash retirement home in the mountains. Granted, it was for some future date but the honor it demonstrated was astounding. Such invitations don't come often. A relationship was built.

As foreigners all conversations eventually turn to why we are in the country. Explaining this without endangering our status in the country can be like dancing a fast jig, and I'm a poor dancer. But we talked about it. We talked about following God's leading. They asked questions. We answered and they began to understand. A deeper relationship was planted. A relationship with a spiritual foundation was laid for future building.

Jesus talked about foundations. Some of His most hard-hitting parables discussed foundations. Paul expanded the picture. The apostle knew different people built on other's foundations. The key was a good foundation. A good foundation is set on the solid rock, and that rock is Jesus Christ.

As we left the party, I was exhausted, I knew others might build on this spiritual foundation with our neighbors. They both work in building construction so they would understand Jesus' word picture. Maybe the Lord will open more doors for us to share and build on this foundation. We pray it'll be built into a complete house of salvation in their lives, whether we are the construction workers or someone else.

As Christians, we are sanctified construction workers. Sometimes we get to build from the solid rock to the roof top. Sometimes we only lay the foundation while others put up walls and ceilings. But the master builder has His plans and we just follow the blueprints. Maybe we need to rise each morning and ask God, "What will it be today Lord? A foundation, a wall, or a roof?"

Light in Darkness

In him was life, and the life was the light of men. The light shines in the darkness, and the darkness hasn't overcome it. (John 1:4-5 WEB)

I, Beth, know there's debate about when to celebrate Christmas. I don't know all of the scholarly research and although I haven't read all of it I must say I am thankful for the choice of December 25th. I've read that part of the reason for picking December 25th was because of the darkness and winter solstice.

For fourteen years our family lived on the island of Guam. Bobbing around the ocean at thirteen degrees north of the Equator, Guam was wonderful with plenty of sunshine and summer weather all year round. Each December we gathered at the beach to celebrate Christmas with snorkeling and a barbecue. With copious sunshine, and sometimes forgotten sunscreen, tropical winters gave a whole new meaning to Santa's red suit! We were soon used to the warm winter weather of the tropics. However, things change.

Jingle Bells, coconut shells, Santa's coming now!
Instead of driving eight reindeer he rides a caribou!

The next assignment with the mission saw our family move to Vienna, Austria, forty-eight degrees north of the Equator. That put an end to the tropical winters and December barbecues on the beach. We traded in our flip-flops for furry warm boots, our t-shirts for sweaters, and our raincoats for thick warm jackets. Instead of snorkeling in December we made snow men and battled the world with snowballs. Sunburned noses were replaced by cold winter red noses. It became a new lifestyle with new traditions. As our first November in Austria rolled around we experienced seasonal changes and a lack of sunshine. Not just sunshine, but daylight appeared to disappear.

It's amazing what you forget when you live one place long enough. You know this, as do I, but the implications didn't fully sink in for a while. One thing I forgot was the darkness of the winter months.

I grew up in Maine and upstate New York. I realize some people object to Christmas being celebrated around the winter solstice and its possible relationship to pagan rituals. Still, I again say, I am thankful! When it is darkest and the days are the shortest I can understand "light in darkness" better. It lifts my spirits greatly.

When Jesus walked the earth, His light was so different many didn't believe but shielded their eyes. They were familiar with the darkness. Even today, when people see what Jesus' light reveals, people turn their heads so they don't have to look. "The people who walked in darkness have seen a great light. Those who lived in the land of the shadow of death, on them the light has shined." (Isaiah 9:2 WEB)

Believers, when they are in the midst of trials, search for the light. Once you have experienced long, consistent days of light a shorter day seems oppressively dark. When a believer finds himself in the darkness his love for the light of God takes on a more profound understanding.

Praise the Lord for Christ's birth, the Word incarnate. In the short days, in the long darkness of winter, I am reminded and reflect more on the sacrifice of God in sending His Son. When darkness is greater than light I'm anxious for each bit of light, each ray of sunshine, I can find in a day. When the darkness rolls away I thank God again for His love. Of course, this awe and celebration and worship can happen all year and anytime we reflect on His saving power!

Again I rejoice! In our home we celebrate with colored lights, candles, decorations, warmth and family at the darkest time of my year. We get up in the dark and it gets dark early. When the winter darkness is here we have lots of snow and fog. We seldom see the sun. I am glad the celebration of light in darkness is shown clearly in my roots and traditions with colored lights, candles, decorations, warmth and family to celebrate! How do you celebrate in the darkness? Do you see the light shining?

Again, therefore, Jesus spoke to them, saying, "I am the light of the world. He who follows me will not walk in the darkness, but will have the light of life." (John 8:12 WEB)

Driving

"Trust in the Lord with all your heart, and do not rely on your own understanding." (Proverbs 3:5 NET.)

I've always liked cars. I should say I've almost always enjoyed riding in cars. I say almost because some drivers qualify as design artists for the house of horrors. I've left my fingernails in the dashboard of more than one prospective demolition derby hopeful car. Hair raising experiences aside, I enjoy a nice road trip. It doesn't really matter where I'm going. If I'm the driver it's even better.

It should be noted I'm not a car fanatic. I can't distinguish one make, model, or year from another unless I surreptitiously sneak a peek at the emblem on the fender. I don't drool over sleek sports models or dream of a car more expensive than a thirty-room mansion. I'm just as happy to drive an old "bug" as a modern Lamborghini. I once saw a Lamborghini parked on the street as I walked to the office. Nice, smooth design and I'm sure it costs more to start than I make in a month. I've learned to use the right phrases and even point out a cool car driving by so I don't appear too dorky. But my real love is driving.

It probably began with Sunday afternoon drives through the countryside. This was just when interstate highways were starting. Most Sunday afternoons we, my brothers and I, would fight for window seats in the back of our big Chevy. Window seats were important since there was no air-conditioning. The roar of the wind and cool, hurricane force gale through our hair made for some interesting struggles as we climbed in the car. Since seat belts weren't required or in vogue, the seating sequence would change from time to time throughout the trip.

Dad would point the car out of town on some long-forgotten highway and he'd drive. He enjoyed it. Where were we going? Nobody knew, not even Dad. When we arrived at our destination we'd turn around and drive home. Highway markers were only useful if we got lost coming home. No need to ask directions, just point your nose home and let it lead.

We'd enjoy the scenery scrolling by on a lazy Sunday afternoon drive. No better experience than feeling the smooth roll of the wheels and swaying of the car on corners. If we spotted a dip in the road we'd chime in for Dad to go faster and provide a short lived, but exciting, weightless moment in history. It was great!

When I left home for college and then married my sweetheart I continued to find Sunday afternoons and other opportunities to just cruise the highways and byways. Then we answered God's call to missionary work and moved to Guam. We'd pile our children into the car and enjoy the swing and sway of

313

the island's roads. Thirty minutes later we found ourselves back at our door. The island wasn't that big and didn't have that many roads.

Later we moved to Europe. Wide open highways and autobahns provided a chance to drive for more than thirty minutes and not end up at home. It's like Heaven on asphalt. We've driven across the continent several times. One day our family was on the highway in Germany when the boys asked how fast the car would go. I decided to find out. We were on a flat, straight stretch, and it was a sunny, dry day, so I shouted, "Here we go, boys!" I floored the accelerator and waited. We hit the 192 kph mark! (120 mph) The first and last time I floored it to the max. The boys were thrilled. After my nerves calmed down we resumed our 100 mph journey.

It may be obvious that speed is not what enthralls me about driving. It's the event. The control as I conquer the corners and hills to see another beautiful vista prepared by God's meticulous hand. With rare exception I'm always ready to take the wheel when it's offered. Apparently, my driving isn't too bad either. Most of my European travel is confined to the continent. Thus, I drive a lot. On most trips I'm asked to drive by my colleagues on a regular basis. I'd like to think it's because they trust me and feel safe in my hands. As I get older I'm not as sure as they are, but I still love to drive.

One thing I don't appreciate is a backseat driver. I prefer to make my own mistakes without nervous prompting over my shoulder. Once on a trip, a couple people were both telling me to go this way and that. Finally, in desperation and confusion I pulled the car into a side street and stopped. Since I needed some direction in this new town I said, "One of you can talk. The other one be quiet!" Things settled down and we arrived at our destination with fewer side trips.

I think my children have caught sight of my driving infatuation. At least they've joined my colleagues when it comes to a designated driver. My lovely bride and I were recently in the USA visiting our children. Fortunately for us most of them live in the same small town. Our fourth is in the Army but took a couple weeks off to see his missionary parents while in the country. It was a great family reunion complete with food, fun, playing with our grandson, car troubles, normal family stuff and housing changes.

It was the housing changes that tugged at my driving enthusiasm. My youngest son needed to move from out in the country to a more citified location. His assumption was Dad knew how to drive anything, including a moving truck. I became the designated truck driver. I do have experience moving across the USA in the capable cab of a U-haul truck. Then again, that was thirty years ago. Not wanting to squelch my son's trust in my abilities I agreed and we picked up the truck.

Honestly, it was great! It took a few moments, a little careful evaluation of the size and protrusions on the truck to figure things out. I backed into country driveways, navigated city streets and came out without any new scratches.

314

Forty-foot moving trucks are interesting beasts to drive on narrow country roads but it was fun! When we returned the truck, I was relaxed and my driving itch had been scratched another day with a new experience.

The problem with itches is that they often come back unexpectedly and demand to be scratched. Five days later our daughter and her husband moved about four blocks to a bigger apartment. Dad was still in town, so my skills were once again called to the front. Interestingly when we picked up the forty-foot rental it was the same truck I used earlier that week for our son. In and out, up and down, back and forth we went until their worldly goods were transplanted from a college-oriented apartment complex to a more family slanted venue. Ah, it's great to scratch an itch now and again.

I'm glad my family and my co-workers trust my driving skills. Thanks to that trust I have more chances to get behind the wheel and spool off more mileage of satisfying driving. My wondrous bride and I more than once headed out on Sunday afternoons for a drive through the winding roads of the Alpine foothills near our home. We didn't know where we were going but always enjoyed the destination when it was reached.

We no longer have a car. They're just a bit too expensive to maintain where we live. Thankfully the area has great public transport. For the most part I have to put my trust in someone else to get me from place to place. My driving is limited to furlough or mission related trips. I still enjoy each adventure and others still trust me to drive. It's nice to be trusted. For something so easily lost it's also easy to maintain. Someone who breaks our trust often must work hard to regain it.

I'm glad God hasn't lost my trust. I know it'll never happen. He told me to, "Trust in the Lord with all your heart, and do not rely on your own understanding." (Proverbs 3:5 NET.) When others trust my driving, without backseat interjections, things go well. When I trust God in everything, without my sanctified backseat prompting, things go well. I can look out the window, enjoy the scenery slipping by and know I'll reach His destination, wherever that may be, and love it when I get there.

Missionary Mama and the Ten Little Cakes

What if you lived in a land with no cakes?

"NO cakes?????" you say "IMPOSSIBLE!!!"

This is the story of the Missionary Mama who lived in a land where there were no cakes.

There were no cakes like we have in America, like she had when she was growing up.

There were no cakes like we have for our birthdays.

Most of the time the Missionary Mama and her missionary kiddies didn't miss the birthday cakes because the land they lived in had lots of really, really good food. The only times they thought about birthday cakes were . . . well . . . at birthdays. Then the Missionary Mama and Papa did what they could to get happy birthday cakes from America for their missionary kiddies. Sometimes it wasn't easy, but they always found one.

As the years past the Missionary Mama learned how to make all kinds of wonderful things in the land where they were living and didn't even always make birthday cakes for birthdays. But one day some people from America were going to visit the Missionary Mama and Papa and they said, "What can we bring from America in our suitcase for you?" Well, they thought and thought and said, "A birthday cake, please?"

"A BIRTHDAY CAKE?????" they thought. "DON'T THEY HAVE BIRTHDAYS? OH NO! WE SHOULD BRING THEM A BIRTHDAY CAKE." So, they packed their clothes . . . Two blue shirts and two pink shirts and two purple shirts and two red green shirts (one for the Mr. and one for the Mrs.) And then they packed a birthday cake. . . And thought . ". . There is more room so we can bring two birthday cakes." And there was still more room and they put in two more and then two more. There were two chocolate and two yellow cakes and two pink cakes . . . You see, the Mr. and the Mrs. liked things in twos . . . And they ended up with 10 cakes in their suitcases.

Can you imagine 10 little cakes all ready to go to a foreign land and take birthdays to the Missionary Mama? Well, they filled up the suitcase so much the Mr. and Mrs. had to take out some clothes and the cakes were starting to get heavy so they got friends to bring their clothes and their friend's daughter to help carry the cakes. Then they all got on a big airplane with their suitcases and their clothes and the 10 little cakes. Oh, I almost forgot, they also brought a rabbit to make the airport people look at him so they wouldn't look at the 10 little cakes and say, "NO cakes in this land!!!!!"

When they came to the foreign land the Missionary Mama and Papa picked them up at the airport with a borrowed car and you know what? It wasn't big enough for so many people and 10 little cakes and a rabbit!!!! There were people and suitcases and cakes and rabbits everywhere. Wowie. They had a great visit and went to all the nice places in the land and ate lots of really good food and the rabbit met lots of nice people and then Mr. and Mrs. and their friends and their friend's daughter took their empty suitcases home and with the rabbit had plenty of room.

Then the Missionary Mama thought ". . . 10 little cakes what will I do with 10 little cakes????? We don't have 10 little cabinets and we don't have 10 birthdays. I know, I'll share the cakes with people who miss happy birthday cakes like we do. Or maybe, I'll share them with people who have never had a happy birthday cake. This is going to be fun."

The first little cake was made and it was a yellow cake with chocolate frosting and the Missionary Mama and Papa and Annamarie ate it just to make sure they were OK to share with others. I mean they needed to know that it still tasted good, right?

The second cake was made for a family from Switzerland and Canada and they had five children, so the confetti cake was the best.

The third little cake was chocolate with chocolate icing and it was for a Missionary Mama and Papa party with Americans so they could practice their English and tell funny stories in English. There were some American missionaries and Canadian missionaries who hadn't had a birthday cake for a long time.

The fourth little cake was a yummy spice cake with cream cheese frosting and Missionary Mama made it for the team that met to plan all the work. Those poor people were in long meetings all day and they needed a treat sometimes. Some of them liked the cake, and some thought it was too sweet, and some thought it was too fat, and some thought it was just right. There was a big Russian man and a happy Swiss man and a quiet German lady, a really, really tall man (I think he ate two pieces) and a strong Serbian man who told funny stories and liked cake, too.

The fifth cake was pink - I mean really very pink - and the Missionary Mama made it for the baptism in the Danube River. I don't know why she made the pink one but the people from Africa and the people from the Philippines and the people from Iran and the people from Austria all ate pink cupcakes and said, "Yummy, yummy, yummy. Let's go to the river and get baptized."

The sixth little cake was pink, too, and the Missionary Mama gave it to a little missionary girl who liked "muffins with cream that are pink" (that is what they call cupcakes there!!!!!) for her birthday.

The seventh little cake was chocolate and the Missionary Mama made it for a happy birthday cake for Jesus on Christmas. Her little missionary son ate it for dinner and lunch and breakfast. He also shared it with our friends from Hungary, and Canada, and Cameroon. (But I don't think he wanted to.)

The eighth little cake was carrot and the Missionary Mama made it for a missionary kid Christmas party and it had cream cheese frosting, yuummmmm. But one little boy said, "Yuck," and Naomi said, "We forgot to pray," and then she and the Missionary Papa prayed and she said, "I like the cream!!!!!!!" There were children from all around Europe at the party and they liked to sing "Happy Birthday" to Jesus and then eat the cake.

The ninth little cake was for a ladies' prayer group and it was lemon and very yellow and pretty. I hope it made the ladies strong so they could really pray for the families and the children.

The tenth little cake doesn't have a place to go yet. What shall we do????? Maybe you can think of a place to take the yellow cake with chocolate frosting on it??????? It sounds yummy but the Missionary Mama is all out of places to take it right now. So please help me to think, and think, and think of the best place for the little cake because it is sad to be all alone in the cabinet and needs a nice party to go to.

Living Legacy

Grandchildren are like a crown to the elderly, and the glory of children is their parents.(Proverbs 17:6 NET)

I remember sitting with my best friend, Doug, on the front porch stoop in Ohio. We would contemplate such deep conversations as, "Hey Doug, what do you want to do?" "I don't know Bob, what do you want to do?" "I don't know Doug, what do you want to do?" This could go on for hours until we gave up and actually went and did something. Occasionally we would think about other things like the changing of the century. We wondered if we'd be alive at the dawn of the new century. I'd be ancient at forty-eight. That just sounded so, so, . . . OLD!

One year I was in the USA for furlough. Some fine folks think of it as a vacation. Since we work daily on relationships, support raising, travel a lot (13,000 miles) and share the ministry often (preaching 49 times in 12 weeks) I can't see how this would qualify as vacation. But, that is another story. Well into my fifties, well past the turn of the century, the old conversations seemed so . . . dated. I had made it. So had Doug, by the way. And not only did forty-eight not appear so old, being a grandparent required a new view on life and aging.

On our home assignment we were thrilled to see our grandson again and meet our two granddaughters for the first time. What an absolute delight to cuddle, hug and spoil my grandchildren. Near the beginning of our US assignment we, Beth and I, spent time with my mom. My brother had retired to the area and my other brother came to visit from the west coast. It was the first time in about 20 years we had all been in the same place at the same time. A little family reunion was in progress.

Into this gathering my daughter, her husband, and their daughter came to visit. Ellice sat next to her grandmother, holding her daughter while I stood behind them for a generational photo. Four generations! I know there are families with more generations in a single photo but for me it was something new and exciting. I thought living to the turn of the century was dubious and here I was with four generations. I loved it.

Here I was looking at an example of a living legacy. My mother, and father passed along their beliefs and views of life to me. I learned, modified and developed my own version tempered by the era which influenced my thinking. I passed them along to my daughter, plus our three sons, who modified them with into their own version tempered by the era in which they lived. And now she was starting to pass them along to her daughter.

One generation after another. As we watched our children grow, build their own families and lives, we hoped they learned the good things and not the bad. They did things differently than we did. That's to be expected. But, regardless of differences we hoped our relationship was like the Proverb.

We knew our grandchildren were our crown as we grew older. Just think of all the photos we could share with the unsuspecting passerby. We never tired of beaming with pride as we inundated others with their cute smiles and rattled on about their adventures.

On the other hand, we hoped our children could take pride in us as their parents. We made mistakes, no argument there. We watched and prayed that the good of the Lord worked through us to shape their lives. So far, so good.

Jesus tells us eternal life is all about who you know (John 17:6). I suspect the present life is knowing your grandchildren. Watching a living legacy grow this side of heaven is what the present life is about. Thanks, God for allowing me to experience this living legacy in my life.

Almost Full

He who has an ear, let him hear what the Spirit says to the churches. To him who overcomes, I will grant to eat of the tree of life which is in the Paradise of God. (Revelation 2:7 NASB)

As I write this Beth and I are only a few days away from celebrating twenty-seven complete years serving the Lord overseas. In all those years we took care to remember many of our homeland celebrations and introduce them to our children. There's Independence Day, New Years, Easter and Christmas and there is Thanksgiving. Thanksgiving was and is a big event in our home. Last fall, during furlough, we celebrated Thanksgiving in our homeland for the first time in twenty-five years. It was great.

We were in Kentucky where most of our children live. Pies were made, turkey was cooked to perfection and almost everyone was available to enjoy the celebration. James and his family were conspicuously absent. He was overseas with the Army and his wife and their two-month-old daughter couldn't wrangle the trip. We missed them. The place was definitely almost full, but more would've been better.

A couple days before Thanksgiving we were at Ellice, Brad and Laurana's for a pie day. Beth helped Ellice and one of her friends make a whole passel of pies. Laurana made comments from her seat on the counter.

On Thanksgiving Day Evan picked up some rolls and side stuff. Beth, Joel, Sonya, and Hayden cooked the bird in their apartment. Hayden was a hoot when it came to helping in the kitchen. Maybe he'll become a chef.

We gathered at the apartment with all the goodies and breathed deeply the wonderful smell of a perfectly prepared turkey turning a beautiful brown. While the bird was simmering in its sauces we enjoyed cookies and playing with our grandchildren. Joel has a nice big screen TV which provided a marvelous display of the Macy's Thanksgiving Day Parade.

It had been a long time since we watched a parade live on TV. Beth and I both remember those special Thanksgiving mornings watching the parade as children. Beth watched the parade and cried. I didn't cry but it was a wonderful feeling to see old familiar floats wafting along with some of the newer renditions.

Meal time was a blast with everyone passing fixin's and food around the table. Needless to say, we were very thankful to be in one place to share with most of the family. There were plenty of leftovers to be sure, but they wouldn't last too long.

After the meal, it was football time! I didn't really care who won or which team played. It was nice to watch a "live" game and pick a side to cheer on without already knowing the results. Watching a live game on Thanksgiving brought a tear to my eye. Beth didn't cry. To each his own, I suppose.

When the game concluded, we gathered everyone for some family photos and to divvy up the leftovers. It was a full day with full bellies and full schedule of events. How fulfilling is that? We were just about full up.

There was only one piece missing. That was James and his family. More than once my mother has commented on not seeing all her family in one place for many years. I'm beginning to understand this more and more. It's all part of life I suppose and should be expected.

Me, I'm looking forward to a grand reunion one day. It'll be at an unbelievable banquet held at God's dining table. The dining table won't be in an apartment in Kentucky but in the Paradise of God. The main dish won't be a succulent turkey but fruit from the tree of life.

Until then, I'll settle for a great Thanksgiving celebration with as much of the family as possible.

Emergency Baptism

. . . one Lord, one faith, one baptism, . . . (Ephesians 4:5 NET)

One year I was able to experience a first in my ministry. I performed my first bathtub baptism. Normally baptisms for our church in Vienna were held at the Old Danube river. We even had one scheduled that summer with a number of people on the list to publicly declare their faith in Christ. So you might wonder, *why baptize someone in a bathtub when we had one scheduled at the river?* (I'm tempted to start singing "Shall We Gather at The River?")

This what we call an "emergency baptism." I know, that sounds weird. You might wonder if the person was about to die of some dread disease? No. But time was limited. This person came to us through the son of their best friend who happened to be in Austria. The young man put them in contact with our church through one of our ministry folks.

The candidate was in town for only few days and wanted to be baptized. She would be headed back to her home country in only three days. Theo, one of our other elders, and I talked and decided we could use the bathtub of one of the ministry folks. The bonus would be that they could also provide translation from the candidate's native language into either German or English. (It turned out to be into German :-)).

We arranged to meet the candidate at this gentleman's home and talk. If things went well, if we were assured of the candidate's faith, we would proceed. Fortunately for me, the candidate spoke a modicum of English, making things a little easier. We listened to the story of living in a country and a culture inundated and controlled by another religion. As a child the candidate heard about Christianity from some family and friends who were Christians. But there was no gathering where they could learn more.

You see, such a gathering, when the candidate was young and still today, was and is forbidden. There are believers in the country but unless their spouse, or close friend, is also a believer they live as an island in a dangerous land. This is learning to lean on God and God alone. After growing up and a failed marriage, the candidate realized her cultural religion didn't work. There were too many things which seemed contrary to living and there was no hope. The candidate remembered what she heard as a child and started seeking this Christian God.

To make a long story short, the candidate came to salvation several years before. He met and married someone who is also a believer. The candidate's visit to Austria was short and she wanted to be baptized before returning. Gathering as believers for church, worship, and Bible study was and is forbidden in her homeland. Baptism was and is also forbidden. The candidate wanted to make a declaration among witnesses of her faith in Christ and her desire to live faithfully for Him. This was her one big chance.

We listened to the story with many more details and knew the candidate was part of God's family. The tub was filled with warm water (a definite improvement over the cold Danube). We gathered in the bathroom, those of us who could fit. Imagine six people with a bathtub in a room the size of a coat closet.

The candidate sat in the tub, scrunched to one end. We asked a few questions and she made a declaration of her faith in front of the witnesses. Then back she went, under the water. With praise in our hearts and on our lips, a new family member rose out of the water declaring to the world, to her homeland, to her past culture and religion, that she was now and forever a child of God. She was saved by God's grace through Christ's blood. We're talking big smiles and excitement.

This was a testimony to God's work even in the face of cultural and national adversity. (I think this is the first baptism where I didn't get soaked :-)). I was thrilled to provide her the opportunity to declare before witnesses her faith. I hope one day we'll have the chance to baptize her spouse as well.

As I wrote this, this new family member was back in her homeland, living in a land diametrically opposed to her faith but assured of God's grace and strength. Pray for her walk with God, strength when opposition comes, and assurance of God's constant presence.

God is amazing. We sometimes just need to be reminded through the testimony of others.

Retreating

Be at rest once more, O my soul, for the LORD has been good to you. (Psalms 116:7 NIV)

Contrary to some well-intentioned but misguided ideas, furlough is not a vacation time for the missionary family. It's a time where we're on display and representing the ministry 24 hours a day, 7 days a week. Even when we're not preaching from a pulpit or sharing the ministry in a Bible study, we're working. Living out of suitcases for months, without a place to call your own, takes its toll on you spiritually, mentally, and physically.

Because of this stress and strain, missionaries often jump at the opportunity to get away from it all even for a day or two. The chances aren't too close together, so you take what you can when you can. On our last furlough, we were hoping to use a mission home for a while but that fell through. However, a friend of a friend knew of a new retreat center that might let us come and stay.

I sent off e-mail messages and asked about certain days. Being the consummate furlough missionary, I planned the retreat days to coordinate with other trips near the retreat center. We'd stay there a few days, run off to see some friends, family, and supporters a few days, and then back for a few more days of "retreat." When, during our communications, we got down to brass tacks, how much would it cost, we were thrilled to learn it cost nothing. It was a ministry funded through other sources for missionaries, pastors, and other Christian workers who needed to escape a bit.

Our trip to the retreat center was exciting as we followed the GPS pathway through winding country roads in a heavy rain storm. Beth thought the GPS was trying to kill us but I'm sure it was the shortest route, maybe not the best, but the shortest. We arrived, a bit tired, and met our hosts in their home which also served as part of the retreat center.

When we arrived there were two options, staying in their home/lodge or at a country manor. The manor was filled by a wedding party, so we chose the basement apartment. Our hosts offered to talk, feed us, or allow us to be hermits and get away from the world. We chose to be hermits. That sort of worked. The apartment was fully furnished, had a kitchen, bath, very comfortable bed, satellite TV, and a great place to relax.

People who run retreat centers are very helpful. They always want to provide services, comfort, counseling and just entertain. The concept that a visitor truly wants to be a hermit is hard to reconcile with the ever-present desire to provide assistance. Several times a day our host would pop his head in the door at the top of the stairs to call out with an offer for some form of entertainment, an invitation to a Bible study or service, or a call to join them for dinner. They were very giving people, with big hearts for ministering to their guests. Leaving someone to fend for themselves was hard to accept.

We joined them in some meetings including a great children's Christmas presentation in a local church. We were taken on some tours of the area and shared a few meals together. Even though our intention was to hide away we enjoyed the ministry of our hosts beyond the simple physical accommodations. When we completed our little retreat and headed out we were rested and ready to take on another portion of our furlough.

Sometimes we try to manipulate our surroundings, thinking we know what is necessary for our own rest and relaxation. This is where the Lord knows better. In truth, He always knows better even though we often miss this simple fact. God sometimes sends along those we least expect to meet the needs we don't always know we have. Why should I be surprised when God does things like this?

Perhaps what we consider a retreat from the world should be a retreat to God's hands. Then we will recognize when God takes what we put in place and works with it to the good He has promised. Go figure!

One Small, Two-Syllable Word

Or don't you know that all we who were baptized into Christ Jesus were baptized into his death? We were buried therefore with him through baptism to death, that just like Christ was raised from the dead through the glory of the Father, so we also might walk in newness of life. (Romans 6:3-4 WEB)

I love to see new believers make their faith public. To be baptized in the baptistery at church is one thing. Being baptized at a public beach, on a hot day, with hundreds watching, . . . that is a public statement of faith.

This was the place for our Vienna church baptisms. One Sunday I had the privilege of baptizing ten believers from Iran. The day started with our regular worship service. Then we all headed to the park at the Old Danube.

There we had plenty of food and a great time of conversation. When everyone was fed we gathered around with the candidates to one side.

The candidates previously shared their testimonies in church over the last few weeks. Now it was time for me to ask a few public questions before we headed to the water.

My first question is something like, "Do you turn away from Satan and . . ?" I asked the question. The translator converted it into Farsi. The candidates looked at me. As a group they said, "NO!" They were very adamant. I was confused! I looked at them. They looked at me. I confirmed with the translator that they all said, "No."

Interesting, I thought... not the response I was expecting from new believers. I asked the translator again and received the same response. Then I had a thought, one little word may have been lost in translation, the word "away." I asked the translator to pose the question once more, "Do you turn AWAY from Satan . . . ?" I emphasized the word "away" and I explained to the translator it meant to no longer seek or follow but to change. He thought about it, confirmed it was a negative and then translated again.

This time they all responded with a hearty, "YES!" Much better! I asked more questions about faith in Christ, walking a faithful life, and others. All received unanimous and hearty affirmations.

When we, as elders, were assured of their responses they sang a song of faith in their language . People from around the park were already gathering about to see what was happening.

We headed down to the water with a myriad of sun-seeking curious bystanders watching our every move. From the land, from boats, from the water people watched to see this public declaration of faith. Some understood, some chuckled, but those whose lives were changed forever rejoiced and the church with them.

I like words and sometimes it's hard to realize how one small word, one little two-syllable word, can create confusion and misunderstanding. I need to be sure I'm careful with all my words, even the small ones, when sharing about God's grace and salvation. As Christians we need to be mindful of our selected words. The last thing we want is confusion when it comes to salvation.

The Reality of the Routine

Do everything without complaining or arguing, so that you may become blameless and pure, children of God without fault in a crooked and depraved generation, in which you shine like stars in the universe (Philippians 2:14-15 NIV)

I was a missionary living outside my homeland for many years. I was there because I knew God called me to use the skills He provided to bring His word of salvation to the world. It was that simple. What wasn't simple was filtering through the mental pictures and ideas people have about missionary life.

While missionary work began with the apostles, who left their homes to share the Gospel in foreign lands, the modern Protestant missionary movement is relatively young. In the last hundred years, the publications of the lives of modern missionaries have fascinated, encouraged, called and otherwise thrilled the church. From this many have built up the idea that "true" missionaries are pounding through sweaty jungles, Bibles in hand, pith helmet donning their furrowed brow, wagging their fingers at the heathen while pleading for them to accept the grace of God. I love these books and have read many. However, these only described the lives of a handful of faithful servants. What about the rest?

I'm one of the rest. I've had some interesting adventures for sure, but for the most part, my life was and is routine. I should clarify that by saying my ministry life is, for the most part, very routine. What makes it routine you ask? Let me describe most of what I've done and currently do.

For years, I've work in the technical side of things. I was a radio engineer when I joined this ministry and have worked with transmitters, antennas, studios, and a host of other electronic stuff throughout the years. At one point I was given a computer. I figured out how it worked. I learned how to program it. Now I administer computers systems, networks and all that modern high-tech stuff. Most of my days are spent tweaking, upgrading, installing and keeping our network secure, up and running.

Don't get me wrong, this is very important for the ministry. Without a stable and efficient computer network our ministry would grind to a halt. All our ministry programs go through the computer network to reach someone's home with the Gospel message. What was once a nice tool for tracking spare parts inventory has become the cornerstone of our ministry. If it is laid out and working correctly God's message reaches people. If it is askew, things go wrong. I try to keep things from going askew.

This is the routine. No pith helmet, although I once saw one with a solar fan on the front which looked great while living in the tropics. No slogging through mosquito-infested jungles to find half-naked heathens in need of redemption. Most days I do my work from a desk using a keyboard, mouse

329

and lots of thinking. Even work for offices in other countries is routinely done from my little office.

Am I reaching the world with the Gospel message? For sure! But the tools and methods have changed over the years. The underlying work to keep things going constantly changes. Even the missionary trudging through the jungle needed time spent on the basic needs of life. In the same way, I'm providing the tools and roadway (technological, of course) for the same message to reach places closed to the missionary in a pith helmet.

Am I a missionary? Without doubt I've departed my homeland, been separated from family, friends, grandchildren and my mother tongue. I've lived solely on the grace and provision of God through His people. I have been "sent" by God to live elsewhere to accomplish His purposes. But, the day to day work I do is . . . to put it bluntly . . . routine.

The father of our mission's founder wrote a great pamphlet entitled, "The Glory of the Grey." I love that thought. That's right where I work and live. Unfortunately, many people, including churches, don't understand this concept. Unless a "missionary" is establishing churches, or running evangelistic crusades, or hacking back the palm trees with their machete, they are not real missionaries. Sorry, folks, perhaps a little change of perspective is necessary.

Is the church secretary not doing ministry because she isn't preaching, just typing sermon notes and keeping the church updated? Is the janitor not doing ministry because he isn't leading the youth group, just keeping the building fit for meetings and worship? Is the business man who attends your church faithfully not doing ministry because he doesn't head the elder board, just supporting the church and demonstrating Christ in his business? Is the missionary not a missionary because he isn't standing in a pulpit or preaching on a street corner, just keeping the message flowing and the ministry connected? These are all rhetorical questions in case you didn't catch that. The answer to these should be no.

The reality of life is that most of life is routine, including the work done by missionaries. Once we accept this, and stop thinking everyone needs some new adventure, like the latest and greatest TV show or movie, then life becomes easier. Once Christians discover God wants us to minister by reflecting his grace in our day to day activities, walking faithfully becomes easier. We can breathe a sigh of relief. If Christians would live their lives rejoicing in this truth it would be a great witness to the world. Once we discover this for ourselves we can recognize it in others: the secretary, the businessman, the janitor or the missionary.

How to Win a Grandparent's Heart

Do not be anxious about anything, but in everything, by prayer and petition, with thanksgiving, present your requests to God. (Philippians 4:6 NIV)

When our children were young we told them we had a plan for their lives. This involved several steps and many years. First, they were to grow up and leave home. We figured by the time they left home we'd have taught them all we could. Next, they were supposed to find a loving mate, who didn't give Beth bad vibes, and get married. Finally, they were supposed to have children so we can spoil them on a regular basis. It's a simple plan for life.

Things are going along right on schedule. We have four children, three of them married (with good vibes), providing us with four grandchildren. Our youngest is still in college but looking to continue his part of the plan. The only problem with grandchildren, at this time, is that they live in our homeland and we live on another continent. This makes regular visits, our part of the plan, a little difficult. So when we do have the chance to visit we're more than glad to spoil them.

A while ago, when we were visiting, I was sitting watching some silly show while Beth and Sonya worked hard in the kitchen. They were in the midst of baking cookies, a favorite of mine, and had the able assistance of our grandson Hayden. He was almost two at the time. The preparation process was interesting. I could hear dishes clink and pots clank as I busied myself in the living room. Then I heard a loud yell from the kitchen, "OPA!"

Hayden repeated my name a few times followed by, "Opa, come here." Now I'm not the type of person to perform on demand but when my grandson calls, I answer. I found Hayden stirring water in a bowl. He pointed to another bowl, handed me a spoon and said, "Stir." I stirred and stirred and stirred. We added water, we removed water. We stirred until we had to vacate the counter in preparation for the cookie dough.

Oma took over the counter, spreading the dough evenly in preparation for cutting. Hayden worked alongside of her. He took some dough and smashed it, crashed it, squished it, and squashed it all over the counter, his shirt, the floor and just about anything within reach. He was very helpful. Even the most helpful can sometimes get in the way of progress. Then it happened.

In the middle of mashing another lump of dough onto the counter, with bits and pieces flying everywhere, he looked up at Oma and said, "Hayden loves Oma!" He smiled at Oma, she melted and decided he could make as much mess as he wanted after that heartfelt declaration. It doesn't take much to win a grandparent's heart. Just the right word will do the trick. The occasional hug, kiss and wiggling doesn't hurt, either.

When the cookies were on the tray and being cycled through the oven Hayden went back to his mixing bowls. I was quietly occupying myself back in the living room, just a stone's throw away. Then I heard it again, "Opa!" I tried to pretend I didn't' hear it. Then it was repeated several times, louder and louder, until I couldn't resist anymore and came to see what was up. There was more careful stirring of water in mixing bowls. There were wet pants and shirts. There was more fun for Opa and his grandson in the kitchen.

By the time the cookies were done, the kitchen was cleaned (thanks to Oma and Mama), it was about time for Oma and Opa to leave for the day. No worries. It was a great day. Just a couple expressions of love and joy were all we needed to be won over, once more, by our grandson. Like I said, it doesn't take much.

I suspect my Heavenly Father is the same way. Sometimes we think He wants us to show Him some grand work we've accomplished for Him. I think all He wants is for us to show our love and joy to him. Simple expressions, thanks, calling for help even in the smallest of tasks, these are just signs of our love for Him and our trust that He will respond.

I'd Like to Exchange That

Therefore, there is now no condemnation for those who are in Christ Jesus, because through Christ Jesus the law of the Spirit of life set me free from the law of sin and death. (Romans 8:1-2 NIV)

Exchange: to give and receive reciprocally, to replace one item with something better. When I was growing up I remember my mother exchanging ill-fitting garments for the proper fit at the local department store. This adventure, led by my fearless mother, usually occurred after Christmas or a birthday. I always wanted to trade in those extra skivvies and scarfs for some toy or game. But I was taught to exchange it for the same item with a better fit.

The last couple of weeks I've been working on exchanging an Exchange for an Exchange. That's not a typo. Exchange, with a capital "E," is a mail and information exchange system which we use in our ministry. Without getting into a debate over which software is best, I'd like to say I like Exchange. It does what we need done quite well. For the user, it's rather straightforward and effective. From the administrator's point of view, it's great when it works, and a nightmare when it doesn't.

Most of the time things go well. But after several years it was time for an upgrade to the latest and greatest version. The new features and stability would improve our operation. The trick is to migrate from 2003 to 2010, a seven-year change of software, with little or no impact on the users. We're not an enormous ministry with thousands of mailboxes but we have a good number of folks to keep happy.

The project also needed to be coordinated between continents so both servers were at the same level. With the assistance of my counterpart in the US we went to work. Step by step we exchanged one version for another and cautiously moved services from one computer to another. I exchanged my Exchange in Europe while my US colleague exchanged his Exchange in the USA. It takes time to set things up, test them out, and then move the data.

It's when we move the data that things get touchy. During the transition process a user has no access to their data. After the transition, most users are automatically directed to the new server while a few need a helping hand to change their settings. Most of the transition was done in the middle of the night, when I should've been sleeping, but some moves required daytime activation.

I had a touch of trepidation as we proceeded. The last thing I wanted was 100 plus people ringing my phone or Skyping me that something was wrong. With careful planning, step by step procedures, and tests along the way, things went quite well. There were a few quirks with the Public Folder migration. Occasionally a recalcitrant account or program setting reared its ugly head.

But overall things went well. In the aftermath, it took time to iron out the last wrinkles which were sure to crop up as the system assumed regular service.

It appeared the newly exchanged Exchange was a better fit for our ministry and proved a good exchange. Now we can exchange email with the world seamlessly as well as several other nice features. I've exchanged my work on one Exchange server for a new set of tools on a new Exchange server. Overall, it's an excellent exchange.

I'm reminded of Paul's words about exchanging one life for another, one law for another. We've been given a spirit of life which frees us from the spirit of sin and death. Just as the exchanged skivvies from Christmas fit better, the newly exchanged Exchange server fits our ministry better.

Now that I've exchanged Exchange for Exchange I need to learn the new tools and make use of them to be more effective in my ministry. In the same way, I need to concentrate on living in the spirit of life to be more faithful in my walk with God. I need to exchange my old habits for new.

Pieces of Christmas

Today your Savior is born in the city of David. He is Christ the Lord. (Luke 2:11 NET)

Once we moved overseas it was 25 years before we were again in the USA for Christmas. That was quite a while. During most of those years we had children at home to celebrate the incarnation, the fun, the songs, and the family time. Over the years, the children have grown up, left home and established their own homes in the USA. Along with their new homes and families, our children are married and have their own traditions.

I love family traditions, especially for holidays. There are good traditions like candy and presents I think everyone enjoys. There are the "not so good" traditions such as one of the children being sick every holiday season. Christmas probably has more traditions than any other season. I love special decorations which bring back enjoyably memories. I love the smell of Christmas cookies baking. I love the smell and look of a "real" and perfectly decorated Christmas tree. I love to throw tinsel at the tree while the family tells me to stop.

Our first Christmas on furlough in the USA with our children married and grandchildren was an exercise in diplomacy, bartering, and great joy. Just about every Christmas I remember someone was sick. That year was no different. I don't remember who was under the holiday weather but someone was. Maybe it was me. Nah.

Diplomacy was the first skill to be exercised. Now that Mom and Dad, those missionaries who lived overseas, were in town the routine of spending the holidays with the "other" in-laws was in jeopardy. Who would go where, when and with whom so no one was left out or hurt that the "norm" was being interrupted? This worked out just fine with a little shifting of our children's holiday routines to squeeze us in.

We then moved to bartering. God provided a small home for us to occupy during the holiday season. Since it was normally used by families with terminally ill children in local hospitals it was a bit lacking in holiday spirit or decoration. So, we started bartering. We borrowed a tree from our daughters-in-law along with some decorations. We borrowed more decorations and stuff from our son's family and Beth even picked up a few new items. In the end, we had a very "family" oriented tree decorated with stuff from everyone we were related to in town.

Beth baked cookies with our daughters and there were plenty of goodies to go around. There were too many and I was hard pressed to eat them all. We found presents for all the children, in-laws, grandchildren at the various shops around town. And they even put some presents from themselves to us under our tree. It looked very festive.

On Christmas Day the traveling began. Two of our children and one of our grandchildren came to our little borrowed house in Kentucky. We opened presents, ate cookies, had fun, had a nice meal and enjoyed family.

It was great to see most of our children for the holiday. There's a sense of relief and calmness in revisiting traditions now and then. When we arrived in town nothing was in place. We had to piece things together from family, friends, and shops to attempt building a touch of tradition while living out of suitcases. I think it worked pretty well.

Along with family holidays I find I've developed traditions in my Christian walk. Traditions (some call them habits) can be found in my prayer life, my study life and even how I approach worship on Sundays. I think it's our human nature that finds comfort in things we understand and things which hold good memories. We need to take time to build our traditions, to find those places of comfort which help us press forward in our walk with Christ. Jesus grew up surrounded by traditions which impacted his earthly life. The same is true for us. What are our traditions?

The Incredible Enchilada Incident

Rejoice in the LORD, you righteous,
And give thanks at the remembrance of His holy name.
(Psalms 97:12 NKJV)

In life milestones present themselves unexpectedly. They become etched in our memories quickly and are removed slowly. There are things we struggle to remember. Fond memories often slip from our grasp as we find ourselves playing out bad memories over and over. Some, usually unexpected, are a mixture of joy and sadness with the emphasis on the joy.

It all started on the first of April. In the midst of a day for fools and pranksters we decided to hold a Mexican food celebration with friends. The planning went on for weeks. Folks were invited, schedules were checked and plans put into place. We all looked forward to a fun evening as the days passed by slowly. To make things more festive we would celebrate the birthday of a friend.

Beth spent the day getting our little apartment ready. She made a special trip on public transport into Vienna to a special shop just to get the right fixings. She came home and started to work. She prepared taco salad, chips and salsa, refried beans and cheese. R brought his homemade enchiladas. We were excited about these fat, tasty, chicken-filled delights. Our previous dinner with these delights was a good memory. The oven was hot, things were cooking or warming up as everyone finally arrived. I remember the enticing smell emanating from the kitchen.

It was a great south-of-the-border feast. Laughter erupted often as we talked about a variety of subjects in a variety of mixed languages. We piled our plates high with all the goodies. We savored every chip, enchilada, salad, and bean. To say we were full after the first tray of enchiladas would be an understatement. We were stuffed. I remember feeling like a turkey on Thanksgiving Day.

I can't remember the gamut of topics we covered, from the spiritual to the mundane. From raising children to raising Cain we talked about whatever came to mind. Sign language (wild hand gestures) and multi-interpretations helped span the gap to cross multiple languages. Lots of memories were created in our joyous banter.

After our dinner settled a bit Beth announced we had dessert. Since we were also celebrating C's birthday, a cake was brought out. The lemon cake with lemon icing looked delicious. In fact, it was delicious. All that sweet, with a touch of lemon, was something to remember.

We continued to chat, laugh, and enjoy the evening when we heard a loud bang. We all stopped talking. We looked at each other wondering what was wrong. Then Beth said, "Uh-oh," and got up. She headed to the kitchen. There was a groan as she found the source of the big bang. There were no theories about this, the Pyrex dish, containing the next batch of enchiladas, had exploded!

The dish was on top of the stove. Unfortunately, the stove burner was not completely off and had heated the dish continually the last few hours. Did you know that Pyrex explodes when it gets too hot? We know that now.

There was enchilada everywhere. The unexpected explosion tossed chicken, cheese, and sauce up the wall behind the stove. It projected the contents across the kitchen to the other counter and wall. Pieces of Pyrex glass spotted the kitchen floor from end to end and out the door into the hallway.

After shaking our heads over the damage, we remembered the enchiladas. I'm not sure which was the greater loss, the dish or the enchiladas. They were great enchiladas! C said she would definitely remember this birthday celebration. I don't remember pyrotechnics being part of the celebration planning, but we had them. And we'll definitely remember that night. We all laughed about the unexpected fireworks and cried over the loss of the enchiladas.

As Christians, we remember many things as God leads us through life. Some are good memories and some are bad. Some are a mixture of both. I'm reminded of the psalmist who calls us to remember, rejoice, and give thanks for the name of the Lord. It might be time for me to look back on my memories and recall the good things, not just the bad. In those memories, I'm reminded over and over of God's care, grace and love.

Day After Day

Day after day they pour forth speech, and night after night they display knowledge. (Psalms 19:2 WEB)

As a youngster and even as a young man I had dreams of adventure. I wondered what I could do with my life that would earn the respect of the world around me. That's what life was supposed to be about. I thought about being a musician with dreams of writing that one special tune that people would remember forever. I thought about writing the theological masterpiece that would convince anyone and everyone to accept my view of God. I considered writing the great American novel. Over the years, a number of ideas came and went.

I haven't done any of those things. Yes, I wrote songs but don't ask me to sing them. Trust me; you don't want to hear them. I wrote numerous sermons and articles on theology but nothing to shake the religious foundations of the world. I even wrote a few stories along the way for fun and family. The closest I came to my dreams of adventure were the travels I had around the globe. But even those were just doing normal things day after day. As the world appears smaller and smaller folks aren't as impressed with world travel as they were in my youth.

So, what do I do? As a missionary, some folks think I'm always on the cutting edge of converting the masses to Christ day after day. In one sense I am. Day after day I do my work, my ministry, to bring the message of Christ to the world in as many ways as I can. In another sense, I'm not on the cutting edge of ministry. Day after day I do my work, my ministry, to bring the message of Christ to the world by carefully doing my work. No mysterious techniques, no miraculous presentations, just getting done what needs to be done. I remember many a normal day while living and serving in Austria.

When I went to the mission day after day I usually saw the same things. I experienced the routines of life. I walked out my door and down the street. Most mornings I'd say good morning to the older gentleman walking his long-haired dachshund. I smiled at him and he smiled at me. When I reached the bus stop day after day I'd see the same people pass by. The young folks were headed to school. Some walked, some waited for a bus, some rolled along on their scooters or roared by on their motorcycles. A young mom came to the bus stop with her daughter most mornings. She helped carry her daughter's extra bags to the stop and then sent her off fully loaded for a day at school. She read the Salzburger News on the bus each morning and got off somewhere after my stop.

There were shops near the bus stop which opened as I waited for the bus to arrive. Day after day they had their routines. They opened their doors. They met the delivery truck and unloaded enough to stock the shop. They put out the signs for the day or rolled the garment and shoe racks outside to catch the eye of the passerby. As the bus approached, the driver smiled and nodded. He knew who I was and didn't ask to see my pass. We greeted each other as I got on board and said goodbye when I exited.

When I walked beside the train platform I'd see the same group of people waiting for the train. I'd work in the same office and do the same things day after day. Sometimes the unusual or unexpected crept into the day but it was normally very routine and uneventful. But it was the routine which kept the staff working. It was the routine that sent the message of the Gospel from its source into our system. It was the routine which sent the message of God's grace from our system to its destination. It was the routine which brought a message of hope to people in need. It was completing the routine which declared God's glory day after day.

As the heavens declare God's glory, day after day, they only display what they are in God's creation. We forget this sometimes. I forget this sometimes. Like the heavens, we declare God's glory not because of who we are but because of who He is. It's not a matter of composing some memorable song, or organizing the theological interpretations of the world or writing a great novel. It's a matter of allowing God to demonstrate His glory in us because we are His. When we go about our day after day business, remain faithful to the Father, complete the things He has placed in our lives, we declare His glory and the world can look on us and see Him.

Repetitions

Impress them on your children. Talk about them when you sit at home and when you walk along the road, when you lie down and when you get up. (Deuteronomy 6:7 NIV)

I'm not young but I'm not elderly. At least it makes me feel better to think that way. I was thinking the other day, dangerous I know, about what I remember thinking when I was younger about those who were not young but not elderly. I'm not sure about others in the world but I have a predilection to allow the changes which take place in my life to be ignored and considered normal while considering the same change in others as evidence of their age. I think it's a case of mental self-preservation.

When I was a young man I loved hearing stories from my parents about when they were young. It was also great to hear of experiences they experienced throughout the "normal" activities of life. There's a lot of humor, wisdom and confusion when you look closely at everyday life. Needless to say, these stories come to mind when we find ourselves in similar circumstances. It's only natural to share them so others are forewarned.

Now that I'm older, but not old, I find that I share such tales with the young folks I meet as well as my own children who are now grown and living away from home. When I'm with their spouses or friends some event will trigger a memory from my past I think will be fun to share. So, I share it.

It's like furlough for a missionary. After so many years on the mission field I've got a treasure of numerous situations or events which others might consider interesting, informative or funny. While bopping around the country sharing our ministry with churches, family and friends I use this collection of tales to fuel many conversations. But the problem is my memory isn't quite what it used to be.

It's not that I forget the salient points of the story. It's not that I forget my wife's name or my grandchildren. It's that I can't keep track of who I've told what, when or how often. We share our ministry and stories at churches across the nation. The advantage of speaking in different locations each week is that you can repeat a sermon or story and it's a different congregation. The embarrassment comes when we're having lunch or just relaxing with different families in the church, with our family or our friends. I can't remember what tale I've told.

Unlike lies which we often forget and thus get us into trouble, forgetting what story you told someone doesn't land you in hot water but in the lukewarm conversation of repetitions. I was gently reminded of this in a recent visit with family. Walking along I was reminded of some funny event centered on where we were and shared it. My marvelous daughter-in-law chuckled and said, "Now I know where he gets it."

"Who gets it?" I queried.

"Your son," she replied.

"Gets what?" I asked

"The habit of repeating stories he's told me before," she said and giggled.

"Oops, did I already tell you that?" I asked, looking down at the pavement under my feet.

"Yes, but that's OK. I'm used to it. I let him go ahead. It makes him feel good."

She smiled, gave me a hug, and let me repeat more stories the rest of the day. I don't know how many stories were repeats because I honestly can't remember what I've told who, when or how many times. I suppose some stories are good to repeat and some get boring. I think it comes as a combination of getting older and making way too many presentations of our work throughout the years. Hopefully the stories I repeat the most often are the good ones which help someone else walk with Christ or liven up their day with humor.

God wasn't afraid of repetitions but I think He remembered who He told what, when and how often. His instruction to the Israelites was to repeat His laws to their children every which way, everywhere, and all the time. I sometimes get so involved in other conversations about life I forget that God is part of everything I do and should take the center in every tale I tell. Honestly, they wouldn't be the stories they are without God.

Whirlwind!

Your thunder was heard in the whirlwind, your lightning lit up the world; the earth trembled and quaked. (Psalms 77:18 NIV)

The first time we departed for the mission field we had two children and sixteen suitcases. Back then extra luggage wasn't a problem and there were no extra fees. Things have changed since then. When we moved back to the US, it was our third international transfer and the whirlwinds swirled around us.

As prices soared and planes fought for income we were limited to a single suitcase and a reduced weight limit - for the suitcase, not us. Unfortunately, it's difficult to move to a new home across the ocean and put enough stuff in a single suitcase to get started. Add in my guitar and we definitely needed additional baggage. Thankfully, our ministry helped with the excess baggage fee so we had three suitcases and one guitar. I thought, "That's enough to keep things moving for a few weeks."

In the last couple months before our departure we were very busy. Getting things turned off was a challenge. Most companies want you to move your account to a new address, not terminate their services. One actually had a "disconnect" fee which amazed me. Then there was the container packing. It was great to hear the company had to pack everything for insurance purposes but a little strange to sit around the house and watch as they did all the work. In two days our home was packed in boxes and brown paper and loaded into a container headed for the USA. If all went well we'd see the stuff again in a few more weeks. Now the question was where to store it at the other end.

Storage became a necessity as God provided for our first nine months living back in the States. A missionary colleague and his family were headed to Guam for nine months. He needed someone to housesit and we needed a place to sit. It worked out quite well and gave us plenty of time to decide where we wanted to live and what type of housing we'd like. This would be like a nine-month furlough trip except our household stuff would eventually arrive, so we'd have access to whatever we could find in the boxes in whatever storage facility we used.

With initial housing out of the way we hit the ground running. First, we needed cell phones. It was quite a shock to see the cost of the new plans available after the less expensive cell phone contracts in Europe. But we needed to talk with family and friends, so we took the plunge and were modernized in our phone communications. Next, we needed an automobile. Beth carefully investigated the options via the internet before we moved. Using this information, we visited a number of dealers and took a number of test rides.

343

We settled on a little car where I could get in and out without my head hitting the roof. Some of the smaller fuel-efficient cars were just too small for me to get in and out. Beth said I looked like someone escaping his mother's womb when I climbed out of some cars. That was settled and arrangements with the auto dealer took all of day two. Now we had a car and a way to communicate.

Day three back in the USA. Next, we turned our sights to a new mattress set. Our old one served us well for many years, but we wanted something a little more comfortable and with a little more space. It was time to find a king-size bed where we could rest for the future. We were staying in our mission's lodge the first few nights and I figured moving into our temporary home would help us get settled. But we didn't want to sleep on the floor. After visiting a few places, we found what we wanted, including a bargain, and they said they would deliver right away. What that meant was they were at the house waiting for us when we drove across Raleigh to the house. They were fast.

One day of rest and then we were off to visit our children, daughters- and son-in-law and grandchildren in our new car. We were still running and looking forward to all the hugs and kisses as well as eventually getting back to our temporary home and enjoying our new bed. I didn't think we'd feel settled until we were there for more than a couple nights and became accustomed to the new location, where to find things, how to get here and there and returning to some sort of a routine.

When we got back we need to rent a storage facility. I think we did well for less than a week back in the country. Phones, car, mattress, housing, and visiting family and friends were a lot in less than seven days. I felt like Dorothy being swept up in the tornado watching the world go by. I wasn't sure where we would land but knew the ground would come up soon enough.

Through all this we saw how the Lord provided day after day. We were ready for a little rest but until God stopped the whirlwind we pressed forward. We were thankful to rest comfortably in God's loving arms and watch Him get that first week of a new chapter of our lives in order. Now, where are those silver slippers, Dorothy?

Rapunzel Tangled!

He said, "Please show me your glory." He said, "I will make all my goodness pass before you, and will proclaim the name of Yahweh before you. I will be gracious to whom I will be gracious, and will show mercy on whom I will show mercy." (WEB Exodus 33:18-19)

I love a parade. It's been a while since I watched a good Christmas parade up close and in person. There were parades now and then in Austria but nothing like the full steam ahead, floats, cars, horses, bands, beauty queen, and grand marshal affairs I remember from my youth. When the chance came to go downtown and enjoy a local Christmas parade I thought it was a great idea.

To add to the fun, one of my two-year-old granddaughters joined us at the celebration. In case you haven't been around a two-year-old lately they have a lot of energy (more than me) and a very short attention span. They like to be entertained. With this in mind, we expected Lily to be distracted during the two plus hours the parade marched by our seats. But a little distraction from our granddaughter isn't really a distraction, it's fun.

We got up early and made our way through the traffic to a back-street parking place. We walked past the line of traffic-snarled cars to join our friends on the parade route a block from the start. It was a cool and sunny day and the crowds were gathering. Vendors weaved their way up and down the street to offer us hot coffee and get us going with donuts, all for a nominal price. Lily watched the people coming and going and started to wake up and enjoy the morning. Then the parade started.

Beth and I were amazed. We expected a tag team approach to keep track of Lily when the initial excitement of the parade gave way to the short attention span of a two-year-old. Nothing close to that happened. From the first trumpet of the first band through the final police vanguard at the rear of the parade, she sat enthralled.

She clapped for the bands, waved at the people on the floats and said hi to everyone who walked, rode or marched along the parade route. When she saw a young lady dressed in a long gown she would shout out, "Rapunzel Tangled!" (We didn't know that was the phrase until later when she was interpreted by her mom.) She smiled, she giggled and laughed and was entranced from start to finish. There were horses, cars, dogs, dancers and folks in large costumes.

Then the first of a couple big balloons came floating by and she was beside herself with joy. She'd look me in the face and say, "Big balloon." Each time a float appeared she put her hands to the side of her face and exclaimed, "Another one!" I really enjoyed the parade, but I also enjoyed watching her excitement and thrill as the various schools, businesses and organizations shared in the holiday celebration.

I can just imagine God watching Moses' face while He displayed His glory before the patriarch. I can hear Moses clapping his hands in excitement as each aspect of God's glory rolled by in a divine parade. I think God was thrilled that Moses was thrilled with what he saw.

I think it will be fascinating and more than we can imagine to see the wonders of heaven and experience a glimpse of God's glory. Just think of the parades we'll enjoy watching as they wind their way down the golden streets of the New Jerusalem. We'll be filled with excitement as we wave at Michael and shout hi to Gabriel and the other angels as they reveal God in each step. That will be a truly grand parade.

Until then I look forward to my next parade. I look forward to sharing more of these joys with my grandchildren. I look forward to a touch of wonder this side of Heaven while I wait in anticipation.

Groceries in the Hall

If we have food and covering, with these we shall be content. (1 Timothy 6:8)

When we moved to Europe we changed from living in a concrete house to a concrete apartment building. It was a great place in the foothills of the Alps overlooking the plain and city of Vienna. At the end of the road past our building sat the Vienna Woods with all the beauty, trails and history. Many times we'd walk up to the woods and then hike along the ridge before descending to the little town of Perchtoldsdorf. There we'd refresh ourselves with Italian ice cream and then take a bus back up the hill to our apartment.

While the apartment was nice, including a wonderful fireplace and spectacular views, it was in a town without a grocery store and lacking most other shops. With three boys still at home it was important to constantly acquire a large stock of food for the larder. To keep the kitchen filled with important items such as peanut butter, cookies, snacks, chips, drinks and various other non-healthy essentials, Beth was required to purchase quantities too large for her to carry up the stairs. Did I mention we were on the fourth floor and there was no elevator?

To compensate for the lack of a lift, Beth would stash her grocery bags at the bottom of the stairs. Then, when the boys or I came home we'd gather what we could and lug it upstairs. This worked pretty well and was the same approach others used in our stairwell. The only problem was when we weren't sure which bags were our groceries and which belonged to our neighbors. They apparently had the same identification problem.

One day, Beth went shopping and left several bags inside the entrance waiting for one of us to come home. I arrived first and buzzed the apartment. She told me to bring up the bags. When I stepped inside and looked around there were no bags to gather. I thought maybe the boys picked up everything, so I climbed the 49 steps to our apartment.

I came through the door and Beth asked about the groceries. I told her there weren't any bags in the stairwell and the mystery began. Where were our groceries? Theft, at least of groceries, was not a problem in our complex. We figured someone else must have picked them up by mistake. Sure enough, there was a knock on our door.

We opened the door to find G holding our bag of groceries. He looked sad and said, "I thought M left our groceries downstairs, so I picked them up. Once I opened the bag I knew it couldn't be our groceries. Inside were fun things to eat like cookies and snacks and chips. I don't get to eat those things." He bowed his sad-looking head and handed us the bag. We thanked him. He left. We closed the door. We chuckled. Later we shared some of our cookies with him.

I like cookies, so I can sympathize with G's downcast appearance. I also like finding special little treats in my life. Sometimes they're for me and sometimes I just pick up something meant for someone else. Then I need to remind myself what's really important and that's really hard. Where do I find contentment? Is it with cookies and snacks or with the fun little extra things in life? According to Timothy it's not the snacks but the essentials of clothing and food. I can live with that. I can be content with that.

I'm not claiming to hold some higher plain of spiritual existence or that I'm always content with food and clothing. Some days I am, other days I'm impatient for that little extra goodie. It's good to remind myself when I look in the cookie bag and find someone else's name inside that I can still be content with God's care and grace, even without a fattening cookie.

A Boat on the Water

They immediately went out, and entered into the boat.
That night, they caught nothing (John 21:3b WEB)

For many years my family lived in the little town of Greenhills, Ohio. It was a Greenbelt community setup by the government when I was a child. The city was surrounded by the trees and wonders of Winton Woods and protected from development that would extend its boundaries into the forest. A city surrounded by a belt of green. I loved living there. You could walk a few blocks and start exploring the creeks, forest and hidden valleys.

Not only did Winton Woods contain woods but it also contained Winton Lake. We skated on the lake and ponds in the winter, skipped rocks across the surface and fished from its banks. Occasionally we'd have the chance to take a boat out on the lake. At one point in history there was a little paddle wheel boat, adding an attraction for tourists.

Years later, I was grown, our children were grown, and our oldest son arranged for a family gathering on Norris Lake in Tennessee. Ten adults, five grandchildren under the age of four, one house and lots of food made for a joyful family gathering. We ate, we played games, we laughed and one day we went out on the lake.

There were two boats to hold us all. I was captain of the pontoon boat. This floating family room was great for the little ones with its high rails and a roof covering half the deck. The other boat, captained by our oldest son, was a speedboat that ran rings around my slower pontoon boat. That didn't matter. I was the captain of my ship! A big tube was attached to a long rope behind the speedboat; several members of the family climbed onto the tube to be dragged at high speed across the water. It was a blast.

At one point we dropped anchor in a cove so those inclined could take a swim. Thanks to the lifejackets everyone, except me, took a dip in the lake. There was some concern on the part of the little ones about the water and a few cries of resistance. One granddaughter didn't like the water because it wasn't blue. She wanted to swim in blue water, not green water. Our son's fiancé tried hard to convince her the water was fine. She even talked about Nemo as a possible resident of the lake, but it just didn't assuage our little granddaughter's fears of the water that was the wrong color.

After several hours of wind, heat and reflection on the water, most of us were tired if not sunburned. The day was fun, but it was exhausting at the same time. Eventually we dropped most of the family off at a dock near our rental home while a few of us returned the boats to their rental dock. By the time we drove back to the house we were more than ready for a good night's rest.

I can't imagine the impact of being on the water all day and working at the same time. A day on the water having fun was exhausting and I spent most of the day just driving the pontoon boat. I can imagine the exhaustion the disciples experienced after an all-night session of net fishing on the Sea of Galilee. Then in the morning along came Jesus telling them to toss their nets one more time. And they did it!

When I get exhausted, whether from physical labor or just having fun, the last thing I want is someone asking me to do something else. And that's just what happens almost daily. Then I remember the results. The disciples pulled in more fish in one toss than they had all night. Who knows what God will do when I put aside my exhaustion and respond to those around me? Perhaps He'll use me to pull a net of seekers into His kingdom. I just need to be ready for that extra toss.

Pruned

"Every branch that bears fruit, he prunes, that it may bear more fruit." (John 15:2b WEB)

There were a lot of trees on the property of my childhood home. I remember my dad tossing a rope over a high branch then attaching a tire so we could enjoy a good swing in the shade. I've always enjoyed the shade of a good tree but sometimes a branch starts to die and needs to be pruned from the trunk. The stub is then tarred over to keep it from growing back and sapping (any pun you'd like to apply) the tree of vitality. That's what I remembered about pruning.

Then I spent a number of years in "wine" country with grapevines almost everywhere you turned. I learned there's more than one purpose for pruning. As a child I learned you pruned to get rid of the dead wood. As an adult I learned you could also prune to increase the fruitfulness of the vine. Not only grapevines but a number of shrubs, flowering plants and other beautiful vegetation can be improved by careful pruning.

Sometimes I thought it looked brutal when trees were pruned down to just a stump. Grapevines are pruned of almost every branch until they look like naked stalks. But that's one of the secrets. When a branch first bears fruit it might not be the best. The art of pruning back the branch so it regrows actually improves the harvest of fruit.

I'm reminded of Jesus' sermon about the vines. One verse comes to mind: "Every branch that bears fruit, he prunes, that it may bear more fruit." (John 15:2b WEB) It's interesting Jesus tells us that bearing fruit is like an invitation to be pruned. It's not a bad thing but for our benefit. The art of pruning in our lives allows us to bear more fruit. We don't always understand this when God suddenly moves us from what was a fruitful ministry into a new place. Beth and I experienced this several times in our lives.

We were involved with our church in the USA and bearing fruit in music and teaching when the Lord called us to be missionaries. We were pruned from that ministry to head overseas. Next God allowed us to bear fruit on Guam in youth work, music, leadership, teaching, and training and then we were pruned from the Guam ministry. God then allowed us to bear more fruit in Austria in music, preaching, leadership, training, pastoral work and teaching.

Next, we were pruned once more from a fruitful ministry in Austria. We then looked forward to what God had in store. We grew in a new land but were connected to the same vine. Each time God applies His pruning shears we learn more about ourselves as we watch God work in us, and the lives of those around us.

351

Our fruitfulness in local church ministry also impacts our global fruit as we bring the message of God's grace and hope to the world via media as missionaries with TWR. The two ministries build upon one another and help us to grow as God's servants. It would be easy to be sad and wonder why God would remove us from a fruitful ministry to start over. But it becomes an encouragement when we consider Jesus' teaching about the vine and the branches

It's not bad to be pruned. It's not trimming of the bad branches. It's trimming our branches so we have the chance to grow back and produce even more fruit. God prunes in wisdom. The vinedresser knows what He's doing and does it for our own good and the growth of the kingdom. When we're pruned we need to look forward to a new harvest of fruit for eternity.

Lost in the Czech Republic

It happened after three days they found him in the temple, sitting in the midst of the teachers, both listening to them, and asking them questions. Luke 2:46 WEB)

Prague is a beautiful city full of history both good and bad. For those who read mystery novels, the act of defenestration has its origin in the infamous Czech courts of Prague. While visiting this famous hall of judgment in the castle, we looked out the window only after ensuring no one was behind us. All I could think of was "ouch" when I considered the quick stop at the bottom of the castle wall.

Aside from this unique form of punishment, we enjoyed touring Prague several times. Once, we enjoyed a beautiful and new guesthouse just below the castle. That wasn't planned but much better than the internet advertised place I originally located. That's another story altogether. On our second visit we stayed in an old seminary located at the outskirts of town.

Our family combined with our visitors couldn't all fit in our little van. So we decided the older boys could take the train and meet us there. We drove up to Vienna and dropped our son with our friends' son at the train station. They had the right tickets and so we left them there and drove onto the autobahn and headed north.

It's a beautiful drive through the Czech countryside. The villages and castles along the way provide for that perfect holiday photo. We arrived on time and made our way through town. We found the seminary, checked in and took a bus back to town for a little sight-seeing. It was a blast. From the grave of Good King Wenceslas to the home of reformer John Huss, we tromped through the streets of history.

As the afternoon waned we waited to hear from our sons that they arrived safely. We waited and waited and waited. Then my phone rang. They missed the train station in Prague, not fully understanding the name of the station and were headed north into the countryside towards Germany. Needless to say, I was a bit worried as it was late in the afternoon, we didn't know where they were, and we didn't know how to get them back.

For the next hour or two we exchanged phone calls until his phone ran out of money. Then we were in the dark, wondering if our sons were going to have to sleep in a train station. As evening approached we headed to the seminary, hoping they would find their way back and the right bus. We went to the bus stop every time a bus came. There we waited for the last bus of the evening, expecting no one to exit.

But we were surprised when the two young men stepped off the bus with a young lady. It seems they met her on the train and she was on a backpack trip through Europe. They explained that when they missed Prague they left the train after a few stops and a kind gentleman who understood German showed them which train to get back to the city. Praise the Lord they had just enough money for the ticket and the bus to the seminary. The young lady didn't have a place to stay so they said she could stay with us. Our friends had room in their apartment with their daughter, so it worked out just right.

I'd like to say I was calm and collected throughout the day but that wouldn't be true. I was definitely upset that our sons were lost in a foreign land, without communications and I had no way to know where they were to retrieve them. I wonder if Joseph and Mary felt the same way when they looked around and Jesus was missing from their caravan. No phones, no trains, no van, no way to know where to find their son. I can just imagine Joseph going from door to door, from shop to shop, retracing their steps to find Jesus.

And there he was, sitting in the temple calmly conversing with the elders. Amazing! From what I could learn our sons were calmly enjoying their trip through the countryside until they could get off the train and find their way back. Joseph and Mary were relieved to find Jesus. We were relived to find our son. I think God was telling me to calm down and just wait on Him. He knew were our sons were and how to get them back. He knows where we are and how to get us where we need to be.

The Shadow Knows!

But we speak God's wisdom in a mystery, the wisdom that has been hidden, which God foreordained before the worlds for our glory, (1 Corinthians 2:7 WEB)

Although radio dramas were popular before my time, I've heard about them and the fun of gathering around the wireless to listen to the serial adventures of some super hero or master detective. When my children were little, there were a number of Christian radio programs still on the air. I enjoyed the stories and listening to them with my children. There is a sense of excitement when you use your imagination to put the sounds, voices, and story into a mental picture. This gave way to more television and eventually the draw of computer games.

One of the characters I heard about on the old radio serials was The Shadow. In later years there was a movie to emblazon this odd crime fighter's exploits across the big screen. I must admit I enjoyed the movie. One of the famous quotes went something like, "Who knows what lurks in the heart of men? The Shadow knows!" That's a great tagline.

It's nice to have a great tagline and be seen as a crime-fighting hero. This isn't something I've had the opportunity to develop in my life. I'm not much of a sleuth outside of sifting through computer problems or transmitter failures. But an encouraging card I received from a colleague surprised me. He was congratulating me on my birthday when he wrote, "Often I am sure you are more *perceived as a shadow* rather than being present until something goes wrong and we suddenly realize how much you are part of a very essential reality!" (Emphasis mine)

Cool! I just might be a crime-fighting hero after all. I've always wondered what it would be like to be a superhero character. What's it like to always be ready when there's a need? You never know where I'll show up. I'd have secret abilities, which only appear when needed and just in the nick of time. Way cool!

My colleague was talking about working in IT and keeping things moving so smoothly they only realize I'm working when something breaks. That's a compliment, I think. Maybe I should wear a big hat, trench coat and scarf across my face to hide my identity. I could be lurking in the myriad bits and pieces of computer technology. Just when you think it's time to reboot I can jump out, fix the problem, and then disappear into the shadows of your office.

Working with IT is sort of like working in the shadows without the nefarious connotations. If I do my job right then no one should know that anything has changed or, even better, was broken and then fixed. Most folks haven't a clue what I did to fix something after I came and resolved an issue.

They're just glad it worked again. In the IT department we do a lot of work in the background keeping things secure, up-to-date, and making necessary adjustments to keep up with the relentless forward march in the technological world and continuous barrage of attacks from the outside world.

All of this is done to bring a message of hope to the world. It's a message from God's heart to His creation. When I think of the frustration computers can bring, I'm amazed that God allowed us to discover how to make and use these electronic marvels. But He always knows what we need to accomplish our calling. It's just a set of tools and I'm called to keep them working in proper order. When we fly we usually think about the pilot and not the ground crew who work in the shadows to ensure the plane is safe. When we boot our computers and send emails we think of the message, not those who keep the servers, network lines and software running so the message reaches the recipient.

Sometimes it's nice to be a shadow, mysterious, effective, only a glimpse out of the corner of someone's eye. That's when I get things in order; out of sight in preparation. As a Christian I try to allow God to use me for reaching others by just being faithful. If I pay attention to what I do before I talk with someone then I become more effective than ever. Perhaps we need to stop for a moment while we're in the shadows and make sure we're walking faithfully with God, make sure things are in order. Then when we're on display it won't be much different than when we were invisible because we're walking the same faithful walk.

The Pirates Who Do I.T.

I press toward the mark for the prize of the high calling of God in Christ Jesus. (Philippians 3:14 KJV)

I once played a pirate in a couple children's musicals. I was a friendly Christian pirate whose goal was to help people, not rob them. My patch would mysteriously move from eye to eye between scenes during the performance. Even a pirate needs a little fun.

Recently I was sitting at my desk, in my cubical, in my corner of the office working on a project. At some point I experienced binary bifurcation of purpose (aka the computer didn't do what I thought it should) and so I let out an "argh." I wasn't wearing a patch but my colleague in the next cubical asked, "Is this talk like a pirate day?"

In truth, it was close! There is an official "talk like a pirate" day in September. I was a few days early. Then I started listening to others expressing their reactions to computer disobedience and discovered pirate talk from different corners of the I.T. department all day. I think every computer geek has uttered some form of pirate talk, intentionally or unintentionally, more than once in their career.

Even the casual computer user understands when there's a wayward program, unexpected patch, or other signs of a computer's resistance to the operator's insistence that a particular function should be performed. I don't want to list all the possible permutations of pirate speak here for fear of offending some sensitive analog lover who's never ventured into the exciting waters of computer technology.

The idea came to me to make a sign for our department. Every department these days has a sign which proudly displays the name of the department and their statement of purpose to help rescue the world through their diligent and heartfelt work. I think a sign like "Computer Department" or "I.T. Department" would be just too plain. It wouldn't be expressive enough for the deep running emotions of electronic ministry. So, I figured it should read something like this:

I.T. Department
We are the pirates who do I.T.
Bring us your recalcitrant, wayward computer
and we'll teach it what for.

We could all get eye patches and expand our pirate vocabulary to include some technical derivations beyond the demonstrative "argh." Instead of "blast it all" we could say, "binary it all." We couldn't threaten users with "walking the plank" but with "disk disconnection." It wouldn't be "waterway congestion" but "Ethernet excess." I'm sure there are plenty of particularly pointed platitudes which could be included in this theoretical thesaurus of pirate speak.

But, ours is not to develop an alternate alliterative language but to keep the forecastles and gunwales of the computer ships running properly so that the sweet message of the Gospel of Christ can smoothly sail the electronic oceans of the world. We have a goal on the horizon and no copious pirate platitudes will dissuade us from the destination. Unfurl the mizzenmast, pull up the anchors, shout out orders to one-eyed Jack and shipshape Sam and turn her into the wind. We've got to get this ship in shape for the rough waters ahead. The enemy has many schemes and frustrating our intentions, even electronic ones, is one of the tools in his arsenal.

If another language helps, go for it!

Bats in the Belfry

And we know that all things work together for good to them that love God,
to them who are the called according to his purpose. (KJV Romans 8:28)

Over the years, I've stayed in a variety of places. These ranged from storage rooms in the back of broadcast complexes, to private homes, hotels, castles and palaces. Yes, I've stayed in a palace or two. The first palace I stayed the night in was with my wife and sons on our trip west toward the castle Neuschwanstein. While it was considered a "hunting" lodge at one point, it eventually was renovated to the status of palace. By the time we arrived it was a retreat center but still spectacular. We stayed in the queen's room. Yep, the room we occupied was the room normally reserved when the queen came to visit. It was large, luxurious and just the intricate wood designs in the walls and on the ceilings impressed us as we brought in our plastic suitcases and two energetic boys.

Fortunately, it was updated with modern plumbing and heating. We enjoyed the thought of being temporary royalty as we strolled around the room and the grounds. We were traveling with friends who enjoyed the cushy comfort of their own royal chamber.

The second palace we enjoyed a few years later was also converted into a retreat center. In this case it was operated by a Christian group running retreats and summer camps for Christian youth and the occasional adult group. Considering the massive number of steps we had to climb just to reach our room, I can understand why it was more youth-oriented than "older" adult-oriented.

Beth and I enjoyed the tallest tower on the south wing. Our room covered two floors within the round tower with a spectacular view of the surrounding valley. We were above most of the rest of the palace with a spire on top of our nice room. The bath and toilet were by the entrance. A few steps up from there was the kitchen and dining area. From there we climbed steep steps (aka a ladder) into the living area. To reach the beds we crawled through a triangular door (like the Krell construction on Altair) where two single sleeping mats were laid head to head. The ceiling over the beds was the roof of the adjoining building, giving just enough room to slide in for the night. In truth, I couldn't sit up without hitting my head on the ceiling. Ah, the comforts of palace living.

Snuggled in for the night, a hot night at that, we eventually fell asleep. I'm not a big fan of sleeping on futon beds but that was what we had. I like a little more padding. Part way through the night we were awakened by a noise in the living area. Since a youth retreat was in progress we thought maybe someone had wandered in thinking the room was vacant. Beth and I crawled on our elbows like the two-legged Krell and looked out the portal.

There, flitting back and forth in the living room, were a couple bats enjoying the darkness of night. Apparently, they were doing us a service by gulping down the little critters who were flying around the room looking to feast on us for dinner. The bats, although spooky to watch, were keeping us off the menu for the night. Thank you, bats!

I've heard the phrase "bats in the belfry" many times in life. That night it took on a whole different meaning. Granted, this wasn't a bell tower but it was close enough. When we arose we carefully peeked out the Krell doorway and assured ourselves they had departed during the morning hours.

I wonder about what God allows to cross the path of my life. Sometimes I get annoyed or distracted as things can flitter this way and that disrupting what I think needs to be accomplished. I want to shoo the distractions out of the way and get on with things. Now I'm inclined to think these "distractions" are at times little helpers to clear away other obstacles from my walk with Him. The have their unseen benefits, like eating insects we couldn't see in the night, and protect us from hidden obstacles. Next time I'm in a castle with bats I think I'll just watch them for a while and think of God's protection.

The Massive Meatball
Massacre of 2015

Come now, you who say, "Today or tomorrow let's go into this city, and spend a year there, trade, and make a profit." Whereas you don't know what your life will be like tomorrow. For what is your life? For you are a vapor that appears for a little time, and then vanishes away. (James 4:13-14 WEB)

I like Christmas parties. They usually are festive, fun and have lots of tasty food available. When it comes to departmental work holiday celebrations it's one of those chances to see a colleague's family and enjoy some fellowship not related to a work project. The IT department often held an evening of celebration with food, fun and an expression of thanks from our supervisor. Many times, the gathering was in the supervisor's home.

It's an interesting prospect when spending time in your boss's home. You get a glimpse of his private life. You learn something of the things he enjoys not related to the ministry. Looking at family pictures, on the wall or in frames, can be fun and at times the source of some interesting stories. Checking out his books gives insights into his penchant for fiction or nonfiction and, in the case of ministry, his favorite theologians and preachers. Then there is the quick perusal of the music library, assuming he still has CDs or records and hasn't gone entirely digital; these things tell you a lot about your hosts and what decade impacted them the most.

A few years ago, we attended the IT Department Christmas party at our boss's home. It was a wonderful time. We laughed, we ate, we were entertained by one another. The children present provided an additional layer of fun and excitement as we chatted or played with available toys. Our boss read his annual poem about each one of the department and their unique skills expressed in a unique and humorous way. When the evening was winding down Beth and I packed the car.

We brought meatballs to the party in a Crock Pot. This made things easy to heat up for the evening. There weren't many left in the pot by the time we departed. I carefully placed the Crock Pot in the trunk surrounded by a few items. It was almost empty, so the center of gravity was low on the device. Things looked good, we were bundled in our winter coats and headed out of the neighborhood.

Pulling out onto the main road can sometimes be tricky. There is a lot of traffic even at night in December. After waiting an appropriate amount of time for the stream of cars to whisk by, I saw my chance and pulled across the road, turning left toward home. Perhaps I accelerated a little faster than I anticipated. As we completed the arc to enter the lane we heard a tell-tale thump from the rear of the car. Oh no! At the first chance, I pulled into a side road on the right and stopped the car.

Cautiously I moved to the back of the car and opened the trunk lid. I couldn't see a thing. Of course not! It was dark outside and there's no light in the trunk. I pulled out my cell phone and clicked on the flashlight. That's when I saw the carnage. There were meatballs everywhere covered in the requisite red sauce. The remnants of unconsumed sauce were oozing out of the pot across the trunk. Some meatballs were intact, having rolled clear of the pot, while others apparently were trapped with other trunk objects and smashed or sliced into meatball oblivion. It was not a pretty sight. I up righted the pot and corralled the wayward contents as best I could back to its still-hot embrace. It would be a long time, with lots of cleaning, before the trunk would be restored to a non-Italian food condition.

As Christians, we sometimes put things away carefully, hoping they'll make the trip through the rest of our life. But then there's an unexpected turn in life and things start rattling around and making a mess. We corral the pieces we can reach in a futile attempt to put them back where we had them. They never seem to fit back in their original packing.

I'm glad God doesn't have this problem. He knows where everything fits and how to keep it in place in our life. If I can remember He's the one in control, then I can put all the pieces in His hand. Once He has packed them where they belong, they stay put. I think that is a better way.

I'm Content

But godliness with contentment is great gain. (1 Timothy 6:6 WEB)
No matter what people may think, I'm content with my life, my family, my work and my faith; so, stop telling me I need something more. I was thinking about this while lying awake in bed one morning. When I look at things in my life and consider what I've done, where I've been and what I've acquired (physical stuff, experiences, etc.), I'm content. Unfortunately, sometimes when my frustration over things around me percolates to the top of my patience, I might present a temporary persona that doesn't portray a contented soul. But that's another subject.

One of the first things I thought about was my wonderful wife quietly asleep beside me. It's the precise planning of God that brought us together at the right place and time to embark on an amazing, busy, full and fantastic life. Two-thirds of our lives we've been together and I'm looking forward with anticipation to undertaking together the next 40 plus years of life and adventure God has planned. Like most married men I know, I often wonder how my love tolerated me all these years. But I'm content knowing God was gracious to me and gives her lots of patience.

We've lived through raising four children, watching them leave the nest and start a life of their own with their own families. I like my children's spouses. I love them all and I believe they like me. Our children are doing well in a variety of jobs. We've got service managers, restaurant managers, teachers and soldiers carrying on the family line. I'm proud of them all. They've had their problems, we haven't always seen eye to eye, but as family we work through things. Thanks to them I have a number of grandchildren that I love dearly. I think they love me as well. I know why God gives us grandchildren. It's to ensure we still have that delightful spark of innocence to encourage us in life. They have good and bad days; they're little children and I wouldn't trade them for the world. I'm content with my family.

I've spent the majority of my life serving and working with the same organization in various places around the globe. I'd like to say everything was rosy and delightful all these years, but the truth is there were hard times along with good times. Still, I'm content with what God has been able to accomplish through my work around the globe. More than once I felt ill-equipped for the job. It was then I watched as God stepped in to show His grace and let me know that I can do all things through Him. I can't say I never had doubts about what I was doing. They would raise their ugly heads now and then until I reset my vision on the one who gives me strength. I can say I never had doubts about God's calling me to this life. I'm content in my work and ministry.

I can't count the number of times I've turned to God and asked, "Why?" Sometimes I found the answer. Some questions remain unanswered. I've railed at God in my frustration and anger and praised and worshipped Him at all times. Yes, even when I was furious I still worshipped God. I didn't understand what was happening at the time, some things I still don't understand, but I trust in God in all things. I'm comforted understanding that I can come to God with praise, anger, questions and the small issues of daily life and He listens. He shows me grace, especially in my stupid times. He loves me always, even in my disobedient times. I'm content with my faith in God.

In all this I find myself wondering why I would consider not being content. I can stop and think and realize that this is a great life God has provided and like the verse above I have great gain. Sometimes people think I'm discontent because I'm frustrated with things or get angry over an encounter with massive stupidity. So I wonder if we're not confusing contentment with emotionless living. Are they the same? I don't think so. God gave us emotions to help us deal with life on this spinning rock. We can let them get out of hand but to dismiss them as ungodly just doesn't ring true for me. There are some things, regardless of my godliness or contentment, which I suspect will always increase my blood pressure.

There are inconsistencies in the behavior and reliability of computers, an area I've worked with for over thirty years that make me want to test the aerodynamic characteristics of the device from any open window (which I have done). There are vehicle drivers who apparently didn't attend driving school, forgot all they learned or had incompetent teachers. Some folks standing in line for ten minutes or more to pay for items wait until they reach the counter to fish through their fifty-gallon purse looking for their credit card. Sometimes I just sigh and roll my eyes. Other times, for whatever reasons, I just get frustrated or angry.

Then there's the modern church. As a faithful member of the congregation we're never doing enough "for God." We hear preaching about contentment and at the same time a message of "do more" which creates discontent because we're not doing enough, in the eyes of the local church, to justify our claiming to be faithful believers. Rubbish! I'm concentrating on my walk in this world as a faithful follower of Christ. Just walking faithful with God through normal activities of life is doing something "for God." Where that intersects with a church ministry, such as being a full-time missionary, I'm glad to go as God leads. I don't doubt some future heavenly residents might need a little fire under their backside to get them moving but who lights the fire, God or man? Without getting into a pet peeve let me say I'm content with the ministries where God has place me and I'm not looking for more. If He gives more I'll undertake it. Otherwise I'll be content with the here and now.

That's probably where contentment lies. It lies in knowing you are where God wants you to be. It's understanding the abilities God has given for the particular task and being content that God knows what He's doing. Does it remove all emotion so we can be like good southerners and just say, "Bless their heart" when they do something ridiculous? At times it might. At other times life boils to the top and we are reminded we are humans, designed with emotions, by a God with emotions, to live in an emotional world. I'm content to live here, with all my foibles, until He takes me to that perfect mansion. Are you content?

Lady of Little Faith

For the whole law is fulfilled in one word, in this: "You shall love your neighbor as yourself." (Galatians 5:14 WEB)

When my son Evan came to visit us in Austria, I asked him to bring me some books. Since he worked in a bookstore it was a great chance to get some reduced prices. I like sales! Anyway, I'd decided to read some of the major works I'd avoided over the years in lieu of reading theology and Christian ministry related books, not to mention the computer, radio, audio, and numerous other texts relating to my ministry.

He lugged the massive, even in paperback, copy of The Brothers Karamazov, to our home. I'd read excerpts from Fyodor Dostoevsky and references to his characters in other texts and decided it was time to take the plunge and see if I could work my way through the 776 pages of the tome. I found it fascinating how Dostoevsky rambled in his prose style. Way too many words for my succinct engineering mind. But, I still enjoyed his presentation of the people, culture, and theological mindset created in his literary version of Russia. So, I just stopped and made a note of a passage that caught my fancy.

I was in part I, book 2, when I met the monastery elder Zosima. Interestingly described, with great detail to the historical installation of elders, with that wizened presence which instills confidence in those around him. Several encounters were described which served to demonstrate his amazing, clear evaluation of those seeking his blessing and advice. Then I came to a lady of little faith. Without reiterating the depth of the text, he made the following statement, to the lady, concerning her desire to love those around her.

". . . active love is a harsh and fearful thing compared with love in dreams. Love in dreams thirsts for immediate action, quickly, performed, and with everyone watching. Indeed, it will go as far as the giving even of one's life, provided it does not take long but is soon over, as on stage, and everyone is looking on and praising. Whereas active love is labor and perseverance, and for some people, perhaps, a while science. But I predict that even in that very moment when you see with horror that despite all your efforts, you not only have not come nearer your goal but seem to have gotten farther from it, at that very moment – I predict this to you – you will suddenly reach your goal and clearly behold over you the wonder-working power of the Lord, who all the while has been mysteriously guiding you."

I wish I could take credit for such a clear statement, but alas, I can't. While translated from the original Russian this seems a concise description of many Christians in today's church. I was caught off guard when I realized the times

I too have sought to be loving for the joy of the spiritual applause my fellow believers provided.

We, even Christians, even missionaries, like an audience that appreciates our efforts. The lady in the story confessed to seeking advice, on how to express love to others, for the joy of being praised by the elder. I like to think I'm selfless and giving fully of myself in serving others. This may be true at times. But, at other times I sulk and am tempted to stop when my ego isn't bolstered with words of encouragement and praise.

Maybe you can identify with me, maybe not. I must confess, I was chastised when I read the sentence, ". . .active love is labor and perseverance, . . ." countered against the condemnation, "Love in dreams thirsts for immediate action, quickly, performed, and with everyone watching." Ouch, that hurts!

So, I guess I need to look a little more closely, even as a missionary, at the reason I do this or that. Am I being "nice" because I should, because it is Christ-like? Or, am I looking for worldly approval? Tough questions.

So, a new week begins, my mind has been challenged. We'll see how things go. Maybe somewhere in the days ahead I'll draw closer to my goal of loving everyone around me, as Christ loved me, even in the midst of my mistakes and, at times, wrong attitude. We have a wonder-working Lord and it is a wonder what he does in me day to day.

Morning Meltdown

I'm not sure where it all began. Throughout my life I've had good and bad days with frustration and angry outbursts. Sometimes I win, sometimes I lose. Fortunately, the results of these physical outbursts are directed toward inanimate objects, not people. A number of years ago I was at the edge of depression and struggled hard to avoid burnout. It was only through the presence of God in my life, understanding His grace and love toward me, and the effective patience, love and grace of my wife, that I made it through those years. But I didn't reach the shore without some long-lasting effects.

Even as I write this my nerves remain frazzled and I struggle to remain calm at times. I think I've done okay the last few years striving not to go ballistic over something ridiculous. My wife is a more realistic judge of that than I am. But there are a few things I know grate on me and I avoid them as much as possible. I can only take a throng of people all talking in one room for a limited time before I have to escape into a quieter, relaxed space. I will quickly pull my head into my turtle shell when a "conversation" is carried by the person who asks and answers their own comments and questions. But this isn't a recitation of my quirks, annoyances and foibles. This is background to a morning meltdown.

I've worked with computers for years. Anyone who works with them (most of the modern world) knows they are incredibly annoying, frustrating and recalcitrant devices designed by humans and imbued with just enough human personality to grate against the nerves. Working with computers in administration has the additional human element. I deal with people trying hard (sometimes hardly) to also tame these silicon-based beasts. The other day my little notebook refused to be cooperative after a numerous attempts, calls, inserted disks, drives, and the resources my thirty plus years of computer work could apply and I succumbed to a full-fledged explosion. In short, I lost it.

I finally did something I've talked about for years. I decided the computer needed to test its aerodynamic capabilities. It failed its test flight. I failed as well. Needless to say, the electronics were no longer useful when it finally landed, dispersing its parts far and wide in the process. Did I feel any better? In one sense, yes. The annoying computer was dead. In the bigger picture, I felt worse. I disappoint myself when I lose it. It doesn't help me. It doesn't help those around me. It doesn't help resolve technical problems.

I'm not making excuses. It shouldn't have gone so far as to turn a notebook into a glider. But frustration and anger are realities in this world. Even our Lord got angry and cleared the temple. God's anger burned in the Old Testament. We're implored not to let the sun go down on our anger which to me indicates that we, even as believers, will get angry at times (Ephesians 4:26). We're also encouraged to put away anger (Colossians 3:8).

It's like Paul's struggle. He wants to do what is right and finds himself doing what is wrong (Romans 7). It's the constant battle as the old nature rears its ugly head. I know some like to distinguish between righteous anger and worldly anger. I don't see it. Anger is an emotion God gave us, God experiences it, Jesus experiences it and it's another evidence that we are truly created in the image of God. I'm more impressed when someone reminds me that anger isn't the sin, it's what we do as a result of getting angry. I guess tossing a dying piece of electronics doesn't look too good.

All in all, I think I learned a few things that morning. First, computers, even sleek notebooks, don't fly or even glide well. Second, I shouldn't try to resolve some issues when I'm already frazzled. I can usually tell when I'm on edge but then I think I can get over it with my own will power. NOT! Third, listen to your wife when she says it's time to do something else. Fourth . . . I could make a long list.

Looking back after a couple weeks, I realize being angry isn't sinful, it's natural. I can stop beating myself up over that part. However, what I do (what I did) in my anger can get me into trouble if I'm not careful. I hope I don't condemn others for getting angry; that's normal. I hope I wait to see how it works out before I start pointing fingers. Fortunately, anger is usually short lived. I'm comforted when the psalmist writes about God, "Sing praise to Yahweh, you saints of his. Give thanks to his holy name. For his anger is but for a moment. His favor is for a lifetime. Weeping may stay for the night, but joy comes in the morning." (Psalm 30:4-5 WEB)

Digital Selection

Sometimes I feel young at heart even though I'm getting older. When it comes to modern technology I usually feel ancient. Although I work with modern computer systems and know more about the systems than most people I meet, I'm still like a dinosaur when it comes to using these devices in the modern social media inundated digital age. I'm into Facebook (to keep tabs on my children and grandchildren), email (a dinosaur), texting (formerly SMS), cloud storage, and a host of modern technological marvels which attempt to improve my life. I think I've got it figured out until I start interacting with the next generation's immersive lifestyle of technology.

My wife coined a great phrase, "Digital Selection." It started when some young upstart commented that finding such and such on the ministry's home page was simple and intuitive. It was then we decided their definition of simple and intuitive was different than ours. I figured with my extensive background in computers, web page design, and the like, I could find what we were looking for. No success. I've become a victim of Digital Selection.

What is Digital Selection, you might ask? It isn't using a search engine to find the cheapest price for a new tablet or notebook or to decide the proper resolution for your new high definition television. It's when the ability to easily wade through modern technology to the desired destination is hampered by an aging understanding of how things work in the digital world. We've been Digitally Selected to be out of touch with the younger generation. Beth says, "They're going to put us on an iceberg and float us out to sea."

Originally electronics and computers were purely logical. That I can understand. Unfortunately, with the proliferation of social media infecting the mental growth and processes of the next generation, what used to follow rules has been reprogrammed to follow the circuitous pathway of the younger mind in a media saturated generation. Pure computer logic has given way to what can appear as random chaos, similar to a planned life giving way to "going with the flow." In my mind, the algorithm of the program isn't easily discovered, almost like the perfect security cypher.

For those raised in such an environment it makes perfect sense. All the pieces fit together smoothly in their concept of the digital age. Unfortunately, it leaves the older generation confused trying to put the square pegs into the round holes. Sometimes we just don't see the connection. We are therefore Digitally Selected to be relegated to the outer circle of fellowship and communication. While I poke fun at this the centuries have demonstrated the division of one generation from another almost proportionally related to the advancement in technology.

When I was young the use of electric guitars, electronic pianos and electronic organs started insinuating themselves into the fabric of modern rock and roll music as well as creeping into bastion of the classic orchestra and even, gasp, into church music. This confused parents who were familiar with the smooth tones of classical wind and string instruments, pianos and pipe organs. It was a new sound and while some parents embraced the changes, many of their generation relegated it to the deepest depths of degradation and evil. There was an error of Electronic Selection threatening to drive a wedge between two generations.

Other things have separated the ages. Changes in cultural beliefs and activities, the redirection of skills from rural to urban work spaces, and any technological advancement from the steam engine to the multicore processor have created segments of selection. Often the selective nature of these advances isn't perceived as a change by the generation in which they develop but as the norm. The concept that the older generation might not comprehend this shift doesn't seem to motivate the new generation to understand the change and work towards an effective stitching together of the two worlds. So, it falls on the ousted to decipher the recent technology and introduce it to their lives in a way which will once again connect them with the new generation.

Things move forward. I'm sure there is more ahead of me to learn than I dealt with in the past. I just hope I have the where-with-all to comprehend and make use of the advances which become so ingrained in our lives. I don't want to be Digitally Selected forever. In the church, we must be careful not to Digitally Select (exclude) those interested in helping because we have some new high-tech sign up site which appeals to the young and confounds the less young.

As a Christian, I'm glad God doesn't use a Digital Selection scale for eternity. I'm looking forward to simplifying things and reducing my digital footprint. I figure if I'm in the presence of God I don't think there's a need for a Facebook status for Him to know what I'm doing. But for now, . . . I guess this is the season of the tablet, phablet, smartphone, social media and whatchamacallit and I better keep up with my skills to avoid Digital Selection.

"For everything there is a season, and a time for every purpose under heaven:" (Ecclesiastes 3:1 WEB)

Crispy

The heart of the wise instructs his mouth, and adds learning to his lips.
(Proverbs 16:23, WEB)

Crispy can be applied to many things and its definition doesn't seem to be standard. When it comes to food there are crispy fries, crispy chicken and the top of the list is crispy bacon. I was thinking about this while enjoying a nice, crispy, piece of bacon at breakfast this morning. It's a Saturday so it's the cook's day off (me) and we go out for a nice morning meal. I like traditions, which include the best meal of the day with someone else doing the cooking.

The bacon this morning was great. It's what I consider crispy. This is important to a breakfast aficionado like me. Let me describe crispy. When the bacon is cooked slowly and fully it will darken, smell great, and become rigid so you can hold the end of the finished product and it doesn't droop. This does not include bacon burnt to blackened carbon residue. That's beyond crisp. I've had what others consider crisp.

While in Europe I discovered a number of dishes that included bacon. Sometimes the restaurant described it as crisp bacon. They were wrong. I don't consider taking a piece of bacon and cooking it in a skillet for 6 seconds on each side to be crispy. I consider that raw. If they didn't include the crisp description it was only cooked 3 seconds on each side. OK, I might be exaggerating but bacon that doesn't break when bent isn't crispy and bacon is best when cooked to a crispy deliciousness.

Others might not share my fondness for this pig product but if I'm going to consume it I want it to be properly prepared. I also understand the definition of crispy applies to other foods. Consider the ubiquitous and marvelous French fry. A properly prepared potato strip is crispy and golden brown. Some of the frozen French fry varieties are golden brown before they reach the oven so that aspect isn't foolproof. But from scratch they end up golden brown with a slight crunch on the outside when consumed. Fried chicken is crunchy on the outside as well and soft and juicy on the inside, when properly prepared. The term crispy doesn't include uncooked exoskeleton or coating. Understanding the definition of the term is crucial.

Just like ensuring a customer receives his crispy bacon properly cooked we also need to be sure we are not misunderstood when discussing salvation and redemption with others. There's a special language that infects the church just as every business has their own special terms for describing internal events and processes. Someone new to the company, or church, is quickly confused and feels disconnected from others until they discover this secret language.

I've been in the church and Christian ministry so long I sometimes forget the implications of using terms which are either unknown to the outside world or have a definition contrary to my faith. Many terms we think are simple and easily understood are often so vague they don't clarify our thoughts but muddy the waters.

Take a term such as *moral* and you'll get a wide list of things people consider to be moral. These lists from inside and outside the church may have some similar items but also many items that stand opposed to one another. One politician once quipped, "My definition of that term isn't the same as yours." How can we have profitable interaction with one another when our definition of the words in our own language differs? Unlike the specifications described in technical documentation, the spiritual specifications and understanding of the terms of faith are apparently open for a wide variety of interpretations in the world.

I've learned to describe to the waiter what I expect when ordering crispy in order to receive that culinary delight with my breakfast. In this way we are using the same language and I've a better chance of getting what I want. Likewise, I've learned to check my language when talking with others about faith. Even brothers and sisters from other churches sometimes use different definitions of ecclesiastical and spiritual terminology. When I use a term I feel I know so well I have to check myself and ask to be the other person understands correctly what I intend. I don't want to lose the Gospel in misunderstanding.

Toothache

Your boasting is not good. Don't you know that a little yeast leavens the whole batch of dough? (1 Corinthians 5:6 NIV)

It all started in elementary school with the infamous health classes which were intended to teach us good personal hygiene. There were lessons in what to wash and how often. There were sessions on how to sit up straight and walk upright so we didn't look like gorillas swinging down the hallways. And there were lessons on how to brush our teeth, up and down, regularly and with fluoride toothpaste.

I tried to pay close attention as long as a butterfly didn't distract me when it flitted about outside the classroom window. The last thing I wanted was a mouth full of decaying, disgusting, blackened, crooked and chipped teeth. Most of the lessons made a lasting impression as they were repeated in subsequent school years, complete with disturbing photographs and videos. Only a few fillings and almost sixty years later I'd done pretty well. Then it started.

In the middle of December, I had a toothache. It was painful enough to warrant a visit to the dentist. The dentist said something about pockets being too deep for her to clean and I was pawned off on a periodontist. When I visited the periodontist's office the pain wasn't as bad (lots of Ibuprofen helped). They took measurements and agreed deep cleaning was necessary but couldn't schedule anything for several weeks. So, I did the logical thing. I went on vacation to visit some of our children for Christmas.

It was holiday time with the family and I had a toothache. A week later, after frowning regularly and chewing carefully, acting a touch grumpy if truth be told, we were home and I decided I couldn't wait for the appointment and scheduled the first of four stages for the next morning as an emergency patient. At this point I really didn't care what they did, as long as the pain went away. Then the snowball started rolling downhill and getting bigger and bigger.

Before the anesthetic was injected and the process started they chose to measure my blood pressure. 220 over 140 was a tad on the high side! They wanted to postpone but I didn't see that as an option. I convinced them to proceed and I'd visit my doctor about the BP afterwards. Thankfully they did the first and most painful area of my mouth, relieving me of most of the pain. The next day I went to my doctor without grimacing in pain each time I closed my mouth. Even though my blood pressure was back down to normal levels (pain can have that effect) I was put on hypertension medication.

There were still three quadrants and five months of chiseling, scraping, grinding and cleaning to go. In the end, the pain was reduced to a dull roar surrounding one tooth. That one wasn't cooperating but appeared in good shape otherwise. So, there was some cut and paste for the gum along with a bone graft to keep things in place. A few weeks after the last debridement we discovered the tooth had died.

Thus, there was a root canal and a crown. Things still weren't in good shape and the tooth next door to the new crown needed attention at the gum level. More cut and paste. Both were successful but still the tooth was an issue.

To cut this short, a year later, after many attempts at keeping the long tooth, we had to give up and pull the puppy. During all this time, I didn't feel the best. Sort of a pain all over and sometimes in areas which caused other fears. Now the tooth was in the periodontist's pliers so we could look closely.

There they were. Two lateral cracks, top to bottom, carefully channeling infection into my jaw but invisible to dental x-rays. More digging, drilling and bone grafting and things were in order sans one tooth. A few days after the brutal attack I started feeling better. In fact, within a week I felt better than I had in years! The small hidden infection had impacted my body head to toe. I'm glad that is over.

It's like bad yeast permeating the entire loaf as it grows and mutates in the warmth of the oven. What we think is small in our Christian walk, or what we don't even recognize in ourselves, can grow to take over our life and make us grumpy and frown regularly while chewing carefully on God's word to keep from causing us pain. We become useless to others and for God. It takes an expert with the right tools to set things in proper order. My periodontist put his sword, aka scalpel, to work in my mouth to separate the bad from the good. And it worked.

"For the word of God is living and active. Sharper than any double-edged sword, it penetrates even to dividing soul and spirit, joints and marrow; it judges the thoughts and attitudes of the heart." (Hebrews 4:12 NIV) Maybe we need to be applying God's sword to our lives to separate the bad from the good. It works and the pain goes away.

Ministry Thoughts or How to Inspire a New Generation

"We are therefore Christ's ambassadors, as though God were making his appeal through us." (2 Corinthians 5:20a NIV)

When I consider all the events of the last few decades, how do I sift through everything to determine what's encouraging and exciting to share with others and what's boring? Another question is; how much detail do I include about technical matters I take for granted? Some folks like all the technical details while others soon have a glazed look in their eyes. It's a fine line to balance when writing anything about ministry years.

As I think of it there's also the question of security. Security is an issue when dealing with an evangelical ministry which brings the Christian Gospel message into countries who are religiously, culturally, politically and historically opposed to the message. Like a spy would say, "I'd tell you everything about my work but then I'd have to shoot you." It's not quite that bad in ministry but some things are best left unsaid outside of the work place for the safety of others in dangerous locations.

The impact of electricity, the booming electronic industry and the growth of media platforms in today's ministry are enormous. Today's young missionaries take it all in stride. They are part of the "connected" generation. They don't remember life before the internet, cell phones and social media. Seasoned missionaries, aka us older folks, are a bit reticent to apply the latest and greatest technology to our ministry. We see the good and the bad from personal experiences. Unfortunately, we often downplay a potential expansion of our ministry in fear or due to a lack of understanding of the new media platform. The younger missionary candidate doesn't see this problem and can easily race forward without carefully considering the fallout caused by a brash approach to distribute the message of salvation. There are bridges to be built and barriers to overcome from both sides of the age barrier.

I'd like to encourage the younger generation to commit their lives to the ministry of reconciliation. I'm not talking about just putting a toe in to test the waters. I want them to take the great leap of faith and jump in full body to see what God can do through their full commitment. The problem I've witnessed with toe testing is that they never get used to the water, they never adjust. It's only when they're willing for God to use them both in their comfort zone (work they're familiar with or trained to do), and out of their comfort zone (work they've never done or where they have no training), that they experience the full reliance on His guidance, grace and care. How do I share this with a culture effectively speaking another language?

I'm reminded of the mechanism I use to prepare sermons in a multi-language, multi-cultural environment. I write the sermon using the vocabulary I know best. I try to be concise and succinct with a careful selection of words and phrases. Then I give the written message to my wife. She sifts through the message and strikes out culturally specific phrases, complicated word combinations, or "big" English words from the text. I have to go back and find more common phrases and better words to ensure the translator and the listener will understand my point. It takes a lot of work and the results make it worthwhile. So how do I apply the same approach to sharing the ministry with young folks?

I want the next generation to understand the amazement I feel when I see God supply, in unexpected ways, everything I need. He even supplies some of the things I just want! My desire is for another generation to see and long for that feeling of total dependence on God to provide. I want them to learn to not rely on their skills or training to be faithful. How do I convince them to hand everything to God and allow Him to manage their lives? How do I convince them that their training, schooling, and experiences are good tools, but nothing is better than allowing God to choose what to use and what not to use? How do I share the experience of being dropped into unknown territory and relying completely on God to provide the skills, knowledge and application we need to accomplish His goals?

How do I do all this without losing contact, without driving them away, without creating confusion instead of clarity? Something to think about . . .

Antenna War Zone

"You are my hiding place; you will protect me from trouble and surround me with songs of deliverance." (Psalm 32:7 NIV)

In high school, I studied and earned my first Phone Engineering license. It was a grueling day of tests in the Chicago FCC offices, but I passed all three sections in by noon and was thrilled to call my father (a radio engineer) and tell him the good news. Shortly after I returned home I acquired a job as an evening/weekend/night transmitter engineer at a local radio station. Money in the bank for all that high school senior year fun! Woo-hoo!

Things went along well, and I enjoyed my shifts which were limited due to child labor laws. I adjusted transmitters, tuned antenna systems, made all the necessary legal entries in the station logs and read a lot of books in the quiet of the late shifts.

One aspect of the work was the evening antenna current ratio check. This involved going to the doghouse (the small building at the bottom of an antenna containing the tuning unit and current meter) of all four towers and manually reading the in-line antenna current. From these readings ratios could be determined which would indicate whether the directional pattern was in compliance with the station's license.

The station's main building was in a valley and the five towers were on the hill behind the station. You could see the towers from the station but the doghouses were hidden behind the ridge of the hill. So, I decided it was a nice evening for a walk and headed around the hill, up the dirt road and over to tower number one. One is always a good place to start.

As I was turning the corner toward tower one I notice a vehicle out near tower five and some young folks standing around the open doors. This was private property, posted, and so their presence was unexpected.

I casually walked to the tower one doghouse, unlocked the door and stepped inside. I pulled the meter switch and noted the reading on my log then returned the switch to its neutral position. It was then I heard the ping and the light bulb outside the door went dark.

I glanced outside the door and the light bulb was in pieces on the ground. Then I heard another ping as something hit the side of the building. I quickly turned off the internal light, not wanting to be a target outlined in the doorway, and scrunched down behind the door. These clowns were actually shooting at the building. Worse yet, they were shooting at me!

Fortunately, there was a local phone in the doghouse which connected to the main building for when we were adjusting the antenna array. I picked up the phone turned the hand crank which rang the studio building. No answer. I tried several times as I heard more projectiles pelting the heavy metal exterior of the doghouse. Apparently, the disk jockey was either talking on the air, indisposed or just too oblivious to notice the phone ringing.

Not someone who likes being the target in target practice, I weighed my options quickly. I could stay and hope they ran out of ammunition and went away. I could keep ringing the studio hoping the disk jockey would rise from his music induced stupor. I could make a run for it and hope for the best. I was young, energetic, felt I was on top of the world (or at least the hill) and decided foolishly to make a run for it.

I peeked around the door toward the car and the villainous youth and edged out of the building. Being the conscientious fellow, I was I even closed the door slowly and put the padlock back. I then made a mad dash for the hillside, heading for the studio building down below. I didn't realize how steep the hill was or how tall until I flew over the edge into what seemed like certain ignominious death in the high grass with all the snakes slithering here and there.

I ran, fell, rolled, jumped and scampered down the hill across the parking lot to the back door. Digging for my keys I realized I wasn't hearing any more shots being fired as I unlocked the door and flew inside on the floor. As I was lying on the cool tile floor, catching my breath, the disk jockey came sauntering around the corner looking at me like I was crazy. I ignored him, jumped up, ran to the desk and called the cops.

About thirty minutes later there was a knock at the back door. It was the police. They came to thank me for calling. Apparently, the vehicle had been stolen earlier in the evening and they were able to retrieve the vehicle and arrest the young, armed joy riders. I suppose you could say I did my civic duty for the day, but my heart wasn't in it. As a matter of fact, my heart was till racing hours later when my shift was over and I drove home.

I always thought God provided special angels for children, missionaries and fools. I've been all three and that evening I think I was in the latter category. As I was flying down the side of that hill I think I could hear songs of deliverance. It's nice to know God has my back.

Customized Custard

For I am persuaded that neither death, nor life, nor angels, nor principalities, nor things present, nor things to come, nor powers, nor height, nor depth, nor any other created thing, will be able to separate us from God's love, which is in Christ Jesus our Lord. (Romans 8:38-39 WEB)

I like ice cream, I like frozen yogurt, I like frozen custard, and all of these are readily available near our home. However, the local iconic dessert for this small region is frozen custard. Not just any frozen custard but Goodberry's frozen custard.

There are two shops within a short distance of our home and we enjoy the cool treat a little more frequently than I think we should. But it's good! It's delicious. It's refreshing. On a hot summer day, you have to be fast to keep the delicious concoction from melting. They have concretes which are custard mixed with other delights, my favorite being Heath Bar. We love to meet friends to slurp, lick, chat and enjoy fellowship in the small seating area in front of the store. Open air tables are just right with a cool breeze.

One evening we called our friends, arranged a meeting time and arrived simultaneously in the parking lot. We greeted each other and walked to the order window. Then we looked down. There were dead and live cockroaches everywhere! Some were attempting to climb the outside wall and fortunately were unsuccessful. Others would run across the tables or over the brick walls which defined the outside dining area. Even to me, after all the things I've seen and eaten overseas, it was a touch on the gross side.

Nevertheless, we purchased our dairy delights. The young lady behind the window let us know none of those crawling pests were inside so the product was still consumable and empty of unexpected crunching. She was actually a little casual about the whole thing. She explained the company sprayed the exterior grounds for bugs about an hour before we arrived.

This created a mass exodus from the underbrush and woodchips of these creatures in their vain attempt to escape the grim roach reaper. If this was the North Carolina State Fair they may have been immersed in hot grease and served fried. But, they were not part of the frozen custard topping list.

As we lapped up our delights we watched other patrons arrive. Their reaction to discovering the critter congress was fun to watch. Some just glanced around and shrugged. Others would scrunch up their shoulders and make funny faces over the unexpected intrusion into their afternoon plans. The children thought it was fascinating and little boys liked to try and chase the roaches until their mothers discovered what they were chasing and ended up chasing the boys. Occasionally we had to flick a wandering Blattodea species from our shoes who made it to the parking lot.

And yet, even with the otherwise gross appearance of these creatures, people came, they ordered, they ate, they left. About the only thing they excused themselves from doing was sitting down at the tables or standing near the brick walls. These people are faithful to their culinary delights. It's the place to be for afternoon enjoyment and socialization. Come high water, come cold weather (open all year), come cockroaches, they still braved the obstacle to buy, eat, chat and socialize. Now that is dedication!

In the Christian life, we are called to be faithful in all things. We are called to be dedicated to God and God is dedicated to us. Unfortunately, there are often distractions or deterrents between us and what we're called to do. We sometimes think similar obstacles or deterrents can come between God from our sphere. God is faithful. Nothing can keep Him from us. Nothing can keep us from Him. God's love comes through in any and all situations, distractions, deterrents and insect infestations.

Maybe we need a little of the North Carolina dedication to dessert so we're not distracted or deterred from God's love. Keeping our eyes on the goal makes a difference. Remembering the sweetness of God's love, remembering the wonder of God's grace should make us persevere through and around anything that bugs us and threatens to separate from God.

Fan the Flame

Remember therefore from where you have fallen, and repent and do the first works; or else I am coming to you swiftly, and will move your lamp stand out of its place, unless you repent. (Revelation 2:5 WEB)

Building fires is a lot of fun. I remember gathering wood and starting a warm blaze during many camp outs. There was always a comforting peace sitting around the fire each evening. We told tales of grand exploits and adventures. There were songs of joy and fun raised over the multi-colored flames. Friendships were created and strengthened while watching the fire give its light to the night.

Fires can also be a lot of work. One day on Guam, after the children enjoyed a swim, I decided to barbecue at Talafofo Bay. What a disaster! All the matches, charcoal, lighter fluid, gasoline, wind breaks and frustrations couldn't light a fire in that breeze. Often, when camping in the woods, I was reminded of the work fire demanded. There was the fuel to gather, the ground to clear, the coaching to get a reliable flame and constant attention to keep it from failing.

To keep a flame going I provided the proper fuel. Occasionally I would fan the fire or blow on the coals to rekindle a dwindling flame. Too much wind would blow the fire out while too little would be useless. It took practice to start and maintain a good camp fire.

As a believer, I need to consider the fire burning inside of me. I need to see how high the flame of God's love is burning in my heart. I was so excited when I was saved. The fires of God's love were bright and blazing in my life that day. But what has happened since then? God has not left me. His Holy Spirit still works in my life. Where have the first flames of love gone?

The church at Ephesus was reminded of its failure in this area. They were called to repentance, called to rekindle that first love and excitement (Revelation 2:4,5). How many times have I failed to share with others the Gospel? When I was first saved I couldn't wait to start a conversation leading to a testimony. Now I consider, with the world's encouragement, whether that person wants to hear the Gospel. How far have I fallen from my first love, that first excitement? "What is contrary to salvation is not sin but habit." Charles Péguy.

The Israelites were instructed to return to God (Jeremiah 2:2). Jesus told his disciples the world would turn from God and grow cold in their devotion (Matthew 13:12,13). John reminds his readers to avoid loving the world (1 John 2:15,16), just the opposite of today's advertising.

But we are new creatures, alive in Christ, born into a new life. We are instructed to avoid loving the wrong things and be content with what we have (Hebrews 13:5,6). We are to understand Christ's presence in our lives for eternity. We are reminded of God's faithfulness even when we are faithless (2 Timothy 2:11-13). We are encouraged to work for God, not for salvation but because of salvation (James 2:16).

I've known the Lord as Savior for more than twenty years. Am I gathering or scattering, living in Christ or existing in Christ? Am I being persecuted for seeking to live a godly life in Christ? It is easy to look at the evil world around and become defeated in the heart as things go from bad to worse (2 Timothy 3:12,13). Still we must stand strong in the Lord (1 Corinthians 16:13).

Is the Lord speaking to your heart today? Maybe you have lost some of the luster of your first love. Perhaps you need to rekindle the first flames of salvation. A little spark in the right tinder box can generate an unstoppable blaze. A simple breeze on a small flame can start a forest fire.

Become a player, not a spectator. Teach a Sunday school class or Bible study. You don't need theological training, just a love for God's word and a desire to learn. Attend a Bible study and Sunday school. There is a great wealth of spiritual growth hiding in our weekly Sunday school classes and Bible studies.

Is someone near you in need? Provide what you are able. Does work need to be done at church or a fellow believer's home? Jump in and provide help, work. Don't rush out after the service, be encouraged and encourage others in fellowship with your brothers and sisters in Christ.

Let's work together to build a bonfire. Let's fan the flame together to light up the skies around us with the Gospel. Where is your first love today? "The pains of being a Christian are all growing pains, and growing pains beset only the growing." Carrol E. Simcox.

A Passage I Love

I recently received an e-mail from a friend who works the site http://missionary-blogs.com This is a great place to see how folks are serving the Lord around the globe. He asked me, as well as others, to post a blog with our favorite Scripture passage and why it is a favorite. So here goes:

My favorite passage is in my favorite epistle, Philippians. There is so much practical application intertwined with foundations of faith in this short letter I could ramble on for days. . . but . . . I won't. The passage I reference most often is:

"Brethren, I do not regard myself as having laid hold of it yet; but one thing I do: forgetting what lies behind and reaching forward to what lies ahead, I press on toward the goal for the prize of the upward call of God in Christ Jesus." (Philippians 3:13-14 NASB)

To state it simply, without expanding this into a sermonette, this passage demonstrates the Christian life in this world, and a perspective which is essential to seeking God's direction and following faithfully.

Too often we burden ourselves with our past, in particular our past mistakes, sins, errors, whatever adjective/noun you would like to apply. It makes us lame, limping through life unable to run or even walk the Christian life. Paul had plenty to feel guilty about. But he knew, and we know, God forgives so we can move forward.

Our vision in this earthly life should be on the goal, seeking God, seeking His direction, seeking His purposes. It's there our strength is renewed, and we can mount up on wings like an eagle and bound about the mountains like we have hind's feet on high places. (I wish I could say I invented those cool images!)

We need not walk through life backwards like a dodo bird. If you ever tried walking backwards, without turning around to see where you are going, you soon found yourself tripping on something and crashing to the ground. Instead we need to turn, face forward, and strain toward the goal, the prize, the upward call, eternal life with God!

Sometimes I walk backwards . . . and trip. Other times I face forward, see my Savior beckoning me to the goal, and run with abandon into His loving arms of grace.

About the Author

Dr. Robert "Opa" Chick hails originally from Georgia. Bob and his lovely wife Elizabeth served as missionaries with TWR for over 35 years. This included 28 years overseas, half in Asia and half in Europe.

Bob enjoys writing for fun and occasionally for larger publications outside the family. He is a father, husband, grandpa, an engineer, a musician, a pastor, and a missionary. Holds degrees in engineering, Biblical studies, and theology.

But his greatest joy and accomplishment is his family. They are a delight. He loves them to visit and loves to visit them.

Made in the USA
Lexington, KY
13 December 2019

58515207R00219